DISINTEGRATING THE MUSICAL

ARTHUR KNIGHT

Disintegrating the Musical

BLACK PERFORMANCE

AND AMERICAN MUSICAL

FILM

Duke University Press

Durham and London

2002

© 2002 Duke University Press
All rights reserved
Printed in the United States
of America on acid-free paper ∞
Designed by C. H. Westmoreland
Typeset in Adobe Garamond
with Bodoni display by
Tseng Information Systems, Inc.
Library of Congress Cataloging-
in-Publication Data appear on
the last printed page of this book.
The poem "Downtown Vaudeville"
is reprinted by permission of
the Estate of Gwendolyn Brooks.

IN MEMORY OF

GERALD MAST AND

MARK TUCKER

·⊂━━⊃·

DEDICATED TO

MARTHA HOWARD

Contents

Acknowledgments

Like most writers, I often find writing hard work—sometimes exceedingly hard and even painful work—but writing these next few pages was pure pleasure. The wisdom, examples, aid, support, and friendship of the people acknowledged here kept me going through nearly a decade. They are responsible for this book coming into being and deserve great credit for its insights. I'll gladly take credit for the flaws, since I know learning of them and correcting them will require continued contact with most of those named below.

This book originated as my doctoral dissertation at the University of Chicago. Though he died before I could begin work on the project, Gerald Mast inspired it with his teaching and writing. I hope he would accept it as an elaboration of his own work, and I hope those who knew and treasured Gerald will accept my work as a memorial to him.

Miriam Hansen, who directed the dissertation, Lauren Berlant, and W. J. T. Mitchell, who were its readers, were unstinting in their support and incisive in their comments and criticisms—a valuable combination. They talked me through many of "my" ideas and then read my drafts and commented again, further improving those ideas, now even less exclusively mine than they were to begin with.

At the College of William and Mary, my colleagues in American Studies, English, Film Studies, and Literary and Cultural Studies energetically and kindly extended the work of my teachers, and this book is much better for all they have taught me. For their general support, thanks to my chairs over the years, David Aday, Bob Gross, Terry Meyers, Ann Reed, and Alan Wallach; to Joanne Braxton, Jean Brown, Lisa Grimes (and the staff of the Roy R. Charles Center), Colleen Kennedy, Rich Lowry, Brad Weiss, and Kim Wheatley; and to the many students who have challenged my ideas and shared their own. Chandos Michael Brown graciously made the illustrations possible. For persistently inquiring after my progress, even when it must have been uncomfortable to do so, thanks to Chris MacGowan and Katherine Preston. Chris Bongie (now, alas, of Queen's University, Ontario), too, was a persistent inquirer, but he was also, at a crucial moment, a superb, quick, *and* voluntary critic and copy editor; I am grateful for his service in all three roles. Thanks to Kimberley Phillips for information and stimulating, sustaining conversation late in the game. Extra-special thanks to Grey Gundaker for invaluable information and stimulating, sustaining, life-changing conversation throughout. Very sadly, my friend Mark Tucker, jazz musicologist extraordinaire, who contributed greatly to my work and career and who I was hoping would help me make my musical analyses here much better, got very ill and died in fall 2000; I hope those who knew and cherished Mark will still see his influence on this book and accept it as a tribute to him.

At every step of the way in this project, Pamela Robertson Wojcik, Hank Sartin, and Shari Roberts Anderson read, shared information, supplied advice, and provided friendship and fun way above and beyond any possible call of any duty. Remarkably, it appears that I haven't worn out all their patience—they keep talking to me!—and I look forward to many more fruitful collaborations.

Many others read parts of this book or talked at length with me about it, generously fitting me into their busy lives and diverse careers. In this regard I am particularly grateful to Vince Bertolini, Bill Brown, Chris Brown, Jim Chandler, Dale Cockrell, Loren Council, Corey Creekmur, Tom Cripps, Dennis Dworkin, Bill Falloon, Graydon Fisher, Krin Gabbard, Kirsten Gruesz, Erin Hogan, Loren Kruger, Jim Lastra, Chris Looby, Anna McCarthy, Bruce McConachie, Kevin McMurtry, Eliza Nichols, Pat Ondercin, Judy Parker, Stephen Thomas, Paul Ulrich, David and Kim Van Houten, Ken Warren, Rick Wojcik, and members of the Ethnomusicology and Mass Culture Workshops, both at the University of Chicago. Special thanks to J. Ronald Green for help with the Oscar Micheaux illustrations.

Many institutions and people affiliated with them aided this project. Besides being a challenging and genial place to study, the University of Chicago, via its Division of Humanities and Department of English, awarded me several generous fellowships; thanks especially to Tom Thuerer, Greta Godbey, and Barb Crawford. Rich Nayer and Nayer Construction filled in the gaps in my work and financial schedules over many years, provided much good fellowship, and gave me the chance to learn in detail the terrain, both present and past, of Chicago. The Illinois Institute of Technology awarded me a predoctoral fellowship that allowed me time to develop my project, gave me crucial teaching experience, and showed me still more of Chicago; thanks especially to John Root. The Henry Luce Foundation and American Council of Learned Societies awarded me a dissertation fellowship in 1992–93 that gave me the time to do research and contributed particularly to chapter six. With great dedication and good cheer, staff at the following institutions tracked down crucial sources for me: Regenstein Library at the University of Chicago, the Black Film Archive at Indiana University (especially Gloria Gibson), the Motion Pictures Division of the Library of Congress (especially Madeleine Matz), the Margaret Herrick Library at the AMPAS Center for Motion Picture Study, the Film and Television Archive at UCLA, the Film Library at MOMA (especially Mary Corliss), the New York Public Library at Lincoln Center, the Wisconsin Center for Film and Theater Research (especially Maxine Ducey), the Harold Washington Public Library of Chicago, and Swem Library at the College of William and Mary.

The institution most important to this book has been Duke University Press. Thanks to the two critically and sympathetically minded anonymous readers the press engaged for their thoughtful and timely comments on the manuscript. Thanks to assistant editor Christine Habermaas, assistant managing editor Justin Faerber, copyeditor Craig A. Triplett, and designer Cherie Westmoreland for energetically and efficiently making sure the manuscript became an actual book. And thanks is nowhere near enough to repay the astounding and enduring support and friendship of Editor-in-Chief Ken Wissoker—nonetheless, my heartfelt thanks to him.

I hope the text of this book will make three debts very clear, but I'd like to amplify my appreciation here: first, to the people who made the movies and music I analyze; second, to the many scholars whose work undergirds mine; and third, to the city of Chicago, sweet home, indeed and forever, in spirit if not in fact.

Finally, thanks to the extended family circle. Everyone on both the Gifford and Knight sides of my family helped whether they knew it or not by shaping my outlook and tastes and by having made it clear over the past four decades that they think I'm alright. Starting early, cousin David LaRussa shaped my musical leanings. Uncle Corey and Aunt Shelly Gifford provided exceedingly comfortable lodgings in Washington, D.C., and cousins Julie, Molly, and Katie ferried me around and kept me amused. My Auntie Carno Johnson (my heroine) and cousins

Loie, Greg, and Dennis, and cousin Diana LaRussa made me directly aware of the challenges, rewards, and stakes of integration in the United States. By being my absolutely unfailing, unflinching friends, David Thompson and Todd Zedak have become my brothers. I have come to believe that Todd and David were taking turns holding the light at the end of the tunnel; at least they were the first to point it out, and they never let me take my eyes off it. My mother- and father-in-law, Noreen and Alan Howard, sister-in-law, Emily, and aunt-in-law, Ann, have been boon companions and huge-hearted, sanity-inducing fonts of wit and wisdom, and Big Al read Proust with me and taught me how to play poker, too. My brother Christopher, sister Elizabeth, sister-in-law Kelsey, and brother-in-law (and great friend) Jim were always there— thank heavens.

As for my mother and father, words fail. Thank you for supporting me, in every conceivable way, on this strange path.

My daughters Nora and Djuna were both born and grew considerably while I was researching and writing, and I thank them for reminding me that lots of things—talking about insects, jumping on the bed, holding hands—are more important than scholarship. First among those is my wife, Martha Howard, without whom *Disintegrating the Musical*— and I—would certainly have disintegrated and to whom it is—and I am—dedicated.

Introduction

DISINTEGRATING THE MUSICAL

"What's your work?" the negro asked Stahr.

"I work for the pictures."

"Oh." After a moment he added, "I never go to movies."

"Why not?" asked Stahr sharply.

"There's no profit. I never let my children go."

—F. SCOTT FITZGERALD (1941)

I loved the tough guys, the action, Humphrey Bogart in *Casablanca,* and I loved all that dancing and carrying on in such films as *Stormy Weather* and *Cabin in the Sky.*

—MALCOLM X (1964)

I asked the stranger . . . , "Mister, that paper [the *Chicago Defender*] got musicianers in it?" . . . [He] flipped the page to a picture of Jimmie Lunceford's entire band. Facing it . . . was a picture story of Ethel Waters, whose movie *Cabin in the Sky* we'd seen the week before from the "colored section" in the balcony of the Ritz picture show on Third Street. That did it! I said, "Gimme one."—WILLIE RUFF (1991)

Beginning with the popularization of synchronized sound, Hollywood movies have emphatically linked African Americans with music and musical performance. This link does not have a necessary or direct relation to film genre. Black musicians turn up, play a song or two, and disappear in comedies, melodramas, and *films noir* or, to note some familiar nonmusical classics, in *Jezebel* (1938), *Citizen Kane* (1941), and

Casablanca (1942). Nonetheless, during the "classical" or "studio" era of American sound filmmaking (1927–1959), when Hollywood movies linked blacks with musical performance, they were most likely to make that link in the context of works that producers, critics, and audiences labeled "musical." The first widely distributed synchronized sound feature, *The Jazz Singer* (1927), was a musical that linked blackness to musical performance through Al Jolson's blackface performance, leading one early historian of blacks in American film to exclaim sarcastically, "The Negro had arrived in talking pictures — as a black-face comedian!"[1] Even before *The Jazz Singer,* however, sound-film pioneer Lee de Forest had made short films of black musicians like Noble Sissle and Eubie Blake performing, and soon after *The Jazz Singer,* Hollywood studios supplemented blackface musical performances like Jolson's with "specialty numbers" by black musicians in otherwise white musicals and with many black-cast musical shorts.

By itself this profusion of black musical performance in Hollywood films demands critical, scholarly attention that it has yet to receive. This lack of attention is made more remarkable by the fact that these fugitive performances, which nestle in the nooks and crannies of the musical, are anchored by an unprecedented and unparalleled cycle of eight all or predominantly black-cast Hollywood musicals: *Hearts in Dixie* (1929), *Hallelujah!* (1929), *The Green Pastures* (1936), *Cabin in the Sky* (1943), *Stormy Weather* (1943), *Carmen Jones* (1954), *St Louis Blues* (1958), and *Porgy and Bess* (1959). Not until the brief flurry of interracial social-problem films in the late forties did Hollywood focus so intently on African Americans using another genre, and not until the 1950s would Hollywood produce a black-cast drama or comedy.[2] Simply put, compared with the musical, whether broadly or narrowly construed, no other genre of Hollywood film provided similar quantity of or focused with similar intensity on representations of black Americans.

My project was initially prompted by the impulse to explore Hollywood's propensity for representing African Americans with and through musical performance. It has been complicated by discovering that, like Hollywood films, sound-era "race" films — black-cast films intended for black audiences and made outside the Hollywood system by both black and white filmmakers — also emphatically link blackness and music. Often the link comes in isolated musical numbers in otherwise nonmusical films such as gangster or boxing stories. In some instances, however, the interest of race films lies predominantly in their use of music, which is sometimes quite like and other times very different from that of a Hollywood musical. These "musical" race films have been as underexamined and even less acknowledged than Hollywood's black-cast musicals, specialty numbers, and shorts. They also demand study.

This book capitalizes on the expanding body of scholarship dedicated to African Americans in American cinema but focuses its examination on what seems to be the most widely and enduringly accepted, enjoyed, and even *loved* black cinematic figure, the musical performer.[3] Why were—and are—African Americans so emphatically linked with music and musical performance in the American cinematic imagination, and why was this link so strongly, generically formalized in the black-cast musicals from 1929 to 1959? Why did race-film producers ever pick such a difficult, expensive, and so clearly *Hollywood* genre as the musical? What and how did race musicals mean, and to what audiences? How did race-film musicals interplay, or not, with their Hollywood counterparts? What and how did these varying representations of black musical performance in the most iconic and revered and most frivolous and dismissed of American film genres—"That's entertainment!"—mean and to whom? What and how do they continue to mean, and to whom, today? These are the overarching questions this book will address as it describes and analyzes the black-musical link and seeks to understand the aesthetic, cultural, and social meanings and effects of that link for various—but especially black—American audiences.

"The Gift of Black Folk" Meets Mass Reproducibility

Neither Hollywood nor race-film producers invented the representational link between African Americans and musical performance. From early contacts between Europeans and Africans, through the transport of Africans to the Americas, during more than two centuries of enslavement, and on through decades of de jure and de facto oppression, both white and black chroniclers commented on the importance of music to West African and then African American cultures. Many mechanisms, ranging from slave purchasing to harvest festivals to stage performances, brought African American "folk" music and musical performance into the domain of the commercial marketplace.[4] In the late-nineteenth and

1. W. E. B. Du Bois, outline for *The Gift of Black Folk* (detail). 1924. Used with the permission of David Graham Du Bois and The W. E. B. Du Bois Foundation.

early twentieth centuries, mechanical and electronic recording media—sound recording and broadcasting, photography, film, and then synchronized sound film—added apparently indexical, verisimilar documents to the chronicle of the important place of music in African American culture. As mass reproducible, mass marketable, and particularly in the case of film, mass audience media, these recording media took on special importance in their relation to—and of—African Americans, their "minority" culture, and that culture's marketable music.

W. E. B. Du Bois is a writer well situated both to represent music's importance in Afro-America and to supply us with tools for analyzing that circumstance and its stakes at the threshold of mass mediation. Du Bois—ardent activist, sociologist and historian, aesthete, and champion of folk and high art—might seem an unlikely companion of the musical film, but he is not. Du Bois wrote only two film reviews in his prolific career. One was of *Birth of a Nation* (1915); not surprisingly, it was negative.[5] The other, just over a decade later, was of *Hearts in Dixie* and *Hallelujah!*, Hollywood's first two black-cast musicals; Du Bois's review was positive—especially about the films' use of "Negro folk music."[6] I have more to say about Du Bois's particular response to these early black-cast musicals and to other forms of black musical performance in later chapters. Because they stand behind his thinking on the black-cast musicals and because they have informed so much subsequent thinking about African Americans and music, I concentrate here on his broader ideas about music.

For Du Bois, at least during the first half of his long career, music was at the pinnacle of the "gifts of black folk," the gifts "we"—black folk—had brought to America and "mingled . . . with yours." The black gift of music, "a gift of story and song," occupied this crucial position for two reasons. First, it emblematized the other crucial black gifts of "Spirit" and of "sweat and brawn." In the form of "sorrow songs" or spirituals, black music stood as both testament to and matrix for black belief and endurance, and in the form of work songs, it served the same functions for black labor. Second, black music provided "soft, stirring melody in an ill-harmonized and unmelodious land."[7] This gift of music, through contrast, both criticized and reimagined the dominant, profoundly unequal order of the United States.

Du Bois's choice of the word *gift* is a complex one that, for ends both polemical and analytic, bears several meanings. Gift carries the sense of some thing given beyond compulsion and outside the marketplace, a thing valued both for its intrinsic properties and for the manner in which it is acquired. In this sense, gift suggests an alternative moral and ethical economy of mutuality, reciprocity, and acknowledgment; one gift calls forth another, and gifts become ties of communication and community. However, gift also carries with it the sense of a unique talent or skill, something "god given," a quality possessed. In this sense, gift suggests a kind of property. So "the gift of black folk" is both a possession of African Americans and something they have shared—"mingled"—with white Americans; it is something that cannot be taken from African Americans and something that must be acknowledged, and should be reciprocated, as already "given" by blacks to whites.

Du Bois insisted that the black gift of music was both passive and active. The gift is something very nearly "essential" to blacks, a crucial part of black cultural identity, something that "black folk" *have,* and, at the same time, the gift must be maintained through giving, through use, through sending it out into the nonblack, nonfolk world. So for Du Bois the emblematic black gift of music was at once black and not black. Du Bois chose music as his emblematic black gift because it so clearly arose from the material, social circumstances of the people who made it—in the United States, socially and legally defined "colored" bodies—and because it seemed uncontained by those circumstances, because it could seemingly float free of those circumstances and bodies.

These complexities suggest that control of the black gift is crucial.

With *the* black gift being music, control has as much—perhaps more—to do with the sight of music and the stories that are told about it than it does with the sound of music. What musical performance looks like and the narratives that explain those looks matter crucially to how music sounds and what it can mean.

Mass mediation such as print notation, sound recording, broadcasting, and film throws the black gift into crisis. By materializing the split between giver/producer of music and its receiver/consumer, mass mediation makes acutely problematic the control of the gift through its affiliated look and story. Under mass mediation, music does not simply float as sound carried through air away from its giving, producing, social bodies; rather, it is captured and carried away, to be re-presented under circumstances whose relation to the sound's "original" affiliated sight and story may be very different. As a consequence, music can seem to become wholly invisible, disembodied, and sui generis. In the combination of mass media and mass market commodity capitalism, this differential distance between giver and receiver comes to be almost ensured and to mimic the very social and legal hierarchies it promises to transcend, escape, or collapse. The potential moral circuit of the gift that Du Bois desired becomes, at best, the abstraction of selling and, at worst, "property" theft. The capital-intensive mass media are beyond ordinary black control and access, and the gift of music can slip away through alienation or be stolen away through appropriation. Langston Hughes succinctly expressed the problem of Du Bois's "gift" in the era of mass-market mass reproducibility this way: "You've done taken my blues and gone."[8]

Here is where musical film enters. Like any other mass medium, synchronized sound film separates producer and consumer, but unlike print, sound recording, and broadcast, synchronized sound film may reproduce the (re)union of recorded sound and sight moving emphatically together in time. Though synchronized sound film offers many possible uses, its dominant use quickly became a way of restoring sound to sight. When musical performance was the object of reproduction, however, sound film became a way of restoring sight to sound. In sound film, the reproduced, synchronized sight of African Americans performing could be (re)attached to the sound of (black) recorded music. And when sound film conjoined with already established patterns of Hollywood feature-length narrative filmmaking, one important generic result was the musical, a type of movie that used the qualities of sound film both by embedding musical performance in a story and by developing a story that would account for musical performance. The musical, then, could not only represent African Americans performing; it could also present stories that purported, more or less explicitly, to "explain" why African Americans would (or should) perform music, stories that would evaluate, even as they commercially conveyed across mass-mediated spatial and temporal distances, Du Bois's "gift of black folk."

Sound film not only *could* rejoin "colored" sight to "colored" sound and tell stories to explain the joining—as I've already suggested, *it did so,* and quite often, in the musical. Because of its properties as a medium and a mode of commerce, musical film became an especially important site of contention over the meaning of African American music and musical performance as the gift of black folk, in all the senses of Du Bois's phrase. Emerging from a web of other media (e.g., sound recordings) and modes (e.g., all kinds of live performances, including stage musicals), the musical film became a locus around which crucial debates about the sound, sight, and stories of black music—and, thus, symbolic debates about African Americans and their culture(s) in America—could play out.

It was because the musical could be such a locus that both Hollywood and race filmmakers used black musicians so often and, at the same time, in such constricted ways. This is why blackface mattered and why it wasn't simply rejected out of hand by many black performers, critics, and audiences. This is why Du Bois and other black intellectuals and critics felt compelled to comment on *Hearts in Dixie, Hallelujah!,* and the other black-cast musicals; why Walter White, director of the NAACP, helped Lena Horne get a Hollywood contract; and why Horne, Paul Robeson, and Dorothy Dandridge left Hollywood while other black stars like Louis Armstrong, Duke Ellington, and Cab Calloway continued to return. And the intricacies of the musical account for why cultural producers of radical "racial" political intent—whether "race" filmmakers like Oscar Micheaux, the left-liberal makers of *Jammin' the Blues* (1944) or, more recently, African American filmmakers like Michael Schultz in *Car Wash* (1974), Julie Dash in *Illusions* (1984), or Spike Lee in *School Daze* (1989), *Girl 6* (1996) or *Bamboozled* (2000)—have so often used, revised, expanded, and dis/integrated the musical.

Integration: Industrial and Sociocultural

The word *integration* has three important senses for this book. The first of these, which in its specifics concerns me least, names efforts of the Hollywood film studios to rationalize, control, and expand the production and consumption of movies. These efforts at vertically integrating the businesses of film had as their aim creating and maintaining the largest possible audience. Consequently, these efforts not only affected economic decisions (e.g., decisions to invest in all the layers of production, distribution, and exhibition as well as in ancillary industries like music publishing) but also influenced the forms film would take and, crucially, the types of spectators these forms imagined and tried to posit for themselves.[9]

Of course, film industry efforts to create a mass audience that would be homogenous enough, or at least consume homogeneously enough, to be an efficient market for its integrated business structure would at least in theory run afoul of the fact that across the classical era of filmmaking much of the United States was legally segregated and virtually all of it was informally segregated by race. Congruent, then, with the rationalist, capitalist business impulse to create homogenized markets arose the civil rights impulse and language of racial-social "integration." This is the second sense of the word *integration* that is important to my analysis, and once more W. E. B. Du Bois both represents the term's importance and supplies tools for analyzing it.

In 1934, the Board of Directors of the NAACP fired Du Bois as the editor of its magazine, *The Crisis,* over a dispute about the meaning of the word *integration* and the potential socioeconomic consequences of pursuing integration as a strategy for black civil rights. In his April 1933 *Crisis* editorial, "Right to Work," Du Bois had analyzed the "American industrial system" as one that organized production and disorganized consumption—or, more accurately, made consumption purely an act of "cooperation" between the individual consumer and the (often oligopolistic) producers of goods. Under such a system, a socially "despised minority" becomes nearly infinitely exploitable, at once needing or wanting the products of the system and being uninvited—by law, custom, and economic rationale—into it as anything more than a consumer and expendable low-wage worker. Sounding surprisingly like Booker T. Washington, but with an explicit socialist bent, Du Bois wrote: "What can we do? We can work for ourselves. We can consume mainly what we ourselves produce, and produce as large a proportion as possible of that which we consume." Without using the phrase, Du Bois proposed—in contradiction of NAACP policy and his own policy in the past—racial self-segregation. Du Bois proposed the purposeful construction of a legal but alternative "black market."[10]

"Right to Work" did not get Du Bois fired, but it started the process. What precipitated it was his April 1934 editorial, "Segregation in the North." Du Bois repeated his analysis and argument, but this time he used direct language of imposed segregation, self-segregation, cooperation, and boycott. The concluding section of Du Bois's essay is titled "Integration." He agrees with "extreme opponents of segregation" that "complete integration of the black race with the white race in America, with no distinction of color in political, civil or social life . . . is the great end toward which humanity is tending." "So long," writes Du Bois, "as there are artificially emphasized differences of nationality, race and color, not to mention the fundamental discriminations of economic class, there will be no real Humanity." These are long-term goals, however, to which contemporary social and economic practices and organization are, in Du Bois's estimation, inimical. Consequently, Du Bois argues, "it will sometimes be necessary to our survival and an ultimate step toward the ultimate breaking down of barriers, to increase by voluntary action our separation from our fellowmen."[11]

The NAACP board disagreed vehemently, condemning all forms of "enforced" segregation, whether the enforcement was legal or social and informal. Du Bois's May 1934 editorial first outlined his colleagues' disagreement with him and then responded with a list of questions aimed at the NAACP's official resolutions on segregation. Du Bois wondered what the NAACP "believed" when it confronted the reality of the segregated American world and all the social, economic, and cultural results. His final, freighted question returned, at what Du Bois clearly believed a moment of profound crisis, to a familiar Du Boisian subject and symbol, one that from another writer and in a different, less charged era might seem a non sequitur: If the NAACP board does not "believe" in or "approve" of any kind of segregation, Du Bois asked, "does it believe in the Negro spirituals?"[12] For Du Bois the question is rhetorical. The spirituals, which in his view would never have come into being had black slaves and freedmen only aimed to integrate with white society and culture, prove to Du Bois that unthinking integration is bad and that specific instances of segregation can be good—or yield good, critical results.

Throughout this debate Du Bois never mentioned the movies, but they may well have presented the knottiest version of what he envisioned as a racialized crisis of confluence between mass industrial integration and racial-social segregation. Comparatively, the hiring of "Negro clerks" by the stores in metropolitan "black belts," an example Du Bois does mention, is easy and straightforward. By and large, for blacks in 1934 (but also 1944 and 1954) the movies meant attending segregated but white-owned and managed theaters that played films employing mostly white performers and made by companies owned and controlled by whites.[13] Under the circumstances, not going to the movies, like the "negro" who appears briefly at the center of F. Scott Fitzgerald's *The Last Tycoon,* would seem easy: "There's no profit."[14] Boycott, which Du Bois defined as "the use of mass action by Negroes who take advantage of segregation in order to strengthen their economic foundation," would seem automatic and beyond the necessity of consumer "co-operation" and "organization."[15]

However, not going to the movies would be harder if the theater were comfortable, convenient, away from family control ("I never let my children go," says Fitzgerald's negro, almost ensuring that they will want to), modestly priced, staffed at least partly by African Americans, and often featured black live performers. Not going to the movies would be harder if there were not many alternative "equivalent" goods available and if an alternative "equivalent" industry of the sort Du Bois envisioned arising through self-segregation was unlikely because of the special intricacy and capital intensiveness of the movies' dominant form, not to mention the anticompetitive measures of the dominant industry.[16] Not going to the movies would be harder if the films shown did also sometimes employ African American performers, especially musicians—perhaps even respectfully, or in a way interpretable as an apparent gesture of respect and recognition. For the politically engaged, not going to the movies would be harder when one knew African Americans would be represented. After all, such representations might influence how whites were thinking of blacks (and how blacks might think of themselves) and might demand informed, critical response. In differing degrees, all of these reasons probably contributed to the "love" young Malcolm X/Detroit Red/Malcolm Little felt for *Casablanca* (music supplied by Dooley Wilson as Sam, well and respectfully "integrated," in relative terms, into Rick's), *Cabin in the Sky,* and *Stormy Weather.*[17]

In such circumstances—in an economically integrated industry deploying some social-racial integration in a dispersed field where the public sites of consumption need not be racially integrated—what was there to boycott? Where was the economic foundation, especially when the form, the product, at the putative center—the movies—could seem to give back the black gift of sighted, storied song? When Langston Hughes wrote his "Note on Commercial Art," his references tended toward media of mass reproduction, but in fact they denoted live performance:

> You've done taken my blues and gone—
> You sing 'em in Paris
> And you sing 'em in the Hollywood Bowl,
> And you mixed 'em up with symphonies
> And you fixed 'em
> So they don't sound like me.

Implicit here is that "my blues" no longer look "like me" either and, additionally, that their look is no longer easily available to "me." Indeed, a compensating virtue of the movies compared with theater might be that they are also relatively available, making it easier for "me" to gauge the misappropriation and (mis)representation of "my blues." At the same time, movies make the problems of misappropriation and (mis)representation different and potentially more severe, since with overdubbing, for example, "my blues" might no longer "sound like me" yet might still look "like me."

As the processes of giving and taking the black gift of music became entangled with mass media and culture, many Americans found it easy to identify black performers visually and to assume, bearing in mind certain broad restrictions, that the music they performed was "theirs," was "black." In other words, whatever was "black" about the music an African American performer made became a superficial (though far from inconsequential) visual quality. The connection was revocable under certain circumstances—a black pianist playing Chopin, for example, didn't make Chopin black music, although the sighted sound might disquiet racist auditors—but stuck tenaciously under others—a black chorus singing, for example, the "folk" music of Stephen Foster or "Dixie" or any variety of what Hughes saw as pseudo-blues.

Adding poignancy to this (mis)representational dilemma, and to my attempts to analyze it, is that even well informed, passionate critics who felt an imperative to limn a complex sense of the link(s) between Afro-America, music, and American socioculture could not and still cannot fully agree about what, besides black performers, makes black music "black" or about what music(s) earn the label. For instance, though both Du Bois and Hughes would agree that something beyond skin color made some music black, they did not fully agree on the blackness of the blues and jazz. Du Bois found both these forms impoverished compared to the authentic (for him) black music of spirituals, music that represented the social and cultural ideals of Afro-America, but Hughes found them, especially in relation to twentieth-century, urban black experience, more compelling than the old sorrow songs. This overlapping of informed agreements and disagreements about what counts as black music is poignant because, in its nuance and complexity, it often failed in the face of a common sound-image and its frequent associational chain, which went (and goes) like this: "There is a synchronized sound motion picture of a black person (or black people) making music. That music is black. Black people are musical (more so than white people and to the exclusion of other qualities)."[18] A distilled instance of this problematic, with a slight shift in register, might be perceived in the film critic and historian Donald Bogle's conflicted feelings about the black musical performers in classical era musicals. On the one hand, they give him immense pleasure; he claims seeing Dorothy Dandridge in *Carmen Jones* inspired his career choice, and he has spent much of his career chronicling and examining these performers. On the other hand, his categorization of their efforts, controlled as they were by Hollywood and the musical, is despairing; they all contribute to the "Negro Entertainer Syndrome." On a third hand (an awkward figure for an awkward situation), Bogle reprieves these performers from the scathing litany of stereotype, "toms, coons, mulattoes, mammies, and bucks," that provides the title of his widely known and influential history of blacks in film.[19]

One early reader of my manuscript asked me with some dismay, "Are you proposing that we know black music when we see it?" Yes and no, depending always on who (and when and where) the "we" doing the seeing and hearing are. Throughout this book, with Du Bois's concerns about the sociocultural and economic mechanisms of integration(s) resonating in the background, I will outline varying, often competing and contradictory but less often interacting positions on black music, black musical authenticity, and the value of different black musical performances.[20] In the musical and its use of black performers, final judgements of the (in)authenticity or (im)purity of the music they perform are less at stake, in my view, than are the circumstances under which, the mechanisms through which, and the debates around how African Americans and blackness can be seen, heard, and understood at all—particularly in relation to the American mainstream that film, especially in its economically integrated Hollywood mode, aims to penetrate.

Integration: Formal, Aesthetic, and Ideological

The third, and last, sense of integration important to this book refers to a formal quality specific to the musical, defined in the strict sense as a feature-length, narrative stage and film genre. The earliest uses of this sense of "integration" that I have discovered were in 1943. The first was in a highly favorable review of the stage premiere of Oscar Hammerstein II and Richard Rodgers's *Oklahoma!*: "Mr. Rodgers' scores never lack grace, but seldom have they been so well integrated as this."[21] The second was eight months later in an equally favorable review of Hammerstein's *Carmen Jones:* "The stage direction by Hassard Short, the musical direction of Joseph Littau and the orchestral arrangements by Russell Bennett are completely integrated."[22] When these two reviewers refer to "integration," they are referring to a pattern of commensurability, coherence, and appropriateness between the story or drama and the music. Since *Oklahoma!* contains no black characters and *Carmen Jones* contains no white characters, these reviewers clearly do not mean to invoke the idea of racial-social integration, even though this sense of the term was common by 1943.[23] Across the forties, this formal sense of integration rose steadily into journalistic, industrial, and finally scholarly usage, and *Oklahoma!* came to be known generally as the first "integrated" American musical. About the same time, critics began, retrospectively, to see signs of musical integration in Hammerstein and Jerome Kern's *Show Boat* (staged 1927, filmed 1936, revived 1946, filmed 1951), which in contrast to *Oklahoma!* and *Carmen Jones* was also self-reflexively racially integrated. Gershwin and Heyward's all-black cast *Porgy and Bess* (staged 1934, revived 1942, filmed 1959) also receives frequent mention in accounts of musical integration, and when critics later began their search for the earliest formally integrated film musical, they often turned to the all-black cast *Hallelujah!*

I suggest below why it is not just an ironic coincidence that "integration" should rise at nearly the same time into common usage in reference to both race relations and the musical genre, but first it is important to understand more fully what musical genre critics and scholars have meant when they use the term. While not fully apparent in the context of the quotations already cited, in formal musical-genre terms integration describes the relationship between the narrative and the musical numbers in a film or play. One source for the idea is opera, where the form aspires to—and institutionalizes in the recitative of grand opera— a fusion of music and narrative;[24] hence the logical, though overlooked, place of Hammerstein's adaptation of *Carmen* in the history of the integrated musical. A more frequently explicated source for the idea, perhaps because it is more apparently "native" to America, develops out of "folk" music. Here the sense is that different cultures, regions, and communities have a music, that this music or an imitation or approximation of it should be assigned to characters appropriately, and that, in consequence, music and story will seem to have a "natural" or "realistic" relation. Affiliated with this source for the idea of musical integration is the sense, often applied more directly to lyric than music, that the music should advance the story, thus creating a musical drama, a work of serious intent and design if not of tone and plot.[25]

What none of these definitions captures is why integration should be so highly prized—for after *Oklahoma!* integration rapidly became the critical, if not practical, sine qua non of the musical and, especially for the stage musical, it remains so—or what its potential meanings and effects are. The four contemporary historians and theoreticians of the musical, Gerald Mast, Rick Altman, Jane Feuer, and Richard Dyer, who suggest answers to this question, do not do so in specific terms of "integration," although Mast, Altman, and Feuer do all use the term. What all four writers agree on is that the successful musical suggests the utopian feelings that would result if genuine problems of "social tension, inadequacy, and absence" were resolved.[26] The musical does this at the level of plot by symbolically joining opposing forces in a wedding or romance.

More specific to the genre, the musical amplifies the dual plot at the level of form by conjoining—in Altman's terms, "dissolving" between—narrative and number, visually dominated and aurally dominated passages. The cleverness, novelty, and apparent ease with which such difficult conjunctions or dissolves are created fuel the utopian feelings the musical conveys and provide the analogue for how life would feel if all more "serious" conflicts and contradictions could be similarly resolved.[27]

Integration would seem, then, to be an amplified or extended instance of what Mast, Altman, Feuer, and Dyer see as a more general quality of the musical. Indeed, returning to the reviews of *Oklahoma!* and *Carmen Jones,* it seems that integration can make a spectator feel good enough to forget some very bad, nonutopian events in the plot, for example, the tragic ending of *Carmen Jones* and the killing of Jud Fry in *Oklahoma!,* both of which go virtually unmentioned in the reviews. Altman argues that such plot events are best seen as ritual sacrifices that serve, through contrast, to secure the utopian feeling inspired by the musical.[28] Put differently, the key reason the integrated musical became so highly prized critically and popularly is that through the drama its audience *earns* its utopian feelings, comes to deserve its entertainment—though, crucially (at least if the reviewers are at all representative), the audience also gets to forget, as part of the integrated musical experience, the costs of that earning or deserving.

For these scholars, the integrated musical is a response to the alienating, disorienting, and violently contradictory aspects of mass industrial integration and social integration.[29] As my analysis of Du Bois showed, industrial integration, with its simultaneous needs to create all subjects as predictable consumers and to maintain a newly hierarchized labor pool, and social integration, with its desire to overthrow traditional hierarchies, both do and do not fit with one another. The integrated musical shifts and aestheticizes the terms and the stakes of this crisis under the rubric of entertainment, and this shift allowed the integrated musical to "resolve"—or erase—the contradictions between industrial and social integrations.[30]

What Mast, Altman, Feuer, and Dyer do not agree on is the cultural, social, and political values of the musical and its characteristic aesthetic, textual effect. Ultimately, Feuer finds the genre conservative, and Altman sees it, finally, as deleterious because it discourages individuals' attempts to create moments of utopian feeling through their own ordinary musical performances.[31] Mast and Dyer, however, are more optimistic because they also take into account live as well as filmed musical performance, the social and cultural identities of key performers and producers of the musical, and the "excesses" and extensions (through, for example, popular songs) of the genre as much as the coherence of its individual narrative texts. Mast sees the American musical's "refus[al] to know and keep its place" in U.S. sociocultural hierarchies as proof of the genre's liberal and liberating potential.[32] Dyer is more circumspect, but also sees the potential for the musical, perhaps uniquely among entertainment forms, to "organize the possibility of changing reality."[33]

But Dyer, Mast, Altman, and Feuer all assess the genre assuming a general audience "drawn . . . from the widest possible spectrum of the public" and "all but coterminous with the American public as a whole."[34] So no matter how differently they evaluate the musical's narrative/number conjunction, dissolve, or integration, these critics see the genre's audience in the abstract — as socially and racially — *because* industrially — integrated. This probably was the case, in aggregate, for the audience for Hollywood musicals and Hollywood film in general, though that varied significantly by region, and it certainly was not true for Broadway musicals, but it is important to remember what such an assumption hides. From an African American perspective the so-called integrated musical — whatever its powers and pleasures — was manifestly *not* integrated. In fact, as the originating texts of *Oklahoma!* and *Carmen Jones* along with *Show Boat, Hallelujah!,* and *Porgy and Bess* suggest, the creation of the ultimate utopian feeling in the integrated musical relied on an explicit social-racial segregation, and no quantity of formal invention could hide that.

In a perverse way, through its specifically circumscribed "utopian" aspirations the "integrated" musical clarified in narration, song, and dance an important and for African Americans painful American circumstance of long standing. For African American performers and spectators, however, the starkness of the contradiction between a formally expressed desire for integrated wholeness and its manifestation in such critically applauded, even idealized, segregation also offered liberating — or, more accurately, persistently illuminating — possibilities. In the face of the integrated musical, African American performers, spectators, and critics developed methods of dis/integration, sometimes taking Du Boisian advantage of segregation always watching and listening for — and often seeking to create—failures of utopian form and feeling out of which new forms and feeling might emerge, and seldom giving up on the complex possibilities of the "gift"—sometimes refashioned as a joke, assault, or evasion—of African American music. Recently, Rick Altman has argued that "genres must be seen as a site of struggle among users," a contest among variously interested producers, critics, and audiences.[35] However reluctantly, musicals—perhaps especially in their "more randomized, more fragmentary forms" like specialty numbers, shorts, and marginal productions[36]—offered African Americans access to these processes and remain as evidence of struggle, evidence that we should not allow the overdetermined appeals of overlapping idea(l)s of integration to conceal.[37]

Dis/integrations in Practice: *Hooray for Love*, "Old Man River," and "Singin' in the Rain"

This book is divided into two parts of three chapters each. Both parts are synoptic, considering from different angles the period from 1927 to 1959—the entire classical sound era and an era that begins with a flourishing black cultural renaissance and ends with increasingly visible and insistent black struggles for political, civil rights. While each part begins broadly, each also moves to chapters that attend closely to individual films made in the charged moment near the end of World War II, when new possibilities for African American aesthetic, social, and political representation—all of which were often distilled into or symbolized by music—seemed to open and then close. This organization is meant at once to convey an historical narrative of the currents of production and reception of black film-musical performances; to capture the fissures, ruptures, and struggles in that narrative; and to complicate the lures of both cockeyed optimism and the (pseudo)blues.

Part one aims squarely at the dilemmas of black musical (mis)representation by taking seriously the quip I cited earlier, "The Negro . . . arrived in talking pictures—as a black-face comedian!" I examine first the use of blackface by black stage performers in the first forty years of the twentieth century and suggest that black performers, critics, and audiences took blackface quite seriously and that, while opinions varied widely regarding blackface's viability and value for African American culture, none saw it as simply inauthentic. Next, focusing primarily on the films of Al Jolson, I track the many instances in which Hollywood musicals conjoined black performers with blackfaced white performers and analyze these instances in relation to black press coverage in order to trace shifting African American understandings of the potential meanings and effects of such unions. The first part closes with analyses of four films that feature blacks in blackface: Oscar Micheaux's race films *The Darktown Revue* (1931) and *Ten Minutes to Live* (1932), the Shirley Temple vehicle *Dimples* (1936), and the Hollywood black-cast monument *Stormy Weather*. These films suggest ways in which black blackface could be wielded as a critique of repressive racial categories in general and whiteness in particular, but I also explore how this critical potential was blunted by mass mediation, which took black blackface out of the control of the improvising performer, by sociogeneric constraints like the all-black cast, by the naturalization of whiteface (i.e., a constructed white racial identity that comes to be transparent), and by the impossibility of black whiteface.

If part one focuses on what, from our contemporary perspective, are the improbabilities of blacks in blackface, part two focuses on the obvious—on musical films cast entirely or predominantly with black performers and on the ways in which black musicality is made generic. The most obvious of the obvious are the eight Hollywood black-cast musicals, and I explore these both through the lens of their shifting and often conflicting African American critical receptions over time and through their remarkably consistent and ultimately constraining use of the "folk" (as opposed to "show" or "fairy tale") musical genre conventions.[38] Much less obvious, in the sense of being less known, are race-film musicals, and two examples of this subgenre—Oscar Micheaux's *Swing!* and Million Dollar Productions's *The Duke is Tops* (Lena Horne's first film), both made in 1938 near the peak of race film production—are the focus of my next chapter. Placing these films in their sociohistorical context and reading them in light of one African American critic's attempt to develop black mass cultural critical standards, I examine them for their comments on problems of black cultural authority. Both at the time and since, critics have agreed that the short film *Jammin' the Blues* (Warner Bros., 1944), which is provocatively cagey about whether its cast is all black, succeeded impressively in representing the mood and mechanics of a great jazz jam session. My last chapter anatomizes this carefully crafted and singular success and explores the possibilities and limits of "artistic," musical crossover as a model for racial-social integration.

A coda expands from the book's core period to limn the continuing life and resonating presence of the black musical performer in American film and culture. Since 1960, Hollywood has not made black musicals—or any musicals, really—in quite the same way that it did from 1927 to 1959. Nonetheless, a bit like Porgy at the end of *Porgy and Bess,* the last classical-era black musical, the musicalized black figure in American film seems ever on the brink of departing for the "Heav'nly Lan' "—which for Porgy might mean either death or New York City—but is never quite either comfortably here or gone.

Since key components of my subject are "randomized . . . fragmentary forms" and the tracing over time of the evanescent responses of their shifting audiences, this book is, despite any synoptic impulse, incomplete and open. To clarify what I've left out, to illuminate some of my methods and assumptions, and to point to my topic's continuing significance, I end by touching here on some of the gaps in *Disintegrating the Musical.*

Despite its abiding interests in the "specialty number" and in issues of reception, this is not a comprehensive study of specialty numbers or of black reception of musical film. Yoking these topics together may seem odd, but they are joined thematically—if not logically—by their ubiquitous elusiveness. I long ago had to give up trying to catalogue and account for the myriad instances in which a black person plays a song in a film; even restricting attention just to obviously musical film forms does not help much.[39] Beyond their plethora is the fact that specialty numbers wander. As excisable, free standing units, they have fueled many film shorts (chapter six touches on this), "jazz on film" festivals, documentaries, late-night TV intervals, and compilation videos, and as a consequence provenance is often murky. In the face of these circumstances, I have chosen the relatively derandomizing, defragmenting strategy of attending to only a few specialties and always in the context of a larger film (most often feature-length) and a larger issue (either blackface or the black cast). While this choice aids the coherence of the analysis, it also downplays an important mode for (re)presenting black musical performance in film and, perhaps even more, on TV.

As importantly, downplaying the specialty number may downplay a key mode of black reception. The circumstances in which African Americans saw movies and what African American writers said about them are recurring concerns here, and my sense of alternative, African American modes of reading cinema informs my interpretations throughout. Miriam Hansen has argued, in relation to silent-era female spectatorship, that alternative modes of reception "cannot be measured in any empirical sense" but that their "conditions of possibility can be reconstructed."[40] I have aimed for such a reconstruction, but as musician Willie Ruff's recollection of his youthful enthusiasm for the *Chicago Defender* suggests,[41] one important condition of possibility for alternative black receptions may be the association of fragments, a condition that is difficult to draw with certainty out of the archive of black public commentary and its sporadic attention to movies.

To bolster my claims for the existence of alternative, African American receptions and their ties to the fragment and to underline the elusiveness of the archive, consider the most complete account of a historical instance of African American reception I have ever found, from the entertainment page of the 17 August 1935 *Defender:*

> The picture, *Hooray for Love,* with the one and only Bill "Bojangles" Robinson . . . was shown this week at the local theatre where standing room was at a premium.
>
> This picture was an added feature at the Main Street [a movie palace in downtown Kansas City] when Cab Calloway played that house recently and this correspondent heard the praise then for Bill Robinson, that grand trouper. Bill has tapped lightly on this same stage many times and his name is synonymous with genuine entertainment, but it was at the local theatre that the "lines" heard comments to the effect that without Bill Robinson there was no *Hooray For Love.* . . .
>
> A restless audience sat through the newsreels, the shorts, and a few wholesome laughs were heard in the unreeling of the film, but when Bill's Harlem scene flashed, the applause was deafening. It was as if Bill was on the stage in person, smiling in response to the welcome, as if he knew and understood that he was the asset necessary to the happiness of the audience.
>
> I believe the manager of the Lincoln Theatre felt an additional admission was due because so many sat through the picture twice. . . . Many grumbled because there wasn't more to see, but the manager smiled in understanding. He knows how Kansas City feels about Bill Robinson.[42]

Even allowing for some journalistic hyperbole, this account is remarkable. Several things stand out. This moment of reception depends on a complicated array of relations—intertextual, social, geographic, and economic—that extend well beyond the confines of *Hooray for Love* and the walls of the local theater. It also contains an emphatic component of identification; the audience feels recognized and recognizes itself in this musical moment. But this identification does not rely on narrative or character; Robinson plays "himself" and has no connection with the rest of the film's characters or backstage plot. Neither does it rely in any clear way on the "blackness" of the music, which is a song, "Livin' In a Great Big Way," by the white songwriting team of Dorothy Fields and Jimmy McHugh. Rather, this sense of identification relies on Bill Robinson's stardom, on his performance style (which, with its constant manipulations of time, rapid shifts of register from, for example, virtuosity to silliness, and call and response with pianist and co-star Fats Waller, is arguably a classic instance of black performance), and on the sense that Robinson is both recognized by and *better than* the rest of the movie, that he is deservedly *in* but at the same time not *of* the movie. And finally, this enthusiastic moment of reception is also critical; members of the audience recognize that their access to and Robinson's presence in *Hooray for Love* are limited, and they qualify the signs of their satisfaction through grumbling and overconsuming (i.e., underpaying). Was this complexly expressive Kansas City audience representative? My analysis does not assume so, but it does assume that such an audience was always possible.[43]

Bill Robinson's looming presence in *Hooray for Love* suggests another potential axis of organization for this book and, more importantly, a way in which African American audiences may have organized their attention to the random, fragmented film musical forms that so often represented them, namely, the star. My choice to privilege struggles around genre over the study of black stars and stardom was spurred by the fact that genre—blacks as musical and hence in musical films—crossed over more emphatically to white audiences than did individual black stars, who never crossed over unless they were musical performers. Indeed, the rise of Sidney Poitier, the first crossover black star who tried explicitly to disavow musical performance as part of his star persona, marks the end of the period I am considering—and Poitier did do a film musical, *Porgy and Bess*.[44] Nonetheless, following genre rather than stars leads to some lacunae. The most serious of these is Paul Robeson, who shows just how seriously the musical could be taken by various audiences and how dangerous attempts to make political use of the genre and attendant stardom could be.

Show Boat both made Robeson a star and contained him. At the moment of its first production in 1927—and in important ways still—*Show Boat* was astonishingly political. It uses an interracial cast, the members of which interact with one another; it makes several opportunities to comment directly on racist inequities, particularly of opportunity and labor; and it uses the malevolent social construction of racialized and miscegenated identity to drive its secondary plot. At the same time, several aspects of *Show Boat*'s structure undermine its progressive features. Most obviously, the black characters disappear as the main plot proceeds. We follow the romantic lead couple of Magnolia and Gaylord Ravenal, and in the face of the need for their story to resolve satisfactorily, the black characters become problems. Julie, the mulatto who sacrifices her own singing career so Magnolia can have an opportunity, is an explicit social, as well as a plot problem; Queenie and Joe ("Old Man River"), who have supported Magnolia and provided her with distinctive musical materials, are excess plot, but also perhaps social baggage. All three are absent at the end, though different versions of *Show Boat* display their guilty consciences about this by gesturing toward "black" music at their finales—for example, a number that employs some black chorines in the 1936 film version (in which Robeson played Joe) or a reprise of "Old Man River" (offscreen for Robeson in 1936, onscreen for William Warfield's Joe in the 1951 film). More subtly, *Show Boat* gives its black characters only Jerome Kern's music and Oscar Hammerstein's and P. G. Wodehouse's lyrics as "theirs." What makes this erasure of black musical material—for instance, say, the spirituals or work songs that "Old Man River" has in its background—particularly powerful is that Kern and Hammerstein did freely interpolate white music they had not composed (e.g. "After the Ball"). Thus, black resilience or protest has only one compositional voice, that of Kern and Hammerstein, while white resilience is given more texture.

The voice that Kern and Hammerstein provided Paul Robeson, in the combined form of the song "Old Man River" and Joe's stage and film image as enduring and long-suffering, is one Robeson struggled through-

2. Paul Robeson shown in jail during "Old Man River" in *Show Boat* (1936).

out his career to turn to his own radically critical but broadly integrationist ends. Many African American critics were disappointed by Robeson's decision to portray Joe in *Show Boat* on stage and even more sorely disappointed when he reprised the role in the 1936 film, and I have discovered no countervailing black critical celebration of Robeson in either instance. Partly in response, and partly due to a paucity of roles, Robeson absented himself from Hollywood and Broadway to concentrate on concertizing and his British films. When he returned to Hollywood in the black musical episode of *Tales of Manhattan* (1942), Robeson's disappointment matched that of his earlier critics (he famously picketed his own film), and he swore off movies altogether because he could not control the medium. Meantime, he attempted to contain the damage by constantly refiguring "Old Man River." He set it in his repertoire of world folk and protest music, including black spirituals and work songs, and he manipulated Hammerstein's lyric to make it more aggressive, revising, for example, "You gets a little drunk and you land in jail" to "You show a little grit and you land in jail" and "I'm tired of livin' and scared of dyin'" to "I keep on fighting until I'm dyin'." But Robeson couldn't escape the refrain, "he just keeps rollin' along"; he couldn't escape the song's isolating solo-voice structure; and ultimately, he couldn't escape the song, which he sang until the end of his career. And his legacy can't escape the film musical version of "Old Man River," which replays more frequently and widely than anything else Robeson ever recorded, symbolizing him—and Africans Americans more generally—as musical, of course, but also as integrally peripheral to the real, main story of white America.[45]

In the early 1990s, as I was just beginning to think about this book, I went to see the jazz and blues singer (and sometime grandfather on the then current *Cosby Show*) Joe Williams in a benefit concert for the Jazz Society of Chicago. It was staged at the Illinois Institute of Technology on the South Side of the city. The auditorium, in a Mies van der Rohe high modernist building, was at the corner of the recently dedicated Sammy Davis Jr. Boulevard and State Street, just across the street from the old offices of the *Chicago Defender,* only a few blocks from the (defunct) Regal Theater, home from the 1930s to the 1960s of both Hollywood films and great black bands (*Meet Me in St. Louis* and the Duke Ellington Orchestra had shared a bill in 1944), and on the old location of the most vibrant musical strip in Chicago—"the stroll"—where Louis Armstrong had played in the pit band of a silent movie theater when he first came north. It was also now surrounded by some of the most dense and depressed public housing in the city, maybe in the country, a kind of minimal storage place for the black "underclass."

Near the end of the concert Williams, who sang accompanied only by a pianist, just as Paul Robeson had famously done before him, introduced an improvised song he called "Pretty Blues." On a twelve bar blues structure, Williams laid out some astounding scat singing, very free in rhythm and melody yet at the same time emphatically dignified, calling to mind art singers like Robeson rather than, say, more apparently lighthearted scat forebears like Louis Armstrong, Cab Calloway, or Bill Robinson. As his song built toward its climax, Williams suddenly but smoothly dropped into "Old man river, that old man river," then he stopped entirely (the pianist kept playing) and said, "wait a minute. We don't have to sing that one any more!" The racially integrated crowd surrounded by the deeply segregated milieu of Chicago's decaying "Black Metropolis"—we?—went crazy. We cheered and laughed. But I think we also wondered. Is it true? Don't we? Who are we? If we don't have to sing "Old Man River" any more, do we still have to remember it and the conditions that called it forth, the work it and black performers who wrestled with it could and couldn't do? What would happen if we stopped and forgot? And since one of the films of *Show Boat* would almost certainly be on TV again soon, could we forget or stop?

Since, as I write, the Internet Movie Database tells me that the 1951 *Show Boat* will show on Turner Classic Movies tomorrow night, I think the answer to this last question must be "no." So how to remember? That is this book's largest lingering question. A fugitive moment from a few years after my experience of Joe Williams's "Old Man River" perhaps hints at an answer.

At the 1996 Academy Awards show—directed by African American musician and producer Quincy Jones and, because of the dearth of black nominees, boycotted by Jesse Jackson—tribute was paid to Gene Kelly, who had died barely a month earlier. Kelly, who had been an outspoken left liberal during the forties and fifties, was a clear progressive on race matters in the United States, but he also had complicated, unacknowledged, or at least not very boldly credited relations with the African American dance traditions and the African American dancers he drew from.[46] To eulogize Kelly, Jones and his collaborators staged a version of Kelly's famous dance from *Singin' in the Rain* to Kelly's recording of the title tune. The song played, Kelly sang, and a mysterious tap dancer, fedora pulled low to obscure his face, performed an amazing homage to and elaboration of Kelly's dance. At the end, acknowledging the crowd's applause, the dancer turned and removed his hat. Savion Glover was probably immediately familiar to a significant number of viewers because of his regular appearances on *Sesame Street*—he was black. In front of a good part of the world, Glover had just dis/integrated, even as he forcefully integrated, one of America's most famous musicals, one of its best-known icons.

This revelatory revision may or may not look and sound like progress some time from now. Indeed, textual traces in home video recordings of Glover's performance have probably all but disappeared. But Glover's dance did once more reassert the musical—a reassertion Glover and his collaborators continued in the more traceable forms of the stage musical *Bring In Da Noize, Bring In Da Funk* (1996) and the film *Bamboozled* (2000)—in all its splits, fragments, fissures, and spin-offs, as a site of performative argument about and a site of remembering how America—especially, though not exclusively, white America—might see and hear and be both more and better.

1

1

Wearing and
Tearing the Mask

BLACKS ON AND IN BLACKFACE, LIVE

downtown vaudeville

What was not pleasant was the hush that coughed
When the Negro clown came on the stage and doffed
His broken hat. The hush, first. Then the soft

Concatenation of delight and lift,
And loud. The decked dismissal of his gift,
The Sugared hoot and hauteur. Then, the rift

Where is magnificent, heirloom, and deft
Leer at a Negro to the right, or left—
So joined to personal bleach, and so bereft:

Finding if that is locked, is bowed, or proud.
And what that is at all, spotting the crowd.
—GWENDOLYN BROOKS (1949)

Does blackface make everyone who puts it on white?
—SANDER GILMAN (1991)

When *The Jazz Singer* (1927) finally came to the Black Metropolis of Chicago's South Side in early May of 1928, it came without synchronized sound. Even so, *The Jazz Singer* was not "silent." Reviewing the event, a writer for the *Chicago Defender* reported that the African American organist at the Metropolitan Theater sang the climactic song, "My Mammy," while the blackfaced Al Jolson performed it on the screen.[1]

The next fall, after the Metropolitan had been wired for sound, *The Jazz Singer* returned. This time the mechanically reproduced Jolson sang for himself, but the feature was supplemented by a sound short of the great black musicians Noble Sissle and Eubie Blake, authors of the music for the seminal black stage musical *Shuffle Along* (1921) and tuxedo-wearing vaudevillians who had long and famously refused to wear blackface.[2] At least on the South Side of Chicago, then, Jolson's most famous cinematic blackface performance never proceeded without being twinned, visually and aurally, by an African American performance.

These varying conjunctions of black and blackface performance were perhaps uniquely local and not inherent in *The Jazz Singer*.[3] However, beginning in 1930 with another Jolson film, *Big Boy,* at least twenty musical films—from at least seventy-two Hollywood movies containing self-conscious blackface, that is, blackface that draws attention to itself as a mask—internalized similar conjunctions by including both blackface and veritable black musicians or comics.[4] Two of the last three classical-era Hollywood films to use blackface performance also staged this conjunction: *Torch Song,* starring Joan Crawford, and *Walking My Baby Back Home,* starring Janet Leigh and Donald O'Connor, were both made in 1953 and each featured their white stars blacked up along with veritable black performers. A knowledgeable fan would have noted the absence of this conjunction in *The Eddie Cantor Story,* the third blackface film of 1953. Cantor had become a star performing in blackface in the Ziegfeld Follies with the monumental, black and blackfaced comedian and singer Bert Williams, but this specific facet of Cantor's career is elided in his biopic, perhaps literalizing Cantor's claim—intended as a compliment—that Williams was "the whitest black man I ever knew."[5]

In this first part of my analysis, moments of conjunction between black and blackface performance will be my primary texts, and understanding the possible meanings of such moments will be my primary aim. In this chapter, focusing on the period from the late twenties to the early forties, a period that saw the proliferation of blackface in cinema, I examine the complicated responses of black writers to black blackface as a live performance tradition. The second chapter considers the same period, but focuses on the conjunctions of white blackface and veritable black performance in films that live black blackface would have been competing against; here I pay especially detailed attention to Al Jolson and black responses to his work. Finally, the third chapter analyzes the few instances we have of black blackface in film. Eric Lott has called the presence of blackface in Hollywood musicals "minstrelsy's somewhat baffling after-life."[6] Understanding the extent and relative vigorousness of this afterlife and where it took place should help make it less baffling. It will at least delineate our bafflement.

The films that I will discuss in the following chapters serve to disprove two frequent assumptions about cinematic blackface performance that prevail in American film scholarship. The first and more general of these assumptions is that blackface performance disappeared from the American cinema after *The Jazz Singer*. This assumption probably arose from a combination of the growing feeling, beginning during the rise of the Civil Rights Movement, that blackface was a profoundly embarrassing, racist practice of the American "past" and the fact that most blackface performances took place in isolated musical numbers in what have come to be obscure musical films. Feeling and "fact" can reenforce one another, though, so that what has grown embarrassing becomes obscure—as, for example, when television stations cut "Abraham, Abraham," a number which pairs a blacked-up Bing Crosby with Louis Beavers, from the very familiar *Holiday Inn* (1942) or when scholars of the ideological effects of American movies ignore *This Is the Army* (1943), which is among the most financially successful musicals ever and which featured Ronald Reagan, Joe Louis, and a blackface number.[7] The assumption that blackface ended, more or less, with *The Jazz Singer* denies the term "blackface" any historical, material specificity and, instead, recreates it as an empty, metaphorical term of disapproval. "Stereotyped" black performances in films and on TV, white performers playing black characters but without using darkening make-up (e.g., Susan Kohner in the 1959 *Imitation of Life*), and many white musicians who appropriate black music-making practices (Elvis Presley, Mick Jagger, Vanilla Ice) thus all become "blackface more broadly understood."[8] One purpose of these next three chapters will be to rediscover, then, through analyzing a full range of blackface practices in American musical film, the historical and material specificity of blackface as a performance practice and as a descriptive term throughout the middle of the twentieth century.

The second and more specific assumption films conjoining black and blackface performance disprove is that blackface, along with appropriated black music and gesture, "only denotes African American absence from the screen."[9] This assumption is convenient because it suggests simple measures for white appropriation and clearly demarcated, always visible and audible boundaries across which appropriation takes place unidirectionally. But, as the examples from this chapter's opening suggest, such a belief is far too easy. Crucial foundations for the U.S. economy, society, and culture were set with the appropriation of black African bodies and labor, and most strands of white U.S. culture have sustained themselves by further appropriating elements from black cultures. Blackface performance stands as a particularly stark and obvious marker of such appropriations, and cultural critics and analysts need to recognize this obviousness. "It could be argued," Carol Clover has claimed, "that there was a perverse honesty to traditional blackface."[10] We need to recognize that white appropriations of black culture, along with their blackface marker, did not only or always indicate *absence* of (and for) African Americans; rather, they indicate a complex, relational, multivalent, though virtually always constrained and unequal *presence.* That presence needs to be described and analyzed. Apropos of nineteenth-century uses of blackface, music historian Eileen Southern has noted, "No one forgot who was behind it all"[11]—and sometimes African Americans were literally, materially behind it all. African Americans blacked up, too, and not just for white audiences.[12] To impute this practice only to the force of racism or wholly to false consciousness on the part of many black performers verges on the racism such claims are meant to combat. A second purpose of this chapter, then, is to understand in a more complex, historically grounded manner the varieties and interconnections of blackface*s* and representations of "veritable" blackness—interconnections that were not stable or constant but, rather, shifted with audiences and across historical moments.

My argument is not that blackface is not embarrassing and racist or that there are no continuities between self-conscious blackface performance and other (mis-) representations of African Americans. Rather, it is that blackface is not *simply* embarrassing and racist and that its continuities with other forms of representation cannot be assumed to be clear and direct. If scholars and critics permit discomfort and distaste to dominate (as opposed to inform) history writing and interpretation, then we risk reifying past practices and, consequently, reproducing the worst aspects of those practices as their opposites. As Stuart Hall puts it: "However deformed, incorporated, and inauthentic are the forms in which black people and black communities and traditions appear and are represented in popular culture, we continue to see, in the figures and the repertoires on which popular culture draws, the experiences that stand behind them."[13]

The pairing of black and blackface performance in film musicals provides a limit case to Hall's claim, since it thematizes what, from a present-day perspective at any rate, seem to be the extremes of deformation, incorporation, and inauthenticity. Consequently, some of the questions that will organize my study in the following chapters are: What, specifically, was blackface performance? What did it look like and sound like? What was its history in relation to the American film musical, and what were its incarnations in the film musical? What black experiences "stand behind" blackface performance in Hollywood musical film? What happens when the experiences embodied in the figure of the black performer stand not behind but *beside* or *within* the blackface mask? How does the conjoining of the "authentic" with the "inauthentic" work, and toward what effect? What forms does it take, and what were the meanings of those forms to white and, more importantly, black critics and observers? Who sees (and hears) what behind and through the deformed form?

Black Critics of Blackface

By the time *The Jazz Singer* was released, blackface, as a self-conscious, professional, theatrical practice in the United States, was over a century old, and since at least the turn of the century both black and white cultural critics had been variously predicting and lamenting or calling and hoping for its demise.[14] As a complete, self-contained form, the blackface minstrel show had ceased to be popular in the cities by the late 1800s. The minstrel show, largely performed by African Americans, did continue in rural areas, especially the south, into the 1950s. One writer for the black press estimated that in 1930 there were "twenty odd" minstrel shows and one hundred plantation shows and carnivals employing African American minstrels, but increasingly in the early decades of the twentieth century, "minstrelsy" had come to mean blackfaced "specialties" or "singles" in variety, burlesque, and vaudeville.[15] By 1927 blackface seemed at once thoroughly residual (and, to many, retrograde) and tremendously resilient. Blackface showed this resilience when it appeared in early sound film, bringing Carl Wittke to conclude his celebratory history of minstrelsy, *Tambo and Bones* (1930), with this vision: "Here the story of the decline of American [blackface] minstrel shows might end, were it not for the fact that the 'talkies' promise a revival of this venerable art. . . . The future of minstrelsy seems to lie in the lap of Hollywood."[16]

Partly as a consequence of this revival at the hands of Hollywood, blackface came under intense scrutiny as critics tried to understand its origins and development and championed their ideas for its future.[17] Studies as diverse as Wittke's, James Weldon Johnson's *Black Manhattan* (1930), and Constance Rourke's *American Humor: A Study of the National Character* (1931) all explored blackface and its legacies in some detail. What was unique about this moment of reflection compared with earlier reflections on blackface is that it now included the voices of black critics, critics who often had significantly different ideas about blackface than white writers—never purely celebratory, though not necessarily only stringently critical.[18] So the renewal that mass media offered blackface also resulted in African American attention to blackface that was unique both in its concentration and in the fact that via the growing black press this criticism, too, was mass mediated.

A common concern of African Americans writing about blackface was (re)asserting and tracing the *black* contribution to Carl Wittke's "venerable art." This common interest in black contributions to blackface led to questions of origins, extensions, appropriations, and evaluation, issues on which there was much less agreement. In a vein characteristic of the moment and of the concerns of many African American critics, James Weldon Johnson wrote in *Black Manhattan:* "Negro [i.e., blackface] minstrelsy, as a form of professional entertainment, seems dead; nevertheless, its history cannot be reviewed without recognition of the fact that it was the first and remains, up to this time, the only completely original contribution America has made to the theater. Negro minstrelsy, everyone ought to know, had its origins among the slaves of the Old South."[19] Johnson had no illusions about blackface minstrelsy and what it meant for black performers: "Minstrelsy was, on the whole, a caricature of Negro life, and it fixed a stage tradition which has not yet been entirely broken. It fixed the tradition of the Negro as only an irresponsible, happy-go-lucky, wide-grinning, loud-laughing, shuffling, banjo-playing, singing, dancing sort of being."[20]

It is easy to see why Johnson would want blackface "dead." Still, since the death of the form did not mean the death of that form's constrain-

3. Black comedian Bert Williams in blackface for the musical comedy *Under the Bamboo Tree* (1921–22). Used with the permission of Wisconsin Center for Film and Theater Research.

ing effects, it was also important, for Johnson, to recognize what the form permitted: "Nevertheless, these [blackface black minstrel] companies did provide stage training and theatrical experience for a large number of coloured men. They provided an essential training and theatrical experience which, at the time, could not have been acquired from any other source. Many of these men, as the vogue of minstrelsy waned, passed on into the second phase . . . of the Negro on the theatrical stage in America; and it was mainly upon the training they had gained that this second phase rested."[21] Bert Williams, still wearing blackface, was among the avatars of Johnson's second phase, which saw the rise of the black musical theater. Sissle and Blake—who refused blackface, but who created *Shuffle Along* with Flournoy Miller and Aubry Lyles, who did not—would be the avatars of the third phase. Johnson seems to say,

"Blackface minstrelsy is dead, long live blackface!"—though he certainly thought the place it should "live" was in the memory of the African American roots of this "completely original contribution America has made to the theater."[22]

Johnson's colleague W. E. B. Du Bois attempted to be clearer and more proscriptive in negotiating the intricate terrain of blackface. For Du Bois minstrelsy was the "nadir" of representations of the Negro, and black-face was to be avoided at all costs—it was a thing of the past.[23] Still, like Johnson, Du Bois ran into difficulties over the issue of blacks in black-face and over how to make—and keep—the past really past. Du Bois recognized the blackfaced and black "Great Funmakers" who, working within the constraints of their time, had helped prepare the ground that made his own critical attitude possible.[24] Eulogizing Bert Williams in 1923, Du Bois suggested that Williams created "the smile that hovered above blood and tragedy; the light mask of happiness that hid break-ing hearts and bitter souls."[25] The word "mask" here recalls Williams's blackface and also Paul Lawrence Dunbar's famous poem, "We Wear the Mask" (1896), but in Du Bois's elusive syntax it seems to refer most directly to Williams's *audience* and his effect on them. And, indeed, Du Bois did not want to claim, with Dunbar's poem, that Williams "grinned and lied" or that he caused such behavior in his audience. To Du Bois, Williams's performance was "the top of bravery; the finest thing in ser-vice"; crucial in the struggle for equality, and worthy of "highest praise." Consequently, in relation to Bert Williams at least, Du Bois had to find a way to revalue, temporarily, the blackface mask he so hated.[26]

Du Bois revalued the blackface mask by acknowledging the complexity —rather than clarity—he believed it had when used by the Great Fun-makers. He coupled "mask" with the term "light," precisely the term that described both Williams's skin and the skin of his white audience at the Ziegfeld Follies and precisely not the word that would describe blackface. By doing this, Du Bois created a conjunction that values the (black) blackface mask because it permitted Bert Williams to create for and install on his (mostly white) audience a "light mask" to "hover[. . .] above [*their*] blood and tragedy" and "hid[e] [*their*] breaking hearts and bitter souls"[27]—a white mask for white people. In this formulation, the light, hovering, and hiding mask also reveals to its wearer, and to canny observers like Du Bois, what is underneath, and this is what made Bert Williams a "great comedian," a "great Negro," and a "great man." The blackface mask could be effective, then, through multiplying maskness, but for Du Bois, hater of masks, the desired effect was the destruction of *all* masks, whether material or metaphoric.[28] By this logic, the effective mask leads through proliferation to its own destruction, and Williams, who died at age forty-six in 1922, becomes a weird mixture of martyr and suicide—most weird because, as Du Bois knew, blackface in 1922 was not dead, not past, and the masks of race were far from destroyed. Despite his firmest desires, Du Bois ends up saying, opposite Johnson, "Blackface lives, long may it die!"

The African American scrutiny of blackface was not limited to elegant polemics like Du Bois's or to reasoned and researched studies like Johnson's. Spurred by the cinematic mass mediation of blackface, this scrutinizing also took place on the less polished but also widely circulated pages of black newspapers. Since these newspapers were likely to advertise performances by black blackfaced performers, their writers found themselves not so much hoping for the end of blackface, at least not as explicitly as Johnson and Du Bois, as wondering about its longevity and its meaning(s) for their readers.

In 1931, the same year that saw the publication of *Black Manhattan*, a headline in the *Richmond Planet* wondered: "Does Blackface Acting Exert a Magic Spell Over American Audiences?" The author, George Santa, does not answer this question but rather concludes with a paragraph whose syntax suggests clenched teeth, an expression of critical feelings very different in style and argument from Johnson's assured smoothness and Du Bois's rhetorical savvy, though it is perhaps less different in sentiment: "The tragic condition of the American Negro in the popularity of the blackface artists [e.g., Jolson, Eddie Cantor, and Amos 'n' Andy] paradoxically gives rise to a much more hilariously funny type of entertainment than any situation in the United States. Nor does the acceptability show any signs of abating."[29] Santa's critical ambiguity arises, at least in part, from *his* take on the fraught issues of origins, extensions, and appropriations: "The late 'Bert' Williams [was] conceded by the most 'hard-boiled' critics to have been the greatest comedian of all times. He, it was, who began the now prevalent custom of blacking the face. It was rumored that this master actor hit upon the idea accidentally but there can be no doubt that the custom has become a deeply imbedded essential to American stage humor."[30]

Wittke, Rourke, Johnson, and Du Bois would have agreed with Santa's assessment of Bert Williams's greatness, but none would have agreed with his claim that Williams "began the custom of blacking the face." Starting in small-time minstrel shows, Williams worked in blackface from 1893 until his death in 1922, after years of work in black musical shows and, finally, in the Ziegfeld Follies. By all accounts Williams hated blackface, worked to avoid it in his early career, and would have given it up once he was a star had he thought his predominantly white audience would accept him without it.[31] With only a little research, Santa could have known these facts, and perhaps he did. The significance of Santa's article is not in his inaccuracy, however, but in his desire to reclaim black-face for a popular, black readership. For him, unlike for Johnson and Du Bois, blackface continued as a living, moneymaking practice.

This operation results in critical, cognitive difficulties that share a pattern with but are different from Johnson's sense that blackface was both good and bad, enabling and limiting, black and white, or Du Bois's sense that blackface was bad, except when it was good, obfuscating, except when it revealed the (white) heart. By moving the "origins" of blackface into the recoverable, directly attributable past, Santa hopes to avoid this ambivalence, and the case of Al Jolson seems to provide just what he is looking for: Al Jolson "received his inspiration from the inimitable Bert Williams years before Jolson had ever received the acclaim and, of course, the wealth that has fallen his lot. Perhaps more than Jolson's unusual ability to 'put over' a song, it was the blackfaced scene in the *Singing Fool* that brought such widespread success to that weeping picture."[32] This case seems clear, though perhaps not as clear as could be hoped: Williams was "inimitable," but Jolson, who is merely "unusual," still manages to imitate him, and it is "perhaps" this—especially Williams's blackface—that wins Jolson his acclaim and wealth.

The case of Miller and Lyles, "the most colorful Negro exponents of blackface acting," is even more acute and critically difficult for Santa because Miller and Lyles, along with their ostensible imitators, were still alive and working. The pair was innovative, successful, and famous, and "it has been rumored that Amos 'n' Andy have directly pirated their comedy from this popular pair." Nothing new here, "but," Santa continues, "no one has ever been able to confirm this report." Santa's story seems to follow the same pattern as his exposé of Jolson, until it suddenly switches gears: "Whatever may be the truth of this report, Amos 'n' Andy have gone much farther in the development of their idea than Miller and

Lyles. They have employed a serialized method of presentation and have coined many catchy phrases that are no doubt totally original. Nevertheless, the enchanting humor of the blackface appearance has undoubtedly carried 'little Lyles' and 'big Miller' to the top of stage pairs in this type of work."[33] Here the pattern of analysis is surprisingly reversed. "Whatever may be the truth," Amos 'n' Andy deserve their acclaim, and the black Miller and Lyles owe *their* success to blackface. Perhaps because he was aware of Amos 'n' Andy's popularity among sections of his readership, Santa's search for clarity, his desire to demystify blackface's magic, leads to further complexity — or, more accurately, disorientation.[34]

"Just Where Did 'Blackface' Comedy Get Its Start?," an article written by Henry Brown for the *Chicago Defender* in late 1932, takes a different tack from Santa's piece. Rather than seeking clarity, it celebrates blackface's lack of clarity as a sort of community adhesive. Like Santa's, Brown's piece sees — and was in part inspired by — blackface as a continuing performance and mass media practice: "While the [live] minstrel man seems to have run his course, there is yet a laugh left in the blackface, even for sophisticated audiences, as the talking pictures *Mammy* and *The Jazz Singer* and others of that type have shown in recent years."[35] Unlike Santa, however, Brown focuses on the impossibility of uncovering the "start" of blackface: "It's up again! How it starts nobody seems to know — it is known only that the argument again rages as to the origin of 'blackface' comedy and the old minstrel. One man says the first person to use cork to put over a song and dance was an English 'Varieties' artist; his friend says he knows better — he says that the original blackface was actually a former slave and that he sang his song to a stable of Kentucky thoroughbreds as he groomed them daily in Louisville."[36] These two myths of the origin of blackface continue to have currency.[37] Again, though, the accuracy of Brown's historical account is less important than the relationship he suggests that his readers have with blackface. Instead of worrying as Johnson and Santa do about the black relation to blackface, Brown suggests that his readers have already (re)claimed blackface through their recurring debates: "Still the argument may rage in our barber shops as to where the first burnt cork comedian drew his first laugh from an American audience. But, after all, it's a good argument, and like the old question as to whether the chicken or the egg arrived here first, or who was the first exponent of what we call jazz, it helps to fill the wintery evenings where good fellows get together to reminisce and to engage in pleasant banter."[38] In Brown's account, then, the ambivalence surrounding blackface is productive.

From the perspectives of Du Bois and, to a lesser extent, Johnson and Santa, Brown's position seems too sanguine, a pronouncement of cock-eyed optimism in the face of a persistent nineteenth-century racist practice. But Brown's optimism is not simply naive. It works to reclaim an important reality in 1932: In addition to white media stars, African American performers continued to use blackface. To emphasize this fact, Brown's essay carries photographs of Johnny Hudgins, a black blackface performer of the twenties and thirties. Brown knew—and felt impelled to acknowledge—that blackface was not dead. He knew that his readers could, and apparently did, go out to see Jolson and Cantor films or listen to Amos 'n' Andy on the radio and that they could see black blackface performers like Johnny Hudgins. Johnson and Du Bois tried to ignore or deny the continuing presence and power of blackface, especially for black audiences, and Santa found this circumstance confusing and apparently distasteful. Brown tried to see it as affirmative, as a potential opening for black cultural expression.

The Reformation of Blackface, 1927–1953

Brown's position raises several questions that need to be answered in order to fully understand the conjoining of black and blackface performance in film musicals: How much black blackface was there from the late twenties to the fifties? What did black blackface mean for its black consumers? And what was a self-conscious "race" man or woman—the ideal writer for and reader of the *Defender* or the *Planet*—to make of the continuance of black blackface, let alone its coexistence and frequent coincidence with cinematic white blackface?

Anything approaching an empirical answer to my first question is impossible, given the fleeting nature of most live entertainment, the multiply "marginal" nature of much black entertainment in this period, and important regional variations in African American entertainment. Nevertheless, a careful examination of the entertainment pages of the *Chicago Defender,* supplemented by more cursory examinations of other African American periodicals, gives some sense of black blackface's changing presence in African American communities. Since most Afri-

4. The black comic Johnny Hudgins in blackface. "Just Where Did 'Blackface' Comedy Get Its Start?" *Chicago Defender*, 31 December 1932;

(below)
5. "Folks We Can Get Along Without," *Chicago Defender*, (detail). 28 November 1936.

THE "COMICAL DARKY" WHO, FOR THE SAKE OF A LAUGH FROM A WHITE MAN, PROCEEDS TO MAKE A MONKEY OF HIMSELF

can Americans would witness both live and filmed blackface performances in segregated, community movie theaters, this context is especially important to understand.

On the South Side of Chicago in the late twenties and the thirties, black blackface was a prominent and regular feature of the entertainment scene, as it had been from at least the turn of the century.[39] By 1927, when *The Jazz Singer* reinvigorated blackface for mainstream audiences, it was not uncommon for blackfaced black performers to appear in the publicity photographs on the entertainment pages of the *Defender*.[40] Alex Lovejoy, a blackface performer, was part of the 1928 gala opening of the Regal Theater, a palace in the Keith-Albee cinema chain that would be a center for South Side entertainment for over three decades.[41] In 1929, blackface performer Marshall "Garbage" Rogers began a semiregular five-year stint on the Regal bill.[42] Not long after Rogers died in 1934, the blackfaced Dewey "Pigmeat" Markham began similar work for the Apollo Theater in Harlem and then other major black theaters around the country.

Examples like this exist for the entire decade, but one last example should suffice for showing the familiarity of blackface in black communities in the thirties. Each year the South Side witnessed at least one charity minstrel show.[43] These shows, which could be front page, society page, and entertainment page news, featured both professional and amateur performers. Though they were vaudeville shows or revues rather than minstrel shows in the traditional, nineteenth-century sense, each show featured at least one blackface performer and often more.[44]

Records of such "nearly anonymous" performers and their ephemeral performances do not exist, so it is impossible to know exactly what these performances were about.[45] What places did black blackface take in the various programs in which it appeared? What were the contents of these acts? How were they received? Since all that remains of these performances are a few photographs, scant promotional newspaper coverage, and a small body of oral history, we must be cautious in our analyses. At the very least, however, it seems fair to suggest that black blackface formed around—and worked to release or ameliorate—a knot of anxieties, tensions, pressures, and contradictions in the lives of blacks in America. This knot was staged as a set of apparently stacked binary oppositions: black/white, dark/light, south/north, country/city, powerless/powerful, lower-class/middle-class, male/female. But the various potential links across these oppositions, as well as with the triad black/light/white, worked to ensure that black blackface never settled into a stable, clear, fully legible, monovocal practice.

Eric Lott, in *Love and Theft*, examines the complex cultural work of blackface, but strictly in the nineteenth century and almost exclusively from white, mostly working class perspectives. He concludes that, although minstrelsy started as a dynamic, potentially explosive form in which all these binarisms interfered with one another, it stagnated after the Civil War into a stable, repressive form in which these same binarisms lined up in a system of oppression. In other words, for Lott (and also for Michael Rogin in *Blackface, White Noise*), minstrelsy seeks to resolve the middle term of the triads white/light[ethnic]/black or upper-class/working-class/slave-under-class so that diads result. For blacks, blackface insisted on the middle terms, both as representatives of all the potential gradations and as a method for questioning the alignment of various gradations with hierarchies of social power.

Dance historians Marshall and Jean Stearns argue that performers like "Garbage" and "Pigmeat" were "country comics," who "spic[ed] their down-home characterizations with sophisticated comments on city life —and eccentric dancing [and singing]." The Stearns go on to claim that "the inside nature of their humor made possible some extremely blue and bawdy remarks, which only those in the know could understand."[46] While the Stearnses are oblique here, "sophisticated," "blue," "bawdy," and "inside" mean, at least in part, critical of white America. Lorenzo Tucker, an African American stage and race-film actor who worked from the twenties through the fifties, claimed (here in his biographer's words) that many of the "interlocutors"—nonblackfaced straight men—"in the black vaudeville shows of the late 1920s were light-skinned black men," as was Tucker. According to him, "the audience knew these interlocutors were sometimes symbolic of the white man, and [they] were often the objects of thinly disguised racial ridicule from the blackface endmen."[47] At the same time, though, these interlocutors were also well dressed, well spoken, well mannered black men—symbols, perhaps even embodiments, of the African American middle and striving classes. For instance, in one show in which Tucker served as the "white" object of black-blackfaced criticism, he also controlled the pace of the show (another of the interlocutor's jobs) and served as blues diva Bessie Smith's escort onto the stage. In this last role, wearing the same fine suit he wore in his other two roles, Tucker was a theatricalized paragon of African American male attractiveness; *and,* in the residual guise of "white" man, he was a racy jab at any illiberal white (or black) people in the audience.[48] At any moment, then, the interlocutor could be seen as white, black, or a mixture of both.

These category shifts were activated in large part by the black-blackfaced country clowns, who were also black, though blacked up —blacker black—which meant nothing and everything, depending on one's way of seeing. These "country clowns" could range from a Women's League amateur to Sweet Papa Garbage (to invoke Marshall Rogers's full and fully complex stage name), the old pro who, "contrary to his billing," dressed impeccably when he performed.[49] For a black audience, these clowns were black people entertaining black people—and getting paid. For a different, white audience they could still (invisibly) "be" all these things and remain "niggers." Given this complex web of significations, Henry Louis Gates's characterization of black blackface as "a double negative" seems simultaneously apposite and inadequate.[50] Gates's description captures the dominant U.S. idea of race as a hierarchized duality, sees how blackface supports that model, and sees how black blackface might also be critical of the model, but it also simplifies the radical—and unpredictable—qualities of black blackface negation.[51]

Of course, there were African American critics, like W. E. B. Du Bois, for whom the multiplicity of black blackface collapsed functionally into a single negative, especially because blackface was also (predominantly) a white practice. If much of the *Defender's* "reporting" on black blackface performance seems to have been implicitly approving (most of it, after all, falls under the category of publicity or promotional material rather than criticism), other writing in the paper, usually located on the editorial page and less frequent than the publicity material, did criticize black blackface. Unlike the pieces by Du Bois, Johnson, Santa, and Brown I analyzed earlier, these criticisms focused strictly on present practice and, hence, were not anxious about maintaining a sense of the black past; but like Du Bois et al., the more casual critics made their criticisms in the name of supporting *the* race. However, the (black) blackface mask revealed all the ironies, complexities, and contradictions in that monolithic "the."

In the first such instance that I have found, Thelma Lee Wallace of Chicago wrote a letter to the *Defender's* editors, who ran it during October

1927 under the title "Our Musical Shows": "When you have seen one you have seen them all, the same thing over and over again, the same blues singer, the two male tap dancers, the advertizing of forty people when in reality there are about sixteen (why pick forty?), the same men who labor under the impression that black makeup and baggy trousers make a comedian, the heavily painted chorus girls who sing with no thought of letting the public know what they are singing about, the usual court scene, and last but not least in every one that I have witnessed the old plantation scene."[52] Wallace does not approve of black blackface, but neither does she single it out for scorn. Rather, black blackface stands in the midst of other performance practices that all coalesce into something repetitive and distinctly low class or second rate. Wallace is abashed, if not ashamed, by what she perceives as her association, her possession of and by these—"our"—shows. She wishes to distinguish herself and her taste and to push "the race" to higher levels of achievement. Nevertheless, the final sentence of the quotation implies that she has seen a fair sample of these shows, and the authority of her critique rests on this implication: Thelma Wallace has been a supporter of "our musical shows"; now she demands and deserves better. That implicit "better" rejects blackface.

Three and a half years later, the *Defender* published an article that suggested the critics like Thelma Lee Wallace (along, perhaps, with W. E. B. Du Bois and James Weldon Johnson) were having an effect on black performers. The article, "Hudgins Cuts Black Face [*sic*], Proves Point," seems to respond directly, if belatedly, to Wallace's 1927 letter:

> Blackface in the world of a comedian is not the open sesame to success, neither is it a guarantee that the man behind the make-up can put over his material unless that particular actor is clever.
>
> Johnny Hudgins seems to be a case in point. Theatergoers have been used to seeing Johnny in dilapidated silk hat, his grotesque frock coat, ungainly shoes, and his face all blacked up.
>
> But have they seen him recently minus the black face and that funny little red hat?[53]

This article does not mean to suggest that Hudgins was not a success wearing blackface. Rather, it means to suggest that he was "clever" enough to do without blackface and experience continued success. Blackface is not in itself explicitly condemned, only its habitual, careless use.[54]

Hudgins does not seem to have proved his point, since the *Defender* carried no more reports like this and many more reports of black blackface performers in the coming years of the decade.[55] In fact, over a year after Hudgins had supposedly dropped blackface, the *Defender* illustrated Henry Brown's "Just Where Did 'Blackface' Get Its Start?" with a photo collage of the blackfaced Johnny Hudgins, "the Modern Exponent of 'Blackface'"[56] (see Fig. 4). It is unclear whether or not this choice of illustration and caption means that Hudgins had returned to wearing blackface or that the *Defender* was being sloppy.[57] What is clear is that no point about the aesthetic or political merits of black blackface was categorically proven for black audiences and performers in 1931.

The *Defender* tried a more direct attack in 1936, suggesting in an editorial cartoon that the "'comical darky'" was someone "we can get along without" (see Fig. 5), but after that it lapsed into complete critical silence.[58] "In those days," Lorenzo Tucker says of 1927, though things were not so different in 1937, "the blacks [*sic*] were trying to get rid of the old minstrel shows, but they couldn't get rid of the minstrel openings [i.e., the black blackfaced comedians] to save their souls."[59] For an old pro like Dewey "Pigmeat" Markham, the fact of his clinging to blackface should not be surprising: With no more authority or protection than his ability to make people laugh, Markham and his ilk had worked in places that Thelma Wallace or W. E. B. Du Bois would seldom—and probably never happily—frequent. Blackface may have been habitual for both Markham and his audience, but it was not careless. Markham knew firsthand, even if the younger, urbanized, or more middle-class members of his audience could not or would not remember, the complex and black history of black blackface.

Why exactly South Side society would continue to use blackface in its charity benefit shows is more puzzling. This tradition appears to have culminated in 1939 with an all-female "minstrel show" at the Savoy Ballroom for the benefit of the Illinois Children's Home.[60] Among the three photographs accompanying this report, two show the women without blackface, but the third reveals that this was not a minstrel show in name only. In this photo, three young women wear blackface and what appear to be angel costumes as they cluster around a microphone. Unlike some of the professionals who performed in benefits, these women did not make a living blacking up, and these same women must have been at least familiar with—and perhaps to—the *Defender* editors and with national luminaries like Du Bois, whose visits to Chicago were carefully monitored by the *Defender* society pages. Nonetheless, in the name of supporting the black poor, they chose to adopt a mask that their peers felt whites had used over and again to caricature blacks. These female reformers flirted briefly with becoming "people we could do without." On the one hand, this suggests the continuing ludic power of the blackface mask: wearing a mask that in black performance practice was reserved almost exclusively for men, the high-toned, northern, middle-class, and safe Women's League got to play at being low-toned, southern, poor, and dangerous. On the other hand, that these women could take up this mask also suggests that for larger, working- and lower-class black audiences its potential for meaning was waning and that even when blacks wore blackface before black audiences the mask was ossifying, here along class and possibly caste lines, into the token of mean-spiritedness and oppression its critics had long felt it to be.

Anthropologist John Szwed has argued that minstrelization, "the process by which the low are characterized or emulated within a carefully regulated and socially approved context" and for which blackface is the exemplar, serves as a sociocultural protection for the "high" group.[61] Minstrelization permits "safe" contact—though, in Szwed's analysis, the protection is always incomplete, permitting "high" to embody "low" behaviors unawares. Black blackface suggests that this protective effect was multidirectional: Blackface might protect whites from too close or too much contact with blacks, but it also protected blacks from whites. When paraded before white audiences, black blackface performed a cultural sleight of hand, permitting easy laughter at the "simple" clown and setting another mode (in many estimates the gem) of black cultural expression—the music that invariably accompanied the blackface performance—in a protected sphere by gauging and governing the attention the music would receive.[62] In front of black audiences, black blackface was critical, puncturing white and perhaps black aspirant pretensions.[63]

By the time of the 1939 benefit minstrel show for the Illinois Children's Home, when political struggles to integrate the booming defense industries and public housing and cultural struggles to integrate jazz and Hollywood (see chapters four and six) were in full force, such protection was no longer as desirable for many African Americans as it had been. It was hoped that white hostility and injustice were ebbing and/or that African American power and moral suasion could make them ebb. And indeed the Children's Home benefit seems to have been the last of the South Side benefit minstrel shows.[64] Some vestigial black blackface performance continued into the forties. It is unclear when, exactly, Pigmeat Markham dropped blackface from his routines—some say it was in the late thirties, others put it in the forties—but beginning around 1937 critics, especially in New York, put increasing pressure on him to cease the practice.[65] In 1945 the *Defender* published a letter to the editor lambasting a black blackface performer who appeared in a downtown (white) theater with the (black) Fletcher Henderson Orchestra: "I was disgusted with the blackface and the 'jokes' he pulled. It is a disgrace to the race that such acts as this one are allowed to represent us on the stage, especially in these days when we are trying so hard to prove to the world that we are equal to any other race in culture and refinement as well as everything else."[66] By 1949 civil-rights spokesmen would criticize Louis Armstrong for applying the mask of the King of the Zulus in the New Orleans Mardi Gras, a mask that *does* look a bit like blackface (though with more balance between the black of the face and the white around the eyes and mouth) but one that also serves a "ritual function" in a very specific and contained event.[67] Certainly by 1950, black blackface was dead as an ordinary performance practice, though white blackface continued in amateur theatricals, parades, and, for a few more years, Hollywood musicals.[68]

For African American movie audiences, it was into the midst of these intricate and changing circumstances that self-conscious and almost exclusively white blackface in cinema emerged, and it is in relation to these circumstances that the next two chapters will examine film musicals combining black and blackface performances.[69] While it is crucial to understand and analyze the continuing appeal of blackface to Hollywood and the general, American (white) audience, it is as crucial to understand and analyze how blackface in film, especially in combination with black performance, could appear to and work for black audiences.

2

"Fool Acts"

CINEMATIC CONJUNCTIONS

OF WHITE BLACKFACE AND

BLACK PERFORMANCE

"I Can't Believe Al Jolson Would Humiliate the Race,"
Noble Sissle Writes. — *Pittsburgh Courier* headline (1936)

Most of its critics assume that blackface is a white phenomenon. Consequently, they analyze how blackface expressed white racist, supremacist ideologies and oppressed black people—how, in Eric Lott's terms, blackface shored up the color line and "infected" black culture with its stereotypes or how, in Michael Rogin's terms, blackface worked to permit white social mobility by enforcing black stasis and "mak[ing] African-Americans stand for something besides themselves."[1] Some of these critics complicate their analyses by examining how, alongside its powerfully oppressive qualities, blackface also expressed utopian yearnings for an interracial collective—how, again in Lott's terms, blackface also crossed the color line, creating a "dance" or allowing "intercourse" between white and black people in the United States.[2]

I find these analyses compelling and useful but also limited. As the previous chapter demonstrated, while blackface was predominantly practiced by white performers for white audiences, it was not exclusively so, a fact worth attending to and interpreting. In other words, we need to pay more attention to the unwilling or, in some instances, differently willing African American partners to Lott's blackface "dance." This kind of analysis has been done for parts of the nineteenth and early twentieth centuries,[3] but not yet for the mid-twentieth, when the audio-visual mass mediation of sound film profoundly altered the terms of any such dance, especially for African Americans.

Unlike mainstream theater and vaudeville, Hollywood film was widely available to African American audiences, especially in cities and, most especially, in northern cities.[4] We know from the stories that opened chapter one that African American audiences went to see Al Jolson in *The Jazz Singer;* this chapter will show that for decades after *The Jazz Singer* these audiences had many other opportunities and perhaps some particular incentives to see other white blackface performances in Hollywood musical films. This general availability of white blackface was novel. So, among other things, sound film meant that for relatively little money and relatively free from white surveillance black audiences could see, hear, and judge the meanings and qualities of self-conscious white blackface performance—a type of performance that supposedly represented them and that many African Americans saw as having highly charged connections with and implications for black entertainment and culture.

The Cinematic Transformation of Blackface

Sound film also wrought some formal changes in blackface performance practices: By both spectacularizing and "narrativizing" blackface performance, it altered the frames in which blackface had been ordinarily placed and understood. With some notable exceptions, about which I'll have more to say later, blackface performers appeared in most films both with and without their makeup, foregrounding a diegetic shift from "natural" character to "made-up" performer. This practice contrasted sharply with blackface minstrelsy and vaudeville as well as with unselfconscious, dramatic, impersonating, and illusionist uses of blackface in both theater and film (e.g., *The Clansman* on stage or *The Birth of a Nation* on film), which did not explicitly reveal the transformation to blackface.[5] Moreover, sound film frequently *showed* blacking up (or, sometimes, deblacking) as a transition, a process, the donning of a mask, and made that process an attraction, in addition to the blackfaced comic or musical performance itself.[6] The change into blackface—either shown, via an abrupt cut, as a transformation or, through a continuous shot or scene, as a process of transition—is a crucial generic marker of the blackface film.

When shown as a transition, this change often supplies the film's most charged moment, though the effects of this charge must have varied from

6. Eddie Cantor
with black valet
blacking up in *Kid
Millions* (1935).

audience to audience, especially when a veritable black performer was
on hand for comparison or comment. In *Kid Millions* (1935), blacking
up for a shipboard talent show, Edward Grant Wilson, Jr. (Eddie Cantor) catches the eye of his black valet and says, "This is tough to put on
and take off . . . you know, you're lucky." How spectators responded to
Eddie's "joke" would perhaps depend on how they felt about his character's implicit namesakes: Ulysses S. Grant, northern Civil War general,
Republican president, and supporter (and unwitting destroyer) of black
reconstruction, and Woodrow Wilson, southerner, Democratic president, and supporter of segregation and *Birth of a Nation*. It would almost
certainly have depended on how enthralled they were by the Nicholas
Brothers, who made their feature-film debut in *Kid Millions* dancing
rings around the blackfaced Cantor.

I put the word "narrativized" in quotation marks earlier because, while
it's true that, unlike minstrelsy and vaudeville, blackface films place
the blackface performance within an extended narrative flow of events,
these films seldom motivate the transformation or transition into blackface.[7] In the few instances in which the change is motivated, the motive
is always disguise. Usually such disguise scenes take place in an anarchic comedy, and consequently the disguise is often an improvised and
ultimately unsuccessful attempt to elude authority:[8] Eddie Cantor gets
blackened while hiding in a stove in *Whoopee* (1930) and while hiding in
a mud bath in *Roman Scandals* (1933); lamenting urban modernity—including the police—Al Jolson gets "mud" on his face in *The Singing Kid*
(1936); in *Dimples* (1936) Frank Morgan, while backstage at the theatrical

debut of *Uncle Tom's Cabin,* hides by pretending to be Uncle Tom; hiding from the police in *A Day at the Races* (1937), the Marx brothers apply axle grease to their faces; casting about for a way to keep a needed theatrical job despite a blackened eye, Bing Crosby (playing Dan Emmett, a pioneer of nineteenth-century minstrelsy) blacks up in *Dixie* (1943); looking desperately for a way to restart his singing career, Larry Parks (playing a young Al Jolson) substitutes for a drunk blackface performer in *The Jolson Story* (1946).

In these instances, the change to blackface is motivated but not really explained. The rationale for the disguise is obvious but anterior to each film's narrative: blackface is thoroughly other and othering; it is a thick, obscuring mask; it is a convention and it is convenient. Of course, this reasoning fails to explain in almost all of these instances how accidentally applied soot or mud magically and comically becomes the conventional blackface mask. More importantly, such reasoning—that blackface is a convincing disguise—is always mistaken. No one in any of these scenes is fooled, at least not for long. What makes blackface work comically in these films is that it does not work narratively. The disguise has no reason.

As the instances of *Dimples* and *The Jolson Story* already hint, except as an (assumed, presumed) amusement, a performance, a part of the backstage milieu common to the majority of films that include it, blackface is most frequently left out of the narrative chain of cause and effect. In most blackface films—*The Jazz Singer, Babes in Arms* (1939), or *Torch Song* (1953), for instance—blackface performance *just is;* it is assumed as a tradition, a fashion so old as to be "natural." Because these films also draw attention to blackface as a process, however, the tradition, the only reason for the blackface mask, is opened for question or at least explicit view, and a space—small, perhaps even virtual, but nonetheless extraordinary in American cinema—is made for examining and perhaps altering the ways in which racialized identities are delimited and maintained through sight and sound.

Michael Rogin, the only scholar who has worked extensively on blackface in cinema and, specifically, scenes of blackface transition, would almost certainly claim that my assessment is too optimistic. In Rogin's analysis, "Blackface operates as a vehicle for . . . [white] ethnic mobility at the price of fixedness for blacks."[9] Rogin acknowledges that the transition scene, which he sees as a "primal scene" for white American identity,[10] *does* "complicate ... descriptions of classic Hollywood's illusionist, narrative realism."[11] In fact, Rogin argues, by "calling attention to the figure behind the mask, blackface ... exposes the illusion that the individual was in charge of his or her voice, that it issued from an authentic interior," "it expose[s] the illusion that the individual was speaking [singing?] and not being spoken for — whether by language, capital, mass consumption, or the locus of all three ... , talking pictures Hollywood." In Rogin's assessment, however, Hollywood movies contained this threat to expose the mechanisms of American racialized identity/ideology using a number of strategies that developed between 1927 and 1953: confining (white) blackface to the musical genre (where performance *is* authenticity); making claims of verisimilitude to put veritable blacks in "the parts minstrelsy had prepared"; (seeming to) substitute for the fetish of color, which is revealed and consequently defetishized in the transition scenes, the never questioned fetish of selfmaking; and, finally, eliminating "traditional blackface" altogether in favor of a "universalized" blackface "more broadly understood," a category that seems potentially to encompass everything, all mechanisms of ideology.[12]

Still, despite all the anxious containment strategies of blackface films, which he describes, interprets, and decries persuasively, Rogin perhaps sees more possibility than he would like to admit:

> Unlike other racially stigmatized groups, white immigrants can put on and take off their mask of difference. But the freedom promised immigrants [and, by extension, assumed for native whites like Mickey Rooney and Judy Garland] to make themselves over points to the vacancy, the violence, the deception, and the melancholy at the core of American self-fashioning. *The films make us wonder:* Do cross-dressing immigrants buy freedom at the expense of the imprisonment of peoples of color? Or does that freedom itself look less like consent and more like the evasion of crimes, less like making a new self and more like endless disguise? [Emphasis added.][13]

For Rogin, however, the "us" is restrictive — us right now, right here (in the academy), not them — "mass audiences," "complian[t]" blacks and enthusiastically rac(ial)ist whites in the twenties, thirties, and most of the forties.[14] Rogin's refusal to argue "resistance" — a by-now tired cultural studies trope — is laudable but his refusal is, finally, undernuanced: resistance to resistance. The positions and practices I analyzed in chapter one reveal more complicated black responses to blackface than either acquiescence or some easy-to-describe resistance. Rogin is right that "making wonder"—raising questions—does not automatically unmask ideology and for many (white) people making wonder very likely even enforces it. In some instances, however, making wonder enabled African American audiences to critique and reformulate U.S. culture and their claim on and place in it—a process with no guaranteed outcome. Considered in light of its African American reception(s), the career of Al Jolson suggests that whenever white blackface and African American performers were paired the space for an African American critique of American cinema and its mechanisms for constructing identity got slightly larger and more revealing.

"Mistah Jolson, Yo' Is Just as Funny as Me"

The displaced ur-text for cinematic conjunctions of blackface and black performance appears in "Al Jolson's Own Story: The Jazz Singer in Real Life," the centerpiece of the original souvenir program for *The Jazz Singer.* Sandwiched between a prose synopsis of the film's story and a piece on "The Making of *The Jazz Singer*," this "biography" motivates and explains Jolson's blackface—information missing from the film itself. "The Making of . . ." makes clear that the Warner Bros. publicity machine (which authorized and authored the program) intended this: "One of the most unique features of *The Jazz Singer* is the fact that it nearly parallels the actual life of Al Jolson, envoy extraordinary of the blackface, minister plenipotentiary of the mammy-song."[15] Any information a viewer collected about Jolson, the program suggests, could be imported into the film.

Here, then, is the blackface scene that was left out of *The Jazz Singer:*

> The turning tide [in Jolson's flagging career] was a chance conversation one night with an old darky. The man was a southern negro who assisted the comedian when he dressed. Jolson was extremely fond of him and appreciative of his loyalty through the lean days of his vaudeville tours. In Washington [growing up] Al had acquired a sympathetic interest in negro life and had learned to mimic the accent of the race.
>
> One night when the two were preparing for a performance in a small theatre in Brooklyn, the actor confided to his old dresser his misgivings as to the merits of his act.

"How am I going to get them to laugh more?" he mused.

The darky shook his head knowingly. "Boss, if yo' skin am black they always laugh."

The idea struck Jolson as plausible and he decided to try it. He got some burnt cork, blacked up and rehearsed before the negro. When he finished he heard a chuckle followed by the verdict.

"Mistah Jolson, yo' is just as funny as me."

Jolson in blackface was an overnight sensation.[16]

"Al Jolson's Own Story" updates tales of minstrelsy's origin for a postbellum, postslavery, postmigration, black Renaissance-infused, urban America. It is impossible to know if this souvenir program was available at *The Jazz Singer*'s belated appearances in Chicago's Black Metropolis and other black neighborhoods; it seems unlikely—though any black cinemagoer in Chicago, or a number of other northern cities where segregation was de facto rather than de jure, could, hypothetically, have acquired one for the requisite twenty-five cents at the film's downtown premiere. Despite the program's (remotely potential) interracial audience, it reads as a set of instructions for a white interpretation of the film. Certainly, as Rogin would predict, though the story's main purpose is to promote Jolson and his putatively amazing range of performance, its flipside seems to be to control unwieldy social forces through stereotype and denigration. As Eric Lott has suggested for the nineteenth-century origin tales of minstrelsy, however, this urge to (pre-)interpret blackface reveals that other readings are possible.

In the nineteenth-century origin story, which exists in many variations, a white performer, usually T. D. Rice, overhears (and sometimes oversees) a black man singing and dancing "Jump Jim Crow." He slightly modifies the black man's performance, blacks up, presents his "new" performance to a white public, and receives immediate, overwhelming acclaim.[17] Surveying the versions of this story, Lott identifies "two narrative paradigms," "one in which [cultural] mixing takes place by an elision of expropriation, through absorption . . . , the other in which it takes place by a transfer of ownership, through theft (or occasionally payment)."[18] According to Lott, by eliding cultural miscegenation, the first paradigm served to forestall white anxiety about sexual miscegenation and, by substituting "comic" cultural theft or "borrowing," the second served to forestall white anxiety over slavery. But, Lott argues, these narratives also always failed in their purposes, revealing what they were supposed to repress—namely white anxiety about the unequal and charged relations between whites and blacks in antebellum America, about white "love" of and "theft" of *and* from African Americans.[19] By 1927, with African Americans no longer property but hypothetically equal if mostly separate U.S. citizens, empowered to respond to white theft (less so to white love), the anxieties had somewhat altered—perhaps they were no longer just white—and so had the story for and possibilities of assuaging them. Moreover, in contrast to most nineteenth-century minstrelsy and its origin stories, which appeared in all-white "popular" venues, "Al Jolson's Own Story" and *The Jazz Singer* were part of a mass—but by no means homogenous—culture, which further complicated their potential meanings.

Unlike minstrelsy's tales of origin, in which "there is rarely any actual meeting between racial representatives,"[20] "Al Jolson's Own Story" not only allows this meeting but focuses on it and turns it into a relationship. In addition, again unlike the nineteenth-century stories, in the Jolson story the white member of this relationship finds himself bereft of ideas, and the black member deliberately and self-consciously supplies the white with an (old) idea, the idea that blackness is funny, at least to "them," an idea that does not initially strike the white as anything more than "plausible." In final contrast to earlier models, the white submits to black approval of his performance, which leads to a claim of equality—"Mistah Jolson, yo' is just as funny as me"—that is at once ordinary (or stereotypical) and startling.

This assertion of equality supports three overlapping readings. First, at its most progressive (and unlikely for a white audience), it culminates the story's acknowledgment of a black contribution to Jolson's blackface performance. It tells of black cultural worth and testifies to autonomous black initiative. Second, and more important in the context of a promotion for Jolson, the dresser's assertion signals Jolson's authenticity—the genuineness of his performance, the actuality of cultural exchange—even while this context suggests that the dresser's claim is patently untrue. The dresser's claim of equality is funny and pathetic because it is wrong—or rather comes to be wrong; Jolson is the one who, by *turning black,* becomes the star, not the dresser, who merely remains black. Modifying the dresser's claim and making it all the more ridiculous is the fact that, in the story, Jolson has already long been a sympathetic mimic of "the race"; Jolson had absorbed blackness before the dresser tendered his advice or rendered his verdict. If the first reading of the dresser's claim asserts an intentional black contribution to Jolson's art, the second reading neutralizes this intention. The third reading of the dresser's claim does more than neutralize the subversive statement of equality; it refuses and reverses the claim. This purpose appears in the story's use of the mechanisms of minstrelsy—dialect, appellation, geographical specificity, the substitution of "fondness" and "loyalty" for economics—to create its unnamed "southern negro" (with a small "n" that was significant in 1927), who turns into an "old darky."[21] And the "old darky's" immediate disappearance from the story after his claim, a simultaneous punishment of the character and a recognition of his unimportance, emphasizes this third reading as the "preferred" one.[22]

As in the nineteenth-century tales, the preferred reading of "Al Jolson's Own Story" works to manage white anxieties about race and the borders between white and black in America. Perhaps because it combines both Lott's paradigms, however, it cannot maintain even the contradictory resolve of those tales. The story attempts to manage twentieth-century anxieties over potential black autonomy, white unfairness, and non-proprietary forms of black/white interdependence by effacing the conditions of hierarchy with paternalistic, plantation-myth-like familiarity. But this does not suffice. In the nineteenth-century story, the black man is either stolen from or paid. Here the "old darky's" compensation for his loyalty is Jolson's fondness, but he also gives Jolson gifts—an idea, his judgement, his color—and for this he is rendered superfluous and disappears from the story, along with the vaunted familiarity. The "darky" must disappear to avoid hints of cultural miscegenation, but he vanishes too late. Jolson *is* culturally miscegenated: a Jew who yearns to be a WASP while consorting with blacks. This is a far cry from the earlier tales in which blacks were heard more often than seen—and in which blacks were never engaged in conversation. Again, then, as in the nineteenth-century tales, "Al Jolson's Own Story" does not escape being revealingly contradictory, but because it combines Lott's two paradigms, its contradictions are amplified: What eases anxiety over black/white economic interrelations—familiarity—is precisely what exacerbates anxiety over social interrelations, but the solution to familiarity—disappearance—undoes the possibility of inexpensive black labor (and white, paternalistic largesse).[23]

That these contradictions were growing especially severe in this period is suggested by one more important aspect of "Al Jolson's Own Story." Before his conversation with the "old darky," Jolson is described as "[s]till in white face, [where] he continued to meet with indifferent success."[24] This is a tiny but nonetheless remarkable violation of Richard Dyer's oft-cited pronouncement that whiteness "secures its dominance by seeming not to be anything in particular,"[25] and it at least hints that "white face" is as much a construction as blackface. But if whiteness is (or can be) a "face," a costume, then the usual stability of transparent white identity is troubled.

None of this would seem as significant if the "negro" had disappeared as entirely from Jolson's career as the "old darky" in "Al Jolson's Own Story." In continuity with his stage revues, however, Jolson's films of the thirties increasingly brought black (as opposed to blackfaced) people into their frames. Since Jolson's films beyond *The Singing Fool* (1928) were less and less financially successful, it seems likely that (among other things) they revealed, without resolving, the American racial tensions and contradictions expressed by blackface; that, in Jim Pine's word, the films grew more and more "decadent"—and whites turned away from the spectacle.[26] But at the same time as Jolson's popularity was waning across the middle thirties, the African American press—spurred by his use of blackface and his employment of black performers but also by his aspirations to play roles written for black performers—was paying more and often critical attention to "America's black-face favorite."[27]

There *is* an African American in *The Jazz Singer*: Mary Dale's maid, caught at the edge of the frame while Jack Robin courts her mistress. In Michael Rogin's reading, she stands as a "residue" of a "too risky" plan to show Jack wooing Mary in blackface. *The Singing Fool*, Jolson's next film and his biggest hit, took that risk, and also kept the African American "residue."[28] The film tells the story of Al Stone's climb to stardom, the dissolution of his unhappy marriage, and, finally, the death of his much-beloved young son. In the climactic scene, the grieving Al blacks up in preparation for the premiere of his new show. As Al applies his cork, his black valet moves about the room, casting seemingly sympathetic glances at his employer. Meanwhile, Grace—Al's (potential) girl-friend—entreats the stage manager, Mr. White, to cancel Al's number, but Mr. White refuses. Just before Al leaves his dressing room, the film cuts to a stunning shot: In medium close-up and slightly left of center, Al's blacked-up face—evenly dark black with only slightly exaggerated

7. Al Jolson with black valet blacking up in *The Singing Fool* (1928).

lips, especially relative to minstrel precedent, and a close, "woolly" wig—looks directly into the camera while over his shoulder, just out of focus, the valet looks at Al. Of this moment, Jim Pines writes: "Obviously, if the two had in fact appeared in the same shot in focus the result would have exploded the inherent pretentiousness of Jolson's blackface pathos. Instead, the viewer's attention is directed to the parody." [29] But this shot is not "obvious." After all, the shot could easily have been set up to exclude the valet or to put him completely out of focus. [30] Certainly this juxtaposition of Al in blackface with a black supernumerary does not "explode" anything, but it does set up a double reading: For some audiences, this sympathetic proximity would cement the authenticity of Al's blackface persona; for other audiences, the comparison would delegitimate the imitation.

This remarkable moment is capped by the very final shots of the film. Verging on hysteria, Al sings his number, a reprise of "Sonny Boy," while subjective shots from his point of view have Al seeing the ghost of his son superimposed over the crowd. When the curtain at last closes, Al collapses, and Grace and Mr. White rush to his aid. With White looking on, the long-suffering Grace, who has been the right woman for Al since the opening scene, embraces Al. As their clinch tightens toward what appears to be an inevitable kiss, there is a cut from a medium shot to a slightly more distant shot rather than the close up we expect, and precisely at the transition, Al guides his face past Grace's and onto her shoulder. By also giving the audience Grace's frustrated desire (and frustrating our desire for the close shot), the film ups the emotional ante.

And it does not stop there. By playing this scene as deadly earnest and placing its "interracial" aspect under the gaze of Mr. White, the film creates for some viewers one conundrum: Would we rather maintain racial purity or have the satisfaction of the kiss?[31] And for others a different conundrum: Why can't we see even a patently fake "black" man kiss a white woman?

Jolson's next blackface films, *Mammy* (1930) and *Big Boy* (1930), push the complexities of race and representation(s) apparent in *The Singing Fool* even further. In *Mammy* Jolson, this time as Al Fuller, plays "Mr. Bones," one of the two traditional comic endmen in a minstrel show.[32] In the complicated plot, Al tries to aid a romance between Nora, the daughter of the troupe's owner and a girl whom Al himself apparently loves, and Westy, the interlocutor (the only member of the troupe not to wear blackface), and he works to thwart the attentions of Tambo, the other endman, to the same girl.

As a consequence of this unusual romantic quadrangle, in which the two frustrated principals are half "black" and the romantic winners are all white, Tambo sets Al/Bones up to shoot Westy on stage in the middle of their regular routine. The routine begins when Al insists that Westy tell him what is bothering him. Westy demurs, but finally tells Al that his sister, Little Nellie, has run away, his elderly mother is distraught, and the farm is in hock. By the end of this story, both men are weeping, Westy quietly and Al very emotionally. Then Westy asks Al to lend him five hundred dollars, and Al, seemingly in sympathetic agony, starts to stumble toward Westy. Instead of pulling money from his pocket, however, he pulls out a gun, which Tambo has loaded with real bullets instead of the usual blanks, shoots Westy, and delivers the punchline: "I had to do it folks—he was breaking my heart." After the laugh he offers Westy a hand in getting up, saying, "Pals to the end."

If, as "black" men, Jolson's characters were prevented from consummating ("interracial") romances in *The Jazz Singer* and *The Singing Fool,* then here Bones gets some measure of vengeance, though it is Tambo who has made Bones' ordinary mock vengeance into genuine violence. Bones performs a comically violent act while the white man—Westy, the American frontiersman, no less—asks for *his* help in supporting the sacred white women. (And who did Nellie run off with, anyway? Al asks: "Traveling man?" Instead of taking offense, Westy says, "We don't know yet.") It seems likely that at least some African American specta-

8. Jolson as "Bones" shooting the white interlocutor (by mistake) in *Mammy* (1930).

tors cheered when, extemporizing until the stage can be cleared from the accident, Al/Bones declares, "When I shoot 'em, they stays shot."

Certainly *Mammy* works to drain as much critical meaning as it can from this scene, piling standard minstrel stereotype upon accident upon sentimental characterization. Al flees the scene of his crime and rides the rails until he reaches his mother. In her wisdom, she advises him to return and trust justice. By now, the same audience that might have cheered the shooting would probably have booed her bromide, "If anyone says anything against you, make 'em prove it." (The *Variety* reviewer quipped, "sound[s] like chorus girl talk in a dressing room.") The film makes clear that it does not believe this pronouncement by having Al return to find that he does not *really* need courage and conviction. In his absence his problems have been solved: Tambo has confessed, Westy and Nora are engaged, and the troupe needs him back.

If this were the end of *Mammy*, it might not merit much further thought, but again, as with *The Singing Fool*, the final moments make it clear that multiple readings of this film's explicitly racialized aspects are encouraged—or at least possible. In the last scene, Al and his troupe (sans blackface) advertise their forthcoming show by staging a street parade. As the parade and film near their ends, Al glances into the enthusiastic crowd and yells, "Mammy!" A cut reveals what he sees: Not his mother (who, throughout the film, Al has called "Mammy"), but a classic, stereotyped mammy: a dark black, rotund woman wearing a head rag and looking pleased but abashed. Alone, this image would cement the film's most racist leanings—and almost certainly did so for

9. The black "mammy" and her companions in *Mammy.*

many audiences. Mammy, however, is not alone. She is flanked by two younger African American women, who are conventionally attractive (nonmammies) and considerably lighter skinned. The joke here is that Al would ever mistake this woman for his mother. Surely the world is safe from such insanity, even if the absurdity of the thought is meant to make us laugh, and Al's mother returns in the film's very closing seconds just to make certain we got the joke. Still, the presence of the two attractive "daughters" complicates Al's notice of "Mammy":[33] Which of these women caught his eye? Is Al really the mammy lover he claims to be? Is the audience (and which audience?) made up of mammy lovers? The light skin of the two nonmammies also extends these questions into a further, more provocative question, one usually repressed by the white American obsession with supposedly rampant black-male lust for white women: If that's mammy, then who's "pappy"?

Big Boy (1930), the last film Jolson made as an acknowledged though rapidly fading star, pushes still further the contradictions of recognizing and yet participating in American racism — to a point where spelling out a "doubled," racialized set of readings is no longer necessary: even the reviewer for *Variety* drew *Big Boy*'s critical potential to his readers' attention. *Big Boy* capped 1930 as Hollywood's most blackface-intensive year to date (and, as it turned out, ever) and, along with other 1930 films like *Mammy* and especially Gosden and Correll's (Amos 'n' Andy's) *Check and Double Check,* helped focus the black and white critical (re)appraisal of blackface that I analyzed in the previous chapter. An adaptation of one of Jolson's stage successes, *Big Boy* also elaborated for a mass media audience Jolson's interest in playing a "black" rather than a blackfaced character.[34] This desire to play black, a desire Jolson would express repeatedly in the early and mid-thirties, especially attracted the attention of the African American press and helped inspire African American critical (re)considerations of the stakes of blackface representation in mass culture.

Big Boy is a double articulation of the myth of the contented "darky" — with the twist that here part of the darky's contentment stems from his (carefully directed) uppityness. In the main story of the film, set in the present, Jolson plays Gus, a groom and jockey working for a wealthy Kentucky family. The center of the film flashes back to the postbellum era in which Jolson plays Gus's grandfather (also named Gus), a just-freed slave who occupies exactly the same position on the plantation as his grandson. Both Guses perform loyal and heroic service for their masters, in the face of the whites' doubt and (for contemporary Gus) dismissal, to save the family honor and fortune. All of this is typical in the extreme, but several aspects of *Big Boy* stand out from this typicality and demand attention because of the possibilities they open up — but do not fully realize.

Each Gus has a community. There are other veritable blacks in the world, and each Gus interacts with them — a fact noted in the black press.[35] At the same time, these communities are delineated briefly and in broad strokes as all male, happy, and humorous, and Gus's most important and extended relations are with whites. Each Gus's longest exchange with another "black" character is, in fact, a conversation with a distinct (stereo)type: Contemporary Gus makes fun of an eyerollingly witless groom; the elder Gus has a long exchange with another blacked-up white man. And despite the fact that the Guses are the heroes of the story, they end alone, unmated and divorced from whatever possible community their stories had offered.

More palpable in *Big Boy* than black community is black(faced) criticism of white oppression. The contemporary Gus cracks wise at the expense of many white characters and undoes the sometimes explicitly racist machinations of the film's villains. These individual and seemingly idiosyncratic behaviors are anchored in a collective "history." In the flashback, Gus joins a veritable black chorus in a medley of antebellum songs.[36] A seemingly spontaneous entertainment on the lawn for the guests of the plantation, the medley begins with "Dixie's Land" (i.e.,

"Dixie," the anthem of the South), but it then moves to spirituals. First comes a sprightly "All God's Children Got Shoes," with its emphatic yoking of the spiritual and material, the invisible (God, singing voice) and visible (shoes, skin [color]). The medley concludes with the sorrowful but demanding "Go Down, Moses" (i.e., "Let My People Go"). This medley means to certify Gus's "blackness" and Jolson's ability to act "black." The same process that asserts white hegemony and black quiescence ("Dixie"), however, also reveals black critique and reminds the viewer of Jolson's Jewishness. "Go Down, Moses," which hinges on the equation of blacks with Jews and whites with Egyptians, opens a vertiginous complexity of identity and identification. It seems at once to suggest that the Jewish Jolson is metaphorically black—before or without or beyond blackface, and that surface is all—the black face, and that depth is all—a common (though not shared) history of oppression, the "soulful" voice. But this complexity is not exactly a critique, and even if it were, it could not make the American stigma of blackness or the power of whiteness disappear.

The medley is succeeded by a scene in which Gus the elder, paired with the other blackfaced "black" in *Big Boy,* has a series of "comic" confrontations with Bully John Bagby (Noah Beery), a proud and violent racist. The humor in this situation is supposed to arise from Gus's wavering and confused defense of his rights in the face of Bagby's demands and Gus's immediate abandonment of those rights when facing physical violence. A few moments later, however, after Bagby kidnaps the young mistress of the plantation, Gus rides Bagby down and drags him back behind a horse. Gus may be motivated to act by his love for his white folks, but by doing to Bagby what Bagby had threatened to do to him and by demanding that Bagby recant, he expresses his rage at racist treatment.[37]

As with *The Singing Fool* and *Mammy,* the ending of *Big Boy* is particularly important. While the endings of the two earlier films are important because they emphatically recall, highlight, and support previous aspects of the films, the ending of *Big Boy* casts a new light on what has come before. And against the endings of *The Singing Fool* and *Mammy,* which I read as potentially progressive, depending on the resources and attitudes of the audience, the ending of *Big Boy* is strongly regressive—a fact that did not go unnoticed by at least one reviewer. Here is an extended passage from the *Variety* review, which both describes and interprets the film's final minutes:

> An anti-climax bit takes something away from the story, but probably was figured desirable for other reasons. At the finish . . . , Jolson does a quick switch [through a match dissolve] from blackface to straight whiteface and in his own person addresses the audience from the screen, observing that a Jolson picture ought to end with a song. . . .
>
> Reason for the device—which comes as a bit of a jolt—probably is that during the play Jolson's stable boy character has been pretty free with the wisecracks at the expense of the white characters, and it was deemed advisable to establish the feeling that it was only the clowning Jolson after all, not a colored stable boy figuring in the free and easy episodes. Whether such a device will make the picture acceptable in the south is another question.[38]

The critical—or offensive—aspects of Jolson's Gus were plain to see and hear in *Big Boy,* at least those aspects that might offend whites. What the *Variety* reviewer does not, and could not, make clear is whether African Americans were also offended by Gus, whether they saw his offensive acts as affirmative of black critique, or, most likely, whether various African American viewers felt various combinations of these feelings. What seems certain is that Jolson's return to whiteness at the end of *Big Boy* and his explicit apologies for Gus's behavior could only have contradictory (and, from the commercial standpoint of *Variety* or Warner Bros., probably undesirable) effects: Reminding audience members who may have been offended by Gus's behavior of that behavior and drawing attention to what was most offensive in it—namely the character's refusal fully to accept racist hierarchies—was likely a poor ending strategy. And for an audience that approved of Gus's behavior, apologizing for it would not be viewed kindly.

White reviewers considered Jolson and his film outmoded, and overall the film was a financial failure.[39] I have found no direct evidence of *Big Boy*'s reception among African American audiences. Certainly, *Big Boy* played in black neighborhood theaters, as did all the Jolson films. In fact, unlike *The Singing Fool* (which was a huge hit) and *Mammy,* which each had extended South Side runs, *Big Boy* had only two runs on Chicago's South Side, though it's hard to know how exactly to interpret this.[40] In comparison, the Amos 'n' Andy film, *Check and Double Check,* which arrived in Chicago only a month after *Big Boy,* played three times

10 and 11.
Jolson's transition
(accomplished by
dissolve) out of
blackface in the
coda of *Big Boy*.

on the South Side. *Check and Double Check* featured the white comics Gosden and Correll in blackface, playing their well-known black characters. Despite this similarity to *Big Boy, Check and Double Check* bore none of the explicitly fraught and contradictory impulses of the Jolson film (and it had the added attraction of the Duke Ellington Orchestra, which figured heavily in the *Defender* ads). In live appearances in 1929, Gosden and Correll had, by using a special lighting effect, changed from blackface to whiteface, too.[41] In general, however, and certainly in their film, these comics—both native-born gentiles—maintained America's color line much more carefully than the immigrant, Jewish Jolson. *Check and Double Check* was a general hit,[42] and if the ad copy of the South Side's Michigan Theater is accurate, when *Check and Double Check* was brought back it was "by popular demand."[43]

After *Check and Double Check,* Gosden and Correll returned all their attentions to their successful radio show, which, under the cover of the medium's invisibility, maintained the guise of being "all-black," a guise that listeners understood as a guise but accepted, embraced, and then perhaps forgot about because it was utterly consistent.[44] In comparison, after *Big Boy* Jolson was somewhat at loose ends. Attempting to remake his career, Jolson further emphasized his ability—or desire—to play real "black" characters. I argued in my previous chapter that *The Jazz Singer* and *Amos 'n' Andy* along with other instances of white blackface in early sound film and radio had spurred renewed attention to blackface, especially by black critics and performers. Jolson's new resolve to cross the line between blackface and black representation sparked still more attention from African Americans, and understanding that attention will help further articulate African Americans' senses of how black American identity existed in a world where blackface (and "black" voice) could be mass (re)produced, mass marketed, and broadcast.

"Goin' to Heaven on a Mule"

Black writers and the black press had noticed with enthusiasm whenever Jolson took an interest in black talent.[45] When Jolson began expressing interest in playing black roles himself, however, roles that, unlike Gus, were not his inventions and did not derive directly from minstrelsy, he got a different kind of attention. In June of 1931, the *Defender* reported with alarm, "Al Jolson Buys Film Rights to *Green Pastures*." The body of the article was more precise. Jolson, who intended to take the role of "De Lawd" in this musical "folk" drama about black spirituality, was on the "verge of" buying the rights.[46] The next week the paper reported with satisfaction, "Al Jolson's Offer for *Green Pastures* as Talkie is Refused by Producers."[47] Later in 1931 and 1932, Jolson was back in favor. The *Defender* noted several times that he had hired the black dance team of Chilton and Thomas for the tour of his stage show, *The Wonder Bar*. Then, in 1933, the *Defender* blasted Jolson:

> Like a bombshell to the lovers of Race talent in the theater, came the news last week that Al Jolson, white mammy singer, will play the title role of the George Gershwin musical version of DuBose and Dorthy Heyward's play, *Porgy*. . . .
>
> Which reminds Colored theatrical followers that Jolson, with all the

cockiness in the world, two years ago wished to play the part of 'De Lawd' in the talkie version of *The Green Pastures*. Marc Connelly and Howland Stebbins laughed in the face of the Broadway clown, who would inherit the mantle of that great [black] artist, Richard Harrison.[48]

Early in 1934, with only slightly less vitriol, the *Defender* claimed, "Al Jolson Pleads for Lead in 'Emperor Jones' on Stage," and the same piece criticized him for playing Jones and Porgy in radio broadcasts.[49]

Into the midst of these criticisms came *Wonder Bar* (1933), Jolson's attempt at a comeback film for Warner Bros. This adaptation of his last stage success varied from all but one of Jolson's previous films by containing not even a supernumerary black performer.[50] Chilton and Thomas from the stage tour were nowhere to be seen. This absence of veritable black performers would be much less noteworthy were it not for the film's particular choice of a blackface production number: a Busby Berkeley spectacle choreographed to a Warren and Dubin song burlesquing *Green Pastures*. In case anyone missed the point, the song and number were titled "Goin' to Heaven on a Mule," and it was the film's finale. Warners made the number the centerpiece of their advertising campaign: "'Goin' to Heaven on a Mule,'" the film's trailer announced, "is a musical creation so startlingly different that to show you *one single flash* of its forty-two unforgettable scenes . . . would be to rob you of the greatest thrill you've ever had in the theatre."

"Goin' to Heaven on a Mule" *is* startling. It takes the working conceit of *Green Pastures*—that rural black "folk" would imagine an all-black heaven that is an idealized version of their surroundings and customs—and turns it into an all-white, blackfaced minstrel number. Jolson, as cabaret owner and performer Al Wonder, sings the role of a sharecropper who takes his trusty mule to a blackfaced heaven replete with pork chop machines, watermelon, craps, and Stephen Foster's Old Black Joe, the nineteenth-century minstrel stage adaptation of Harriet Beecher Stowe's Uncle Tom, *and* O'Neill's Emperor Jones. The only moment in the entire turn that recalls a glimmer of Jolson's play with identities is when Al, in blackface character, reads from a Yiddish newspaper. If it does nothing else, "Goin' to Heaven" certainly makes clear why many African Americans accepted and applauded black roles like Emperor Jones, Porgy, Joe in *Show Boat*, and De Lawd or even the "black" Amos 'n' Andy—given what the alternative was.

12. Jolson blacked up with "The Emperor Jones" (also in blackface) in "Goin' to Heaven on a Mule" in *Wonder Bar* (1933).

Despite an advertising campaign that included serializing the story of *Wonder Bar* in the *Defender,* the film played just one engagement on the South Side of Chicago and sank, leaving dignified silence as its only trace in that paper.[51] A year later, though, Jolson was back. The *Defender* again announced, "Al Jolson Certain to Get Lead in Film's *Pastures.*"[52] The *Richmond Planet* was more cautious (and accurate), saying Jolson *might* play the role, but it quoted at length the "withering criticism" delivered by the associate secretary of an important African American church council: " 'Can you imagine the Christus of Ober-Ammergau spending nine years on the variety stage and the tenth portraying the life and death of Jesus of Nazareth?' she asks. 'I do not question his (Jolson's) ability. He may try to enter into the spirit with which Mr. Harrison imbued the play. But he has played his minstrel part too long and too well to step into the shoes of Richard Harrison,' she concludes."[53] Michael Rogin interprets the endings of *Big Boy,* which also contained jokes about Jolson's Jewishness, and "Goin' to Heaven on a Mule" in *Wonder Bar* as "immigrant Jewish self-assertion" built on "disavowing" blacks and sees this continued self-assertion as the key to Jolson's fading career.[54] This may be so, but from an African American perspective "disavowal" looked different—less like a forgetting and more like a preemptive, displacing, and perhaps poisonous embrace.

The reporting undergirding these criticisms of Jolson was accurate; Jolson did indeed lobby to play the roles of Emperor Jones, De Lawd, and Porgy.[55] Why, however, should (some) African Americans have cared so ardently? Each of these three roles, after all, were "folk" characters written by white, cosmopolitan, progressive authors, and for these reasons, each of the plays, along with their lead characters, had met already with at least some ambivalence from black critics. However, all three plays were also immediately recognized by the American literary establishment as important works, and with *The Emperor Jones* (1920) as the oldest among them, these three works represented a new and tenuous trend in mainstream American drama. None of the three plays explicitly ridiculed its black characters as minstrelsy often did. More importantly for black critics, all the roles Jolson wanted were strongly associated with highly regarded black performers: Emperor Jones with Charles Gilpin and Paul Robeson, Porgy (in the dramatic rather than musical-operatic form) with Frank Wilson, and De Lawd with the revered Richard Harrison. These roles and the plays that contained them represented in distilled form the American "art" of Broadway theater versus the entertainment of minstrelsy, vaudeville, revue, and perhaps films. Despite the fact that the various productions of these plays were not available to a wide black audience, for many black critics these roles and the men who played them represented the high possibilities for black achievement and sociocultural dignity and for black-white collaboration. Wanting to play these roles, Jolson was proposing to remake a barely established circle of black-white collaboration into the far too familiar circle of white-white collaboration and, most significantly, to co-opt and compromise these ambivalent and tenuous black achievements. "Disavowal" would have been preferable.

Once more *Amos 'n' Andy* provides a useful comparison to Jolson, one anchored by the commonalities of *Big Boy* and *Check and Double Check*. In 1930, *Amos 'n' Andy* had been the object of an energetic, though finally unsuccessful and perhaps even divisive, African American protest led by the *Pittsburgh Courier* and opposed by the *Chicago Defender*.[56] In contrast to Jolson, Gosden and Correll had made several choices that helped assuage or disarm their black critics: They had created their characters, discouraging one-to-one comparisons between themselves and black performers (though, as we saw in chapter one, some critics did compare them, ambivalently, to the black comics Miller and Lyles) and continuing the old white minstrel tradition of which blacks may not have approved but to which they were fully accustomed. They did not aspire to share black musical skills. They played almost exclusively on the radio, de-emphasizing the visual and (traditionally) public aspects of their performance. Finally, they cultivated their black audience with public appearances (without blackface), often for black charitable organizations.

Jolson did not play Porgy or De Lawd—though this fact probably had less directly to do with African American criticisms and more to do with George Gershwin and Marc Connelly. Each man apparently sensed or perhaps was informed by black collaborators that casting Jolson to play "black" would be, despite the popularity of *Amos 'n' Andy* and the continued presence of blackface in film and theater, a step backward.[57] Nothing suggests that Jolson understood the various resistances to his taking these roles. After *Wonder Bar,* though, still searching to revive his still flagging film career, Jolson returned to and finally surpassed his earlier forms of playing with race. This probably insured he would fail with the general audience he and Warner Bros. wished to win back, but it ultimately put him back in favor with African American journalists and perhaps with a larger black audience.

"Who's the Swingin'est Man in Town?"

Go Into Your Dance arrived in theaters in black communities in the summer of 1935 during the height of concern over Jolson's desire to play black roles, so very likely it did not contribute much to rehabilitating his image or interest for black audiences.[58] *Go Into Your Dance,* however, does finally consummate the "interracial" blackface kiss that had been pending since *The Jazz Singer.* At the film's climax, which shows his triumphant return to stage success, Al romances the woman who has (literally) saved his life (Ruby Keeler, Jolson's wife and a bigger star in 1935) while wearing blackface. "If I didn't have this black on, I'd kiss ya," he says, and she replies with Warner Bros. showgirl spunk, "Don't let a little black stop you." Al kisses her. No doubt this was still a controversial and provocative gesture in 1935, but its power was diminished in *Go Into Your Dance.* The earlier Jolson films contained scenes and built themes—albeit themes that probably eluded majority audiences—that could amplify such gestures. But *Go Into Your Dance* gave its viewers "Snowflake" (Fred Toones) in a "coon" performance as the only available veritable black substitute for the blackface figure, a nostalgic rendition of "Swanee River" to spur the blackface, and a final line of dialogue— "You ain't heard nuthin' yet!"—to make it clear that this film was more interested in reclaiming a past than projecting and perhaps provoking an altered future. All of this is encapsulated in the fact that when the blackfaced Al kisses Dorothy Wayne (Keeler), she stays perfectly white.[59]

Jolson's last film as a devalued star—the last film he was expected to carry—returned to and attempted to exceed earlier Jolson form. *The Singing Kid* (1936) was concerned with maintaining what was best about Jolson—his immediate, uncontainable energy, which revealed and sought to transcend the ordinary physical and social boundaries of what a performer or a voice could do—while also linking him to a new, amplified, multimediated speed and energy. The film wanted to stage an explicit autocritique of the old-fashioned content of Jolson's past while maintaining some of his modernist form and style. It wanted to both erase and celebrate boundaries and difference, including most emphatically the color line. It is this impossibility that makes *The Singing Kid* interesting, incoherent, and a commercial failure.

After a montage of Jolson singing his greatest hits, at first in blackface and then not, *The Singing Kid*'s narrative opens with the multimedia star Al Jackson (Jolson) singing on the balcony of his sleek, modern penthouse. From another penthouse across the way, Cab Calloway and his band join in, and the song, "I Love to Sing-a," develops into a duet between Al and Cab (Calloway plays himself). This number introduces the negotiations the film attempts. The lyric is about the past. It refers to Jolson's career highlights ("Blue Skies," *The Singing Fool*) and celebrates the Jolsonian verities (love of nature and song, romance, the South, the nation, mammy). Jolson sings the lyric—including a syncopated, punctuating, and accurate line, "microphone's got [i.e., ruined] me!"—in his characteristic old-fashioned, premicrophone, declamatory style. But the music is about the present and about moving speedily into the future. It "swings." When Calloway begins singing in *his* characteristic style—in which the words are tools for exploring rhythm and stretching melody—it becomes clear that American culture is changing around Jolson and with (and through) Calloway.

Al's second number with Calloway, an extended medley of three songs, serves as the thematic key to the film. Portrayed as a piece in Al's long-running Broadway show, the number is prefaced by the standard scene of Jolson blacking up, though here he does so while being told by his doctor that he will die if he does not take a rest. Al's problem is that even as he sings nostalgically about quieter times past he (over) embodies modern,

13. Jolson blacked up with Cab Calloway in "Save Me, Sister" in *The Singing Kid* (1936).

industrial energy, and his "nerves" cannot take it. As Al moves through the backstage, we cut to Calloway and his band, who perform "Hi-De-Ho in Your Soul"—a fast-paced, collectivist party song (and written, unlike the rest of the film's music, by Calloway)—in an all-black nightclub.[60] Al enters, and the song shifts to "Who's the Swingin'est Man in Town?," which Al performs as a call and response with Calloway and the black extras. This song is interrupted by the arrival of a blackfaced angel, who cues a shift to the mock sanctified "Save Me, Sister," a song that interweaves with "Swingin'est Man" and also interweaves the very different voices and demeanors of the angel (staid and quasi-operatic), Jolson (declamatory), and Calloway (fluid, improvisational, and wild). Unlike "Goin' to Heaven on a Mule," this medley seems meant to take seriously, if very superficially, the potential in black culture(s) for interconnecting "opposites"—in this instance the secular and the religious, "swing" and "spiritual."[61] "Hi-De-Ho/Swingin'est Man/Save Me" culminates by showing Al and Cab "saved," even as—or, more accurately, *because*—they switch styles from the religious to the secular. If "Goin' to Heaven on a Mule" mocked African Americans more pointedly than Jolson ever had before, the medley suggests that African American culture—embodied by Cab Calloway, his band, and the extras and "played" by Jolson and the angel—might offer America something worth attending to, worth seriously imitating.

Calloway is not the only exemplar of modernization in *The Singing Kid*. Certainly, from the perspective of the story Calloway is secondary. He has no role in the film's story, and he never speaks a word. Other characters—namely the romantic interest, Ruth Haines (Beverly Roberts), who is an aspiring New England playwright, and the crooning quartet The Four Yacht Club Boys—make the most clearly articulated, though also contradictory, cases for Al's need to update himself. Ruth argues that Al should become more honest, less of a performer. The Yacht Club Boys argue that Al needs to become a different kind of performer. Ruth's argument, which is absurd in a musical, ultimately melts under the force of Al's honest performing. The Yacht Club Boys, who like Calloway play themselves and have no speaking roles, use a revised version of "I Love to Sing-a" to criticize Al during his comeback radio broadcast (his "nerves" had affected his singing voice):

> Al: I love to singa . . .
>   [Changing tune] Mammy! Mammy!
> Group: You love to singa?
>   You'd better stick to moon-a and a june-a and a spring-a
>   But not a thing-a 'bout your old black mammy
>   Or the shack in Alabamy.
>   If you're for us, please don't bore us with that same old chorus.
>   There'll be murder if there's a word about. . . .

Al continues to interject "Mammy" and the group continues to protest— "We're through with dix-a [dixie]," "Go to heaven on your mule"—until Al storms angrily out of the studio and into the street, where bystanders join in. The Boys follow and try to instruct the reluctant Al in modern rhythm, which is modeled for him by a line of black shoe shines. Ultimately, the shoe shines mysteriously disappear from the scene and the ever increasing rhythm seems to kill all the white participants in the number except the befuddled Al. In a coda, he and the dead Boys get splashed by a passing car and all end up wearing blackface, which brings the Boys back to life and leaves Al with the last word: "Mammy." The final moment of this number, then, seems to vindicate Al's old-fashioned content and to criticize the elevation of his style—energy—to the level of content. The astringency of the Boys' (admittedly apolitical) critique, however, expressed both in the verbal and physical violence, is not erased so easily.

At this juncture Calloway and his band are nowhere to be seen or heard. Giving lines like "We'd love to stuff the South-a in your mouth-

a" to Calloway instead of the Yacht Club Boys would have been incen-
diary—or would have at least called into question Al's regressive moment. As with *The Singing Fool, Mammy*, and *Big Boy*, if this were all,
if Calloway were never to return to the film, *The Singing Kid* would not
be nearly as interesting as it is. But Calloway and the band—not the
Yacht Club Boys—return for the film's climax. It is the premiere of Al's
comeback stage show, and all he can think of is finding and making
up with Ruth, who is meanwhile trying to find him. (In their comings
and goings, we see that the backstage area is, unlike similar scenes from
earlier in the film, racially integrated; groups of black and white chorines stand around chatting.) Al leaves the theater just as the Calloway
Band begins the show, and a panicky stage manager asks the producer,
"What'll Calloway do when he get's to Al's chorus?" The answer: "Sing
it himself." This possibility raises questions: Would Calloway transform
Al Jackson/Jolson by ventriloquizing him or would Cab be transformed,
playing a meta-version of "himself"? Would Calloway, who's nearly as
white skinned as Jolson (and considerably "whiter" than Jolson when Jolson blacks up) but usually "blacker" voiced, be performing "whiteface"?
Who, indeed, *is* the swingin'est man in town?

This moment does not arrive, so these questions are not really asked,
let alone answered. Instead, Al and Ruth find one another and enter the
theater. Spotting Al, Cab cues the band to "I Love to Sing-a," and Al
leaves Ruth to join Cab on stage. Al sings the song alone, repeating the
lyrics from the film's opening—though this time we can also remember the signifying lines the Yacht Club Boys provided earlier and can, if
we choose to, imagine Cab singing them. Finally, the band segues into
"Swingin'est Man." Now Cab and Al sing in unison and dance a circle
dance together until Al breaks away to step into a medium shot. This
shot of Al with Cab still clearly visible over his shoulder ends the film,
leaving the strong visual and aural suggestion that theirs is the most important and interesting partnership in *The Singing Kid*. The opening of
the film might have put Jolson and Calloway on "separate-but-equal sky-
scrapers" (in Michael Rogin's words) and might be taken as a sign of Jolson's and his collaborators' bad faith, another mark of business as usual
in U.S. culture, with the mingling of singing, entertaining voices but an
enforced chasm between and hierarchy among racialized bodies.[62] However, this closing—which recalls Al with his dresser in *The Singing Fool*,

14. Jolson dancing with Calloway in the finale of *The Singing Kid.*

but bumps that scene to the finale and Jolson out of blackface—suggests that whatever other, usually unequal relations prevail between Calloway and Jolson, they are not "separate."

The song Calloway is singing when Al enters the theater—"You're the Cure for What Ails Me (and You Do Me Good)"—suggests the further intricacy that underlies my interpretation of this ending. "You're the Cure for What Ails Me" raises an immediate question. Who is Calloway singing to and/or for? Within the logic of *The Singing Kid*'s narrative, Calloway is singing *for* Al in every sense. Al employs Calloway; Al is wooing Ruth, and the lyric Calloway sings expresses Al's feelings. Considering *The Singing Kid* as a production, however, this relation is less clearly one way. Jolson needs Calloway's new style to reinvigorate his career; Calloway is the cure for what ails Jolson. Jolson does Calloway good in aiding him in reaching a wider, whiter, more remunerative music market. But Al/Jolson's "doing good" directs the viewer to what ails Calloway, something so obvious it is invisible: nothing. "Nothing" ails Calloway both in the sense that his "character" seems carefree and in the sense that in *The Singing Kid* he has no *character,* no narrative role. *The Singing Kid* was doing Calloway good, but in the process it could not avoid also being an instance of the racial discrimination that ailed the careers of black performers in the United States. Perhaps this is best emphasized by asking another impossible, unanswerable question: Within the fiction of *The Singing Kid,* during an "ordinary" performance of Al's revue, one in which Al was in place for the curtain, would Al and Cab sing "You're the Cure for What Ails Me" to one another?[63] Is this their displaced duet?

For the black press, *The Singing Kid* was more a Cab Calloway film than an Al Jolson film, and, excepting *The Jazz Singer,* it attended to *The Singing Kid* more than any other Jolson film.[64] *The Singing Kid* was a too rare opportunity to see a popular black performer on screen—and on screen for more than just a couple minutes or in a narrative role that straightjacketed him or her in a demeaning stereotype. This might seem like an impossibly small gain. Certainly, from our present perspective it appears pathetic rather than cause for celebration that, over the course of nearly a decade, a significant white performer and the industry promoting him could see their way clear (partly out of desperation over the white performer's career) to include a named black musician in one of his films. Nonetheless, in the thirties and into the forties, black writers and performers did see Jolson substantially differently from how we see him now. While Rogin is incorrect in his assertion that "Jolson himself was never an African American target," it is true that, compared with many whites that black critics attacked, Jolson supplied a target with a specific, productive effect for African American critics.[65]

About a year and a half after *The Singing Kid* played in theaters in black neighborhoods, Jolson turned up again in the black press and for the last time as far as I've been able to determine. This final appearance hints at the significance and complications of white blackface, especially for African American audiences of the period. On 9 April 1938, the *Chicago Defender* carried as its page-one headline, "Al Jolson, Comedian, Invokes Nazi Creed on Folks He Mimics." This article reported that Jolson had signed a restrictive housing covenant in Encino, California, where he lived. By equating the Jewish Jolson with the Nazis this article made its critical point much more sharply than any of the earlier black criticisms of Jolson's "playing" black could have ever done. What is especially interesting, however, is that the *Defender* now felt Jolson's years in blackface as well as his own minority status should make him virtually black. The compelling logic of singling out Jolson from among the many whites (some probably equally famous) who were signing restrictive covenants seems to have been that mimicry constituted affiliation and because of this affiliation as well as because of his own racial/ethnic heritage Jolson have should known better.

In a reversal of the Amos 'n' Andy debates from 1933, the *Pittsburgh Courier* came to Jolson's defense—three times. First, in a front page piece from 16 April 1938, " 'I'm Not An Ingrate' [Says] Jolson," the *Courier* gave Jolson space to defend himself. Ten days later, the *Courier* reported Noble Sissle's outraged response to what the paper called "an erroneous account of discriminatory tactics."[66] Finally, a week after that article the *Courier* published Jolson's remarks to one of their writers. The report was sympathetic, as its headline makes clear: "Al Jolson Gives Morris 'Lowdown'; 'Hurt To My Heart'."[67]

Perhaps as surprising as the *Courier's* defense of Jolson is the fact that any African American newspaper would spill so much ink on so faded a star. By the spring of 1938, Jolson had no prospects and no apparent power in Hollywood and little in show business in general. Yet in an era when many African American performers and audiences were still trying to decide what to do with blackface—recall, for example, the benefit minstrel show on Chicago's South Side in 1939—Jolson was a still powerful symbol. Noble Sissle's and Jolson's words reveal the tensions and contradictions that circulated around this symbol.

In his defense of Jolson, Sissle mostly extols the singer's virtues from a pragmatic perspective: "he was always the champion of the Negro song writer and performer" and "was first to put Negroes in his shows." Less realistically, though, he goes on to assert that, when Jolson sang of "mammy" "with real tears streaming down his blackened face," he "immortalized the Negro motherhood of America as no individual could." This combination of the "real"—both in terms of clear effects in the world, such as employment, and in less measurable terms, like tears—and the represented—"blackened" rather than black or Negro—fuels Jolson's symbolic power for Sissle.

Jolson's own words, as filtered through the *Courier,* suggest that he also saw and actively used this combination of the real and the represented, the real and imaginary. They also reveal how fraught, both for Jolson and his "colored" interlocutors, this combination was. Here is Jolson from the first article:

> "I have always employed colored people and still do. I bought Henry Armstrong [a black boxer] and have never taken a cent of his money. . . . I ask you, would I have any part in discriminating against the race that I was raised among and have made my living from impersonating? I have the

colored race to thank for their superb music and grand humor and I'm not the kind of a heel that bites the hand that has fed me."

Like Sissle, Jolson first asserts his pragmatic connections to black people, though his tone is distinctly that of the wounded paternalist and describing his relationship to Henry Armstrong in the colloquial terms of purchase is perhaps telling and at the very least tactless. If Sissle implies in his defense that blacks should feel indebted to Jolson, the same implication coming from Jolson grates. Jolson's next rhetorical move takes a different approach. He addresses his black listener/reader—"I ask you"—and then suggests two connections: his youthful proximity to blacks and his career impersonation of them. Finally, and most significantly, he reverses the flow of "debt"; it is he who has been "fed" by blacks, and he thanks them for it. As a symbol for African Americans and to himself, Jolson exists in a complex if always unequal web of affiliation.

Some readers clearly remained unmoved by Jolson's (and Sissle's) assertions of a complex connection with black people and culture. In the final article of the *Courier* series, Jolson complains: "Now that I have publicly denied the nasty accusation, my denial is questioned. They question my sincerity." At least according to the first *Courier* article, Jolson *had* behaved sincerely. He had mistakenly signed a petition for the restrictive covenant, and then he had acted within the domain of Encino politics to have the restrictive covenant voted down. Ironically, it was this action that called the mistake to the attention of the black press.

But "sincerity" is a fraught question for a performer, and Jolson's doubters apparently wondered how sincere an actor could be, or had differing standards for the expression of sincerity. Jolson's second attempt to convince blacks of his sincerity extends and amplifies his first defense in interesting ways, which is why I quote at full length:

> I am not a fool. Anyone who is a salesman as I am for a product that is used by everyone, an actor in pictures which all groups attend, cannot knowingly offend any race. Then to top it all off I am a Jew. And Jews, not only today, but for centuries, have been forced to meet segregation. I knowingly cannot condone any form of discrimination, because of my birthright.
>
> As a kid down in Washington there were only two white families in the neighborhood. Mine and another. Why, Bill Robinson and I were kids together. We used to swipe apples. I have used colored people in most of my

shows. It was my show that practically introduced colored artists to Broadway. I took Mary Duson and Johnny Peters from the "Barbary Coast" in Frisco years ago and Chilton and Thomas were in "Wonder Bar." When it was my choice to use any band I wanted in pictures I sent for Cab Calloway. I was raised among colored people. I have used more colored people in my shows than the average actor. I have portrayed the Negro on the stage and screen. I know what colored people have had to suffer. I couldn't knowingly add to their plight. Henry Armstrong, his brother, all have been here to my home and swam in this very pool.

There isn't a colored old timer who has ever worked with me, or a colored person who knows me that could believe me guilty of such a fool act.

Of course, old timers might also remember Al Jolson playing (with much vaunted sincerity) Al Stone as *The Singing Fool* in 1928, and younger readers might have heard Al Jolson as Al Jackson reassert the connection—"I was born a singin' fool!"—only recently in *The Singing Kid*. More importantly, the *Courier's* regular readers might have noted Jolson's even more extreme swings between the pragmatic pressures (or reason) and the imagined or represented. Readers had seen before the assertions contained at the center of his statement—about employing and portraying African Americans—but here these old claims are sandwiched by new ones: Jolson's characterizations of himself as a salesman and, explicitly, a Jew, on the one hand, and his reconfiguration of Henry Armstrong as a house and pool guest, on the other. This relatively denotative information (at least in 1938) brackets more subtly connotative new material: Jolson's description of his family as "white"; his claim—completely mythic and transparent to any half-knowledgeable "old timer"—that Bill Robinson was his youthful companion; and, last, his explicit linkage of imitation with experience: "I have portrayed the Negro. . . . I know what the colored people have had to suffer."

Jolson's most significant addition to his defense, however, is not the new evidence on offer. Rather, it is the awkward and awkwardly repeated adverb, "knowingly"—"an actor cannot knowingly offend," "I couldn't knowingly add to [blacks'] plight"—which introduces the twin specters of ideology and the unconscious. The question Jolson raised emphatically for African Americans in 1938 was this: What is the relationship between "fool act(s)"—blackface donned, "black" song sung, and, perhaps, black people employed repeatedly—in a mass entertainment medium and the more directly political, materially effective world of restrictive covenants and segregated labor markets? For African Americans there was and is no single and clear cut answer to this question. This at least is what I read from the differing responses of the *Defender* and the *Courier* to Jolson's unknowing, political "fool act," their differing interpretations of how it might relate to his theatrical and cinematic "fool act," and their differing senses of the value and meaning of Jolson as an entertainer.

What the *Defender* and the *Courier* share, however, and what distinguishes black and white thought on connections of politics and culture in the thirties (and still does), is the sense that noting and probing such connections are not fool acts. Jolson's meaning for African Americans might not have been clear in 1938, but few blacks seem to have doubted that he and the range of complex practices he embodied had a meaning, one that had to do with African American culture and one that they should actively attempt to extract and (re)shape.

"My Daddy was a Minstrel Man": Beyond Jolson

Al Jolson's career neither rose nor fell because of the ticket buying patterns of black filmgoers. And to attribute Jolson's decline as a star of Hollywood, Broadway, and radio musicals solely to his acutely problematic Negrophilia/phobia would be inaccurate. By the late thirties, Jolson was old-fashioned and the musicals created around him were unconventional enough to seem incoherent. For Hollywood, Jolson was relatively old (fifty in 1936) and unmistakably ethnic, and he carried direct, presentational, hard-sell performance techniques into an era and a medium that, increasingly, gave the appearance of being smooth and suave (e.g., Astaire, Crosby). These qualities made him unsuited as a romantic lead in modern musical comedy, so perhaps his emphatic and repeated linking of his blackface with veritable black performance was simply gilding the lily, but I do not believe so. Rogin credits the shift in Jolson's fortunes to his continued "ethnic self-assertion," but another cause of the shift in Jolson's career and the cause of the considerable, if conflicted, African American interest in Jolson may have been his inability wholeheartedly to disavow blacks or his interest in black performers and black characters.

Jolson carried on a career-long series of winking dalliances with representing white dependence on blacks, black vengeance against whites, and white desire for blacks, and this amounted to a virtual proclivity for disabling the ordinary circuits of romantic Hollywood desire by adding the forbidden element of race. While hardly revolutionary—and, indeed, profoundly confused and duplicitous—these aspects of Jolson's films came closer to acknowledging the complexities, pains, and perverse pleasures of American race relations and racism than any other Hollywood films of the period, especially nonmusical films. Unlike, say, *Imitation of Life* (1934), which makes race a black problem, or *I am a Fugitive from a Chain Gang* (1932) or *Fury* (1936), which deracinate white prejudice, Jolson films at least hint at the constructedness of race and the potential productiveness of embracing difference.

In the absence of a figure who was a clear equivalent to Jolson but did without blackface and connections to black performers, however, it is impossible to prove such a claim. No such equivalent performer seems to have existed, but a few quick comparisons to Jolson's contemporaries and successors and to the "Jolson" who made a comeback in the late forties should help illustrate my claims.

Eddie Cantor appeared in blackface in film six times in the thirties (out of seven films), just one fewer blackface appearance than Jolson, and he resembled Jolson in age, ethnicity, and performance style, though Cantor was a much more anarchic comic than Jolson. As my remarks on Cantor's *Kid Millions* near the start of this chapter indicated, Cantor also sometimes yoked his blackface to black performers. Cantor's films, however, never invested the connection with the same erotic charge or the structural importance it held in Jolson's films: Only in *Roman Scandals* (1933, numbers directed by Busby Berkeley) were blackface and black performers linked erotically, though not romantically, as Eddie cavorted in mudbath blackface among white and black women, and only in *Ali Baba Goes to Town* (1937) did black performers ever figure in the conclusion of a Cantor film. In contrast to Jolson's films, Cantor's films never used blackface in the final, climactic scenes nor did they ever set a blackface number in contemporary America. Where Jolson was absurd as *The Singing Kid* in 1936, Cantor always remained the "kid," and even when he did appear in blackface surrounded by white women, as he did in *Kid From Spain* (1932) and *Roman Scandals* (where the white women are joined by an equal number of black women in an exponential amplifica-

15. Cantor in blackface "disguise" from a mud bath beauty treatment, accompanied by both white and black chorines, in *Roman Scandals* (1933).

tion of Manet's "Olympia"), he seemed more a cute, queer mascot than a (hetero)sexual threat. Indeed, Cantor was explicitly concerned that he not be defined wholly in terms of blackface or by his early connection with Bert Williams, and in contrast to Jolson he had been careful to control his blackface persona so as to maintain his autonomy from it: "I . . . made a resolve that old Black-face must die. In a moment of emergency I had put on his dark mask and he had helped me to succeed. Now the audience knew only this cork-smeared face, while I stood hidden behind it wondering what would happen if the blacking came off. . . . I was not going to be a slave to a piece of burnt cork for the rest of my acting days."[68] Finally, unlike Jolson, Cantor never seems to have garnered much attention from black critics, though his films played black neighborhood theaters.[69] After 1937 he left Hollywood because his health was failing, but he was still a star and continued his career on the radio.

After Jolson and Cantor, the white stars who appeared most frequently in blackface in the thirties and forties were Judy Garland (three times — four if one counts the "tan" make-up she wears in "Minnie From Trinidad" in *Ziegfeld Girl* [1941]), Mickey Rooney (twice, both times with Garland), Betty Grable (twice), and Bing Crosby (twice). Garland and Rooney shared a "hot," theatrical style somewhat similar to Jolson's, but because they were young and unmistakably white, this style translated as exuberance rather than aggression.[70] When they appeared together in blackface numbers in *Babes in Arms* (1939) and *Babes on Broadway* (1941), Garland and Rooney were connecting with a "past" both for purposes of nostalgia and to legitimate their present performance practice. Be-

16. Mickey Rooney's blackface being washed off by a hurricane at the end of "My Daddy was a Minstrel Man" in *Babes in Arms* (1939).

cause the "past" of minstrelsy they were celebrating was hardly past and had racial and ethnic associations, however, they had to overemphasize the (supposed) gap between themselves and it so they could also appear modern and white.

This is most explicit in *Babes in Arms,* in which the two portray children of unemployed vaudevillians who have been displaced by talking pictures. To raise money to aid their parents, they put on a show—a minstrel show, which they initiate by singing "My Daddy was a Minstrel Man." This tune signifies on Eddie Cantor and the Nicholas Brothers' "I Want to be a Minstrel Man" number from *Kid Millions,* but looks back over a generation to Stephen Foster songs and the late nineteenth century "When Eddie Leonard was so great/And [George] Primrose was king," skipping entirely Jews and African Americans in their history— after all, the figure who initiated the parent-destroying talking pictures was a blackfaced Jew. Jews and African Americans are present only by association: beside the blackface, the kids sing one of Cantor's signature tunes, "Ida," and two songs penned by blacks, "Darktown Strutters' Ball" (Shelton Brooks) and "I'm Just Wild About Harry" (Sissle and Blake). But the conclusion of the "Minstrel Man" number is decisive: A hurricane rolls in and destroys the show, leaving Rooney to plead with the audience not to exit, even as the storm washes his blackface away. The film ends with a second show, one free of blacks and Jews, to be sure, but one also free of the blackface and minstrel songs that might recall them. Garland and Rooney became huge stars during the period of *Babes in Arms* and *Babes on Broadway,* but black critics seem to have returned the favor of black displacement from these films by ignoring them, and judging from the advertising *Babes in Arms* enjoyed less of a presence on the South Side of Chicago than any of the Jolson or Cantor films.[71]

Betty Grable's blackface appearances are even more directly nostalgic and more certain about the place of blacks than the Garland and Rooney films. Both *Coney Island* (1943) and *The Dolly Sisters* (1945) are set firmly in the past, the former at the turn of the century and the latter in the teens and twenties. *The Dolly Sisters,* which takes place mostly in Europe, contains one blackface number—again, "Darktown Strutters' Ball"— that trades entirely in stereotype and seems designed to hint at Parisian decadence. *Coney Island,* set as it is in an iconic American location, is more systematic. It begins with a sequence detailing the attractions of the amusement park, including a "darkie" figure that serves as the target in a throwing game and a black singing waiter. After this opening, the film tells the story of Kate Farley's (Grable's) rise from a bawdy singer at Coney Island to a "class" entertainer at Delmonaco's. In trying to transform her, her mentor and lover criticizes her performance style: "you moved around too much, it was too fast and too loud, and you didn't make the words mean anything." Nonetheless, her breakthrough comes in a blackface number, "Lulu From Louisville," that embodies all these qualities in extremis, thereby permitting them literally and figuratively to dissolve along with the blackface in the transition to Grable's first "class" routine and the refrain of the movie: "Take It From There (and Make of It What You Will)." *Coney Island* literalizes this sentiment by climaxing with a plantation number (based on Stephen Foster songs) in which four old-fashioned, African American clog dancers are sandwiched between two "class" (and very anachronistic) routines performed by Grable and her decidedly white chorus. As with the Garland and Rooney films and unlike Jolson (and to a lesser extent Cantor), Grable's blackface appearances use blackface to claim whiteness as a clear and stable category and to marginalize blacks.

Compared with Garland, Rooney, and Grable, Bing Crosby's blackface appearances stood in a different relation to Jolson's. While Garland, Rooney, and Grable were akin to Jolson in their various embodiments of spectacle, Crosby's persona and performance style were utterly different from Jolson's: Crosby was the original "crooner" while Jolson was a "shouter"; Crosby was unambiguously white, middle-class, and nice while Jolson was ethnic, working-class, and difficult; Crosby was "cool"

17 and 18. Bing Crosby with a black eye and the blackface mask concocted to cover it in *Dixie* (1943).

while Jolson was "hot." At the same time, like Jolson, Crosby was often affiliated with black performers in his films (probably most famously with Louis Armstrong in *High Society* [1956]), and this is also true of his blackface films, *Holiday Inn* (1941) and *Dixie* (1943). Unlike Jolson, however, the blackface numbers and numbers performed with blacks in Crosby's films stand not as the climaxes of the story but as incidents in it; in Crosby films, the climaxes are reserved, in usual musical form, for white, heterosexual couple formation. In *Holiday Inn,* while the blacked-up Crosby and Marjorie Reynolds stage a show celebrating Lincoln and his birthday, Louise Beavers and her two children toil ("happily") in the kitchen, from whence they take—without any apparent irony or camp— a chorus. In *Dixie,* a biopic of Dan Emmett, ostensible author of the eponymous song and an early blackface minstrel, the place of blacks is clearer still.[72] Taking a steamer to New Orleans, Emmett (Crosby) hears a group of black laborers singing "Swing Low, Sweet Chariot" and joins in. The laborers, awestruck, stop singing and look around for this unfamiliar voice; they all end up looking heavenward since, as it turns out, Crosby stands on a deck high above them. Once they have found him, the laborers resume singing—now as an earthly choir in support of their godlike soloist. After this incident, blacks disappear entirely from the film. Emmett's motivation for putting on blackface—and the blackface makeup in *Dixie* is arguably the most grotesque of any Hollywood blackface film—has apparently nothing to do with African Americans: He and his partner have had a fistfight and given one another black eyes, and they adopt blackface as a way of hiding this fact from their audience. Blackface serves, literally, to erase the evidence of a displaced, personalized, wholly white "civil war."

I have found no evidence of direct, African American response to *Holiday Inn* or *Dixie,* though given the title of the second it is hard to imagine it meeting with much enthusiasm.[73] And *Dixie* figured in a particularly vivid and ugly historical confluence, parts of which might be seen as signs of a generalized, African American vernacular criticism. The 5 July 1943 issue of *Life* magazine that featured a laudatory piece on *Dixie* and nineteenth-century minstrelsy also featured a long, late-breaking pictorial on the bloody race riots in Detroit, a conflict that began when whites tried forcibly to prevent blacks from moving into a public housing project.[74]

Another image from the same issue of *Life* suggests that the whites were fighting to make sure the(ir) world reflected a Bing Crosby film and that the blacks were struggling to make sure the(ir) world did not. In an article about entertainment in the white sections of segregated military camps in the Pacific (this configuration is simply assumed, never stated), one small photograph shows "a colored band from Army engineers," playing for the white audience.[75] The progression of these sets of *Life* images—from musical entertainments to what a colloquialism from a later Detroit uprising would call "Dancin' in the Streets"; from black performance for (or in front of, at any rate) whites to white performance *as* black to, finally, white refusal of black proximity and black counter-insistence—inadvertently allegorizes American racialist hierarchies and conflicts that emerge in blackface. On the one hand, there is the white

19. "Colored Band from Army Engineers" and their audience in "South Sea Island Scandals," *Life,* 5 July 1943.

effort to use blackface to control and erase—and justify the erasure of—African Americans. White supremacist interpretive logic would suggest that if, as in *Dixie,* whites can perform with and then perform instead of blacks, then even in the constrained domain of entertainment blacks are no longer "necessary" to U.S. culture, though they might be convenient for labor. On the other hand, as my previous chapter suggested, some African Americans had long seen such attempts at displacement and erasure as an opportunity to use blackface as a critical foot in the door of American opportunity. And as this chapter has argued in part, some African Americans saw white blackface as an invitation to pay especially careful attention to white behavior and as an opportunity to remind whites of the continuity of (and responsibility of) races in relation.

Al Jolson's blackface performances of 1927 to 1936 were perhaps second only to the implied blackface of Amos 'n' Andy in prompting black cultural criticism. One important reason Jolson (like Amos 'n' Andy) seems to have functioned this way is that his blackface remained emphatically connected to black performers, to representations inhabited by veritable blacks. When the increasingly conventional narratives of the musical could no longer accommodate this connection (along with Jolson's performance style, age, and ethnicity), he was relegated to spots as a blackface specialty number where he could function conventionally. In *Rose of Washington Square* (1939) and *Swanee River* (1939), Jolson's primary task seems to be to protect the films' heroes from the proximity to blackness that blackface could imply, especially the model of blackface that Jolson had himself promulgated.[76] *Rhapsody in Blue* (1945), a liberal biopic of George Gershwin, reverses this process, and the blackfaced Jolson becomes a stop on Gershwin's path to veritable black talents like Hazel Scott and the cast of *Porgy and Bess*. But what *Rhapsody in Blue* shares with *Rose of Washington Square* and *Swanee River* is an uncomplicated notion of "progress" or (dis)connection. The two earlier films work to eradicate blacks from the lives of their white principals, and the latter film works to eradicate blackface. This is certainly a preferable course, and *Rhapsody* must be given credit for bringing Gershwin into this relatively complicated relationship with blackface and black performance, but finally the film is too easily satisfied with using Jolson and his blackface as a mark of the old-fashioned, a (perhaps) regrettable but necessary step toward enlightenment.

The huge success of *The Jolson Story* in 1946 proved that blackface was not too old-fashioned to be popular. Still, to bring Jolson back required conventionalization: a handsome, young leading man (Larry Parks), a sustaining family life, romance, a moderated performance style (Jolson, who supplied the voice for Parks, learned to croon)—and no black people. Even within these constraints, however, Jolson (or "Jolson") resists complete conventionalization: He "discovers" jazz in New Orleans when he overhears a black band. This is a Bing-Crosby-as-Dan-Emmett moment, it seems, but unlike Crosby (or Don Ameche as Stephen Fos-

20. "Al Jolson" (Larry Parks, in the hat) discovering jazz in New Orleans in *The Jolson Story* (1946).

ter in *Swanee River*) "Jolson" (Parks) sits *with* the black players, listening raptly; he does not join in; he does not show his immediate command of black jazz; when he leaves, he gives the players money; and when he later tries to sell his boss on the idea of performing jazz, he is explicit about the changes he will make to commercialize the idiom. Still, compared with the thirties Jolson, this is minor resistance, and it has been substantially blunted by a preceding scene when "Jolson," like Crosby in *Dixie,* blacks up because of a mistake. He discovers the regular blackface performer in his troupe drunk and, without anyone knowing, goes on in his stead. In *The Jolson Story,* then, blackface and blackness are both connected by temporal proximity in the plot and, especially relative to the earlier Jolson films, separated by narrative causation or "logic" (Jolson does not black up because he's discovered black music). As it is for Gershwin in *Rhapsody in Blue,* blackface becomes something "Jolson" must go "through" before developing a more direct connection to veritable black performers and whiteness, though *The Jolson Story*'s displacement of blacks is more complete than *Rhapsody*'s, and "Jolson"'s blackface lingers in the plot for much longer. Nonetheless, both biopics ultimately go to Hollywood, where all traces of both blackness and blackface are banished.

The black and blackfaced repressed might be seen to return in several abstracted ways in *The Jolson Story.* Most prominent among these returns occurs at the conclusion, when a retired "Jolson" visits a nightclub and gets called to perform. He retastes the pleasure of performance, a pleasure the film has constructed as a sickness, albeit a noble one. This sickness—a sort of reflex to perform—destroys his marriage to the "shiksa,"

who haunts all the Jolson films, and the "sickness" connects the assimi-
lated "Jolson" back to his Judaism, to stereotypes of blackness, and to
expressive "others" in general.

Jolson Sings Again (1949) reverses the pattern of *The Jolson Story* and
thereby completes the work of conventionalizing Jolson. In *Jolson Sings
Again* "Jolson" gets remarried, turns his urge to perform toward socially
useful ends (entertaining the troops), and moderates that urge while at
the same time making a genuine comeback—*The Jolson Story.* There are
no African Americans, not even the marginal jazz musicians of *The Jolson
Story,* in *Jolson Sings Again,* and the blackface appearances are all motivated by *The Jolson Story.*[77] A flurry of blackface (the only blackface in
the film) concludes *Jolson Sings Again,* but this conclusion is twice removed: It is about a three-year-old film that is about a performer who
was more than a decade out of fashion. That was then, *Jolson Sings Again*
says—though it is also powerfully, nostalgically, the "now" of the film.

White blackface, in its most obvious, ritualized, masklike form, still
had not completely run its course in U.S. film in 1949. The last blackface
Hollywood films were made in 1953. In combination with mass mediation, however, blackface had done its critical work for African Americans, who had forsaken blackface as a black performance tradition and
who, at least judging from the printed record, had lost interest in Jolson and white blackface in general. Mass mediated blackface had made
clear for African American critics, and probably for larger black audiences, that pleasure or criticism internal to black communities and audiences could no longer be enough[78]; they had to struggle to articulate
cultural and political alternatives to blackface that would be *obviously*
different from—disconnected from—blackface, even to white audiences
disinclined to see such difference. Bebop, the revision of the swing that
had revised jazz, is perhaps most emblematic of this disjunctive impulse, but within the conventions of the musical, which included the
once critical but ultimately constraining conjunction of blackface and
veritable black musical performance, such disjunctions were unfilmable,
unrepresentable.

3

Indefinite Talk

BLACKS IN BLACKFACE, FILMED

> There is an unwritten law in America that though white
> may imitate black, black, even when superlatively capable,
> must never imitate white. In other words, grease-paint may
> be used to darken but never to lighten.
> —JESSIE FAUSET (1925)

For African American audiences of the twenties, thirties, and into the
forties, blackface was a common entertainment experience. By the early
thirties most radio listeners knew that Freeman Gosdon and Charles
Correll were white, so the black-identified voices of *Amos 'n' Andy* came
in sonic blackface, which was made visual in Gosdon and Correll's public
appearances, their film *Check and Double Check,* and their publicity materials. Consequently, white blackface was exceedingly regular on radios
everywhere, including many black homes.[1] As my last chapter has shown,
white blackface was also ordinary in the Hollywood musicals that helped
fill U.S. cinemas, including those in black neighborhoods. Opportunities for African Americans to experience white blackface live were much
rarer, but they existed. And, as I argued in my opening chapter, black
blackface was, at least through the mid-thirties, nearly ubiquitous and
an important comic and critical mode in black live entertainment.

In this welter, however, mass-mediated black blackface was uncommon. Black blackface on the radio was impossible or, at least, illogical and unattractive to white administrators, sponsors, and audiences.
Radio's divorce of sound from image added a modern, technological
anxiety to America's visually grounded but invisibly "blood"-based system of racism. How could a radio listener be certain of a performer's
race? Insofar as radio was blind, it was also color blind, but in the context of a society that was extremely color attuned, radio's blindness made
masking at once unavoidable and uncertain. Admitting blacks into this
medium could only cause confusion and instability for the highly cate-

A 'Race-Hater' Tunes In

21. "A 'Race-Hater' Tunes In," *Chicago Defender*, 21 November 1936.

gorical dominant "way of seeing," which was certainly not a bad thing to do from an African American perspective. "A 'Race-Hater' Tunes In," an editorial cartoon that ran in the *Chicago Defender* in 1936 makes this situation plain: A white man turns on his radio, relaxes in his chair, and describes himself as "entranced" by the piano performance he hears.

When the announcer comes on and says, "You have been listening to George Johnson the inimitable *Negro* pianist," the shocked race-hater takes an axe to his radio.[2] Admitting black blackface performers — performers accustomed to manipulating the minstrelized masks of racial identity and, perhaps, equipped with an audience accustomed to hearing and seeing them do so — had the potential to increase the confusion of racial categories and hierarchies to intolerable levels.

Synchronized sound film, which (re)joins recorded sound and recorded image, would seem to ameliorate the problems of radio. We might expect then that, as it did with white blackface, sound film would mirror (perhaps even amplify) black blackface's place in live performance culture(s). However, it did not. As far as I've been able to determine, blacks appeared in blackface in only four films: two race films made by the African American director Oscar Micheaux, *The Darktown Revue* (1931) and *Ten Minutes to Live* (1932), and two Hollywood musicals, the Shirley Temple vehicle *Dimples* (1936) and the all-black cast *Stormy Weather* (1943).

The reasons for this dearth were multifold. The causes for the absence of black blackface in Hollywood films were probably not much different from the causes of its absence from radio. There were plenty of white blackface entertainers available for film, and black blackface had the potential to raise too many direct, critical questions about the performance of racial identity and order in the United States. In race film — independent, inexpensive, and, especially in the sound-era, most often white-financed film production for black audiences — the causes of this dearth were more intricate. Partly they were due to timing. Race film production had never been prolific, and with the successive burdens of the onset of sound, which required additional capital and technical expertise, and the Depression it fell off precipitously from the late twenties through the mid-thirties. As a consequence, the opportunities for race film (re)presenting black blackface were few. Moreover, by the time race film production was increasing in the late thirties, live black blackface was starting to wane because blacks were beginning to understand how mass reproduction and distribution took the black image (even more) out of the control of black audiences and performers.[3]

The rarity of black blackface in race film also suggests that race filmmakers may have sensed that the meanings of black expressive forms, usually experienced live, could be profoundly altered by recording. Film would not accommodate the immediate, responsive, and potentially altering call and response relation between performer and audience that much black performance builds on. If my argument in chapter one is correct that the (potential) critical meanings and effects of black blackface resulted from the performer's careful shifting—done in collaboration with his or her audience—between the stasis of the stereotyped mask (the "same" as the white blackface mask) and the fluidity of the identity behind it (now complicatedly black rather than white), then film (and mass media more generally), which eliminates the direct spatiotemporal link of performer and audience, would have serious consequences for the possibilities of a critical black blackface.

This would be especially apparent for African Americans operating from a position of Du Boisian "double consciousness," those who saw themselves simultaneously from inside and outside "the veil" of race in America.[4] Confronted with the recorded image of the black blackface performer—who in live performance might collaborate with the audience to embody multiple consciousness as a concept for critical consideration but who appears frozen on film—the multiply conscious viewer might well feel him- or herself to be in an intolerable psychic echo chamber, a place in which the liberating noise and nonsense of the black blackface performer gets fed back through the ears and eyes of the (imagined) white viewer and becomes dangerous(ly) static.

With these reservations in mind, it becomes especially interesting to analyze the few instances of cinematic black blackface that do exist. Before proceeding with my analysis, though, I should point out that, unlike my analyses of live black blackface in chapter one or of filmed white blackface in chapter two, here I cannot draw directly on any African American critical writing about these scenes; my researches have uncovered none. I have found no evidence that *The Darktown Revue* was released. *Ten Minutes to Live* was available in black neighborhoods but aroused little comment, and the same is true of *Dimples*. *Stormy Weather*, in contrast, received considerable coverage in the black press, both laudatory and critical, but none that I have found mentioned the black blackface number that, at least temporally, is at the very center of the film. This circumstance—this silence—suggests that it is especially crucial to ask what meanings and effects these films might make possible and for what kinds of audiences, and what meanings and effects they seem to foreclose. What sort of (traceless and always uncertain) attention might the inattention they received, at least in print, indicate?

Race Blackface: Micheaux's *Darktown Revue* and *Ten Minutes to Live*

Oscar Micheaux was the most prolific and persevering black filmmaker of the early twentieth century. Micheaux worked completely outside of Hollywood and the mechanisms of even the low-budget end of U.S. fiction filmmaking, and as a consequence, even the basic outline of his career is somewhat uncertain.[5] We know that, after farming and writing a novel, he began making films in 1918 and continued, with an eight-year break in the forties to write more novels, until 1948, but we do not know how many films he made. Fifteen survive, but he may have made as many as forty or even fifty.[6] Micheaux's productions were always extremely low budget, so few prints were ever struck, and those that survive were well travelled and fully used. As an independent, Micheaux encountered perpetual problems with censors and review boards, and prints were changed to meet their demands. Additionally, like D. W. Griffith, Micheaux proved willing to alter his films to appeal to his audiences — or to attempt to re-present old films as new material. Among the prints of the Micheaux films that have survived, then, it is unclear how near they are to Micheaux's authorial and directoral intentions, how close they are to his original films, or most importantly, how exactly they relate to what any audiences saw and heard.

All of these considerations force analyses and interpretations of Micheaux's films to be extraordinarily open ended, but they would seem to place beyond dispute one aspect of Micheaux: In terms of the Hollywood film industry and of film scholarship focused on mainstream American cinema, Micheaux was certainly independent. He received no money from and had no connection with the Hollywood film business. Especially when examining Micheaux's sound-era work, however, some scholars have wondered about Micheaux's racial and ideological independence from the mainstream of American thought, which Hollywood so struggles to represent, and from white capital and consequent influence.[7] Micheaux's silent films are his most consistently and widely regarded works. In the silent era, Micheaux was a fully independent producer who raised all his funds himself; some of his money came from whites, but all of Micheaux's investors were small-time, and hence, presumably none exercised direct influence on his work. With the coming of sound and the Depression, Micheaux's company went bankrupt and was refinanced by a more consolidated group of white capitalists, who owned and ran most of the theaters in Harlem. For critics like Daniel Leab, Pearl Bowser, Toni Cade Bambara, and Mark Reid, this direct financial dependence combined with melodramatic plots, musical numbers, skin color consciousness, and middle-class values (all associated, for these critics, with dominant, white aesthetics and ideology) fatally compromised Micheaux's sound-era productions, especially in comparison with his silent productions.[8]

No written evidence exists to suggest that Micheaux was directly admonished by his investors, but more surprisingly, the films that survive do not suggest a radical (or even substantial) transformation of either Micheaux's themes or his style between the silent and sound eras. In fact, Bogle is wrong when he writes of Micheaux, "He created a fantasy world where blacks were just as affluent, just as educated, just as 'cultured,' just as well-mannered—in short, just as white—as white America."[9] Beginning with *Within Our Gates* (1919) and its horrifying depiction of a lynching, Micheaux refused this fantasy, opting to explore the possibilities of dependence and independence, connection and autonomy.[10] Critics have most appreciated such exploration when it took "serious," melodramatic forms, but I will argue that Micheaux also used comic or, more accurately, emphatically mixed and fragmented forms for the same ends. Here I examine how, for a brief moment in the early thirties, black blackface provided Micheaux another musical and comic—and oblique and ambivalent—tool for his project. When I return to Micheaux in chapter five, I will analyze his 1938 backstage musical, *Swing!*, which allegorizes the complexities of Micheaux's own position by explicitly taking up the relations of white capital and influence on black cultural producers.

The Darktown Revue (hereafter *DTR*) was either Micheaux's second or third sound film, and with its nonnarrative frontality and presentational form, it has much in common with Hollywood's first widely distributed experiments in synchronized sound, the Vitaphone shorts (*DTR* is itself only twenty minutes long), and with early sound period revue musicals like *The Hollywood Revue of 1929* (MGM 1929).[11] Like these Hollywood

22. The Donald
Heyward Choir in
Darktown Revue
(1931).

films, *DTR* is a succession of apparently discrete musical and comedy numbers stuck together. What makes *DTR* interesting is that its succession is carefully patterned by a series of contrasts—contrasts which at first appear simple but build until finally they become complex, critical, and interconnected.

The foundational contrasts of the film are contrasts of mode—music versus comedy, and class—upper-middle versus low, and morality—religious versus secular. *DTR* opens with a number by the Donald Heyward Choir, a group of sixteen formally dressed, decorous young men and women, who perform with crisp diction, unswinging rhythms, and an ordinary, sedate melodic style. The choir is supplanted by Tim Moore and Andrew Tribel, two well known black "coon" comics, who are not wearing blackface. When the comics' turn is finished, the choir returns. This order implies a pattern of simple alternation between contrasts, and the content of the numbers also notices and comments on these contrasts. Moore and Tribel's turn is "Why Leave By the Window?"—Here is the first (and a representative) comic climax of the routine:

> Moore: Outta all dem folks standin' round on dah levee, the man had to come off the boat and walk up and insult me.
> Tribel: How'd he insult you?
> Moore: Ask me did I wanna work?

The choir follows with their own invidious question, "Ain't It a Shame?"

From its very start, however, *DTR* allows room for a complexity that is unrecognized in the choir's (implied) simple, moralistic distinction, a distinction that is perhaps already compromised by the use of the colloquial "ain't". A viewer might wonder, for example, what a choir like this is doing in a revue bearing the stereotypic title "darktown," a title that seems to have more to do with the film's comics. On the one hand, the title places the film in a three-decade tradition of black-produced and controlled black musical shows; it is a mark of pride.[12] On the other, coming near the tail end of this tradition of naming and during a Depression-induced rough patch for the black musical, the title subtly hints at the inescapability of race and racism in the United States; it seems to say, you can dress in formal wear and use crisp diction, but if you are black (which all the choristers "are," though they range from "clearly" black to able probably to pass for white), you still belong in darktown. The choir's first number—"Watermelon Time" interpolated with Stephen Foster's "Swanee River"—resonates with multiple meanings. The number can be heard as calling forth and preparing the way for the coon comics, or a viewer might wonder at the (ironic?) gap between such old Negro songs sung by such a seemingly New Negro choir. Either way, a sense of an expansive interpenetration of the contrasting terms begins to emerge.

DTR does not require its viewers to be so subtle, though. Immediately after the choir's "Ain't It a Shame?" the implied pattern of a succession from music(high) to comedy(low) is modified. The choir remains for another number, "Jazz Grand Opera," which explicitly works to fuse "low"/black and "high"/white forms of music. Here the middle-classness that the choir seems to embody becomes formally explicit as it mildly satirizes both jazz and opera, mushing them together, ultimately, into a bland mix.

Just when a viewer may start to wonder if the bland mixture of "Jazz Grand Opera" will be *DTR*'s conclusion, the place of pride by the conventions of revue structure, the film's true finale begins, and it both returns us to comedy and takes its patterns of contrast and connection in new directions. The number "Is That Religion?" keeps the choir on stage, making its members at once the respondents to and (as the question in song title again implies) the critics of a preacher that comic Amon Davis creates—in blackface. Davis's mask becomes the film's emblem of connection through contrast. The unmasked choir, so markedly different from him, is both with him and against him; they are both black like him and not black(faced) like him, and they sing both in support and

23. Amon Davis in blackface, with the Heyward Choir, in "Is that Religion?" from *Darktown Revue.*

critique of him. Davis amplifies this connective split with his own performance. To be sure, Davis is mocking at least a strand or component of black religion, a purpose that is of a piece with the anticlericalism of Micheaux's *Within Our Gates* (1919) and *Body and Soul* (1927). At the same time, his turn enacts what it mocks. For his "text," Davis takes the alphabet and, through gesture, exclamation, exhortation, rhythm, and tone, turns it into a rousing, engaging "sermon." Suddenly, the answer to the choir's critical question—"Is That Religion?"—is not as simple as it seems. Davis's sermon may not be "religion," but it is a persuasive demonstration of the power of performance style.[13]

Mel Watkins, a historian and critic of African American humor, argues that "while Davis dons blackface makeup and riddles the piece with minstrel-like references and mispronunciations . . . , the use of a nonsensical, abstract text clearly confirms the humor is intentional, a performance and not an instance of naivete or innate idiocy."[14] I would extend Watkins's reading of this moment to claim that blackface in this context is a further—even the primary—mark of intention. It is the combination of black blackface with nonsense text *and* with nonblackfaced blacks and coherent singing that makes the intent certain, though the effect is recursive: What is certain is uncertainty. (To return to *DTR*'s earlier questions: Is it—i.e., the "coon"'s putative laziness—a shame? Why *not* go through the window? And behind that, why work for "the man"?) *DTR* seems to imply that attention to connection as well as contrast is crucial to African American entertainment—and, hence, African American culture's sense of what utopia would feel like.[15] Read this way, *DTR,* a simple revue film, argues against simple judgements. Davis's blackface number makes clear that form and content (here performance and "text") are both always related and always separable, and the form is genius while the content is nonsense.

Micheaux's film, *Ten Minutes to Live* (*TML*), his fourth or fifth of the sound era, is a narrative film that exchanges the concision and directness of *Darktown Revue* for a generic and organizational delirium that verges on utter incoherence. Like many of Micheaux's films, *TML* is fascinated with doublings, both in the formal and in the psychological Du Boisian senses, and with duplicity.[16] *DTR*'s contrastive structure hints at this interest, but that film uses its doublings, along with conventional expectations that the revue be entertaining and comedic, to hint at the possibility of union in difference, the possibility of pairing. By comparison, *TML* is obsessed with doublings of all kinds, and it is not confident that they can be unified or even brought into meaningful, interpretable alignment. If *DTR* used blackface to present the entanglements of contrast and connection at a variety of discourses and levels in African American culture, from modes of black expressive culture to intraracial class and color relations, it did so in a generic frame that emphasized entertainment, with all its utopian overtones. In contrast, *TML* uses its blackface number as an emblem of incoherence, as a mocking suggestion of the potentially tragic—certainly melodramatic—impossibility of full knowledge or complete communication, whether it is inter- or intracultural.

TML encompasses two discrete "Stories of Harlem Nightlife," "The Faker" and "The Killer." Along with their general theme these stories share a key setting, the Libia cabaret, and their lead actress, who plays a crucial role in each. "The Faker" and "The Killer" each center on the idea of heterosexual coupling as both a potential site of pure, true communication and, more often, a site of tragic miscommunication, whether intentional or not. Each story climaxes with a murder. In "The Faker," a woman kills a man—the eponymous character, who is an intentional miscommunicator—to avenge her own wounded heart and revenge a murdered female friend. In "The Killer," a man—the eponymous character, who is a deaf-mute actor (in the story) and whose ability to communicate is restricted—kills a woman, who nearly misled him into the revenge killing of an innocent woman, Letha. Unlike "The

Faker," though, which ends with the murder, "The Killer" ends with Letha leaving Harlem to make a new life with the man who stood by her through her ordeal. Importantly, these interpersonal melodramas are not represented as private or domestic. They ripple out, first through the black-dominated but apparently interracial space of the cabaret, where the climactic murder takes place in "The Faker" and where Letha awaits her narrowly avoided death in "The Killer," and then by implication, through a white-dominated larger world represented by the white audience members in the cabaret, newspapers, and locations — trains, Grand Central Station, Westchester — outside of Harlem. But these are contiguities, not connections. In terms of *TML*'s narrative(s), this is captured best by the fact that, though Letha knows who "The Killer" is, she does not tell the police. Placed prominently at the beginning of the film (and "The Faker"), *TML*'s blackface number presages, in a distilled non-narrative attraction, the difficulties of (dis)connection, (in)coherence, and (mis)communication that become the film's main subject.

Appropriately, *TML*'s black blackface number is a duet and has two sections, a dialogue and a song. The first section focuses on the serious subjects of uplift, freedom, and role models, all of which gather under the general heading of individual agency and all of which are ruthlessly lampooned. For example, the comics open with this exchange, which in the depths of the Depression must have struck especially close to home for many African American viewers:

> 1: I've been tryin' to teach you to keep up with me all the time. What you wanna do is stop talkin' about goin' to jail. Uplift yo'self, elevate, be somebody. Follow in the footsteps of great men.
> 2: Now what's the use of me bein' somebody and elevatin'? What good it's gonna do to me? I wanna go wh . . . wh . . . where I can eat.
> 1: Well, that's all right . . . you elevate, and then you can eat.
> 2: I can't even join the Fresh Air Camp. Fresh air don't mean nothin' to me now. Gimme less liberty and more food. Got a whole lotta freedom and starvin' to death.

The closing of this first section of the routine takes a swipe at the U.S. cult of personality and myths of upward mobility and individual self-reliance when the comics agree that "Lindenbergh" is a great man, "the greatest out of all of 'em" — a list which includes Booker T. Washington, Frederick Douglass, Marcus Garvey, George Washington, and Abe Lin-

24. "George and Gabby," a black blackface duo, in *Ten Minutes to Live* (1932).

coln, all of whom are also ridiculed. Even (grand)mother-wit, which will play a crucial role in "The Killer," is not safe:

> 2: I, I, I never will forget the words my grandma used to tell me. . . . When I was a little boy, she use' to hold me on her lap and look into my big blue eyes. She pushed my goldilocks back from my forehead and said, "Son, my darlin' son, where dere's a will dere's a way."
>
> 1: She was right!
>
> 2: I got a will to eat, but I can't find the way.

In the world created by the dialogue of these two comics, the punchline is always pessimistic. It is a world of gaps—the gap between the two men (1 always positive and 2 always negative), the gap between knowledge and ignorance (the comics are "ignorant" of facts, but they also seem to "know" the limited power of black leaders and American political myths; we know the comics's names, George and Gabby, but we don't know which one is which), the gap between the "goldilocked," "blue-eyed" boy and the blackfaced man, or the gap between the mask and its wearer. This is black blackfaced "humor" as howl.

The second section of George and Gabby's act—their song—seems meant to be less charged. A few individual lines suggest the despairing tone of their dialogue and the interests of the film's narrative. For example, the song's opening line, "You can make love in a flower garden, the daisies will not tell," hints at *TML*'s concern with romance as/and communication, and its final lines, "Why did the boy stand on the burning gate? / It was too doggone hot to sit down," echo some of the logic of the dialogue. As these examples also make clear, however, the overarching sense of the song is nonsense and non sequitur.

More intelligible than the meaning of any line or verse of the song—its apparent content—is the situation that gives rise to it, its performance, and its effects. The transition from the dialogue to the song comes when one comic (the straight man) asks the other to help him finish the song he has started writing. He argues that this will make them "just as great as ['Lindenbergh']." The performance enacts this proposal of partnership. The straight man sings a line, and the other harmonizes with him for two repetitions of the line, after which the straight man drops out, and his partner sings the final (punch) line. Since this is a comic turn, the performance is not supposed to be "great"; rather, it is supposed to be absurd. This performance, however, is also extremely ragged. George and Gabby seem to be both improvising and camera (and microphone) conscious, a disquieting and decidedly unpolished combination that reveals the missteps, risks, and labor in the performance. George and Gabby fall far short of what a Hollywood-trained audience would expect. It seems as though, despite their efforts (both within the fiction of their act and as performers), they are failing to work together, which amplifies the pessimism of the act's first section.

Compounding this sense of failure is the fact that George and Gabby seem profoundly isolated by the framing and editing of the scene. The film establishes that George and Gabby have a diegetic audience in the Libia cabaret, but we seldom glimpse them in the medium-long and medium shots that dominate the scene. When we do see the audience, its members appear stiff, perhaps even mortified. When the camera cuts away from the comedians to focus on the audience, violations of continuity rules create a sense of disorientation and further isolation, and the apparent distraction of the ostensible audience members still further emphasizes these feelings. As the film develops, we discover that compared with the other cabaret performers George and Gabby have not received an especially cold response and that key audience members, seen in the cutaways, have reasons—namely the murder plot—for their distraction. Nonetheless, the effect, which is more depressing than the direct despair of the dialogue section of the act, lingers over the whole of *TML,* so that when Letha and her beau make their escape at the end of the film, it is hard for the viewer to escape a lingering sense of nihilism.

Unlike *Darktown Revue,* where the black blackfaced "preacher" called and the choir provided a response at once appreciative and critical, where blackface served as a contrastive connection, in *Ten Minutes to Live* the black blackface act does not connect but only contrasts, suggesting deep divides of class, color, and gender in Harlem, but also gesturing beyond those divides to the American racial and class orders. *Ten Minutes to Live* neither embraces nor scorns black blackface, as it appears the two comic's diegetic audience members might be inclined to do; rather, it confronts it as a complex cultural legacy and a tool, a critical reminder of the past in the present.

Dimples: Black Blackface as Accommodation

Four years after Micheaux's *Ten Minutes to Live,* the Shirley Temple film *Dimples* (1936) put Stepin Fetchit in blackface for its concluding spectacle and quickly revealed the limits of mass-mediated black blackface. Fetchit in blackface, especially in the context of *Dimples*'s Hollywood antebellum fantasy, is an obvious instance of what the critic Tommy Lott has labelled "cultural malpractice."[17] Perhaps even more than Micheaux's obscurity or intricacy, however, Fetchit's obviousness requires explication especially because *Dimples* was (and almost certainly continues to be) the most widely seen instance of cinematic black blackface. Why is Stepin Fetchit in blackface so clearly just negative, rather than being the more ambiguously, multiply "negative" figure we have seen in some instances of black blackface?

There are two parts to the answer for this question, one having to do with the "star," Stepin Fetchit, and the other more specifically aimed at *Dimples*. In 1936, Stepin Fetchit's nine-year film career was starting to wane. There were several reasons for this. Fetchit was typecast, but he also seemed uninterested in varying that type. At the same time he was labeled uncooperative and, because of his (mildly) scandalous off-screen behavior, more difficult to employ. Because he was an established performer, he was also more expensive than less-established but similar performers, and more nuanced African American performers like Bill Robinson and Paul Robeson began providing audiences a basis for comparison with Fetchit.[18]

Ironically (from a present-day vantage point), performers like Robinson and Robeson or comic supernumeraries like Willie Best or Fred

"Snowflake" Toones may have supplanted Fetchit because they presented a more stable, comfortable, and intelligible presence than Fetchit. While these other performers were simply comic personae—or in the cases of Robinson, "copacetic," and Robeson, stately—Fetchit more and more conveyed the impression of a personality in the process of both fragmenting and imploding. His performances moved from conveying his character's "struggle" with (ostensible) laziness and stupidity to creating a struggle for his audiences, most obviously to understand what he was saying. Donald Bogle sees this as "a complex, contradictory element" in Fetchit's film appearances, and he argues that "the ambiguity in Fetchit's work was so strong that audiences often asked, 'Can he be serious?' "[19] In examining black blackface in Oscar Micheaux's films, I argued that blackface needed to be seen as a marker of comic or critical intent. The (potential) power of Fetchit was in the put on, the uncertainty about intent: Did he mean to act like that? What could make him act like that? Fetchit's blackface in *Dimples* ended the ambiguity of his performance, which, until then, could be read as having both productive and destructive, critical and recuperative effects.[20] But because Fetchit acted the same whether in or out of blackface in *Dimples,* the mask could not consistently convey intention, awareness, or even mutability and skill; for most African American viewers Fetchit's blackface mask conveyed the opposite qualities, and his performance became fully recuperable.[21]

Considered within the specific contexts of the genres and narrative of *Dimples,* Fetchit's blackface becomes still more clearly negative. *Dimples* caps a loose trilogy of Shirley Temple Civil War films, at first progressively modifying but finally recapitulating the ideology reflected in the first two films. The previous installments, *The Littlest Rebel* and *The Little Colonel* (both 1935), are each set in the South during and immediately after the war, and their ideological project is sectional reconciliation. Set on plantations and using interracial casts, these two films secure the stage for North-South reconciliation by presenting racial reconciliation as always already accomplished in the form of Temple's cutely paternalist rule over her black playmates and, most indelibly, through her dances with Bill Robinson. *The Littlest Rebel* assures that such close affiliations do not lead to anything like (even cultural) amalgamation when, in an attempt to disguise herself from Union soldiers, Temple dons blackface and is immediately discovered—she's a good mimic, but not *that* good a mimic. The loving but "appropriate" relationships Temple has with the loyal black characters in both films make clear that there was nothing to fight over in the first place.

Initially, *Dimples* seems like it will pursue a different and potentially more progressive angle on the Civil War. The film is set in New York City before the war. Dimples (Temple) is the leading member of an interracial band of urchin street performers (like the Little Rascals), which serves as cover for the petty thievery of her grandfather (Frank Morgan). Within her gang, Temple is more an equal to her pals than in the previous films, and after the second number—a tap dance with a pair of young black dancers [22]—Dimples, who has been caught in her grandfather's robbery scheme, says to her captor, "I like chocolate and vanilla." Though she is supposed to be talking about cake, the analogy with her egalitarian spirit is clear. Fetchit plays the grandfather's manservant, Cicero, and his first appearance suggests that he is smarter than his impoverished employer. In the face of the grandfather's imperious orders, Cicero does nothing, manages to make the grandfather appear a fool, *and* gets paid. It seems he might be the grandfather's comeuppance for earlier expressing his preference for "vanilla." As the film's plot develops, a rich and kind-hearted matron, who has discovered the grandfather's poverty, offers to *buy* Dimples, and Dimples only avoids this fate by getting a job playing Little Eva in the premiere of *Uncle Tom's Cabin*. All of this suggests, weakly, to be sure, but much more strongly than *The Littlest Rebel* or *The Little Colonel,* some of the racial politics that were at stake in the Civil War.

Dimples vitiates whatever modest progressive stance it developed in its first half not only by making its *Uncle Tom* focus on Little Eva and making Uncle Tom a white in blackface (both of which choices could be justified in the name of "historical accuracy"), but also by allowing its narrative to intersect, farcically, with its representation of the play. Once more on the run from the law, Dimples's grandfather tries to masquerade as Tom, in which guise he is forced by the police to take the stage, causing pandemonium; for a moment, Tom is strangely doubled, but the grandfather is revealed when he attempts to remain "in character" even when he is offstage, while the "real" Tom relinquishes his dialect and mannerisms when he comes off. Equilibrium is restored for the sentimental death of Little Eva, which has the effect of reconciling—in a double romance—the plot's "adult" conflicts of class and taste. But the grandfather's blackface turn has prepared the way for the film's conclusion, a minstrel show celebrating the first year of *Uncle Tom*'s run.

With the minstrel show, *Dimples* creates a final, systematic undoing of the film's earlier progressivism. It begins by asserting an abiding interest in sectional reconciliation (or, since within the fiction the war has yet to begin, compromise). "Out of the South has recently come a new form of entertainment," says *Uncle Tom*'s producer, by way of awkward transition to the minstrel show. "Our company wishes to be the first to present it in New York."[23] A full blackfaced minstrel line takes the stage; Fetchit's Cicero occupies an endman's position. After a noisy, up-tempo instrumental introduction, the line sings the verse to "Dixie-Anna," a love ballad by Tin Pan Alley writers Ted Koehler and Jimmy McHugh about "a lonesome Romeo . . . waiting for his dusky lady love." Dimples, in a white tuxedo and sans blackface, enters, takes the central, interlocutor's position, and sings the chorus. Now the pathos of Little Eva's last words—her request that her father free his slaves—is fully displaced by the white romances called forth by this song of "dusky" romance in the slave South.

But *Dimples*'s regression is not complete. "Dixie-Anna" modulates into "Swanee River," quietly plucked on a banjo, and Dimples queries Cicero/Mr. Bones:

Dimples: Mr. Bones, why does a fireman wear red suspenders?
Cicero (mumbled, slowly and stumblingly): Well, I tell ya, Miss Interlocutor, I don't know . . . how come a fireman wear red suspenders?
Dimples (imitating Cicero): The reason a fireman wears red suspenders is to keep his pants up, I don't know . . .

Cicero, who in previous scenes seemed to be using his "stupidity" as a form of resistance, now is seen to be just stupid. Apparently, he really will do whatever is asked of him—including put on a blackface that is among the most grotesque captured on film—as long as the request is simple enough for him to understand.

As if pinning Fetchit to the worst elements of his stereotype were not enough, *Dimples* ends with Dimples rejoined by her two dance partners from early in the film—her fellow urchins, the "chocolate" she likes as well as "vanilla"—but now they too are in blackface, and like Fetchit, they are not permitted to modulate their performance when they don

25. Shirley Temple with the "Two Black Dots" (without blackface) from the beginning of *Dimples* (1936).

26. Stepin Fetchit in blackface at the end of *Dimples*.

27. Temple with the "Two Black Dots" (in blackface) from the end of *Dimples*.

the mask. *Dimples* thus ensures (as if there could have been any serious doubt within the most progressive Hollywood discourse of 1936) that the audience understands that a child might like both "vanilla" and "chocolate" but still remain thoroughly, glowingly, white and, moreover, that preferring white is easy, understandable, and probably sensible.

Indefinite Talk: *Stormy Weather*'s Blackface and Whiteface

The last of the cinematic black blackface routines is also the most re-markable. In the black-cast, backstage musical *Stormy Weather* (1943), the blacked-up Flournoy Miller and Johnnie Lee perform an "indefinite talk" routine, a type of turn for which Miller, along with his deceased partner, Aubry Lyles, had long been famous.[24] To Mel Watkins, what is most remarkable about *Stormy Weather* is that it puts Hollywood re-sources and techniques into the service of a "type of comedy that was rarely seen outside black honky-tonks, variety shows, theaters, and the occasional race movie." In *Stormy Weather,* argues Watkins, "the 'New Negro', or at least a hip, comic version of that transplanted city dweller, had finally come to the screen."[25] Set in the center of the film, as its only nonmusical number and its only blackface turn, and at once wholly mar-ginal and crucial to *Stormy Weather*'s narrative, Miller and Lee's blackface routine would seem to respond to claims like Watkins's, "(In)definitely!"

Indefinite talk is a mixture of an authoritative tone and obscure con-tent created by the dialogue partners chronically cutting one another off. When the partners are not interrupting one another, their sentences alternate between abstractions (usually because their pronouns have no clear referent), questions (that go unanswered), and hyperbolic pro-nouncements (which are immediately deflated). Along with precise ges-tures and timing, some punning and malapropisms, the deformations of dialect, and a schism between character and tone, what most makes indefinite talk unique (and funny) is that the indefinite talkers always understand one another. While the audience struggles to figure out what the indefinite talkers are (not) talking about, the indefinite talkers them-selves never require clarification and continue as if their conversation were ordinary and comprehensible. A couple of examples from Miller and Lee's turn in *Stormy Weather* should make my description clearer. Wearing blackface and modified tramp costumes and accompanied by

28. Flournoy Miller
and Johnnie Lee
blacked up in "Bum
Garage" in *Stormy
Weather* (1943).

a jazzy vamp from the unseen pit band,[26] Miller and Lee come on stage
in a jalopy, which immediately breaks down:

Lee (the driver): I just had it worked on.
Miller: Well who worked on it?
Lee: The man who's got the garage around . . .
Miller: Well he ain't no good. The man you want's the one what's worked
    on [starts to point offstage] . . .
Lee: I had him [pause]. He's the one that ruined it.

At the end of the turn, after a conversation that wanders (insofar as we
can make it out) quite far afield, the men make a date to go for a drive
with their girlfriends:

Miller: That'll be great! Can you make it on . . .
Lee: Nah. I'll be busy den.
Miller: Well, when can you make it?
Lee: Less see . . . The best day for me . . .
Miller: That suits me. What hour?
Lee: Any time between . . .
Miller: That's a little early, but we'll be there.
Lee: Alright, I'll be seeing you.
[Lee attempts to get back in the car, resulting in a series of small explosions,
    and Miller utters a nonsense salutation and exits, leaving Lee standing
    alone next to a heap of wreckage.]
Lee (mournfully): Bum garage . . . Bum garage . . . [curtain].

Because of its qualities, indefinite talk seems empty of explicit meaning. In this regard, indefinite talk borders on music. It creates—and

represents—affect and thereby meaning of a sort, but it depends on association, timbre, beat, rhythm, and volume, the specifics of (a) cultural practice more than (or in emphatic addition to) specific language; it goes through the motions of communication. Much of the delight of indefinite talk comes through what ethnomusicologist Charles Keil calls "engendered feeling"—"characteristics of an ongoing process" rather than a static "syntax," and "participatory discrepancy"—"the little discrepancies between hands and feet within a jazz drummer's beat, between bass and drums, between rhythm section and soloist, that create the groove and invite us to participate." [27] Indefinite talk, however, communicates through resolute, structural miscommunication (unpredictable interruption being its rule) and creates its humor by playing between syntax and process and by making "the little discrepancies" big. Its invitation to participation is so extensive as to be unclear because it is so "open." It riffs on the conventions of desired intelligibility characteristic of most theatrical and polite, white conversation by weaving complexity into seeming simplicity, and it is, as is most humor and much music, radically contingent and relativist. There is no clear "it" to get in indefinite talk, but nonetheless, some audiences—those who collaborate in the process of filling in the discrepancies—will "get it" and some will not. Moreover, among those that get (or make) "it," the "it" will be very different. "Meaning" seems too strong a word for what indefinite talk ultimately offers up, but humor or laughs, while accurate, do not seem quite strong enough.

For some of *Stormy Weather*'s audiences, Miller and Lee would have appeared simply to be idiots, and members of those audiences could either take that appearance as a (stereotypical) truth or as a (stereotypical) falsity. For those inclined to interpret Miller and Lee's performance this way, their blackface—the mark of representativeness or misrepresentation, depending on the perspective—would have supplied a strong syntactic cue to definite meaning and stopped the interpretive process. For other audiences, those getting the "it" of the indefinite talk in the fullest sense, Miller and Lee's blackface would have cued a more interesting play of surfaces and depths, revelations and concealments, insides and outsides. These audiences would have also seen Miller and Lee in part as idiots or at least clowns. Especially if they were familiar with the traditions of black blackface and vaudeville performance, however, these audiences would have also noticed other salient features to the act—some of which were specifically "black" and some of which were "Hollywood." And they would have noticed the mixture of these features that makes "Bum Garage" and its place in *Stormy Weather* especially provocative.

Because it had to fit into a Hollywood movie, "Bum Garage" was depoliticized. Unlike much stage black blackface, it makes no explicit comment on race or, more specifically, on whiteness. The disadvantage of this depoliticizing is that it makes Miller and Lee's personae more readily available for stereotypical readings as dumb black men. The compensatory advantage is that it permitted "Bum Garage" to be filmed and played for a multiracial, multiclass audience. At the same time, though, drawing on the strengths of the black blackface tradition, Miller and Lee seem like individuals, even within the constraints of the brief comic turn. In contrast to most white uses of the blackface mask, Miller and Lee create personae that exceed the "darky" caricature, and their dialogue "focuses" on the car (which Lee apparently owns), travel, extended family, and relationships rather than any of the standard "darky" subjects (e.g., eating and theft). Moreover, Miller and Lee (unlike, say, Amos 'n' Andy, who owed Miller and Lyles so much) are well matched. Neither character is a particular bully or weakling, and neither is a clear winner or loser (though Lee *is* left with the heap).

In fact, "Bum Garage" flirts constantly with but ultimately rejects the competition, hierarchy, and moral or lesson that underpins so much (blackface) humor. And this, to a discerning eye and ear, is what is most affecting about "Bum Garage":

Lee: I worked with her [M's girlfriend's] brother, and one day on the job, the first thing I know'd . . .
Miller: That was your fault. Now what you should have done was . . .
Lee (emphatically): I did!
Miller (enthusiastically): You see dat?
Lee (uncertain): Uh huh?
Miller: Now dat's why I like talking to you . . .
Lee (smiling): Yeah.
Miller: Cause you an' I can seem to 'gree with one another.

At its core, "Bum Garage" (and indefinite talk in general) holds a utopian vision of clear, total communication through community: Miller and Lee understand and/or accommodate one another in ways that most people simply do not and cannot. This is true at the level of both the performance content and performance practice. Miller and Lee's characters know what they are talking about without knowing what they are talking about; and, as heavily rehearsed but improvising comedians, Miller and Lee themselves know one another's behavior, as well as their collaborative behavior and the behavior of their audiences, more thoroughly than most people ever know their own behavior.[28] As with the many "paradoxes" of African American culture — the elusive doings-and-undoings and intricacies of direct indirection, characterized by phrases like Amiri Baraka's "changing same" or Ralph Ellison's "moving without moving" — Miller and Lee communicate without communicating. For anyone who takes the comic invitation to participate seriously, anyone who can see the discrepancy — the "groove" — between the "real" face and the blackface mask or in the many other gaps in this act, what Miller and Lee communicate is a flexible, inclusive fraternity in the face of economic hardship, hardship which has racial, racist foundations (among others). Miller and Lee and their characters solve no problems, but they suggest ways in which "problematic" lives can be rewardingly led, and beyond that, they suggest that America would very likely be a better place if all — not just black — life were seen as a "problem" needing constant, processual solving. Those who do not get this "groove" are left out — left cold, mad, or in the same place they were when the act began.

So far my analysis has treated "Bum Garage" as a self-contained unit wholly excerptable from the body of *Stormy Weather*. Still, while it is true that, with its setting on a stage, its entry and exit music, and its frontality, "Bum Garage" does not differ substantially from the canned vaudeville of the late-twenties Vitaphone shorts, the number is only semiautonomous from the larger film.[29] "Bum Garage" 's most obvious connections with *Stormy Weather*'s story are thematic: *Stormy Weather*'s subject is the history of black professional entertainment between the wars, and "Bum Garage," as a blackface number, provides an example of one stream in (or perhaps the "root" of) that history. And *Stormy Weather* is a Hollywood musical, which, like most musicals, celebrates community through entertainment and heterosexual romance. With its celebration of community and communication, "Bum Garage" underscores an important thematic element of this genre.

"Bum Garage" however, also ties directly via Miller and Lee to *Stormy*

29. Miller and Lee blacking up in *Stormy Weather.*

Weather's backstage success plot. I will say more about *Stormy Weather* as a whole in my next chapter; for now I'll summarize only the most immediate plot elements: In their inexorable series of successes (we know the series is inexorable because all but the final scene of the film are framed as memories), the protagonists, Bill Williamson (Bill Robinson) and Selena Rogers (Lena Horne), have decided to produce their own show. They have a great array of talent but lack money, and the chorines are threatening to strike the opening if they do not get paid. Bill runs into his old friend, Gabe, a benign, womanizing "promoter" (Dooley Wilson), who suggests that he pretend to be an investor long enough to assuage the cast's worries, open the show, and payoff with the opening-night take. Bill agrees, and Gabe rents a tuxedo and enlists the aid of his cousin, Jake (Nicodemus Stewart), who is a chauffeur—probably for a white man.[30] Gabe's ploy succeeds, and the chorines agree to go on. Flournoy Miller, however, to whom Gabe has been introduced, has the nagging feeling that he has seen Gabe somewhere.

Acting like the angel from a Warner Bros.–Busby Berkeley musical of the early thirties, Gabe works to secure the affections of the chorines, while in cross-cut scenes we see Miller and Lee blacking up and puzzling over Gabe's identity. As with virtually all of the white blackface performers we examined in chapter two, we see Miller and Lee transform themselves, so we know that they are performing, that their selves and their characters are different. At the same time, we also see that Miller and Lee are funny offstage as well as on:

Lee: [Did you see him] in a pool room?
Miller (thinking): No.
Lee: Thought it might give you a cue.

This overlaying of communicative discontinuity and continuity—which will be characteristic, at a different level, of the indefinite talk the two men are preparing for—becomes the organizing feature of this entire section of the film and the most profound "crisis" in its plot. Emphasizing this communicative complication, Miller and Lee are shot from behind, looking at themselves in a mirror, the typical Hollywood manner for filming such scenes.[31] But this scene is not typical: Miller and Lee are black men blacking up; they are not the protagonists of this story (as Jolson and Cantor are the protagonists of theirs); and they are together. Each not only looks at himself in the mirror; each also looks at the other, both directly and in the mirror, multiplying their identities, identifications, and connections manifold.

As he heads back to his dressing room after "Bum Garage," Miller—still in blackface but not in character—finally gets his "cue":

Chorine: Ersa Mae, I believe you've taken a shine to that angel.
Miller: Shine. . . . Did you say shine?
Chorine: Yes.
Miller: Doggone it, I knew I saw him somewhere. He's a boot black.
Chorine: Who?
Miller: That angel—he ain't no angel. He's got a shining stand in Harlem.
    He's shined my shoes a thousand times.

After this revelation, the chorines attack Gabe with items from their dressing room, coating his head with powder—giving him a white face. At this point Miller and Lee, still wearing their blackface, enter (along with the rest of the cast) to see what the fuss is about. Without returning to character, Miller and Lee return to indefinite talk:

Miller (to Gabe): You remind me of . . .
Lee: Nah. He looks worse'n that.

Though the point of indefinite talk is to be "pointless," to be rigorously obscure, here it seems fair—and certainly it is possible—to finish Miller's sentence: "You remind me of a white man." (In this regard, it is worth recalling that, during *Stormy Weather*'s filming and reception, Dooley Wilson was famous as Bogart and Bergman's "boy," Sam, in *Casablanca*. It is

30. Dooley Wilson in "whiteface" in *Stormy Weather.*

also worth noting that "Shine" is a doubled name, a derogatory term in white slang and an African American trickster figure—a "bad nigger"—from turn of the century oral narratives.) How bad, then, does a white man look? And what looks worse than a white man? An equally exploitative black man who lacks the power and resources of many white men? People who masquerade—or only people who "pass," who masquerade without revealing the masquerade?

With the potential for questions like these, *Stormy Weather* reaches the crisis prophesied by its title. It evades this profound-but-implied crisis of communities and identities by staging an explicit-but-fake plot crisis. The chorines again claim they will strike, though Gabe's ruse has already opened the show and brought funds into the box office, something the women could presumably figure out for themselves or, at least, be convinced of.[32] Instead, Cousin Jake returns with money he won while with his employer at the race track, and the show is "saved." The final lines of the scene hint that this solution to this noncrisis is a cover:

Gabe: You mean there was a coincidence?
Jake: What do you mean, coincidence?
Gabe: The right horse came in at the right time at the right track at the
    right hour . . .
Jake (delighted): Yasss.

Whether this exchange between a white-faced black performer and a "coon" (Nicodemus Stewart's specialty) while two black blackfaced "performers" stand by is taken as (bad) comedy or seen to (re)reveal the implicit crisis would be contingent on the audience. On the one hand,

31. Lena Horne and Bill Robinson in "I Can't Give You Anything But Love," the "high class" number that immediately follows "Bum Garage" and the "whiteface" incident in *Stormy Weather*.

coincidences are congruent with musical genre patterns, the character behaviors are stereotyped, and thus this scene is easily digestible. On the other hand, overdetermining the coincidence in this way and expressing it as a concatenation of "rights" *and* putting this expression in the mouth of an impossible figure, the (accidentally) whitefaced black man, addressing (diegetically) this group of African American performers—taken together these details suggest hard questions: Which of these performers will be able to assemble enough "rights" to make it in America, and how will they? Why must these performers experience this particular coincidence rather than, say, the more generic coincidence of "discovery"?

The remainder of *Stormy Weather* shows that these are not idle questions. Any vestige of the rural or low, and certainly any explicit trace of blackface minstrelsy, is banished and replaced by the urbane: Horne, Katherine Dunham, Cab Calloway, the Nicholas Brothers. Bill and Selina split—she for Paris and he for Hollywood, both for continued success. At least some of the questions are answered, but *Stormy Weather* never shows us those successes. It never gives us the film within a film we might expect—since Bill is supposed to have made it in Hollywood—and instead substitutes the double success of a benefit show for the USO combined with Bill and Selina's reunion. Again, this conclusion is generic: It marries old (Bill) and young (Lena), dance and song, southern and northern, rural and urban, "copacetic" and ambitious, but this "utopia" is built to serve two restrictions.

The first and most powerful and obvious restriction is racial separatism. Anyone thinking about it for even a moment knows that Bill's success in Hollywood (or Selina's in Paris) must have involved some contact with whites, but because it implies previous contact and some (at least) cultural continuity between black and white, *Stormy Weather* cannot explicitly represent these successes. Still, this separatism must remain unspoken; otherwise where would it end? Should white audiences see and enjoy this film? Neither can *Stormy Weather* represent a fantastic all-black Hollywood, which might have pleasures all its own. In this regard, *Stormy Weather* is an utter failure: it does not sustain the mythic connection between the represented and real worlds of entertainment; it is neither realistic nor unrealistic enough—or perhaps it is both too realistic and too unrealistic.

The second, more subtle and less common restriction may be more pernicious: a restriction on the range of representational practices available, here specifically to African Americans. *Stormy Weather* represents some practices—black blackface, the blues, innuendo-laden dialogue—left out of most musicals that use black performance. Moreover, it hints at one seldom considered possibility: whiteface. For these qualities it must be applauded. At the same time, *Stormy Weather*'s liberal progressive plot gradually eliminates these practices, flattening (and whitening?) black culture—making the indefinite definite—and leaving no space, not even the space of black blackface, for explicitly considering whiteness, the uniqueness and commonalities of black and white American cultures, or, beyond the magic of the cinematic audiovisual dissolve and the generic coincidence, a sense of how or whether to escape or modify the blackfaced, minstrelizing past, which was still so present.

2

4

Black Folk Sold

HOLLYWOOD'S BLACK-

CAST MUSICALS

De white folks put me in [jail], an' de white folks take me out,
an' I ain' know yet what I done, done, done.
—GEORGE & IRA GERSHWIN and DUBOSE HEYWARD (1935)

It ain't necessarily so.
—GEORGE & IRA GERSHWIN and DUBOSE HEYWARD (1935)

It ain't necessarily so that it ain't necessarily so.
—SUN RA (n.d.)

Al Jolson in blackface introduced "blacks" in sound film under the double stricture of the mask and the extractable, narratively inessential specialty number, and as I have argued thus far, these conventions continued to be important for representing African Americans in American musical film for well over two decades.

Nearly simultaneous with this set of conventions, however, arose the convention of the black-cast musical, a convention that persists into our present moment and one that is more familiar to, more kindly regarded by, and more meaningful for present-day audiences than blackface. Starting in 1929 and coming at semiregular intervals for the next thirty years, Hollywood studios made eight such black-cast musicals: *Hearts in Dixie* (1929), *Hallelujah* (1929), *The Green Pastures* (1936), *Cabin in the Sky* (1943), *Stormy Weather* (1943), *Carmen Jones* (1954), *St. Louis Blues* (1958), and *Porgy and Bess* (1959). Not until the brief cycle of late forties (inter)racial social-problem films were these musicals matched by any other genre, and not until the early fifties were there *any* Hollywood black-cast dramas—and those were very few and low budget.[1]

In U.S. film history, then, these eight films are "among the most un-usual products of 'classic' Hollywood."[2] At the same time, they are also Hollywood's best—that is, most expensive and prestigious, most widely hailed in both the black and mainstream press, and most remembered and reviewed—attempts to recognize and represent the black portion of its audience and talent pool. Consequently, this extended, generically consistent cycle of films and the varied and shifting responses of its Afri-can American critics and audiences demand careful scrutiny.

Two aspects of this group of films are remarkable at the outset. First, seven of the eight are what Rick Altman has described as folk musicals—narratives that emphasize family, home, and nostalgic memory.[3] The ex-ception is *Stormy Weather,* a backstage musical; however, because their casting focuses on and (re)creates an enforced American subcommu-nity, in an important sense all eight of the black-cast musicals are folk musicals.

This restricted casting leads to these eight films' second remarkable as-pect: With the possible exception, again of *Stormy Weather,* all of these films posit and are driven by conflicts from exclusively within the folk community. Moreover, the black-cast musicals portray these conflicts not through a simple dualistic conflict but through a series of dualisms—male/female, sin/spirit, urban/rural—that overlap in varying combina-tions in all the characters and are distilled into the musical distinction—blues (or jazz)/spirituals. Because these dualisms are represented as both internal to individual characters and wholly contained in the folk com-munity, they are resolvable only through an act of the most violent re-alignment. Most folk musicals—indeed, most musicals—resolve their dualistic conflicts with a marriage. Five of the black-cast musicals *do* con-clude with a marriage or reunion (among the other three, one is a tragedy and the other two have open endings). But two thirds of the black-cast musicals hinge on episodes of extreme internecine violence—most often murders—either to create their resolution or to pave the way for the con-cluding reunion or marriage.

By way of contrast, consider the most famous and influential white-cast folk musical, *Oklahoma!:* Its primary dualism seems to be between farmers and ranchers. Aligning with that dualism is the apparently more elemental one of male (ranchers) and female (farmers—even the male farmers are domesticated and hence female by association). But ulti-mately trumping these dualisms—and leading to the dissolution of the other dualisms and the resolution of all conflict—is the dualism of good (pretty much everyone) and evil (the outsider and hired hand, Jud Fry, who is balanced by the good outsider, Ali Hakim the peddler). *Oklahoma!* climaxes with a murder, when Curly kills Jud, but this killing is a clear act of self- (and community-) defense making it both legal and guiltless. The final celebratory community of *Oklahoma!* is untainted by the violence required for its formation; such violence is the exception not the rule in this folk world. But in the black-cast musicals this violence always lingers as a scar on both the individual (usually the male protagonist) and the folk community; such violence is, if not the rule, then always a part of the constitution of both the black individual and group.

The table, which follows on the next two pages, maps these aspects as well as some other key qualities of the black-cast musicals and makes schematically clear the arch of the subgenre's history. This table raises a number of questions: How did the black-cast musical subgenre change —or not—over time in relation to changes in mainstream and African American culture and society? How did these mainstream works (propose to) value Afro-America and how, in turn, were they valued by African Americans? What expressive possibilities did the form of the black-cast musical subgenre allow and disallow?

Probing these questions will be the work of this chapter, but that process can be founded on three main claims: (1) The black-cast subgenre is remarkably consistent in its patterns but at the same time develops into one explicitly set in the past and increasingly divorced, especially in its musical materials, from the "folk" it purports to represent. (2) In this context, the uniqueness of *Stormy Weather* becomes especially clear. (3) The model offered by *Stormy Weather* represents an important cultural road not taken by Hollywood and U.S. culture more generally at a crucial historical moment. That choice still resonates in our present.

The Backstory of the Black-Cast Musicals

Like blackface and the specialty number, the black-cast film musical had roots in musical theater, but it also had antecedents in serious drama and literature. Beginning in the late 1890s, African American cast shows had turned away from the episodic, multipart minstrel show form and

Hollywood's Black-Cast Musicals: A Schematic

FILM	SETTING	PERIOD	TONE
Hearts in Dixie (Fox 1929), B&W, original story	Rural South. Hero goes north in the end	Present	Serious, melodramatic
Hallelujah (MGM 1929), B&W, original story	Rural South. Hero goes to Semi-urban South and returns home in the end	Present	Serious, melodramatic
Green Pastures (WB 1936), B&W, adapted from stage and Bible	Heaven and Earth (rural South)	Mythic past/BC	Quaint, reverent
Cabin in the Sky (MGM 1943), Sepia-toned, adapted from stage	Rural South	Present	Quaint, seriocomic, romantic
Stormy Weather (20th C 1943), B&W, original story	Various mostly urban North and West (Hollywood)	1919 to Present	Romantic, comic
Carmen Jones (20th C 1954), color, adapted from musical and opera	Rural South, Chicago	WWII	Tragic romance
St. Louis Blues (Paramount 1958), B&W, adapted from autobiography	Memphis, New York	1894–1928	Melodramatic, romantic
Porgy and Bess (Goldwyn/Columbia 1959), color, adapted from novel, play, and musical	Urban South. Hero goes north in the end.	1930s	Melodramatic, romantic

Note: My subgenre categories are drawn from Rick Altman, *The American Film Musical* (Bloomington: Indiana Univ. Press, 1987), though I have substituted "backstage" for his term "show."

NUMBER OF DEATHS	SUBGENRE	NUMBER OF WHITES	TYPE OF MUSIC
Two: Mother and sister of hero die of fever	Folk	Two: One in non-diegetic prologue; doctor in story	Mostly spirituals; some Stephen Foster songs
Three: All murdered by hero	Folk	None	Mostly spirituals; some Foster Songs; two Irving Berlin songs
Hundreds; Biblical proportions	Folk	None	Spirituals
Two: Hero and heroine murdered— but in what turns out to be a dream	Folk	None	Mostly original songs, mostly by white authors; one spiritual and one Duke Ellington song
None	Backstage	None	Songs adapted from theater, mostly by black authors
One: Hero murders heroine	Folk	None	Bizet music with Hammerstein lyrics
None	Starts as folk, ends as Backstage	Many (agents, lawyers, audiences)	Handy originals, black folk music
Four: Two murders (one by hero); two deaths in hurricane	Folk	Four (police, lawyer)	Gershwin originals

toward the narrativized musical comedy form. In the late 1910s, a small but increasing number of black-cast or predominantly black-cast dramas joined the trend, the most famous of which was Eugene O'Neill's *The Emperor Jones* (1920). In the same period, though most emphatically during the 1920s, increasing numbers of literary works focused on African American life were published by both black and white authors.

Though it was not adapted to film until 1959, the multiform work *Porgy/Porgy and Bess* drew from these various antecedents. Because of its synthesizing work, its clear artistic ambitions, and its enduring presence in U.S. and international culture, *Porgy/Porgy and Bess* influenced all of the black-cast musical films Hollywood made, until the film adaptation capped the subgenre of the black-cast musical. Moreover, the shifting African American responses to *Porgy/Porgy and Bess* provide a thumbnail sketch of how black responses to mainstream representations of "them" would alter between the midtwenties and the late fifties.

Porgy began its cultural life in 1925 in the form of a novel by white, Southern author DuBose Heyward. Heyward's novel supplied the story, the setting, and the characters that would remain substantially the same through the shift to performance media and three crucial narrative alterations. Set in an indistinctly past time in "Catfish Row," a poor all-black section of Charleston, South Carolina, *Porgy* tells the story of an unlikely, summer-long love affair between Porgy, a middle-aged paraplegic beggar, and Bess, a younger, drug-addicted street girl.[4] Ultimately, Porgy murders Bess's possessive and vengeful former lover, Crown, and is jailed for refusing to identify the body for the police. When he is released, Porgy returns to find Bess gone, lured away to Savannah by unnamed men, and he ends the story defeated and alone.

In 1927 the Theatre Guild mounted a Broadway production of DuBose and Dorothy Heyward's dramatic adaptation of the novel, still titled *Porgy,* which included three key alterations in the *Porgy/Porgy and Bess* story. First, the resolutely sad and undramatic ending of the novel, which has Porgy in his goat cart grieving the loss of Bess "alone in an irony of morning sunlight,"[5] gives way to a more active, romantic ending in which Porgy departs in pursuit of Bess. Second, Bess has been lured to New York—not Savannah—by a specific character, Sporting Life, an urban émigré back for a visit in the South.[6] Third, the vague period of the novel's setting—which seems to be a relatively recent past made distant and "golden" by the looming presence of increasing modernization—

becomes concrete: "the present."[7] Perhaps the most important change in the play, however, was that it amplified the novel's portrayal of music as a component of everyday, black, "folk" life.

These changes have subtle and interesting effects on the potential meanings of the *Porgy* story. While the novel is nostalgic and ambivalent about African American sociocultural change, it still relies for its effects on and ultimately endorses black, American progress. As a novel, *Porgy* is a liberal text. It must be seen in light of the black, modern, and popular dance that dominated U.S. culture during the book's conception and that bore the name of Porgy's home town, the Charleston. By placing the action of the story in the past, the novel implicitly argues that things have changed and are changing in and for Afro-America.[8]

By erasing the gap between the represented past and the present of the performance while amplifying only the markers of the past in the form of folk songs and peasant behaviors, the play presents African Americans as anachronisms, representatives of the past who exist unchanged, unchanging, and unchangeable in the present—not only racial others but temporal others as well. The only African American route of transformation that does appear, represented by Sporting Life, is marked as criminal—and criminal by active choice. Working from the dramatic adaptation of *Porgy,* it would have been difficult for the audience to account for the hard working, law abiding, sophisticated, Northern black actors who were performing the play.

The novel *Porgy* was a bestseller and the dramatic adaptation was a hit, but *Porgy and Bess,* the musical-operatic adaptation of the play by George Gershwin, Ira Gershwin, and DuBose Heyward, is the *Porgy* that many people the world over know and have known since the first successful revival in 1941. In 1935, the first performance of *Porgy and Bess* kept the changes to the novel that the Heywards' dramatization introduced: It ended with Porgy leaving for New York in pursuit of Bess (now to the rousing chorus of "Oh, Lawd, I'm on My Way"), and it was set in the present. Gershwin's famous decision *not* to interpolate any black folk music, however, again altered the sense of what *Porgy and Bess*'s representation of "folk" African Americans in the present could mean. The black characters sang in a full array of musical idioms—folk, jazz, street cries, recitative, and aria—though all were in Gershwin's compositional "voice," and the performers' voices that rendered all these forms were, with an important exception in the 1935 performance, trained operatic instruments. So while Porgy and Bess may have been seen as "primitives"—figures from the past standing in the present—the performers that rendered them were thoroughly modern and accomplished. They, along with Gershwin and his music, represented the "New York" Porgy and Bess would find in 1935.

Two specific choices Gershwin made in the 1935 production lent further dimension to *Porgy and Bess*'s represented texture of modern Negro life. The role of Sportin' Life was filled by the dancer John "Bubbles" Sublett, who brought an "untrained" voice into the show's musical weave and, more importantly, designed his own dances. Sublett entered into the frame of the white-conceived and controlled show a node of nonfolk, black-created black performance; Sublett's dancing provided a standard against which to measure Gershwin's attempts at jazz, and he represented (now in a legitimate venue) another—and crucial—option, besides classical training or "pure" folk expression, for African American creativity. To emphasize this point, Sportin' Life's role in *Porgy and Bess* was made bigger and more important in both narrative and musical terms than it had been in either version of *Porgy;* aside from his dancing, Sublett's Sportin' Life got two key songs: "It Ain't Necessarily So" and "There's a Boat Dat's Leavin' Soon for New York," the first at the very center of the musical, and the second at Bess's exit.

The second choice Gershwin made in 1935 was to have the few white characters in the show not sing at all, not even in the recitative that all the black characters are given as "speech."[9] On the one hand, this choice suggests a wide gap between black and white, but on the other, this choice suggests that the gap is as much—or more—cultural than racial/biological. The choice works simultaneously to make clear the racial identities of the characters—identities that may not have been clear only in visual terms[10]—*and* to suggest that those identities are sociocultural rather than essential or biological. After all, if *Porgy and Bess*'s performers could learn to sing in classical European styles and Gershwin could aspire to compose in African American vernacular styles, then in important ways (though perhaps not *all* ways, as the oppressive presence of the police in *Porgy and Bess* shows) identity could be (re)learned.

An important result of *Porgy and Bess*'s endurance—and one I will take up in more detail when I return at the end of this chapter to the 1959 film—has been the simplification of the 1935 *Porgy and Bess*'s representa-

tion of a black "present." Starting with the show's revival and popularization in the early forties, the setting of *Porgy and Bess* once more slipped
into the past, lodging now in "the 1930s"—a date that places the action
in a comfortable (perhaps comforting) past, a moment where poverty
could be attributed to the Depression rather than (or, perhaps, in addition to) prejudice and oppression, and one that is, at any rate, past.[11]
Moreover, the coincidence of the setting with the moment of the show's
creation, when combined with the cult of Gershwin's genius, emphasized
by his early and sudden death, served to claim for the Gershwin score a
sort of racial-cultural authority—even a strange documentary quality—
that it did not have in 1935. In revival, the use of recitative was jettisoned,
flattening an important distinction between the black and white characters; and the role of Sportin' Life, while often serving as a spot for a star
persona (e.g., Cab Calloway), lost some of its power when relegated to
the past of the show's setting.[12]

Though black response was never monolithic, the general trend of
African American responses to *Porgy/Porgy and Bess* has moved from
favor to disfavor. African American intellectuals were, by and large,
favorably impressed by *Porgy* as both a novel and a play. Champions
of the novel included Countee Cullen and Sterling Brown,[13] but their
praises for Heyward's book were exceeded by James Weldon Johnson's
enthusiasm for the play, which he saw as transformative. "*Porgy*," Johnson wrote, "loomed high above every Negro drama that had ever been
produced" for two reasons: first, for its staging, by which Johnson seems
to have meant its weaving of music with drama, and second, because
it provided "massive and indisputable" evidence of "the Negro performer['s] . . . ability to do acting that requires thoughtful interpretation
and intelligent skill."[14]

Porgy and Bess stirred more debate. Its performers, the musical's first
audience, in a sense, were enthusiastic about it from the start. This has
remained generally true for theatrical productions of the show but was
not true for the film adaptation, as I will discuss in more detail later. The
black press followed the production with interest, and it seems that significant numbers of African Americans did attend the show.[15] After its
initial New York run *Porgy and Bess* toured briefly, and it garnered substantial notice in the black press when its players refused to perform at
the segregated National Theatre in Washington, D.C. until seating was
completely open.[16] In 1935, however, *Porgy and Bess* did arouse two im-

portant black critics: Both Duke Ellington and choirmaster Hall Johnson dismissed *Porgy and Bess* as inauthentic—though in very measured terms, and always with enthusiastic praise for the performers.[17]

In revival during the forties and fifties, *Porgy and Bess* gathered more mixed (and more occasional) attention from black critics. For example, in 1943 the *Defender* took note (via an Office of War Information release) when the German government criticized a Danish production of *Porgy and Bess*.[18] Perhaps most emblematic of *Porgy and Bess's* shifting and shifty place in black critical regard is a front-page *Defender* report from 14 March 1942: "Offensive 'Darky' Songs At Last Get Long-Awaited Boot Out of [Washington, D.C.] Schools." Here the unnamed reporter and the headline writer seem clearly at odds, as the opening paragraph hints: "George Gershwin's haunting 'I've got Plenty Of Nothin',' from the Negro opera, *Porgy and Bess,* has been banned from Washington's public school music [*sic*] after contentions that it contained phrases offensive to colored students."[19] While the headline seems to celebrate this action, the final paragraphs of the article imply that the consequences of banning songs might not be entirely positive. The writer notes that one song proposed for banning, "Carry Me Back to Ole Virginny," was written by an African American and that "Paul Robeson rode to fame and fortune in Kern's classic ["Old Man River"] from *Show Boat* [another song proposed for banning], [and] Todd Duncan of Howard University and Anne Wiggins Brown of Baltimore are renowned for their renditions of *Porgy and Bess*."[20]

By the midfifties, when a company of *Porgy and Bess* embarked on a world tour, the critical polarization between content and performer had formalized in the *Defender* into "Should *Porgy and Bess* Be Taken Abroad Is Question American Negroes Cannot Agree On." The paper supported its claim by publishing two pieces, one con and one pro. As with the piece on music in schools, however, where the definite headline effectively anchored the more ambivalent article, here again the *Defender* layout—including an editorial disclaimer under the title "Says Catfish Row Smells"—subtly suggested that the critical position made the most sense. And in light of Hollywood's five black-cast musicals that preceded this tour, which canonized *Porgy and Bess,* and the three that would follow it, Dean Gordon Hancock's critical position was especially illuminating. While he admitted admiring the music, he argued that *Porgy and Bess* was unintegrated (in terms of race rather than musical theater form) and, hence, bolstered sentiment for keeping the United States a segregated society.[21] Unlike virtually every other black critic of *Porgy and Bess,* he said nothing about the performers. Compared, however, to the Hollywood (or other Broadway) black-cast musicals, *Porgy and Bess,* with its five white characters, was unique in its level of racial integration, and as I suggested earlier, *Porgy and Bess* took some pains to represent the intersection of racism and institutions of power. That this should have become "invisible" to Dean Gordon Hancock by 1954 seems crucial in analyzing how the black-cast musicals had worked in U.S. culture and could continue to work in the last six years of the fifties. Implied in Hancock's critique is the need for endless metacritique: *Porgy and Bess* may criticize racism, but in revival at any rate, it could not, in Hancock's estimation, see itself implicated in the history and processes of U.S. racism.

Turning back now to the black-cast musical films, considered in the order of their production, we will see—to borrow terms from *Porgy and Bess*—that "it took a long pull" to get to Hancock's critical position, and that this was still far from any sociocultural "Promise' Lan'" for African Americans—perhaps farther in 1959, when *Porgy and Bess* finally ended the classical era of black-cast musicals, than in 1943, when *Cabin in the Sky* and *Stormy Weather* marked the high-point of the subgenre.

"Folk Values in a New Medium"?

The first three Hollywood black-cast musicals were conceived nearly co-incident with one another in 1929, in the penumbra of *Porgy.*[22] *Hearts in Dixie* and *Hallelujah!* were created as film musicals and released in 1929, while *The Green Pastures* was written for the stage and, because of its long run and tour, not filmed until 1936, but all three works bear strong similarities; this cycle of the black-cast subgenre is more internally consistent than the 1943 or the 1954 to 1959 cycles. Like the vast majority of the Hollywood black-cast musicals, these early films focus on the "folk"—Southern, rural, and apparently timeless blacks going about what purports to be "a slice of life." Unlike the other representatives of the subgenre, though, these three productions pin their defining generic quality, their music, mostly to pre-existing folk musical forms, primarily spirituals. And this traditional music, performed and arranged by African Americans, intersecting with white controlled and concocted narratives and institutional settings made these films both especially fraught and especially powerful for black intellectuals and critics.

Hearts in Dixie and *The Green Pastures* are joined and illuminated by their shared use of the foreword or prologue as an opening, situating strategy. Both films make explicit at the start that the spectators they imagine will have nothing directly in common with the subjects of the stories they tell; neither film seems to be able to envision a "Negro" spectator, at least not one willing to cast him- or herself immediately into the third person. At the same time, each foreword hastens to assure the spectator that its subjects are captured in "everyday life" and, therefore, exist in the world somewhere beyond representation. These forewords imply that the film to follow is a sort of documentary. They cast their characters in terms not of performance, a category that implies volition and will, but rather in terms of display. These terms dovetail neatly with long-standing discourses about African Americans as "natural" performers to suggest the paradoxical category of the performer who is unaware s/he is performing and who is thus—like a child, an animal, a drunk, or even an inanimate object—outside ("beneath" for the uncharitable viewer, "beyond" for the charitable) consciousness, awareness, self, and subjectivity.[23]

The foreword of *Hearts in Dixie* is the more elaborate of the two and displays the most concern for negotiating between its imagined audience and the people it represents. Because it was produced in the period of transition to sound, *Hearts in Dixie*'s foreword uses synchronized sound as an attraction; in light both of the foreword's contents and of the plot of the film, however, the attraction itself becomes ideologically loaded. A white man dressed in a tuxedo enters the frame by parting a pair of theater curtains. Then, directly addressing the camera and using a mellifluous, carefully articulated voice and very restrained gestures, he says:

> "I trust that in this theater you are forgetting for a brief hour the cares and trouble of everyday life. If the motion picture which follows helps you forget, to relax and enjoy yourselves, it will have served its purpose. To do this, it will show you the joys and sorrows of other people, their happiness and their heartaches. Our manners and our civilizations change, but our emotions remain the same—in all ages, in all countries, in all climes. The same feelings which made our prehistoric fathers and mothers leave the forests and jungles to get food for their child makes them risk their lives to snatch their child from the path of a speeding automobile. [The speaker

puts his left hand in his pocket—his only gesture.] Our manners may differ, our dress certainly does, even our skins may vary in color—white, yellow, brown, red, and black—but we all laugh when we are happy; we cry when we are sad. We sing, we dance, we play, we work, and we love. We're all brothers and sisters in our emotions. So, I will draw the curtain on a slice of life—the life of a race of humans—and present . . ." [The speaker parts the curtain behind him.]

With its opening on "other people," its ending on "a race," and its compressed, social Darwinist narrative all drawn together and softened by the refrain of collectivity ("our," "we") this foreword is a fascinating instance of protesting too much. The enthusiastic though carefully qualified reception of *Hearts in Dixie* by many African American intellectuals suggests, however, that we must seriously consider the progressive aspects of this monologue and carefully consider the liberating potential of even a film whose rationale is at best profoundly conflicted.[24]

When the presenter of *Hearts in Dixie*'s foreword parts the curtain, he reveals the film's title sequence, and that gives way to an opening chorus number. "This Cotton Wants Pickin'" presents a group of folk ending their work day and taking up their leisure activities. After introducing this community, the film focuses on a single extended family, building two competing narrative strands around uses of music as deployed by community and family: In one strand, Gummy, the father of the family, played by Stepin Fetchit, chafes at having to stay (and work) at home, and he finally escapes to the public dance, which employs eccentric dancing and music. In the competing strand, Nappus, the grandfather, played by Clarence Muse, entertains his grandchildren and their friends with "spirituals"—"All God's Children Got Wings" and "Swanee River." What increases the tension between these two strands of the narrative, but also keeps them from becoming a simple dichotomy, is the death of Gummy's wife and daughter. Both men, along with and the surviving grand/son, are aggrieved, but they act on their grief in opposing manners. Unrooted, Gummy grows completely feckless, becoming more and more recognizably "Stepin Fetchit" as the film progresses; his whole character now revolves around nonproductive community relations—avoiding work and pursuing play—and finding a new mate who will allow him such pursuits. Nappus, on the other hand, is now seen formally associated with the church, and he arranges for his grandson to go North with the ultimate hope that he will become a doctor. The appro-

priate music accompanies each narrative path, until in the end the community—including Nappus, Gummy, and the grandson's girlfriend—
reassembles and sings a spiritual (in contrast to the work/play song of
the opening) as a farewell to the grandson.

Hearts in Dixie found several champions of varying degrees of ardor
among African American writers and no absolute critics.[25] Elmer Anderson Carter, the editor of *Opportunity,* wrote coolly that the film "justifies
no . . . high hopes," but his comment appeared in the European avant-
garde magazine, *Close Up,* instead of his own publication, which published an ecstatic review by Robert Benchley. And, while Carter based his
criticism on *Hearts in Dixie*'s lack of any "real sustained story," he allowed
the film "one redeeming feature—the rich resonance of the Negro voices
in speech and in song."[26] In this foregrounding of sound over image,
music over story, Carter was setting a pattern for African American criticism that would run in various formulations throughout the period of
the black-cast musicals.

In the most enthusiastic and sustained analysis of *Hearts in Dixie,* Alain
Locke and Sterling Brown both agreed and disagreed with Carter. Unlike Carter they found the film "a really moving folk idyll on a peasant
level . . . . the truest pictorialization of Negro life to date."[27] Acknowledging that "this [may be a] rather negative virtue," they moved to prais-
ing the performers, particularly the two male leads—a step that will be
recognized from my review of the reception of *Porgy/Porgy and Bess* and
a step Carter had, surprisingly, avoided altogether. Locke and Brown
are especially lavish in reviewing Fetchit: "Of course, most genuine and
spontaneous of all is Stepin Fetchit, who contributes the still more typical quality of infectious rhythm and mercurial change of mood. Indeed
never before had this primitive capacity for becoming an incarnate emo-
tion been more graphically portrayed. Stepin Fetchit in this picture is as
true as instinct itself, a vital projection of the folk manner, a real child
of the folk." Their terms for understanding Fetchit's performance—he
is "incomparable" because he is a "wholly untrained and naive being"—
are in surprising continuity with the racist discourses underlying *Hearts
in Dixie*'s foreword, but Locke and Brown complicate this position by
also appreciating, albeit much less effusively, Clarence Muse's "trained
artistry."

This dualism, which rearticulates the film's narrative dualism, also
leads Locke and Brown to their point of firm agreement with Elmer

Carter: "the greatest artistic triumph [in *Hearts in Dixie*] is that of the Negro voice in song and speech." With this new dualism, the triumph of sound over image, Locke and Brown repair the split between Fetchit and Muse, between untrained and trained, folk and New Negro. All African Americans including Locke and Brown — two urban, sophisticated, and sometimes elitist professors — have a part in the Negro voice. In their approbation, Locke and Brown complete the open narrative of *Hearts in Dixie,* attempting to reconnect via the mass media of film and through Hollywood to the(ir) folk, people who might actually see this film but who were much less likely to read or see, say, *Porgy.*

Locke and Brown are uneasy, though. They never say so directly, but they know that sound cannot simply trump sight in the movies — after all, *Hearts in Dixie* is a "pictorialization" — and this means that voice cannot escape color, which so often means "convention," in the United States. Consequently, Locke and Brown express their anxiety, as well as some optimism, through wondering whether the film resulted from "good luck" or "the rewarded virtues of good management," "happy accident or deliberate insight." For the academic and aesthete (and in Brown's case, artist), the good management and deliberate insight seem desirable, but one can almost hear Locke and Brown hoping for the former — the lucky accident(s) that will let black voice(s) disrupt the deliberate, managed Hollywood image of the Negro.

Locke and Brown further temper their hopefulness by following their review of *Hearts in Dixie* with a briefer, negative review of *Hallelujah!,* 1929's second black-cast musical. "Unfortunately," begins the second part of their essay, "*Hallelujah!* relies heavily on the usual claptrap." For them, the "obvious . . . ambition" of *Hallelujah!* is a double-edged sword. The film's ambition — the facts (which Locke and Brown leave implicit) that *Hallelujah!* was made by MGM, was conceived and directed by well-regarded King Vidor, was technically innovative and produced at some expense, and employed black performers new to film — showed deliberation, but also suggested Hollywood management and, therefore, the strangulation of insight. Ultimately, Locke and Brown significantly qualified their disapproval of the film: "Even so, *Hallelujah!* is important. Its pioneering, its very failures, promise a great deal." As it turned out, this evaluative back-and-forth was a response many African American viewers had to *Hallelujah!,* a response that, in important ways, the film could not avoid cueing because of its shifting combinations of a dual-

32. The black community singing and laboring in the opening of *Hallelujah!* (1929).

focus narrative with dualities between performer and material, sound and sight, music and narrative, and black and white.

In contrast to *Hearts in Dixie* and *The Green Pastures, Hallelujah!* forgoes any sort of foreword or introduction and simply begins in medias res with the protagonist, Zeke, and his family working—and singing—in the cotton fields. As in *Hearts in Dixie,* music is an integral component of this family's world, permeating their work, their leisure, and the ordinary events of daily life. In the first quarter of the film, nothing much happens: The family walks home from the fields talking about the treats each wants when the crop is cashed in; they eat, amuse themselves, take part in a "comic" belated wedding for some neighbors, and, finally, they go to bed. Each of these events is folk musicalized. The family performs work songs, spirituals, "Swanee River" (a Stephen Foster song once again seemingly equated with spirituals), improvised dance songs, and an astoundingly West African–inflected lullaby. Unlike in *Hearts in Dixie,* however, in *Hallelujah!* no clear, immediate moral distinction obtains between spiritual and work songs, on the one hand, and play songs on the other.

The second quarter of the film, in which Zeke and his brother go to town to sell the family's cotton, introduces conflict and the familiar musical contrast of good and bad. After Zeke has sold the cotton, a young townswoman, Chick, uses song and dance to lure the innocent, desiring countryman into a saloon, where her male partner, Hot Shot, fleeces Zeke at craps. Enraged, Zeke tries to shoot Hot Shot but instead mortally wounds his own brother. Zeke returns home with his brother's

33. Zeke (Daniel Haynes) cradles the dying Chick (Nina Mae McKinney) in *Hallelujah!*

corpse and, while mourning, hears the call to preaching. Music permeates these events as well, but here moral distinctions *are* made between what might be called outdoor forms—work songs or spirituals, and indoor forms—jazz and the blues, and the viewer understands Zeke has moved from good to bad in following Chick inside the juke joint.

Crucially, however, these seemingly clear distinctions are muddied by a strong similarity, a sort of sonic blur, between Zeke's and Chick's songs. And, indeed, both Zeke's song, "The End of the Road," which he sings to open this section of the film and which becomes his refrain for the rest of the film, and Chick's siren song, "Swanee Shuffle," were written by Irving Berlin specifically for *Hallelujah!* Both songs are in standard American popular song form and are sung predominantly by solo voices, and consequently, neither sounds much like the songs of the first section. Thus, even in what seems meant to be the clearest contrast in the film— its use of song to crystalize its conflict—there is both a strange unity and the creation of another, implied duality: the Berlin songs sound more alike than different, and they sound white(er) while the rest of the *Hallelujah!*'s music sounds black(er).

The second half of the film follows a rise, fall, rise narrative pattern that mirrors the first half. Zeke rises to prominence as a preacher and converts Chick. In turn, through their sexual attraction, she (re)converts him, and he leaves his family and calling. The fall is completed when Chick, bored with Zeke's piety, attempts to run away with Hot Shot. Zeke pursues and kills them both—Chick by accident and Hot Shot on purpose. After serving time on a chain gang, Zeke returns to his family, which accepts him with open arms, a reunion cemented by the implied union between Zeke and his adopted sister, Missy Rose. The music in the second half of the film maps more clearly onto the narrative pattern than it did in the first half, but confusions remain. Mostly spirituals accompany the first portion of Zeke's rise, and the first stage of his fall is marked by Missy Rose transforming a spiritual into a lament when she discovers Zeke has run off with Chick. Zeke, however, reprises "The End of the Road" to cement his "conversion" of Chick; this mock spiritual, which seems meant to stand for clear redemption and good (for "whiteness" of soul) in the story, presides over the narrative's moment of greatest triumph and danger and, thus, becomes still more ambiguous. It is as though because Zeke has aimed so high—to redeem the most sinful, to sing the whitest song—he must be brought low. Music nearly disappears in the section in which Zeke falls lowest. Having moved with Chick to town and into the noisy employ of a saw mill, Zeke finds music has left the world. When music returns, it is with Chick singing a version of "St. Louis Blues" to lull Zeke to sleep and permit her to escape with Hot Shot. In the concluding scenes, music returns fully, and in its "ideal," moral, outdoor forms. We hear a work song in the labor gang sequence, a folk song as Zeke travels home, and finally Zeke's Berlin-penned theme, "The End of the Road," restored to its affiliation with unambiguous good, which concludes the film.

So strong are *Hallelujah!*'s musical performances, in Locke and Brown's estimation, that they "mak[e] something rich and strange out of even the theme song—'The End of the Road'." Locke and Brown continue, "Such a transformation wasn't easy, because this song has really no connections with any point farther south than the lower East Side." But for Locke and Brown this transformative quality could not overcome "trick plotting," "stale" images, "poorly popularized Freud," and "sentimentality." They preferred *Hearts in Dixie* for its carelessness and superficiality, its more consistent use of folk music, and its unsentimental, unmanichean open end.[28]

In contrast to Locke and Brown, W. E. B. Du Bois, writing in *The Crisis,* preferred *Hallelujah!* to *Hearts in Dixie*—and in no uncertain terms: "*Hearts in Dixie* is a fine film. . . . But *Hallelujah!* is a great drama."[29] Yet, like Locke and Brown in reverse, Du Bois became less enthusiastic about *Hallelujah!* the more he thought about it. By the end of his review, this "great," "epoch-making" drama becomes "fine . . .

entertainment."[30] Since Du Bois believed firmly in the social efficacy and power of art, these shifts in enthusiasm and category are significant. They grow out of Du Bois's feelings about music and race—crucial components of Du Bois's notions of "black folk"—and the way *Hallelujah!* represented both.

After identifying *Hallelujah!* as the latest and among the most "true to life" in the checkered history of black portrayals in "English drama" from *Othello* to *Porgy,* Du Bois listed the "epoch-making" qualities of *Hallelujah!:* the depiction of love and the Negro family, the creation of "the sense of real life," a full range of characterizations, and fine acting. He completed his list of these qualities in his penultimate paragraph: "The music was lovely and while I would have preferred more spirituals instead of the theme-song, yet the world is not as crazy about Negro folk songs as I am."[31] In order to gauge the rhetorical weight of this brief statement, it is worth remembering exactly how "crazy" Du Bois was about Negro folk songs. As I detailed in the introduction, for Du Bois, the Negro "sorrow songs" were the only true art that had originated in the United States; they were, Du Bois had suggested in *The Souls of Black Folk,* "the gift of black folk," the premier example and great symbol of what African Americans had given and continued to give to America.[32] Du Bois hoped that recognition and appreciation of this gift—a gift of sound that comes from within but also goes beyond "color" and the "color line"—would begin to heal the troubled, doubled nation. Compared with this hope, Du Bois's muted approbation of *Hallelujah!*'s music is understandable.

Du Bois's waning enthusiasm for *Hallelujah!* and his tepid response to its music makes more sense when we consider the Irving Berlin "theme-song," as well as the film's Berlin-penned cabaret song. Considered generously, these songs simply substitute for more folk songs. Read more critically, however, the Berlin songs were exploitative and misleading. These Tin Pan Alley songs masqueraded as authentic Negro, "folk" productions, and in so doing they both asserted and hid the color line—*the* problem of the twentieth century in Du Bois's well known view. *Hallelujah!* was a product of a virtually all-white Hollywood, yet it contained no white characters—"although," in Du Bois's words, "it strains the imagination to see a cotton gin or a convict gang without a swaggering white boss."[33] It uses two "white" songs but envisions them as "black," even as, especially in the instance of the cabaret song, they play into distorted white conceptions of African Americans. The Berlin songs are hybrid cultural products (as, of course, is the film), but they (like the film) efface rather than bravely and fully own their complex origins.

In the final paragraph of his review, Du Bois grounds this complexity in his own experience of seeing *Hallelujah!*: "Everybody should see *Hallelujah!* They may even be slightly 'Jim-Crowed' as I was, far forward on the side, where some of the scenes were distorted."[34] Under the circumstances, *Hallelujah!*'s lack of bravery in combination with the slickness and power of its masquerade must have been troubling and contradictory. Because of the genuine hope Negro folk songs embodied for him, Du Bois could only approve of *Hallelujah!*—certainly it was far better than *Birth of a Nation,* the only other film Du Bois ever reviewed. But spurred by the absence of whiteness on the visual track and its presence masking as absence on the sound track, both of which emphasized the color lines surrounding the production and exhibition of the film, Du Bois had to modify his grand, historicizing language—"a great drama"— to the less glowing "fine . . . entertainment." Even for an enthusiast, *Hallelujah!* hinted at the complex limits of Hollywood representations of the folk, which were potentially antiprogressive and could ensnare black performers and audiences in their subtle—and engaging—distortions.

The final mark of *Hallelujah!*'s ambiguous importance to African Americans was the quantity of comment it elicited from ordinary black filmgoers. *Hallelujah!* is unique among all the films this book considers for the amount of writing it prompted.[35] What is most interesting about this common response to *Hallelujah!* is how it shifted the discourse of dualism from a quality of the text and a quality of potential responses to the text to a quality of the black audience of the film.

When it was released in New York in the late summer of 1929, several black leaders strongly criticized *Hallelujah!*, feeling it misrepresented or ridiculed its subjects and, in the words of one preacher, was "an insult to the religious ideal of the colored race."[36] On the other hand, Oscar De-Priest, the only African American congressman at that time, endorsed the film.[37] Word of this controversy reached Chicago, where the *Defender* ran a photograph of a protest against the film outside Harlem's Lafayette Theater.[38] But by the time *Hallelujah!* reached the South Side almost five months later, the *Defender* was fully on the publicity bandwagon. In addition to its ordinary publicity boilerplate and star photographs, it gave away one hundred free tickets (in a contest that twice made the paper's front page and reportedly drew "thousands" of entries), reprinted glowing reviews, and printed its own review.[39] The review, which hailed *Hallelujah!* for its excellent performances, concluded by shifting its focus to the film's South Side audience and reviewing *it* and its expectations:

> Many race patrons made comments which would indicate that they would have much rather seen a picture wherein the dark actors were garbed in fine clothes and drove big cars, and made love in lavish settings, or, in other words, conducted themselves much as their fairer brothers.
> Why should that be?[40]

The pseudonymous writer, Ace, left his question unanswered, and after a brief reassertion of the film's virtues, returned again to the audience: "It seemed sad to hear the cackling of the audience during parts of the picture which were tragic."[41] A significant portion of *Hallelujah!*'s black audience seems to have at once been enticed enough by the film to go to the theater and distanced enough from it to laugh at it (and articulate a desire for something different) when it did not appeal to them.

Ace's question, and his recording of this elusive audience, spurred a run of letters to the editor of the *Defender* that stretched over more than two months and totaled, finally, nine letters and an editorial response. Six of the letters, as well as the editorial, applauded the film as "A Work of Art." The reasoning of the letter writers was diverse, ranging from focusing on aesthetics to invidious comparisons with "some Negro shows" to assertions of *Hallelujah!*'s "accuracy."[42]

The three negative letters were more consistent (two of the three were by the same correspondent). All complained that *Hallelujah!* focused too much on the "low" elements of black life and culture. Both writers also cast this hierarchy in judgement in terms of history and geography, implicitly aligning low—"the depths from which we came"—with past ("memory") and South, and aligning high—"the heights to which we have ascended"—with present and North. Clarence J. McGivens, the writer who felt compelled to write twice, added to this an economic and cultural nationalist position in favor of cultural products made *by* blacks—in this instance, race films. Calling for unity of cultural identity and economic practice, McGivens sought to erase the dualisms and polarities that structured both the Hollywood black-cast musicals and, more importantly, African American responses to these films.[43]

What McGivens evidently did not know is that *A Prince of His Race,* the specific race film he championed as an alternative to *Hallelujah!,* was made by a company controlled by whites.[44] In this regard, then, *Hallelujah!*—whose white, Hollywood roots were relatively clear in context, right down to the crediting of Berlin for his two musical contributions— *was* honest in its polarities. Despite—and perhaps because of—its attempt to erase America's racial duality and displace it on to dualities of morality, gender, location, and musical style within Afro-America and within black individuals, *Hallelujah!* could become a startling, disconcerting, provoking objective correlative of Du Bois's "double consciousness"—an emblem clearly visible (and audible) to its African American audience and at best only flickeringly (and mostly not at all) perceivable to its white, mainstream audience.[45]

By the time it reached film in 1936, *The Green Pastures* certainly did not —and could not—fulfill Locke and Brown's hope that some lucky accidents would let black voices disrupt the deliberate, managed Hollywood image of the Negro. There were three reasons for this. First, as Donald Crafton has shown, by the early thirties, sound production had been completely rationalized and institutionalized in Hollywood. Struggles over the voice, which had been occasioned by the adoption of sound, and which had permitted *Hearts in Dixie* and *Hallelujah!* to be made, were over. Second, *The Green Pastures* was a "property"—a pre-existing, highly esteemed, well known text. This—in combination with commercial concerns about the mass, national appeal of black-cast productions that led to assigning the adaptation a modest budget—militated against change and innovation. Third, and most importantly, like *Hearts in Dixie*, *The Green Pastures* explicitly presented itself as a sort of documentary portrayal of African Americans, but unlike both *Hearts in Dixie* and *Hallelujah!*, *The Green Pastures* wished to portray an interior, psychological (yet also emphatically collective) state—the imagination of, rather than practice of religious belief: "Foreword: God appears in many forms to those who believe in Him. Thousands of Negroes in the Deep South visualize God and Heaven in terms of people and things they know in their everyday life. *The Green Pastures* is an attempt to portray that humble, reverent conception."[46] While this assertion and attempt might be mistakes, it was unlikely to yield the type of "accidents" Locke and Brown were looking and listening for.

Theatergoers had kept the stage play of *The Green Pastures* running on Broadway and on tour for five years before the film was finally made. Though it is impossible to know what proportion of the audience for *The*

FOREWORD

God appears in many forms to those who believe in Him. Thousands of Negroes in the Deep South visualize God and Heaven in terms

34. Foreword to
The Green Pastures
(1936).

Green Pastures was black, African American critics saw the play and often wrote about it in glowing terms. For James Weldon Johnson, for example, *The Green Pastures* cemented the revolution, which *Porgy* had heralded, in black representations in mainstream American theater.[47] The African American press supported the show—and especially its players—with enthusiastic notices throughout its run and grieved on its front pages when the original De Lawd, Richard B. Harrison, died in 1935. And as the Depression deepened, the endurance of *The Green Pastures* represented for the black press one persistent piece of good news, so that even a skeptic like the Afrocentric popular historian, J. A. Rogers, assessing the play when it returned to Broadway in 1935, was moderate: "Impressions of *The Green Pastures* as a play. Stage setting: a delight. Acting: good. . . . Singing: unforgettable, on a par with the best. Humor: rather thin and below the Negro standard of a decade ago."[48] Rogers harshly criticized the story, a "folk" adaptation of the scientifically and ideologically suspect Old Testament: "Thanks to its acting, setting, and music, [this story] has been made the most popular play for the times. Change it to white-face and I'd give it a single night on Broadway, or anywhere else." Nonetheless, Rogers concluded, "See *The Green Pastures* by all means," though he urged his readers to go to MOMA afterward and, by way of contrast, see the display of African art.[49]

The body of *The Green Pastures* is motivated by a frame in which a group of Sunday school children ask questions about Heaven. The bulk of the film then moves back and forth between De Lawd in Heaven and the results of and prompts for his actions on Earth. Using the stories of creation, the fall, Cain, Noah, exodus and captivity, and an apocry-phal tale of human faith, *The Green Pastures* forges a narrative of De Lawd's disenchantment with humanity and his discovery of the need for mercy. The story ends at the moment of transformation from the Old to the New Testament God, signaled by De Lawd's describing the crucifixion as it takes place offscreen. Singing well known spirituals, De Lawd's heavenly choir (played and sung by the Hall Johnson Choir, which was carried over from the stage production) provides entertain-ment in heaven and much of the musical sound track for earthly events. Jazzy secular music is used in three key moments—just before the deluge, just before Moses calls down the plague on Egypt, and during the Baby-lonian captivity—to signify unredeemable evil.

In all of these aspects, *The Green Pastures* is safe. It risks nothing, espe-cially not complexity or anything less than excessive clarity. And by and large it was received with polite enthusiasm by African American critics. Those who protested the film—and there were only two—came from major urban centers (and the middle classes) that had had access to the play. For many African Americans in smaller towns, in the South, and in the lower classes, the film of *The Green Pastures was* an event of some mo-ment precisely because it was an accessible, affordable record of a widely hailed, well regarded, and unprecedented theatrical production. Though no critics articulated it directly, however, many must have felt at least some irony from several possible causes in *The Green Pastures*. Creating a retributative God or an enslaving Pharaoh as black men certainly has ironic potential—one akin to Du Bois's sense of the impropriety of a labor gang with no white boss in *Hallelujah!*[50] This was as true of the play as of the film, but a Hollywood film was more manifestly, directly controlled by whites—the "gods" of Hollywood and U.S. capitalism—than a live performance could (or would appear to) be. More specific to the film were that it marked the end, at least for the foreseeable future, of live productions of the play and that in the film's mass mediated, re-corded form, many of the play's most progressive and delicate qualities could no longer be supported by the activism and care of its cast. As a film, *The Green Pastures* would routinely play at segregated theaters, something the cast of the live show had refused to do at least once; and in a film the dignified, physical presence of the performers could no longer work to ensure that, in James Weldon Johnson's words, the performance fell to the correct side of the story's "so tenuous" "line between the sublime and the ridiculous."[51] Thus the film's accessibility was both a benefit for black audiences eager to appreciate and celebrate black achievement and a potential liability for the same audience's larger political causes.

In light of this contradiction, the attempt on the part of *Jump for Joy*—Duke Ellington's activist musical revue performed in Los Angeles in 1941—to at once invoke and write a critical epitaph for *The Green Pastures* becomes especially interesting. "Have you seen pastures, groovy?" the show's title tune asks. Then, as if in response to a potential answer, the next line asserts, "Oh, *Green Pastures* was just a Technicolor movie." The criticism, especially in the context of the show's general criticism of "Uncle Tom" in American entertainment, is unmistakable: *The Green Pastures* is not groovy. Yet, in its off-handed benignity—it's "just a . . . movie"—this invocation also expresses the aspirations and limits of a cultural politics of black *entertainment:* "to give an American audience entertainment without compromising the dignity of the Negro people"[52]; to build a tenable present, better future, and useable past; to do it with performers with stage names like Pot, Pan, and Skillet, the comedians in the all-black *Jump for Joy.*[53]

"Thanks, Pal"?

"Thanks, Pal" was the working title of *Stormy Weather.*[54] The shift from the declarative to the descriptive, from white-penned thank you note to the name of a white-penned song describing romantic dissolution, hints at some of the most salient features and some of the limitations and successes of the second cycle of black-cast musicals. The tensions and contradictions condensed in this shift also hint at why *Cabin in the Sky* and, even more, *Stormy Weather* were the most successful and are the best remembered of the black-cast musicals. In important ways, this was an honest shift, coming as it did in a moment of profound disease about the place of African Americans in the putatively egalitarian and anti-racist nation. The United States did not seem prepared to say, even symbolically, "thanks, pal" to Afro-America, and it did see African American demands for civil rights as dangerously disruptive of a patriotic national atmosphere, even as, in increasing numbers, white Americans found themselves entertained by African Americans, and especially African American musicians, via live performance, radio, records, and even film. It would be hard—probably impossible—to represent such a complex situation on film; the best that could be hoped for is a kind of perfect imperfection, direct indirection, which I will argue is just what *Stormy Weather* and, to a considerably lesser extent, *Cabin in the Sky* achieved.

Taken together, the two films share several salient features that distinguish them from their thirties' forebears. First, they feature the first generation (or generation and a half) of black multimedia "stars." Ethel Waters, Eddie "Rochester" Anderson, Louis Armstrong, and Duke Ellington were all in *Cabin in the Sky,* and Bill "Bojangles" Robinson, Cab Calloway, the Nicholas Brothers, and Fats Waller all appeared in *Stormy Weather.* None of these performers were movie stars in the usual sense: none would have had his or her name placed above the title or even very high in the credits in the ordinary films in which they appeared, none had a standard star contract with a studio, and none could have lived as well from performing mostly in movies as they did from their other work, but they were all "names" from live performance, radio, records, and, to a lesser degree, film. None of the thirties' films featured any performers of similar magnitude arguably because there were, as yet, no black performers (including all the stars listed above and possibly excepting Paul Robeson) who had much penetrated the cultural mainstream.

Second, both films worked in concert in an attempt to *make* the first black movie star, Lena Horne. Horne, who was a multimedia performer, was not a star—not a name to attract audiences in a way comparable to any of the performers listed above—but she became a movie star when she secured a standard contract, aided by some activist pressure, at MGM. *Cabin in the Sky* and *Stormy Weather* mark the pinnacle of her Hollywood movie career, which had only begun late in 1942 and lasted, with longer and longer pauses between films, until 1956.

Finally, unlike the earlier black-cast musicals, *Cabin in the Sky* and *Stormy Weather* are comic in tone and narrative outcome. No one dies in the story of either film (though we are led to believe otherwise for part of *Cabin in the Sky,* and there are acts of physical violence in both), and each ends with (re)marriage. Like the 1930s films, both *Cabin* and *Stormy Weather* are set in the present, but unlike the thirties films, the two 1943 films make this emphatically clear and, thus, attempt to place contemporary black musical production in a narrative frame. Each film tries to tell a story that makes sense of *new* black music. Added to this, both films—largely because of their use of stars and the types of music these stars perform—at least flex the subgenre of the (black) folk musical. Examining this generic flexion will form an important part of my analysis below. Suffice it to say here that, in combination, all of these qualities verged on creating a revolutionary change in the texture of the black-cast musical.

Cabin in the Sky was the first of the pair to be released, and its publicity benefitted from the film's relative novelty as a black-cast musical and as Horne's first full star turn, from MGM's advertising budget, and from the fact that it was adapted from a moderately successful, modestly known stage musical. In a newly activist era, however, all of these benefits—with the exception of Horne—could become drawbacks to significant portions of the black audience, while the common studio wisdom was that the black cast—and perhaps especially Horne as a movie star—would likely be a liability for much of the white (especially Southern) audience. Consequently, the film had to attempt to balance progressive and conservative impulses and demands, both in terms of form and content. To borrow again from Duke Ellington's assessment of the "problems" *Jump for Joy* had to confront, *Cabin in the Sky* had to figure out how "to give an American audience entertainment without compromising the dignity of the Negro people."

More because it was the first film of Vincente Minnelli, a favorite of auteurist critics, than for any other reason, *Cabin in the Sky* has received the most sustained scholarly attention among all the black-cast musicals. The most attentive scholarly critics, most notably James Naremore and Adam Knee, agree that the film is cleverly and intricately constructed, but they cannot quite agree whether this construction is pleasurable and, more importantly for most critics, (mildly) progressive and antiracist or regressive and racist—perhaps especially so *because of* whatever pleasures the film might hold. Before offering my own descriptive analysis of the film, which will draw from the insights of Naremore and Knee, I think it useful, perhaps more so with *Cabin in the Sky* than any of the other films this chapter examines, to consider the film's reception by black critics and audiences.

In the black press, *Cabin in the Sky* was hyped to the skies (it is impossible to convey the onslaught of press coverage without resort to colloquialism). Hardly an issue of the *Defender* passed in late 1942 and the first half of 1943 without at least one mention of the film, usually via a mention of one of its stars. The publicity began to crescendo when MGM announced the film would premiere in Dallas—"a thing which was thought incredible a few decades ago," crowed the piece making the announcement in the *Defender*.[55] As with the double premiere of *Hallelujah!* in 1929, this choice became an object of interpretation and criticism. A week before the premiere, Al Monroe, a regular entertainment columnist for the *Defender*, took up the meaning of the premiere's location:

> WHILE SOME ARGUE that *Cabin in the Sky* carries much of the chatter and character many Negroes find objectionable on the screen, its stars are performers of the highest type. . . .
>
> What we are wondering is just how well the . . . players who do so much for *Cabin* . . . will be received [when they attend the premiere]. Will the DISCRIMINATION they are bound to face mar their appreciation of the art they helped to mold? MGM has done a fine job we are told. BUT SOMEHOW we cannot help thinking how nice it would be if Blacked Out Broadway could be the first to make the stars feel that they too did A FINE JOB in the picture.[56]

Monroe's piece reactivates a discursive strategy already familiar from analyses of the earlier black-cast musicals: the separation of the stars from the material they perform. In part, this is a prophylactic move against what Locke and Brown had called, a decade earlier, the "usual claptrap." Monroe also adds a critical layer, however, suggesting that different contexts of reception might influence the need for this strategy; on Broadway such separation of performer from performance would not be (as) necessary.

When *Cabin in the Sky* was finally released, it received mostly good notices from the white press. It made a small profit—it was a modest success, as had been its stage forebear—and in all probability it was seen by a considerable African American audience. I have found no favorable reviews in the black press, and in several important black papers, African American critics were unusually blunt in their assessments. Rob Roy, in the *Defender*, "resented Lena's sitting on a piano and lifting her skirt to prove that the clothing beneath her dress was highly colored silk. . . . That simply does not rate in our book of fancies . . . anymore than does the continual display of teeth as in *Cabin in the Sky*."[57] In the *New York Amsterdam News*, Ramona Lewis called the film an "insult." More importantly, she was exceedingly critical in her rejection of the strategy of separating the performer from the work: "Since box office returns convince Hollywood more than anything else that it is in the right, it's too bad the actors [a 'magnificent cast'] didn't have the courage to refuse to make the film in the first place."[58] Reviews like this—especially after the build-up for *Cabin in the Sky*—raised the cultural political stakes of the film musical considerably. This level of attention diminished for *Stormy Weather,* but it presaged much of the black critical response to the last, fifties cycle of black-cast musicals.

Cabin in the Sky courted such a response by not being clearly formally innovative. It lightened the tone of the black-cast folk musical, and in a variety of ways, it attempted to signal its awareness of generic constraint. But, with its story of a devout woman struggling to keep her wandering man from the interrelated, sinful temptations of gambling, jazz, and brassy women, it still appeared to be—especially if distilled into its narrative outlines—a refashioning of *Hallelujah!* by way of *The Green Pastures. Cabin* attempts to replace the solemnity of its generic forebears with comedy by, among other things, casting "Rochester" as the protagonist, Little Joe. It creates a cartoonishly simple evocation of the subgenre's spiritual/secular dichotomy via Joe's apocalyptic dream of devils and angels competing for his soul, which forms the body of the narrative. It attempts to signify on the tradition of the black folk musical via clever casting: Rochester had played Noah in *The Green Pastures,* a wavering character whom we know in advance is redeemed, the same as Joe, though with Joe the audience is (at least formally) uncertain of his end; Rex Ingram is here Lucious/Lucifer Jr., a devil, the inversion of his De Lawd in *The Green Pastures;* and Oscar Polk, Gabriel in *The Green Pastures,* plays the same character—an angel/Deacon—in *Cabin.* And *Cabin,* like *Hearts in Dixie* and *The Green Pastures,* uses a foreword to cement its "folk" quality, but it pushes its foreword to a point of apparent referential incoherence: "The folklore of America has origins in all lands, all races, all colors. This story of faith and devotion springs from that source and seeks to capture those values." This "folklore" is fakelore, it seems—or, at best, it is " 'folklore.' "

All of these qualities are, for James Naremore, legible as "primitivism . . . transformed . . . into a paradoxical sophistication," "a kind of capitalist progress," and markers of "the death of bogus authenticity." In a word, *Cabin* can be seen as "ironic."[59] In a publicity interview,

The folklore of America has origins in all lands, all races, all colors.
This story of faith and devotion springs from that source and seeks to capture those values.

35. Foreword to *Cabin in the Sky* (1943).

Rex Ingram expressed a clear understanding of *Cabin's* revisionist intent: "*Cabin in the Sky* is more grown up than *The Green Pastures*. . . . It is the story of a wayward soul kept on the straight and narrow path by the prayers of his wife, but the treatment is in a happy vein. While good triumphs over bad, there's a lot of fun in the doing of it."[60] Nonetheless, Ramona Lewis and Rob Roy clearly managed to miss the irony and fun, and Lewis argues that white audiences were missing the irony, too, and "believ[ing] this was the normal pattern of Negro life." The foreword may suggest a polyglot American folk of "all," but the image track distills this all to black—America's perennial folk. Adam Knee argues that the film's emphatic but wholly black binarisms, which are twice healed in the film's conclusion (once when Joe's dream ends in the destruction of a nightclub signifying all that is "bad" and again when Joe awakens from the dream and renounces his wavering ways), are a racist diversion from the wounding binarism of race in the United States. From this position, when Little Joe is shot in a rigged craps game and dreams of leaving his body, the film is not asserting an awareness of Du Boisian double consciousness ("I ain't never been twins before!," exclaims Joe) but reasserting the root cause of double consciousness—the American view that blackness is a (black, moral) "problem." For critics like Lewis and Roy, Knee's interpretation would almost certainly resonate more than Naremore's.[61]

Naremore—and from a more interested perspective, Rex Ingram—would as certainly respond that this interpretation, keyed as it is to generic form, misses the nuances of fugitive pleasures and meanings embedded in performed content. Suggestive and complex support for this position comes from an interesting—if unlikely—source. Malcolm X, speaking in *The Autobiography* of the hustling, "Detroit Red" phase of his career, notes his general affection for movies ("Sometimes I made as many as five on one day") and says specifically, "I loved all that dancing and carrying on in such films as *Stormy Weather* and *Cabin in the Sky*."[62] This statement is complex because Malcolm X is speaking of a past he had repudiated, and indeed, in this passage he implicitly links his love of movies to his drug pushing and drug addiction. Yet Malcolm X never repudiated his admiration for the "Negro entertainers"—most especially the musicians and dancers—who so heavily populate the first quarter of his narrative. "Carrying on" in the context of Malcolm X/Detroit Red's life and black life in America in 1943 has multiple possible meanings, none mutually exclusive: inconsequential and transitory silliness, disruptive nonsense, consequential endurance.

A brief examination of the patterns of music and musical performance in *Cabin in the Sky* suggests the potential of "carrying on"—and performances of good "badness"—in the film. For its first two-thirds (and first seven numbers), the film uses mostly standard show tunes composed by the teams of John Latouche and Vernon Duke, and Harold Arlen and E. Y. Harburg—all white, liberal writers. The only exception is a spiritual, "Old Ship of Zion." Save for the sixth number, all of this music is clearly "good" music: the first two numbers are sung in Petunia's (Ethel Water's) church and the next three express Petunia's love for Joe. The first two numbers, motivated by a church service, are—until the very end of the film—the only songs sung in the "real" world; the others take place, we discover, in Joe's dream. The sixth number, "Life's Full of Consequences," is also predominantly a "good" number, but here Georgia Brown (Lena Horne) attempts to seduce Joe ("I'm throwin' nature at your feet"), who successfully resists. Petunia oversees this duet, misunderstands, and kicks Joe out of their house; her sad and melodically unresolved reprise of "Happiness is a Thing Called Joe" concludes the "good" dream portion of the film.

The next four numbers, all set in Jim Henry's Paradise nightclub, are "bad": Duke Ellington plays an extended instrumental, "Goin' Up/Things Ain't What They Used to Be"; Joe's nemesis Domino Johnson (John "Bubbles" Sublett, the stage *Porgy and Bess*'s Sportin' Life) sings and dances "Shine"; and Georgia Brown and then Petunia sing

36. Petunia (Ethel Waters) vs. Georgia (Lena Horne) in "Honey in the Honeycomb" in *Cabin in the Sky.*

"Honey in the Honeycomb." While the "good" numbers of the film are all pleasing in their way, they are all also yoked directly to the story and consequently feel somewhat restrained. In contrast, these "bad" numbers are infused with energy, motion, and "fun." The two versions of "Honey in the Honeycomb" do serve the narrative of the struggle for Joe's affections and soul, but the Ellington tunes and the Sublett number escape obvious narrative purpose or use. "Shine," a song about a carefree character, is strongly associated with Louis Armstrong's "innocent" clowning, but here it is given to Sublett's manifestly "bad" man, perhaps reminding black audiences of the Shine of African American lore, a critical, surviving, enduring trickster. By retying musical performance to narrative and by hypersexualizing Georgia and Petunia, "Honey in the Honeycomb" may restrain the "carrying on" developed by the Ellington and Sublett numbers, but Horne and Water's performances also collapse the hyperbolic good/bad dichotomy the film had been built on, suggesting that music and morality/spirituality are linked shiftingly rather than uniformly. Moreover, the remarkable competition between Georgia (young, trim, and lightskinned) and Petunia (older, plumper, and darker) makes clear that this film can conceive of black (female) beauty and (hetero)sexuality in capacious, inclusive terms.

Cabin in the Sky was not a radical break with Hollywood black-cast musical practice, so its rewards, pleasures, and resistances must be seen as heavily qualified at best. And it will not do to forget that some—perhaps many—black viewers saw no reward, pleasure, or resistance in the

film at all. Although it has garnered virtually no scholarly critical attention, *Stormy Weather*—in the context of the black-cast musical and in the
domestic political context of the summer of 1943—did make a (more)
radical break with its subgenre, one that would remain utterly novel until
the subgenre re-emerged in the poststudio seventies.

In contrast to any of its forebears, *Stormy Weather* made Malcolm X's
"carrying on" its primary impulse and organizing principle. This is most
obvious in the film's generic shift: instead of drawing from the outlines
of the folk musical, *Stormy Weather* fuses the general conventions of the
backstage musical and the biopic; it tells the life story of a showman. The
virtue of this choice is that it allows history and memory into the form
and thus makes carrying on—in the sense of continuing, persisting—a
subject. This sense is further nuanced by two crucial narrative choices
the film makes, choices that permit *Stormy Weather* to register some of
the costs of carrying on and that both flirt with and complicate the conventional alignment of "folk" with black. An important motif of the film
is travel: It begins with black troops returning to Harlem from World
War I; follows its protagonist Bill Williamson (Bill Robinson) from New
York, through the South, and back; sends Bill's romantic partner Selina
Rogers (Lena Horne) to Paris; and ends in present-day Hollywood, from
whence the body of the film is narrated in flashback. Along the way, Bill
both gains and loses friends; fellow performers appear, disappear, and
sometimes reappear—but more often do not (though Selina, of course,
does). Carrying on, it seems, is at once costly to (the black) folk and
constitutive of a new and always shifting show folk life. While *Stormy
Weather,* both as a movie and a song, is not a blues, it does work to evoke
the blues's sense of combined restraint (words) and possibility (music),
lament and celebration.

But this descriptive analysis only gets at the depth of *Stormy Weather*'s
carrying on—not its all-important surface. Besides being a backstage biopic, *Stormy Weather* is also a revue musical. In itself, this subgeneric
quality hardly makes *Stormy Weather* unique; the revue had a long history
on stage and in film, and during the early years of World War II it was
experiencing a comeback in film (e.g., *Star-Spangled Rhythm, Stage Door
Canteen*). Combining the revue with other (and more apparently ambitious) generic inflections, however, and packing all of this into seventy-
eight minutes of screen time, results in a most heavily musicalized musi-

cal.[63] "Carrying on"—in the sense of play, amusement, kinesis—was the order of the day. This could be read as incoherence—or as a criticism of the (racialized) limits of "coherence."

In chapter three I argued, though in slightly different terms, that *Stormy Weather*'s use of black blackface deployed "carrying on" in all its senses, masking a critique of race/whiteness that emerges out of the disruptive qualities of "indefinite talk" through permitting the viewer recourse to the play's apparently disposable qualities. The hyperventilating, interarticulated subgeneric mixing in the film supports this analysis: in contrast to its black-cast musical antecedents, and in particularly stark contrast with *Cabin*, *Stormy Weather* emphatically refused (or was simply unable) to contain its "carrying on" in a conventional(izing), moral(izing) narrative frame. At the end of the film, Bill and Selina *do* reunite, but because the narrative of their union and disunion has to compete with so many other aspects of the film—Bill's personal narrative as well as the revue/review of black entertainment—the reunion seems perfunctory at best. The May-December couple of Selina/Horne and Bill/Robinson does have symbolic resonances in its union of generations, of North (Horne) and South (Robinson), of song and dance, and of light and dark skin, but this couple lodges in memory much less firmly than the Nicholas Brothers, who perform the film's penultimate number. The Brother's dance, set to the Cab Calloway Orchestra's "Jumpin' Jive," caps—and expands on—the film's theme of extensive, expansive performance. If, as I've argued, after the strange centerpiece of the black blackface number, the film threatened to turn constrained, proper, classy, the Nicholas Brothers—impeccably dressed in restrained, proper, classy tuxedos—confront this threat head on. Their athletic, acrobatic dance takes the energies of all the performances that have preceded them, encapsulates and embodies those energies, and attempts—quite literally—to take performance *vertical,* not just to carry *on* but to carry *out,* to carry *over,* to carry *beyond.* They fail to reach escape velocity, but they triumph nonetheless. They survive their heroic, improbable labors to dance another day, and they do so with consummate grace, turning each potentially disastrous landing into another energizing display of skill and refusal of defeat.

Compared with *Cabin in the Sky*—and perhaps in part because of it—*Stormy Weather* received relatively little attention in the black press.

37. Nicolas Brothers in mid-flight from the end of *Stormy Weather.*

Much of the attention it did receive was undesirable. First, in February the black composer-arranger William Grant Still very publicly quit his job arranging the music for the film, accusing the music staff at 20th Century-Fox of denying him resources and, more importantly, of discarding his arrangements for being "too good"—inaccurate in their portrayal of black musicality.[64] Next, in March reports surfaced that the studio was unhappy with the Horne/Robinson pairing and was planning to reshoot and recut the film to minimize (or eliminate) the romance.[65] Finally, the film opened in July and August, during a summer of race riots across the country—Detroit, Harlem, Chicago and a number of smaller cities—beginning in June with the so-called zoot suit riots in Los Angeles.[66]

All of this press crowded out anything like a review of the film in the black press. The white mainstream press was mixed, at best, in its assessment of the film. And yet *Variety* reported that *Stormy Weather* outearned *Cabin in the Sky* three-to-one.[67] Out among that audience was the young Malcolm X/Detroit Red, perhaps wearing his cherished zoot suit—a suit that, because of war rationing, was essentially illegal; a suit that was thus (perhaps only implicitly) meant by its wearer as a stylish "fuck you" directed at a racist government willing to conscript but not employ blacks; and a suit that was consequently taken by soldiers as an invitation to "patriotic" attack.[68] Perhaps Malcolm X/Detroit Red and his cohort were amused by *Stormy Weather,* but maybe it seemed "square," too, drawing its protagonist from 1930s Shirley Temple films

38. Cab Calloway
in zoot suit from
Stormy Weather.

and championing black service in the ranks of both entertainment and military. But, then, in the film's climax—when Selina and Bill are re-united at a benefit performance—there are Cab Calloway and his valet in outrageous, illegal, provocative *zoot suits!* And suddenly—especially with the Nicholas Brothers's dancing in front of Calloway's zoot—Holly-wood "carrying on" becomes legible as *carrying out* (here, from within the government-approved system) a subversive cultural politics of style, one dedicated not just to enduring or having fun, but also to demanding and commanding recognition. As *Stormy Weather*'s final number would have it, "My my, ain't that something?"

My sixth chapter will show how some of the impulses captured in *Stormy Weather*—perhaps inadvertently and certainly without the pol-ished (and limiting) craft Minnelli and MGM brought to *Cabin*—carried over into one specific, gemlike Hollywood film treatment of jazz. That chapter will also suggest, however, that such impulses, especially in terms of politics wed with music, carried no further than the end of the war. To conclude this chapter, however, I'd like to jump ahead to the fifties and the end of the studio-era black-cast musical feature and the films Ellington's *Jump for Joy* may have been attempting to preempt when it mischaracterized the inexpensive, black and white *The Green Pastures* as a "technicolor," hence expensive, monumental, and *fully* controlled (to return to Locke and Brown) movie.

"Stand Up and Fight Until the Fight is Won"?

The three films that concluded the subgenre of the Hollywood black cast musical all looked emphatically backward in a period when African Americans were increasingly looking explicitly forward, from Brown v. Board of Education in 1954—the year of *Carmen Jones*—to the rise of the sit-in and the consolidating of the Civil Rights Movement in 1959— the year of *Porgy and Bess.* All three films were set in the past, but the two most spectacular productions—the "technicolor [and wide screen and stereo] movies" of the bunch—were also the most backward looking: *Carmen Jones* and *Porgy and Bess* were both adapted from old stage folk musicals (*Porgy and Bess* was thirty-four years old and *Carmen Jones* was a decade old, though of course it adapted nineteenth-century sources) in the reverentially lugubrious style of the Rodgers and Hammerstein films that followed in the wake of *Carmen Jones,* just as the plays had followed in the forties. Within the black-cast subgenre, these two films "innovated" by being in color, costing a lot, using dubbed operatic voices in the main singing parts, and completely foregoing black music. The more modest *St. Louis Blues* tried to capture some of the energy of *Stormy Weather* via recourse to the biopic. Consequently, it made use of W. C. Handy's music but despite the fact that Handy, "the father of the blues," was still alive in 1958 *St. Louis Blues* did not have the nerve to carry its story farther than the 1920s.

Still, these three films—and particularly the two more elaborate productions—cannot be casually dismissed because, on the one hand, they deployed the first generation of black movie stars—Dorothy Dandridge, Harry Belafonte, and Sidney Poitier—while, on the other hand, they gave a new generation of outspoken and systematic black critics some particularly knotty material to work over.

Placing the story of *Carmen* in the South during World War II, making Carmen a parachute packer and Joe a G.I., but keeping Bizet's music, *Carmen Jones* was a significant Broadway hit when it was first staged in 1943. As my introduction discussed in some detail, it was also among the first musicals ever to be called "integrated."[69] While the critic's use of this word was meant to describe the show's form—that is, songs that move the drama forward—like *The Green Pastures* and *Porgy and Bess* before it, when *Carmen Jones* went on tour, it also racially integrated auditoriums across the country.[70] Reviewing the film in 1954, *Time* began a glowing review by placing *Carmen Jones* in this tradition, without noticing that it was also displacing it: "The rattle of cash registers does not often serve as the drum roll of social progress. With this picture it may."[71] The social progress *Time* foresaw was more opportunities for black performers in Hollywood—a possibility the *Defender*'s two favorable reviews of the film also perceived.[72] In summing up the mass media for 1954, the *Defender*'s Rob Roy saw *Carmen Jones*'s success in the same light, but did not (initially) see fundamental changes in U.S. social geography—that cities were blackening and that capital was withdrawing to the suburbs and, consequently, that integrating a collapsing public medium like the cinema was relatively inconsequential.[73] Just a week later, though, "Prof Doodle"—a character from one of the *Defender*'s cartoons!—excoriated Roy for his optimism: "I must agree that *Carmen Jones* is a fine picture . . . but I cannot allow myself to scream too loudly about its overall production. It is drawing well, as it should do, but among the things that made it good theatre to Dixiecrats are its many biased avenues."[74] "Doodle" concluded by asserting that blacks should be more concerned about live performance (symbolically), radio and most especially TV (pragmatically).

With the exception of a few scattered pieces of work in the thirties and Ralph Ellison's omnibus review of the late forties racial social-problem films, James Baldwin's scathing *Commentary* review of *Carmen Jones* is probably the first widely disseminated film review by a black intellectual of national stature—in fact, reprinted in *Notes of a Native Son* (1955), Baldwin's *Carmen Jones* review helped secure that stature. Baldwin is relentless in his attack on the film's many contradictions—between the "daring" story and the deadened performances, between the flattened images and the dubbed, operatic voices—which he takes as founded on the competing (white) American desires to see "Negroes" as the "amoral" embodiment of sex *and* to see the (white) self as not nearly so unenlightened. The all-black cast *Carmen Jones* derives its strangeness, in this analysis, from the fact that, while being obsessed with amorality, "it is important that the movie always be able to repudiate any suggestion that Negroes are amoral—which it can only do . . . by repudiating any suggestion that Negroes are not white."[75] With the possible exception of Pearl Bailey, no one and nothing associated with *Carmen Jones* is left standing

39. Joe (Harry
Belafonte) strangles
Carmen (Dorothy
Dandridge) in
Carmen Jones
(1954).

at the end of Baldwin's review, yet he calls it "one of the most important all-Negro movies Hollywood has yet produced." But Baldwin obviously did not have in mind the sort of wavering assessment we have seen elsewhere in this chapter and that even the *Defender's* "Prof Doodle" gestured toward. Rather, Baldwin saw *Carmen Jones* as a sign that America was "very deeply ["inwardly" and "personally"] disturbed." For him this was a good sign, one that meant "that the ferment which resulted in so odd a brew as *Carmen Jones* can now be expected to produce something which will be more bitter on the tongue but sweeter on the stomach."[76] America responded to Baldwin's prognostication by making *Carmen* a commercial success, and, in the guise of the Academy of Motion Picture Arts and Sciences, by making Dorothy Dandridge the first African American nominated for a Best Actress (or Actor) Oscar.

After the flurry surrounding *Carmen Jones,* both the long delay and the content of *St. Louis Blues* were so disappointing that it left almost no trace. Combining Handy's early blues with Nelson Riddle's characteristic orchestrations and Nat "King" Coles's mellow and genteel delivery did not help attract black audiences who, though they were proud and long supportive of Cole, had a different sense of the sound of the blues than this movie could convey, perhaps most especially in Chicago in the late fifties, where the urban, electric blues had been on a steady rise since the end of the war.[77] In Krin Gabbard's estimation, *St. Louis Blues* is interesting for its "striking exception to the conventions of films about black jazz artists." Rather than showing Handy as a natural folk musi-

40. W. C. Handy
(Nat "King" Cole)
on stage in front of
a white orchestra
and a white orches-
tra hall audience at
the end of *St. Louis
Blues* (1958).

cian, it shows him as a middle-class observer of folk performers, one who must work to learn their music. For Gabbard, this exceptional quality is recuperated first by giving Cole a near-white subjectivity and then by using a generic form to cement it that traces back to *The Jazz Singer* and narratives of ethnic repudiation.[78] Further securing this assurance that a black man could be (near) white are Handy's final triumph in a performance that places him between a white symphony orchestra and a white orchestra hall audience, and the fact that a key episode in Handy's life—the theft of his first copyrights, which lead him to found a black publishing and record company—is depicted as being black initiated (through a white minion). Handy/Cole becomes sympathetic (in both senses) to whites through falling prey to a black criminal rather than to the white corporation that, in historical fact, victimized him and, thereby, spurred him to become an activist, "race" capitalist. Symptomatic of the limits of *St. Louis Blues* is that fact that, while Handy died in 1958, the film's narrative ends in the twenties, at the height of his success; Hollywood does not know what to do with the rest of his story.

Plans for filming *Porgy and Bess* had been reported in the black press as early as 1943—at virtually the same moment that the midperiod black-cast films were being released, the school system in Washington, D.C. was banning *Porgy and Bess* songs, and Danes were irking fascists by producing the opera.[79] "Summertime," staged with some members of the 1935 cast, appeared in the 1945 Gershwin biopic, *Rhapsody in Blue*. In his unfavorable review of the *Carmen Jones* film, one that noticed many of the contradictions in form that Baldwin had remarked while also drain-ing them of any cultural political meaning or cause, the *New York Times*'s Bosley Crowther, dean of American film critics, ended with a question that seemed meant to inspire hope: "Has anybody thought recently of *Porgy and Bess?*"[80] In his favorable review of *Carmen Jones* in the *De-fender,* Al Monroe concluded by quoting Crowther at length, and fin-ished his piece by directly answering Crowther's question: "We hope not, Mr. Crowther."[81] From a veteran Negro journalist like Monroe—one seemingly dedicated to championing the mainstream presence of "the race," or "sepians" in his creaky lingo, at virtually all costs—this ex-pression of hostility is especially telling of *Porgy and Bess*'s apparently plummeting status among blacks in the fifties.

A few months later, in early 1955, the *Defender* correspondent Hilda See reported pitching *Porgy and Bess* to Hollywood producers and direc-tors—but a *Porgy and Bess* "sans Catfish Row." She could find none to agree with her that this was a good tactic. In fact, they all asserted that "the story as a picture would suffer if Catfish Row were deleted."[82] Musi-cologist David Horn has argued that, almost since its inception, two broad critical discourses have surrounded *Porgy and Bess*. One focuses on the aesthetic description and evaluation of the show (and often on the question of whether or not it is an "opera") and has been engaged almost wholly by white critics. The other focuses on the "racial politics" of the show and has been engaged mostly by black critics. Horn argues that what is especially interesting is these discourses's "consistent failure to connect with one another."[83] Hilda See's essay provides a unique—and perhaps symptomatic—instance in which the two discourses *do* meet on a potential common ground albeit very briefly and dissatisfyingly. They would continue to "meet" in much more conflictual terms for the next four years leading to the Goldwyn adaptation of *Porgy and Bess,* which would remain, in the title of James Baldwin's review, "On Catfish Row."

The first controversies *Porgy and Bess* started involved—surprisingly—questions of the "auteur," questions that were briefly given a racialized cast. Goldwyn fired his first director, Rouben Mamoulian, who had di-rected both *Porgy* and *Porgy and Bess* in their original incarnations (as well as many successful film musicals), and replaced him with Otto Preminger, who had directed *Carmen Jones* and many other successful (and controversial films) but who was not generally known for his work

on musicals. Leigh Whipper, a black performer who also had an association with the show that stretched back to its premiere, suggested that
Preminger was a racist. This small controversy died relatively quickly,
but it fueled and focused for a number of black critics interlinked questions of *Porgy and Bess*'s suitability for the screen, of how to develop a
unified African American position on cultural politics, and of how to
effectively protest a specific mass cultural text—especially one, like *Porgy
and Bess,* that seemed simultaneously light and heavy, entertainment and
art, ephemera and history.

While all of these questions turned out to be complex, the last, in the
context of the late fifties and mass media, was especially so. Many of the
most effective civil rights initiatives had focused on issues of access crystalized at the site of consumption—going to school, riding a bus, being
served at a lunch counter. What was being demanded and dramatized
in these famous instances (especially in the last two) was a desire for a
change in form rather than content: education that was integrated but
not fundamentally altered in terms of content; any place on the bus, but
not a new bus; any place at the lunch counter, but not a new menu. Theaters and cinemas had a long history of serving such a strategy. But over
the period this chapter has examined, African Americans began to demand not just access to the site of consumption but also access to the
site of production—representation on screen—*and* access to that representation at the site of consumption. In other words, by the time *Porgy
and Bess* went into production, certain African American critics were demanding a seat at the counter, assurances that black labor was being
(well) used, and changes in the menu—all in a moment of, from the
perspective of Hollywood, extreme organizational disarticulation.

In the *Los Angeles Tribune* in August 1958, Almena Lomax ("great Negro
editor") wrote a long piece that lashed out at Whipper for clouding the
issues surrounding the film, Goldwyn for making it, the performers for
being in it, the L.A. branch of the NAACP and its leader Loren Miller
(a black activist for two decades and a journalist and jurist) for defend-
ing Goldwyn and the performers, the white press for colluding, invoca-
tions of "taste" for hiding the genuine "dignity" that might be found in
"America's Catfish Rows," and the Heywards and Gershwins for originating the whole mess—and, secondarily, for not being Duke Ellington.
But even Lomax could not follow her logic to its most astringent con-

clusions and veered at the last moment: "Except for the jobs it will create we would just as soon Goldwyn gave up the whole idea and that they buried *Porgy and Bess* in a bottle out at sea somewhere."[84] As the film neared release in 1959, Sidney Poitier—in the national black forum of an *Ebony* profile—collaborated with Lerone Bennett Jr. to damn *Porgy and Bess* with faint praise and to delineate the challenges of laboring in Hollywood:

> In November 1957, [Sidney] did a revolutionary thing by demanding script approval from Hollywood Titan Sam Goldwyn. Although he didn't get script approval, the fact that he demanded it and the fact that Goldwyn went to such lengths to persuade him he didn't need it indicated that the Negro actor had come into his own.
>
> Sidney is still cautious about *Porgy and Bess.* Asked if he were artistically satisfied with his work in the forthcoming movie, he replied: "I would like to leave that question in abeyance. I want to see first if I am socially satisfied with it. I know I tried like hell to make it so. Artistic satisfaction? Well, it depends . . . on how well it comes off socially."[85]

At almost the same moment, the playwright Lorraine Hansberry engaged Preminger in a TV debate on the "social" and "artistic" merits of *Porgy and Bess*—which she dismissed, along with *Carmen Jones,* thus giving Poitier at least an advance hint of the answer to his question.[86]

See and Roy, the critics for the *Defender,* tried to put a happy face on the film, publishing several publicity pieces each, but they were swimming against the critical tide. In September and October 1959, James Baldwin in *Commentary* and, perhaps more resonantly for potential black viewers, Era Bell in *Ebony* decimated the film. Baldwin's essay does not have the verve and wit of his piece on *Carmen Jones* and in fact reiterates many of that piece's main points before expressing a plaintive wish that Hollywood "tell the truth" (and America accept it) about "Catfish Row." Still, it is a successful condemnation—given some of its power by Baldwin's confession that he "like[s] *Porgy and Bess*" in some of its other versions.[87] Bell's piece, "Why Negroes Don't Like *Porgy and Bess*," was more sweeping, narrating not just the controversies around the film but also the history of black complaints against *Porgy* in all its forms: "to a whole lot of Negroes, drama, novel, or opera, it is 'plenty of nothin!' "[88]

The actual film of *Porgy and Bess* proved incapable of freeing itself from

41. Porgy (Sidney Poitier) murdering Crown (Brock Peters) in *Porgy and Bess* (1959). (Museum of Modern Art Film Stills Archive)

this black critical onslaught, and working from an "artistic" rather than "social" perspective, white critics did not help. Few had anything kind to say about *Porgy and Bess,* catching the piece in a sort of double bind. As Hilda See's 1955 idea of revising Catfish Row out of *Porgy and Bess* suggests, black critics were worried about depictions of backwardness, poverty, and degradation, depictions that Gershwin's music might seem to ennoble and that the presence of black stars might seem to endorse. Conversely, white critics found the settings, costumes, and performances (again, as with *Carmen Jones,* using dubbed singing voices) too blandly polished to be interesting. For many, this quality was unfortunately supported by the overwhelming high-tech presentation of the film, which — shot in Todd-AO, recorded in six channel stereo, and toured as a special, advanced ticket road show — seemed at once aggressive and distant or, in Baldwin's words, at once "overdone" and "discreet." The film's technical, material qualities ensured that it cost a great deal and that it was unwieldy to schedule. Under all of this weight, *Porgy and Bess* died, taking with it the career of Dorothy Dandridge and the black-cast film musical.

Just less than a decade later, the black scholar and cultural nationalist Harold Cruse attempted to write *Porgy and Bess*'s epitaph and, at the same time, criticized the film's critics as too timid: "As a symbol of that deeply-ingrained, American cultural paternalism practiced on Negroes ever since the first Southern white man blacked his face, the folk-opera *Porgy and Bess* should be forever banned by all Negro performers in the United States. No Negro singer, actor, or performer should ever submit to a role in this vehicle again." [89] Even as he wrote, *Porgy and Bess* was being staged, and by the midseventies it was firmly within the canon of American opera. Negro performers continued and continue to "submit" — to *Porgy* and to many of the conventions of black-cast musical — but not on film and often not for black audiences.

The most lasting result — and the most widely valued by popular black audiences — of *Porgy and Bess*'s translation to film (and, hence, perhaps of the black-cast musical film subgenre) was a spate of recordings of the music from the show. Joining older recordings by Todd Duncan and Ann Brown, Billie Holiday and Paul Robeson (on separate recordings), and many others were the new film-cast recording and records by Sammy Davis, Jr., Diahann Carroll, Harry Belafonte, and Lena Horne. All of these African American performers worked to claim Gershwin's music for themselves, to reclaim it by shearing it from the constraining image of Catfish Row, and to permit it to tell a different story. Among this group, five additional recordings stand out: Ella Fitzgerald and Louis Armstrong's version, Miles Davis's recording of Gil Evans's arrangements, Duke Ellington's recording of "Summertime," Sun Ra's multiple recordings of songs from the show, and Nina Simone's recording (her breakthrough hit) of "I Loves You Porgy." The Fitzgerald/Armstrong recording lets these two performers sing *all* the characters and consequently creates complex characters out of *Porgy and Bess*'s more schematic types. The Davis/Evans recording is an instrumental record and, in a long-standing jazz tradition, pays *Porgy and Bess* (and Gershwin) the ultimate black musical compliment of reconstructing it. The Ellington and Ra recordings are deconstructions in the two musicians' substantially differing styles, the Ellington "Summertime" being the more violent of the two, surprisingly, since Ra was a much more overtly "out" musician. While in no way typical of these other recordings, Simone's "I Loves You Porgy" shows what these African American musicians could do with Gershwin and Heyward: Despite the song's official title, Simone makes it "I *Love* You Porgy" in her vocal, correcting all of the lyric's dialect. She takes the song from its source, refreshes it, and gives it back to her audience as a love song for a hoped-for new day—one that was still impossible to represent on film in (and for) the United States in 1959.[90]

5

"Aping" Hollywood

DEFORMATION AND MASTERY IN

THE DUKE IS TOPS AND *SWING!*

So, we must be careful—lest we lose our faith—and
become possessed.—JAMES BALDWIN (1976)

Even when Negroes set out to make literal imitations of
white people, they often seem to find it impossible not to
add their own dimensions.—ALBERT MURRAY (1976)

To name our tradition is to rename each of its
antecedents, no matter how pale they might seem.
—HENRY LOUIS GATES JR. (1988)

More than any of the others, this chapter is a recovery project. Its specific
aim is to recover for analysis two black-cast musical films, *The Duke is
Tops* and *Swing!*, both made in 1938. Race films in general and particularly those of the sound era have only just started to be subjected to extended critical analyses. While there have been a few enlightening critical
studies of historical black film and their number is definitely increasing,
past criticism of these films has generally consisted of either unconsid-
ered condemnation, usually on the grounds that they imitate Hollywood
without meeting Hollywood standards of quality, or tolerance, as long
as they are considered "social" (reflective, transparent) and never "aesthetic" (multiply coded, difficult or pleasing, meaning-*full*) objects.[1] But
does imitation simply equal failure? And do social and aesthetic values
and codes ever meet and overlap? Respectively, no and yes seem to me
the simple answers to these questions, and in the analyses that follow I
will explore and explain the successes and the failures, the structures and
the meanings of *The Duke is Tops* and *Swing!*

As a preface to my efforts to recover *The Duke is Tops* and *Swing!*, however, I will explore the conditions for the disappearance, at least for scholarly criticism, of historical black-addressed film, and I propose to do that in part through the recovery of a "lost" black critic, Loren Miller.[2]

Toward a Critical Matrix for Historical Black Film

Writing for *The Crisis* in November 1934, Loren Miller, an activist journalist and attorney, began his essay, "Uncle Tom in Hollywood," with this paragraph:

> A few years ago I attended a showing of *Trader Horn* [1930], a Metro-Goldwyn-Mayer film, at a Negro theater. One scene depicts the "beautiful"—of course, blond—heroine in the clutches of "savage" Africans. In typical Hollywood thriller style the girl is saved just as all hope is ebbing away. At this particular showing the audience burst into wild applause when the rescue scene flashed on the screen. I looked around. Those who were applauding were ordinary Negro working people and middle class folk. Hollywood's movie makers had made the theme so commonplace and glorious that it seemed quite natural white virtue should triumph over black vice. Obviously those spectators were quite unconscious of the fact that they were giving their stamp of approval to a definite pattern of racial relationships in which they were always depicted as the lesser breed.[3]

This is, indeed, a portrait of an audience *possessed,* and Miller efficiently sketched the outlines of this machine of possession, the cinema. On the one hand, he saw the industrial institution figured by "Hollywood's movie makers." On the other, Miller saw the audience, the assembled social group composed of individual spectators. And binding the institution and the audience was the "excessively obvious" film text of *Trader Horn,* with its specific industrial origin (MGM), its genre (thriller), and its typical, thematic, patterned style.[4] These industrial codes aligned with and organized the overlapping social codes of value, class, gender, and race that the audience and spectator carry to the theater, and at the confluence of industrial and social codes—the cinema—Negro working people and middle-class folk identify with "white virtue" and applaud its victory over "their own" excessively obvious—because obviously *black*—villainy.

Miller's program, however, was not one of despair. He did not see the

only avenues open for the black spectator as passing or masochistic identification with "savages." Miller proposed two strategies to help blacks
exorcise Hollywood's possession of their cinematic pleasure and slow the
traffic of degrading cinematic images. One strategy, the one that eventually became the NAACP's most useful threat, was critical renunciation,
"action against [the] box office" of offensive Hollywood products. Miller
saw hope in this strategy because by 1934 other (sometimes racist) groups
had already used it. Miller's other suggested strategy was the creation of a
16 millimeter " 'little movie' movement" designed to evade Hollywood's
monopolistic control of American cinema. The little movie movement
would be an alternative network of production, distribution, and exhibition of Negro films, films addressed explicitly to blacks and "reflect[ing]
their own lives and aspirations," films that would permit blacks to repos-
sess their cinematic image.[5]

But Miller's vision of a repossessive little movie movement did not
come to pass. Instead, "race film" production, virtually dormant in 1934,
resurged,[6] and in January 1938, again in *The Crisis,* Loren Miller addressed this resurgence in an essay titled "Hollywood's New Negro
Films." The title reveals Miller's skeptical critical regard: the films Miller
considered were recent and did contain black casts, but though made independently, they were all possessed by Hollywood. Certainly they had
nothing to do with the idea of the New Negro fostered ten years earlier
by the Harlem Renaissance and still epitomized, in 1938, by young intellectuals like Miller himself. In his 1934 piece Miller had mentioned the
filmmaking efforts of Oscar Micheaux and other "Negro companies,"
but only to suggest that they "fail miserably because . . . [they] simply
ape the white movies."[7] Hollywood's new Negro movies fell prey to the
same failing. *Dark Manhattan* (1937, Million Dollar) and *Bargain With
Bullets* (1938, Million Dollar) were both in the gangster genre; *Life Goes
On* (1938, Million Dollar) was a family melodrama; *Spirit of Youth* (1938,
Grand National) was a very loose biography of Joe Louis, starring Louis
himself; and *Harlem on the Prairie* (1938, Associated Features) was a singing western. Miller had not viewed all of these films, but the ones he had
seen were not just imitative, "built around trite and shopworn plot[s]";
they were also "weighted down with more than [their] share of technical
faults," making them "distinctly mediocre from an artistic standpoint."
Finding that there were more failed race films in 1938 than there had
been in 1934 and seeing no signs that an economically autonomous little

movie network was possible, Miller turned his attention to how, within existing distribution and exhibition practices, Hollywood's new Negro films—"this problem child"—might become successful Negro films.[8]

Miller believed "movies, made either for the Negro or the general audience, educate as well as amuse," but unlike Hollywood films, Negro films would have to explicitly educate (or countereducate) as they amused. Some might find the results "propagandistic," but Miller kept his explicit standard simple: "All that can be asked is that the pictures tell the truth." Genuine Negro films would be "serious" and "straightforward." They would not "distort reality." They would, like "any art," "help him [the Negro movie fan] understand the world in which he lives and cope with the problems inherent in living in that world." In short, Miller saw it as the "artistic" and "social responsibility" of Negro film to confront and judge "Jim Crow." But Miller was not so naive as to believe meeting his standard would be simple. "Grave problems" confronted "realistic" Negro film. Because of the necessity of using existing, white-controlled channels of distribution and exhibition and because there existed no "signposts to indicate what kind of films Negro fans want," a clear feedback loop between Negro filmmakers and fans would be difficult to establish. Economics (always potentially inflected with prejudice) and the probability that "ninety percent of the fans want gangsters or love stories or success yarns" could easily conspire to defeat educative, repossessive Negro films. More troublesome still for Miller was his suspicion that "the truth," at least as clothed in traditional forms of representation, was ideological: "The Negro's place on stage and screen has been fixed for so many years that the tradition sways the judgement of Negroes themselves and honest whites."

How, then, could Negro film escape prejudicial traditions of representation to create an alternative tradition of truth? Miller proposed a critical matrix based metaphorically on two cinematic processes: "What is required for the job is the simple honesty necessary to *turn the camera around* and *focus it* in such a manner that it will catch the phases of our lives deliberately neglected and distorted by Hollywood for cash and carry considerations."[9] Simply turning the Hollywood camera around and reversing color from white to black would not result in Negro films. This had already been tried and resulted in "aping" Hollywood. Reversal, to be effective, had to be accompanied by refocusing. In fact, for Miller refocusing took precedence over reversal as the critical move for

Negro film. He granted that the ideal would be films as "frank" about "the Negro question" as the social-realist stage play, *Stevedore* (1934), but was certain the existing networks of distribution and exhibition would never tolerate such a film.[10] Consequently, Miller's model became "serious"—that is, refocused, though not reversed—Hollywood drama, films like *Dead End* (1937), *Fury* (1936), and *They Won't Forget* (1937). Even though, like most Hollywood films, these films did place blacks on their margins (in the case of *They Won't Forget*) or displaced them entirely (in the other two cases), Miller seems to have believed that this direct neglect was less important than exposing social problems that disproportionately affect blacks and that it was better to leave blacks unrepresented than to have them badly represented.[11]

In making his case for refocused films as a model for a repossessive film practice, Miller effectively abandons the other axis of his critical matrix, reversal. In part this reflects an idealistic vision. Miller envisions a world in which the casting for films as well as the identification of human social problems would be what we have come to call color blind.[12] But, as I have already argued, Miller's privileging of refocusing over reversal is also, in part, a pragmatic response to what he thought the market would bear. It is this complex combination of idealism and pragmatism that finally unmakes Miller's otherwise canny critique. He recognizes that color is a problem—perhaps *the* problem—for blacks in America. Yet, partly because he feels he must and partly because "white" can seem not to count as a color in the American racial order, Miller willingly accepts, even champions, a singularly colored—that is, white—refocused cinema.[13] In effect, Miller's abandonment of reversal as a viable route for a genuine Negro cinema or as an appropriate critical criterion leaves the Negro audience possessed, with no complete position of identification, unconsciously cheering in the dark for white virtue's typical triumph over black vice—or in a refocused film practice (like Lang's *Fury*), white virtue's triumph over white vice.

As a further consequence of his preference for refocusing, Miller left already extant films of reversal unanalyzed. Since these were "cheap films," which "lean[ed] too heavily on exploiting the thrill that comes to the average fan when he sees the Negro actor on the screen with his hat on his head instead of in his hand and far too little on the[ir] artistic merit," they were easy to dismiss.[14] "Aping" Hollywood and the attendant thrills such artistically inferior products might cause apparently needed no analysis; they were, in a sense, already understood. And this dismissive pre-understanding stems from an assumed combination of understanding, internalizing, *and* rejecting Hollywood standards. Films of reversal fail—must fail—because they are at once too standard and substandard: They imitate Hollywood genres, Hollywood modes of narration and characterization, but in a "technically" inferior manner. This is unacceptable largely because films executed in such a manner will seem like seedy, sad, abject fantasies. *The Duke is Tops* and *Swing!* were both made slightly after Miller's "Hollywood's New Negro Films," but because they are musicals he would have almost certainly rejected them for being (almost by definition) fantasies and for relying too heavily on "the night club [or "cabaret"] aspect of Negro life, so beloved in screen and stage tradition."[15]

Perhaps because the received literary standards of form and quality are more fluid and not dominated by an industrial monolith like Hollywood, critics of African American literature have spent more time than their cinema counterparts analyzing and classifying possible African American literary relationships to, uses of, and revisions of the "standard." For instance, though anxious about "apish imitation," which he never defines, Henry Louis Gates Jr. nonetheless finds "repetition and imitation" of (white) literary criticism a legitimate "moment" in the history of the development of African American critical theory.[16] Further, Gates's master trope of signifying names a continuum of "formal revision" in African American literature ranging from the so-called "imitation" of the "Mockingbird School" of poets to the radical fragmentation of Ishmael Reed's *Mumbo Jumbo*.[17] In other words, the ape's imitating can become the monkey's signifying.

For understanding the relationship of historical black film to the strict standard of Hollywood, however, Houston A. Baker Jr. provides a most useful terminology. Writing of the oft-reported failure of the Harlem Renaissance, sometimes also described as the New Negro movement, Baker notes that when a critic "begins with the notion that a recognizably *standard* form automatically disqualifies a work as an authentic and valuable Afro-American national production, analysis is in fact foreclosed by a first assumption of failure."[18] Baker proposes—or perhaps signifies on—strict binary relationships with the standard by suggesting two possible, "authentic" African American literary tactics for approaching the standard: "mastery of form" and "deformation of mastery." Mastery of form is figured for Baker by the African American inhabitation of the blackface minstrel mask, and it is akin to what I have called, through Miller, "reversal." For Baker, however, this masking constitutes a sort of "double negative" rather than, as for Miller, a simple negative. The African American master of form takes the form the "master" gives him, the mask the "master" projects onto him, and uses it to communicate, with the same "sound" meaning very different things depending on who hears. Deformation of mastery is figured by Shakespeare's Caliban, and is most closely akin to Miller's utopian "little movie movement." The deformer of mastery appropriates the tools and terms of the "master" and uses them for his own ends; in this instance, the consequent "sound" will be nonsense to many but perfect sense to some. In short, according to Baker, the master of form "lies," while the deformer of mastery "scandalizes." The remainder of this chapter will seek traces of these processes in *The Duke is Tops* and *Swing!*

Address and (Re)Possession

Processes of potential mastery or deformation, attempts at repossession, begin long before an audience views a film. Nor is it only the text of a film, or more specifically its diegesis, that constructs its address. As with Hollywood films, a variety of contexts and pretexts, disseminated mostly through advertising and journalism, would have prepared black audiences to attend—and attend to—*The Duke is Tops* and *Swing!* These pre-texts thus both tap and add to a realm of knowledge available to potential spectators. In this section I inspect how this pre-textual realm of knowledge works to address *The Duke is Tops* and *Swing!* for/to their potential spectators, and I will consider the possible repossessive—deformed or masterful—qualities of this knowledge.

The names of the producing companies of *The Duke is Tops* and *Swing!*, respectively Million Dollar Productions and Micheaux Pictures Corporation, suggest their own miniature allegories of possession, though what is possessed and by whom differs in each instance. Million Dollar calls up a fantasy of wealth, and intertwined with that fantasy are attendant ideas of "quality." Micheaux Pictures enacts a different fantasy, one of individual ownership and control. The Million Dollar name does not specify who owns the fantastic capital it names, but it implies (using a less varnished version of the logic of other film industry names like "Paramount" and "Universal") that the benefits of this capital, translated into quality, accrue for the spectator.[19] The Micheaux name implies that Oscar Micheaux controlled, possessed, *his* "pictures," and it suggests (more boldly than the Hollywood compounds of Twentieth Century-Fox or Metro-Goldwyn-Mayer) that one individual's integrity guarantees the quality of his product.

But these allegories of capital and control also intersected with others, not the smallest of which was color. By 1938 Oscar Micheaux, an African American, had been making race films for nearly two decades, always under his own name. Black moviegoers *knew* Micheaux pictures never cost a million dollars, and they felt Micheaux's name did not guarantee truth about black experience. The Micheaux film immediately preceding *Swing!*, *God's Stepchildren* (1938), closed after only a day in New York because Harlem activists protested its racism. And, though it is uncertain how public this knowledge was, Micheaux depended for his capital on white businessmen like Apollo Theater owner Frank Schiffman. In this context, Micheaux Pictures Corporation appears to be an exploitive ruse or a bit of vanity. Million Dollar functioned similarly, hiding white investors and control behind an abstraction and Ralph Cooper, the company's high-profile African American "star" and "general manager."[20]

The industrial, journalistic information surrounding *The Duke is Tops* and *Swing!* was sparse and was disseminated mostly through newspapers intended for black readers. In the mainstream industry press, *Variety* reviewed *The Duke is Tops* five days after its public premiere on 15 July 1938 at the Apollo Theater in Harlem. The headline of the review indicates that the film is first, "All-Negro" and second, "Musical," and the reluctantly unfavorable review goes on to relate all its points to these two observations: "Holds little or no interest for whites"; "collection of musical entertainers does much to improve bad first effect."[21] A few months later, when *The Duke is Tops* reached Chicago, the Regal Theater's first ad in the *Chicago Defender* used less sober language to provide similar but more complex information: "It's Coming . . . /Swing . . . Romance . . . Adventure . . . with Ralph Cooper/In His Newest and Best Hollywood Hit . . . /All-Colored Cast."[22]

Variety's review of *The Duke is Tops* reveals the "obvious"—this film was read through the social codes of race and the textual codes of the musical genre, in that order. In the *Defender* ad, however, the film asks to

42. Second Regal ad for *The Duke is Tops, Chicago Defender,* 10 September 1938.

be read first as a musical containing *a* black performer, second as "Hollywood," and last as "*all*-colored." It would have required a particularly uninformed reader not to recognize from the start that *The Duke is Tops* was a "race" film. But, in an era familiar with the black specialty number in Hollywood musicals and within memory of the few all-colored Hollywood musical productions of the preceding ten years, this particular order of language was unique, not obvious. It spoke of mastery *before* reversal.

The title of *The Duke is Tops* makes manifest the fantasy of wealth and quality that the name Million Dollar initiates by making explicit the film's aspirations to mastery. Read in the reflected light of the ascendent African American musician of the era, Duke Ellington, *The Duke is*

Tops both unquestionably asserts and very specifically refers to a realm of musical stars. (That this "musical" naming is not accidental is born out in the film's story by the heroine's name, Ethel, and the name of her maid, Ella.) Ellington's name carried very specific meaning, even relative to the other stars—Louis Armstrong, Cab Calloway, and Count Basie, for instance—whose names appeared as frequently as his in the entertainment pages of black (and some white) newspapers of the time. Ellington, like his peers, was a success, enjoying considerable crossover fame, but unlike Armstrong and Calloway, his persona projected suave, elegant, masterful (as opposed to deformative or masked) control, and unlike Basie, Ellington was a *composer.* To say that Ellington composed and was composed perhaps captures his persona and music best. He drew his control from—exercised it over—not only his image or his musicians but also his music, his art. Ellington's own progress of names illustrates this control: He transformed his big band from the minstrelized Cotton Club Orchestra to the Jungle Band and finally to, by the mid-thirties, *his* Famous Orchestra. And, beginning in the late twenties, Ellington proved that he took the idea of the "orchestra" as seriously as the idea of the "cotton club" or the "jungle" by expanding jazz to include (and masterfully deform) concerti, suites, and symphonies.[23]

To further cement the logic of the association of *the* Duke with *The Duke is Tops,* the film's producers could rely on three items of "general knowledge." First, entertainment sections of black newspapers in the thirties did not discriminate between types of entertainment; the same two or three pages would carry news and advertisements for movies, concerts, dances, theater, and cabaret. Given this fact, it was almost certain that Duke Ellington's name and *The Duke is Tops* would appear in close textual proximity. Second, in the late thirties most of the entertainment forms listed above were not separable; many movie theaters—especially "palaces" like the Regal—hosted big bands, including the Ellington Orchestra. Third, and probably of most immediate consequence for the purposes of *The Duke is Tops,* by 1938 Ellington and his orchestra had appeared in several shorts and at least three Hollywood feature films, including Mae West's hit *Belle of the Nineties. The Duke is Tops* never claimed to star *the* Duke, but it could not help but capitalize on the affiliations and associations—success, quality, wealth, class, dignity, in short, mastery—that the name-that-is-a-title suggested.[24]

Moving from these broad discursive associations, *The Duke is Tops* draws on smaller, more circumscribed, specialized fields of "stardom" in an attempt to exploit (or expand) and create its own movie stars—its own masterful performers—in the figures of its two featured players, Ralph Cooper and Lena Horne. By 1938 Cooper was probably the biggest star in race film. His reputation rested on his leading roles in two all-black gangster films, *Dark Manhattan* (1937, Randol-Cooper Productions) and *Bargain with Bullets* (1937, Million Dollar). Each of these films received some attention in the industry press and generous attention in the African American press, and Cooper became something of a celebrity. (For instance, in August 1938 the *Defender* found "Blind Wife Sues Cooper, Film Star" a worthy piece of entertainment news.[25]) But Cooper also had abilities and some reputation that extended beyond the limits of the gangster genre. Through the midthirties he had worked as a dancer, comic, singer, and band leader, and in 1934 he had helped develop and was the MC for the nationally broadcast weekly Amateur Night at the Apollo Theater in Harlem. In fact, when Cooper quit the Apollo in 1936 and moved to Hollywood, he hoped to replace an injured Bill "Bojangles" Robinson as Shirley Temple's musical partner, but his hopes for a career in Hollywood studio features were frustrated because the camera did not read his skin as "black"—or at least not black enough for Hollywood, so Cooper turned to race films. Given his dossier, it was natural that Cooper should be the above-the-title "star" of *The Duke is Tops*. But it was also natural that *The Duke is Tops* be a musical, thus allowing Cooper to display his mastery of multiple talents and expand his star image.[26]

In 1938 Lena Horne was not nearly as well-established as Cooper in African American entertainment. Her career had started in 1934 in the chorus at the Cotton Club. She had toured for a year with Noble Sissle's "sweet" (as opposed to "hot" or "swing") band, but she had yet to record any music, and by 1938 she had quit singing and was in retirement in Pittsburgh. Horne, however, was a member of a well connected Brooklyn black bourgeois family whose name "meant something." This fact placed her in a different system of stars, a different constellation (or genealogy) of mastery, than Cooper or any of her other co-stars in *The Duke is Tops,* and it almost certainly helped the film receive its legitimating benefit showing for the NAACP in Pittsburgh.[27]

The more meager journalistic information on *Swing!* provides a counterexample to the information strategy of *The Duke is Tops*. It seems

43. Ad for *Swing!*, *Chicago Defender*, 29 October 1938.

to have completely escaped review by either the mainstream or black presses. The small ad in the *Chicago Defender* placed by the Metropolitan Theater was vague about the film's genre—"Fast . . . Furious Drama! / Catchy Swing Music!"—and the story on the same page was headlined simply "All-Race Movie Opens On Sunday."[28] Here, as was common (and as Loren Miller had complained), reversal precedes mastery.

I have already suggested that in American film practice, mastery descends from capital and has material effects (quality) that lead to more capital. *The Duke is Tops* played the Regal, the newest, grandest theater (3000 seats) in Chicago's South Side "Bronzeville." It opened on a Friday and ran for a week on a double bill with *I'll Give a Million,* a Twentieth Century-Fox program comedy starring Warner Baxter. Two months after its initial run, *The Duke is Tops* returned to Chicago for two-night, midweek runs at the New Michigan and Park theaters. This is typical of the South Side exhibition pattern for standard Hollywood films.[29] In contrast, *Swing!* played the smaller (1384 seats), slightly older Metropolitan theater, opening on a Sunday night for a four-day run. It appears never to have returned to Chicago for a second run.[30]

To American audiences of 1938, *Swing!* was a transparent allusion to the ascendent dance music of the era. Alone the word *swing* certainly in-

dicated the film would be set in a musical milieu and would contain diegetic music, enough to qualify it as a musical in the broadest sense. But
the typography of this title, "*Swing!*," with its quotation marks (which
were standard Hollywood practice) and exclamation point (omitted in
the *Defender* ad) surrounding a generic term, glimmers with deformative possibility. Though its ethnic and racial pedigree is complex and
unclear, swing refers to a type of music initially named and perfected
by African American musicians in the late twenties. Swing rose to its
greatest popular prominence, however, when white bands began to play
it too, and by 1938 Benny Goodman, rather than Ellington or Basie, was
the "King of Swing." This process of appropriation was also reflected in
Hollywood adoptions and adaptations of swing, perhaps most obviously
in *Swing Time* (RKO, 1936).[31] Certainly *Swing!* was meant to capitalize on
the swing craze, but its title records this craze as a command in someone
else's voice or a mimicking of that command: The placement of this term
in quotes marks the ambiguous benefits (relative economic success versus loss of possession) of the appropriative process, and, like the W. E. B.
Du Bois review of *Hallelujah!* I analyzed in chapter four, foregrounds
dis-ease with the "adjectivalization" of music. By calling attention to its
title word, *Swing!* deflects (or reflects on) the certainty of that process and
presents itself very differently—and perhaps deformatively—compared
with the sanguine assertion of *The Duke is Tops*.

The additional extracinematic information surrounding *Swing!* makes
for a short story. None of the performers in the film were stars of any
magnitude. Cora Green, who got a below-the-title credit in *Swing!*, was
a blues singer who had been a staple on the black vaudeville circuit, the
Theatrical Owners and Booking Association (TOBA), and had performed
in three moderately successful all-black musical revues, but those successes had been in the twenties.[32] Several of the other performers had
served in previous Micheaux pictures, but that did not guarantee recognition in any sphere.

Perhaps more important than the lack of name performers in *Swing!*
is the controversy that surrounded *God's Step Children*, the Micheaux
film released earlier in 1938. In May 1938 a coalition of Communist party
members and Harlem community activists picketed and shut down the
premiere of *God's Step Children*, complaining that it was racist. The New
York *Age* paraphrases Micheaux as saying he "realized now [after the
protest] that there were objectionable features to the picture" and that

44. *The Duke is Tops* (1938) MPPDA seal.

he "intended to remedy the situation."[33] *Swing!* was released later in the year, and it may represent Micheaux's intended remedy, a sort of attempt to deform his own historic practice of racial melodrama into a compromise with an audience he had misaddressed.

The last card of the credit sequence for *The Duke is Tops* bears a sign familiar to film viewers from the early thirties through the sixties: the seal of the Motion Picture Producers and Distributors Association (MPPDA). The seal affirms that the film was approved by the Production Code Administration Office and met the standards of the Production Code of 1930, with its proscriptions against representing, among other things, miscegenation and "obscenity" in costume or in dance.[34] *The Duke is Tops* draws on a legacy of African American musical mastery and attempts to translate that mastery into the stardom of its male and female principals, Ralph Cooper and Lena Horne. And *The Duke is Tops* performs these discursive acts within the confines of the law, the Code, of Hollywood and its official association, the MPPDA—the acknowledged legislators of American film form and standards in 1938. *The Duke is Tops*, then, at least institutionally, masters the form of the Hollywood movie.

Swing!, by contrast, does not carry a seal, and this officially indicates that the film is an "outlaw" text unavailable for distribution through wide and/or standard channels. *Swing!* was far removed from the discursive structures of the film industry: it used no stars and carried no seals. Micheaux Picture Corporation occupied multiple margins: It was located in Harlem (as opposed to Million Dollar's Los Angeles base); it could not afford stars who had any currency for African American audiences, and it could not afford to advertise—to create or recreate—those stars; it could scarcely afford to reach, let alone "address" black audiences across the nation. And, aside from *Swing!*, earlier Micheaux products had worked to alienate at least some segments of their "natural" (i.e., reversed—black) audience. Each of these add to the mimic echo sounded by *Swing!* Consequently, in terms defined by the dominant institutions of American cinema—Hollywood, the studios, the MPPDA—and very likely in terms defined by "its" audience, *Swing!* was bound to be a deformation. What remains to be seen is whether the texts, and specifically the narratives, of either *The Duke is Tops* or *Swing!* recognize, in the precise terms of genre theory, that the musical is the form they are mastering and deforming.

Mastery and Deformation of Generic Narrative Form

According to Rick Altman, what defines the American film musical as a genre is not just the presence of music; rather, the defining characteristic of the genre is that its narratives contain a "dual focus," crystalized in an antagonistic heterosexual couple, that is reconciled, unified, or integrated through and in musical performance. The purpose of such narratives is the ritual, symbolic easing of contradictory beliefs and pressures implicit in American society.[35] Any number of contextual pieces of information suggest that *The Duke is Tops* and *Swing!* were meant to be musicals as well as race films (though, as I have shown, the two films are differently invested in these categories), but are their narratives members of the musical genre as it would have been widely understood in the late thirties?[36]

The Duke is Tops and *Swing!* are both set in the backstage or professional milieu of show business—specifically, the business of creating black-cast musical revues—and contain in their narratives motivated musical performance as well as "realistic" acting. More importantly for strict generic considerations, though, both films focus on heterosexual couples and pattern their stories on separation and "remarriage." Further, *The Duke is Tops* and *Swing!* each amplify the divisive duality of their couples with other thematic dualisms of country/South and city/North, of rural and urban communities of address, and of competing rural and urban social values. These explicit divisions are further complicated by the implicit division of black/Harlem and white/Broadway. Three questions will focus my close readings of the narratives of *The Duke is Tops* and *Swing!:* To what extent can these films envision the reconciliation of their dualisms? Are their reconciliations total and totalizing or partial? What roles do musical performances play in (attempted or achieved) reconciliations? And, finally, how does the (differently) implied racial address of *The Duke is Tops* and *Swing!* intersect with and inflect codes and patterns of the musical genre they both claim?

The Duke is Tops was summarized this way by *Variety:* "Story of a girl-boy producer-performer team having to split up when gal gets a N.Y. break. Boy goes down, gal goes up, and then sags. Get together for finale, when combined efforts put them into the big time."[37] However, this excessively obvious, generic, dual focus story bears elaboration. *The Duke is Tops* opens with the "Sepia Scandals," an all-black revue, arriving for a two-week engagement in a small, seemingly all-black town somewhere in the "sticks." The show is written, produced, and directed by Duke Davis (Ralph Cooper) and stars Ethel Andrews (Lena Horne), Duke's fiancée. On its opening night, "Sepia Scandals" is a terrific success. During this performance a New York talent agent (Monte Hawley) discovers Ethel and offers her, through Duke, a chance at larger success. Duke conveys the message, but Ethel rejects the offer, refusing to leave Duke. As the run of "Sepia Scandals" closes, Duke pretends to have sold Ethel's contract to the New Yorker, and devastated, she leaves for the city.

At this point the film's narrative strategy becomes explicitly parallel, shifting between the male and female leads. Duke's theater career fails without Ethel. He becomes a busker with the down-and-out medicine show of his friend, Dr. Dorando (Lawrence Criner), and soon transforms the medicine show into a sensation by adding musical performance to selling elixir. Occasionally intercut with this narrative line are scenes of Ethel's success and, then, stagnation. The evening of Duke's biggest success (measured by the money he and Dorando count) coincides with the cancellation of Ethel's New York show, a fact Duke learns through a radio broadcast. Duke leaves the medicine show and joins Ethel in the city—just moments after she has learned the truth about Duke's pretense of selling her contract. In an extended coda, we see an all-black musical revue—"Music Is Medicine"—performed in a nightclub for a black audience. Dorando is the show's MC, Duke its bandleader and male

45. The conventional finale, with Duke (Ralph Cooper) and Ethel (Lena Horne) kissing, in *The Duke is Tops.*

vocalist, and Ethel its female star. For her performance, Ethel reprises her hit from "Sepia Scandals," a ballad entitled "You Remember." The final image—a close-up—is a fade on a lingering, onstage kiss shared by Duke and Ethel during the curtain call.

Swing! begins in Birmingham with Mandy Jenkins (Cora Green) awakening to face another day of cooking for a (never-seen) white household. Her husband, Cornell (Larry Seymour), a flashy, undependable piano player, is having an affair with Eloise Hawkins (Hazel Diaz), the pampered wife of a violently jealous, middle-class train engineer, Lem Hawkins (Alec Lovejoy).[38] Alerted to Cornell's infidelity by a neighbor, Mandy confronts her husband and Eloise as they dance at a nightclub. The scene fades as Mandy makes good her threats to beat up Eloise.

After the fade, an intertitle informs us that we are now in "New York— many months later [at] a rehearsal." Mr. Gregory (Carmen Newsome), aided by his assistant, Lena (Dorothy Van Eagle), is staging an all-black musical revue, intending to bring it to Broadway. According to Gregory, the difference between his revue and all the others that have come before it is that his revue will be not only 100 percent black-created but also 100 percent black financed. Cora Smith (doubled by Hazel Diaz)— the show's "blues singer and mammy lead"—is causing trouble, however, with her tardiness and drinking. Mandy arrives on the scene at this point, and Lena, who is an old family friend from Birmingham, secures Mandy the job of wardrobe mistress for the show.

In rapid succession, Mandy—with Lena's help—finishes the costumes on time; Gregory and Lena declare their love; Cora is assaulted under the guise of discipline by her boyfriend, Big Jones (doubled by Alec Love-joy), gets drunk, and falls down a set of stairs, breaking her leg; Mandy announces she is quitting her position to help Cornell, who has sought her out, but at Lena's urging Mandy instead steps into Cora's role, with Cornell as her accompanist; a white theater owner agrees to back the show; Mandy is a hit; Cornell sweet-talks Mandy out of some of her money; Lena threatens Cornell with severe harm if he hurts Mandy; and the movie ends with the embrace of the happy lovers—Lena and Mr. Gregory.

The Duke is Tops concentrates its narrative energy on the explication of one couples' separation and reunion. In its course, the film conscientiously eliminates potential competing or complementary couplings: Sam (Charlie Hawkins), the stage manager for "Sepia Scandals" and Ella, Ethel's dresser (Neva Peoples), seem to be a potential couple early in the film, but they are separated by the sundering of Duke and Ethel, and Sam disappears from the narrative. The medicine show sidekicks, Joe and Dippy (Johnny Taylor and Ray Martin), form a comic duo but are left behind when Duke goes to New York. Bracketing for a moment the odd vestigial "remainder" of Dr. Dorando in the "Music is Medicine" revue, the only couple left at the conclusion of *The Duke is Tops* is the original one of Duke and Ethel.

In contradistinction to the clarity of the limited coupling in *The Duke is Tops, Swing!* offers a continuum of possible relationships, ranging from the successful coupling of Lena and Gregory through the tenuous (re)coupling of Mandy and Cornell, to the abusive couplings of Eloise and Lem, and Cora and Big Jones. *The Duke is Tops* tightly closes its narrative with the remarriage of Duke and Ethel corresponding precisely to the success of "Music Is Medicine." *Swing!,* on the other hand, qualifies the remarriage of Mandy and Cornell by counterbalancing it with Eloise and Lem and Cora and Big Jones, and it qualifies the success of its show by motivating Mandy's rise to stardom through the (literal) fall of Cora. (Arguably, the film focuses attention on the negative end of its continuum of relationships by having Hazel Diaz play both Eloise and Cora and Alec Lovejoy play both Lem and Big Jones and by refusing to make clear whether Eloise *is* Cora and Lem *is* Big Jones.[39]) Furthermore, despite the fact that Cornell is supposed to accompany Mandy in her star vocal turn, he never does—their remarriage is not *staged.* And at its conclusion the film displaces the remarriage of Mandy and Cornell onto the marriage—the final kiss—of Lena and Ted Gregory. *Swing!* contains no grand coupling and only partial reconciliation.

The Duke is Tops performs a masterful version of a strict, classic musical narrative. *Swing!,* in its promiscuity, its excess of diverse couples and obvious affiliations with melodrama, is a blatant deformation, a narrative that seems to try to become a musical out of desperation. Does this mean that mastery simply becomes reversal, recoloring Hollywood? Does it mean that deformation lapses into incomprehensibility? Does this mean *The Duke is Tops* is simply a film of reversal, a "pale" (in Daniel Leab's terms, referring to the skin-tones of the stars) copy of a Hollywood musical? Or to return to Houston Baker's terminology and his redemptive reading of Booker T. Washington's *Up From Slavery,* can "deformation" be found resonating beneath *The Duke*'s masterfully imitative "mask"? Conversely, is *Swing!*'s deformation simply a "failure," or does it bear traces of systems of mastery like those Baker finds in Du Bois's deformative *The Souls of Black Folk?*

Baker implies that African American mastery of (white) form is always a mask and suggests that the mask hides what is, in fact, a deformation. If the generic mastery of *The Duke is Tops* is a mask, then the search for that transformative mask must cover the film's visual strategy, its themes of memory and ownership, its narrative excess (embodied by Dr. Dorando), and its reflexive relation to entertainment.

Jane Feuer has described the standard series of shots in Hollywood backstage musicals, which progress from showing the diegetic audience to aligning the film viewer with that audiences' gaze as a "conservative" reflexivity, a move that firmly secures the film viewer's alignment with the (conservative, utopian, reconciliatory) ideology of the musical text rather than one that reveals the spectacle by distancing the viewer.[40] Gerald Mast notes the difficulty *Stormy Weather* (1943, Twentieth Century-Fox), an all-black Hollywood backstage musical, confronts in applying this standard musical genre technique: "In the theaters where black acts perform, the camera deliberately avoids that previously unavoidable image of backstage musicals—shots of the audience enjoying the show, to remind us that we are in a theater and the show is a success. To photograph a theater audience would expose a problem that the film is trying to hide from its own audience, black or white. Is this show produced for a white audience? . . . Is it produced for a black audience? . . . Is it produced for a fully integrated audience? (No such audience exists in 1943, not even in New York.)" [41]

Unlike *Stormy Weather,* the narration of *The Duke is Tops,* using cutting, framing, and camera movement, privileges the viewer to both backstage and audience perspectives. Every number in the film uses this suturing technique, but the opening sequence, showing the opening night of "Sepia Scandals," is most explicit, showing the all-black audience filling the theater, the all-black pit band tuning up, the all-black cast peeking through the curtain to determine the size of the crowd, and, finally, when the show begins, uniting all these groups—and the film spectator—in the performance and appreciation of the musical numbers.

This conventional visual reflexivity in *The Duke is Tops* cannot escape being generic, but it does not follow that it must be considered simply conservative—or conservative in only the "Hollywood" sense. *The Duke is Tops,* through its use of a well established Hollywood musical genre technique, combines the display of performers—stars—with the gaze of an audience to structure a stable "world." And what makes this world exceptional, by American film standards, is that it is peopled wholly by African Americans. The world of *The Duke is Tops* refers to the defunct all-black TOBA vaudeville circuit and other African American venues, and inscribes an alternative, other history of American musical entertainment.[42] Through this history, *The Duke is Tops* makes a more deformative maneuver. Baker suggests that, by unequivocally asserting in the very title of *The Souls of Black Folk* that African Americans have souls, W. E. B. Du Bois was courting outrage.[43] *The Duke is Tops* more quietly recognizes, celebrates, *conserves,* and seeks to extend the gaze of black folk.

Ethel Andrews's theme song, indeed the musical "theme" of *The Duke is Tops,* is a love ballad entitled "You Remember." She sings it early in the film, during the "Sepia Scandals," and reprises it to conclude "Music Is Medicine." While this is never explicit, the story implies that Duke wrote this song, and he uses the title words frequently as shorthand for saying something like, "because of all our mutual experiences you know how I feel about you." Alone, this is unremarkable, revealing and reinforcing as it does Duke's and Ethel's love, but this "memory" of an equal partnership is overwhelmed by a deeper "race" memory of slavery when Duke lies to force Ethel to leave him. Duke tries to couch his efforts in terms of commerce, but Ethel translates Duke's terms into terms of ownership.

When Ella suggests, after Ethel's New York career fails, that she rejoin Duke, Ethel retorts, "You're forgetting a little matter of the five thousand dollars he sold me for." The narrative makes clear Duke's innocence, but it also makes clear (through a seemingly sage adviser) that to force Ethel to leave him, Duke must "cut deep," and pretending to treat Ethel as chattel serves that purpose.

When Duke leaves the "sticks" after hearing of Ethel's New York failure, he leaves Dr. Dorando—his colleague for a year the dialogue informs us—muttering, "from pinnacle to pit . . . bottomless pit . . . that's me." It seems that Duke is again breaking up another team, though through less duplicitous, hurtful means. So, when Dorando returns to introduce "Music Is Medicine," *The Duke is Tops* amplifies its theme of memory as loyalty, effects the homosocial remarriage of Duke and Dorando, and expands Ethel's and Duke's community of two, suggesting that a simple marriage is not enough to guarantee success. However, Dorando's mute presence (he says nothing after his introductory speech but he remains visible onstage throughout) also reminds the viewer of those who have been left behind in this exercise in community (re)formation.

Dorando's presence also motivates the new revue's title and *The Duke's* critique of entertainment. "Music Is Medicine," already carrying both populist and Marxist rhetorical overtones, is an equation that *The Duke is Tops* allows the viewer to extend thus: music = medicine = Dorando's elixir = quackery—the opiate of the masses. This equation can be read in more generous ways (for instance, the elixir could represent the spectatorial souvenir of a good night out), but, no matter what, the existence of such an equation reminds the viewer of the various communities of taste *The Duke is Tops* presents: the genteel small town theater audience that approves of "Sepia Scandals" and rejects Duke's post-Ethel show, the alternately gullible and vicious country rubes who attend the medicine show, and the fickle urban sophisticates who first accept, then reject, then accept Ethel. Only Duke's varied experiences cross all these communities, and the prospect of uniting them in any but the most temporary, illusory way seems impossible. Looked at less generously, *The Duke is Tops* becomes a critical (perhaps even cynical) text, mastering a sophisticated array of techniques to create a facade of cheery community but, unlike its Hollywood counterparts, not allowing its viewer to forget that, even as he or she consumes entertainment he or she is participating in a deformative ritual, a community-rending rip-off.

While *Swing!* is a deformation of generic musical form, it is important to note that it is also obsessed with mastery—both as white racial mastery of the social, cultural, and economic spheres and as embodied by exemplars of the musical form. Instead of beginning with a love song predicting the overdetermined heterosexual dualism of the musical, *Swing!* starts by acknowledging another set of determining relationships. As the film begins Mandy is being awakened by an alarm clock; she grabs the clock and prepares to hurl it against the wall but catches herself, saying, "No, that won't do no good. It ain't the clock's fault. I might as well get up from here and go cook those white folks some breakfast." Before we know anything else about Mandy, then, we know she cooks for white people, and it is this relationship—triply determined by race, class, and gender—that becomes the structuring paradigm for *Swing!* As the narrative proceeds, the absent presence of white people repeatedly impinges on the characters in this film, always aligned with issues of employment. For instance, Cornell hides his affair by telling Mandy he is selling cars for a white man, and Lena explains to an astonished Mandy that black women can get professional jobs in New York, just like white women.

What the viewer discovers, though, is that even in New York racism is a damaging (and often internalized) force. Mr. Gregory, the producer of the revue being rehearsed in *Swing!,* follows the pattern set by his forebears in the early thirties Warner Bros. backstage musicals (e.g., *42nd Street* [1933]) and rallies his company with a speech:

> "I hope you like it folks, but these are only rehearsals. I want you to remember that. If we were to fall in love with our own efforts, often we work so hard for the first night that the heart is taken out of everybody by the bad press notices we get the morning after. Now, we don't want that to happen to our show. You know and I know that while a colored show may be and is supposed to stay within a certain prescribed scope, we must if we hope to get anywhere deliver something within that scope that the public will like and come to see [a discontinuity in the print interrupts this speech here] that is entirely different from what an audience has become accustomed to seeing and hearing. That, my people, is what I hope we're giving them. So I want all of you to do your best. Unbend, relax, give me all that's in you, but don't—oh, please don't—begin thinking how good you are and all that. Just hope you're fair and just give me a show that will get over and the public will like and come to see."

Several things are notable about this speech. First, its placement. Unlike similar speeches in Hollywood musicals, which tend to come just before opening night, Gregory's talk precedes even the securing of a theater and thus stresses the fragility of the entire project. Second, while the language of these generic speeches, especially in the Warner Bros. musicals, tends to be tough and sometimes even despairing, the language here is, to say the least, difficult and contradictory: The "colored" show must work within a prescribed scope, and it must be great within that scope while not exceeding it. This implies a type of implosion—a full, even excessive, inhabitation of a prescribed position, a stereotype, which hopes to use that position for escape even while recognizing the probable futility and the definite frustration of such hope. While in the Hollywood musical the performers may have to fight creditors, competitors, and critical audiences, there is always a sense that the "enemy" without can be conquered by energy from within. In *Swing!* the best a black performer can hope to do is mollify critical (white) forces by delivering a standard product that somehow at the same time transcends the standard.

Gregory's masterful program is based on a knowledge of African American entertainment and economic history. After Cora has broken her leg and it appears that the show will close before it has a chance to open, Gregory says to Lena: "I'll hear it now from all sides. They said I couldn't do it. Of all the colored shows that have ever gone by the boards, no Negro has ever produced one. From Williams and Walker to *Green Pastures,* they've all been sponsored by white men. No Negro's ever been in on the money, or the profits." Gregory's remark recalls Loren Miller's thoughts on the (New) Negro in Hollywood; he knows that "[t]he Negro's place on stage and screen has been fixed for so many years that the tradition sways the judgement of Negroes themselves and honest whites."[44] While it is never made explicit, *Swing!* holds out the hope that Gregory, seemingly with the awareness of the New Negro, and Lena, seemingly a New Woman *and* a New Negro, might turn profits generated through mastery of form into a deformative display.

Ultimately, the reflexivity of *Swing!* regarding show business and race, along with the viewer's best hopes and worst fears, combine at the moment of success—also the moment of full white presence—in *Swing!* Without any explanation and in seeming contradiction of his earlier claims, Gregory enlists the aid of a white backer. Here is the speech the backer delivers to Gregory and Lena:

> "Now you've worked hard; all producers do that. And you've got a fair show, but . . . it's just another colored show. It'll last about as long on Broadway as the average one that's been brought down from Harlem has been lasting. But you've got one spot that is a constellation, and that one spot is the new woman you just rushed in at the last minute, Mandy Jenkins. She is the most original and versatile person I've ever seen. With her in a long term contract, you've got the biggest colored possibility since Williams and Walker, and it's because of her and the spot she is in the show that I am ready and willing to open on Broadway without an out-of-town tryout. And to show you how much I think of it, I am ready and willing to assume all financial obligations of the show from now on and lay in your hands a check for ten thousand dollars advance on your share—and the check can be certified. I'll use the fifty square feet over my theater for the biggest electric sign on Broadway. My only stipulation is that the name of the show be changed to . . . [here the backer assumes a voice and posture redolent of Al Jolson] Mandy Jenkins in 'Ah Lub's Dat Man'."

The film immediately confirms that this deal has been struck by dissolving from the backer to a close-up of the cover of a theater program, which reads:

> Swingland Cafe
> Two Weeks Only, before
> Grand Opening on
> Broadway
> "Mandy Jenkins"
> Original sensation
> "fum Bumin'ham"
> in
> "Ah Lub's
> Dat Man".

Mandy is a hit, so this show is a success. But this success costs internal proscription and affirms the external, social terms for this internal condition, as symbolized by the authority behind the backer's "generosity" and his offensive naming, his insistent minstrelization, of the show.

The songs that Mandy sings to bracket this white intervention illuminate the conundrum of deformation and mastery *Swing!* explores. The first, before the backer appears, is a cover of the Andrews Sister hit, "Bei

46. "Ah Lub's Dat Man" program.

Mir Bist Du Schöen," which was drawn from a Yiddish theater musical. Mandy slows the song down and "blues" it a bit (though there is certainly melisma and pitch sliding in the Andrews Sisters' version too), making the yearning aspect of this love song—the desire to communicate perfectly—the main point:

> I could say bella, bella, even say wunderbar
> Each language only helps me tell you how grand you are
> I've tried to explain, bei mir bist du schöen
> So kiss me, and say you understand.[45]

When the Andrews Sisters sing the song, understanding seems assured; when Mandy sings it, it seems much less certain. To underscore this fragility, Mandy's final song, and the only one we hear from "Ah Lub's Dat Man," is a slow Tin Pan Alley-type tune, "Heaven Help This Heart of Mine (Handle It With Care)."[46] Like all the numbers in *Swing!*, this one is shot simply in a single take, which has the effect of making Mandy's isolation and vulnerability—from the whole concatenation of social, cultural, and personal forces the film has examined—all the more palpable. After her number, Mandy retires to her dressing room, where Cornell rubs her feet and at the same time relieves her of some of her money and prepares to leave. Lena catches him and offers this as the film's remarkable final speech: "Shame on you, taking her money. She loves you, and you ought to be good to her. Because if you're not / I'll have you put on the spot / and taken for a ride / and shot / through the head." Perhaps sensing that the deformation here—the display of unresolved gender and class, as well as larger racial problems—is getting untenable for his chosen form of the musical film, Micheaux has Ted Gregory arrive for a conventional embrace for the finale, but it hardly erases the succession of performances that have led up to it.

According to Houston Baker, "the mask mandates [that] to be a *Negro* one must meld with minstrelsy's contours."[47] For the mask to work, however, this masking must be complete; it cannot let the master—the white—see the mask he has mandated. At *Swing!*'s most deformative moment, it shows this mandate. Unlike, say, *Hallelujah!* or *The Duke is Tops, Swing!* does not create a masterful mimicking of a white world while leaving whiteness out; rather, it continually points to the reality of "race" and, finally, reveals it as the vortex of a constant cycle of mastery and deformation distilled into the presence of a single, representative white man. In delineating the musical genre, Rick Altman claims that even the "color-blind" spectator will see the structuring prominence of the couple in the musical,[48] but, while couples *are* prominent in *Swing!*, they cannot account for this film's deformed—"failed"—musical narrative structure the way that "color" can.

6

Jammin' the Blues

THE SIGHT OF JAZZ, 1944

Music is heard and seldom seen.
—RALPH ELLISON (1952)

W. H. Auden says of music . . . that it "can be made anywhere, is invisible, and does not smell." But music is made
by men who are insistently visible, especially, as in jazz,
when the players *are* their music.
—NAT HENTOFF (1961)

Last year some twit in a British jazz rag proclaimed that
music has never been a particularly visual medium. . . .
What music has this motherfucker been looking at?
—GREG TATE (1992)

In his column in the July 1944 issue of *Esquire,* Leonard Feather, critic,
impresario, and sometime composer of modernist jazz, asked an eclectic
group of jazz musicians and aficionados, "If you had a million dollars to
spend on jazz, how would you use it?" Sam Donahue, "Musician Third
Class, U. S. Navy; tenor saxman, trumpeter and leader of the Navy band,"
answered this way:

"Well, I'd like to make an educational film, debunking the average movie
musical. I'd tear down the studios' haphazard method of sloughing off good
music. Instead of having some chick bursting into song somewhere in the
middle of a forest, accompanied by an invisible fifty piece band from out
of space, I'd work the music in logically and give the musicians a break. If I
could get Duke Ellington or any great colored band, I'd fix it so you could
really see the band and get to know it, instead of covering it up with a lot
of jitterbug dancing and stuff.

". . . I'd have all the recording done simultaneously with the shooting of the pictures, instead of having it dubbed in separately the way they do now. That would help make the music real and spontaneous. Listen, after I got that movie on the market, all the musicals after that would just *have* to be legitimate!"[1]

Clearly Donahue was aware of the conventions for representing musical performance in Hollywood musicals. He was also aware that those conventions depended on and played with the audiovisual split made possible by sound film's dual recording technologies. Further, he understood that these conventions and the technologies they drew on had racial-political implications. Hearing jazz, Donahue's comments suggest, was only part of the experience of jazz; "really see[ing] the band and get[ting] to know it" was another. But, especially if the band was "colored," really seeing and getting to know it was an experience that Hollywood conventionally denied its customers. Donahue felt confident that altering these conventions and letting audiences see as well as hear the music, no matter what color, would be "educational."

In August and September 1944 the recording and photographing were done at Warner Bros. studios for *Jammin' the Blues,* a ten-minute musical short that seems nearly, if imperfectly, built on Donahue's "debunking" model. Produced and distributed by Warner Bros., *Jammin' the Blues* was created by a group of people whose relationships with Hollywood were either unusual or nonexistent. It was directed by Gjon Mili, a *Life* photographer, coordinated by Norman Granz, an apprentice film editor who was also a jazz fan just starting a career as an activist entrepreneur, and it featured performances by jazz musicians of varying degrees of fame: Lester Young, Red Callender, Harry Edison, Marlowe Morris, Sid Catlett, Barney Kessel, Jo Jones, John Simmons, Illinois Jacquet, and Marie Bryant. *Jammin' the Blues* was what would later be labelled a consummate "crossover" product. It combined small group "hot jazz" and "art" photography, inserted them into the mechanisms and forms of Hollywood, and distributed the results to theaters everywhere.

Most shorts came and went without much notice, but after it was released late in December 1944, *Jammin' the Blues* attracted positive reviews from *Time, Life, Esquire, Theatre Arts, down beat,* the *Chicago Defender,* and *Ebony.* Walter Winchell acclaimed it on his radio show and James Agee gave it an equivocal, though finally negative, review in *The Nation.*[2]

It was also nominated for an Academy Award in the one reel short-subject category. In other words, the Hollywood industry establishment, the mainstream press, and a variety of specialty presses all found *Jammin' the Blues* worthy of special note.

If he was paying attention, Sam Donahue must have been pleased; a version of his proposed education and legitimation project seemed to be working. But very quickly his satisfaction would have turned to disappointment. *Jammin' the Blues* may have crossed over, but it did not start any trends. Hollywood musicals, whether feature-length or short, did not become any more "legitimate" from the jazz fan's or player's perspective after *Jammin' the Blues* than they had been before it. Instead, *Jammin' the Blues* passed into jazz lore as an anomaly: "one of the few honest motion pictures about jazz," "a landmark," "probably the most famous jazz movie of all," and "the greatest film to depict jazz musicians in their natural habitat."[3]

Why was *Jammin' the Blues* so successful as an individual film and so unsuccessful in inspiring similar films? This chapter will analyze *Jammin' the Blues* within the multiple, overlapping contexts of its production and reception in the midforties: the jazz scene, Hollywood, and the audiovisual politics of representating race in the arena of American culture. *Jammin' the Blues* provides a unique, densely encoded site for exploring the connections music—and particularly jazz—was thought to provide between hearing, seeing, and "getting to know" other Americans. It provides an opportunity to explore the relations of peripheral and central, repressed and ascendent discourses, discourses about Hollywood film, jazz, entertainment, art, race, and American culture—discourses that standard Hollywood practice worked to control and hold separate but that *Jammin' the Blues* shows sometimes overlapped, sometimes competed, and often were contradictory. Finally, *Jammin' the Blues,* when considered in this context, reveals the possibilities and limits of "education" and "legitimation" through crossover products, products in which the sight of music becomes the object of industrial mechanisms and forms.

Looking at Jazz before *Jammin' the Blues*

What music looks like relates crucially to how it sounds and what it can mean. Whether viewed in performance, depicted on the cover of a score or record, or suggested by program notes or the words of a radio announcer, the "look" of music influences how listeners categorize what they hear: Is it "art" or "commercial claptrap"? Is it music or noise? What is its relation to me, to us? Music's look helps define and answer questions like these.

In the United States especially, a key determinant of the look of any music has long been the race—the "color"—of the musicians who play it. A legal and social construction, built on a physical trait, color suggests where a music comes from, who it "belongs" to, and who its "natural" consumers are. At the same time, and especially in the ages of mechanical and electronic reproduction, music can seem to float free of its players; through imitation, notation, recording, broadcasting, and marketing, music can separate from "colored" social bodies.[4] Music arises out of the material circumstances of the people who make it and can work profound changes in those circumstances, yet music—most oddly, recorded music, "music as a thing"[5]—seems immaterial, audible but invisible. It is intimately bound to the cultures color represents in the United States and, at the same time, easily appropriable, deracinated, dis/colored.[6]

This dynamic makes music an especially complex cultural expression and an especially charged intercultural terrain. In the United States, it has resulted in what Andrew Ross has described as a "long transactional history of white responses to black culture, of black counter-responses, and of further and often traceless negotiations, tradings, raids, and compromises," not to mention "thefts,"[7] and has made music the site of intense scrutiny of and anxiety about color. Consequently, music has become a multifaceted symbol—and a debating ground—for how color is defined and represented, where it belongs in and how it affects U.S. society and culture. Control of the visible in and around music, in all its forms, has become a critical issue.

Jazz was the first indigenous, (semi-)vernacular music in the United States to wrestle with representing, visually and aurally, its "origins" and its transactional quality. It generated scenes, groups of like-minded musicians, critics, impresarios, and fans, which developed discourses for debating competing (though often contiguous) visions of the music, for clarifying views of jazz history, and for struggling with the music's value and status: Was the music black, white, or "mixed," and what would it mean to call a music "colored"? How "transactional" was its history? Was it art or entertainment? Unique, live experience or mass, recorded object? These discourses welded the aesthetic to the political and the cultural to the social across the sound and sight of the music and, in the process, influenced the way jazz was seen and heard—and how color was perceived—in the United States.

When *Jammin' the Blues* was created late in 1944, jazz and its discourses were undergoing profound shifts.[8] The end of the big-band swing era was at hand, and its replacement, small-group bebop, was percolating "underground" (in Harlem), soon to surface. Mediated by the phenomenon of "hot jazz," a small-group genre that was itself split between "Dixieland" traditionalists and swing-inflected "modernism," the shift from swing to bop marked a change in jazz from a mainstream popular music to an explicit "art" music, which was (at least initially) assertively black and (at least nascently) cultural-nationalist. In *Blues People,* Amiri Baraka told the story this way: "Philosophically, [late-]swing sought to involve the black culture in a platonic social blandness that would erase it forever, replacing it with the socio-cultural compromise of the 'jazzed-up' popular song."[9] In Baraka's account, "[t]he willfully harsh, *anti-assimilationist* sound of bebop" was the reaction to this malaise.[10] It was also, as Eric Lott has noted, the music of "a moment . . . in which unpaid historical bills were falling due."[11] According to Lott, the consequent African American "militancy and music were undergirded by the same social facts; the music attempted to resolve at the level of style what the militancy combated in the streets."[12]

A considerable component of bebop's "politics of style" was visual and stemmed, Baraka argues, from "young Negro[es]" realizing that color was irreducible, "that merely by being a Negro in America, one *was* a nonconformist."[13] Still, while bebop could react against swing, it could not entirely escape (white) swing's "involvement of black culture." Swing was wildly popular, tremendously "commercial," yet some of its most successful proponents—most notably the Benny Goodman band—had used their success to gradually alter the racialized, segregated look of jazz. This process influenced jazz discourse in general during the swing era and directly involved many of the people who collaborated to make

Jammin' the Blues. Before analyzing *Jammin' the Blues* and its representation of jazz at the transition from swing to bop, it is worth detailing
the development of the look of swing, especially insofar as that look was
figured as both interracial and "artistic."

Writing in the summer of 1945, the blues poet and scholar Sterling A.
Brown revealed how high the stakes of the look of jazz were and how
complex that look could be in a racist, industrial culture:

> Of all the arts, jazz music is probably the most democratic. Mixed units
> of Negroes and whites have recorded for well over a decade, and most of
> their records are jazz classics. . . . The mixed band meets up with difficulties,
> especially in the South. But completely democratic are the jam sessions,
> both public and private, where Negro and white musicians meet as equals
> to improvise collectively and create the kind of music they love. Here the
> performer's color does not matter; the quality of the music he makes is the
> basis for comradery and respect.[14]

For Brown, visible racial mixing on the bandstand best indicated the
democratic quality of jazz. At the utopian moment of the jam session,
the performer's color does not matter—and, at the same time, it matters entirely. Jazz is democratic because it mixes races and because that
mixing makes no difference. In Brown's vision, because music is simultaneously colored and colorless, it can become a "gift" (W. E. B. Du Bois's
word) given back and forth between cultures, binding them, assuring the
humanity of all parties to the exchange, and ultimately leading to a truly
shared culture where each contribution is acknowledged by all. Brown
is not explicit, but he seems to believe such cultural democracy will lead
to social democracy: The attraction of the sound of colored people leads
to an acceptance of their sight—an acceptance of *them*.

For all the utopian qualities of his vision of jazz democracy, however,
Brown was also a pragmatist. He recognized his vision as a vision—as
specifically reliant on the visible aspects of the music—and recognized
the less-than-utopian circumstances that affected the dissemination of
jam-session democracy. On the one hand, Brown argues, despite the excellence of the sound, some people will resist the sight of mixed jazz. On
the other hand, others will be distanced from this sight by the mediation of private, consumer objects: records shorn of visible information
to become commodified "classics."[15] The tension between performance,
which forcefully connects sight and sound but which is relatively exclu-

sive and can lead to "difficulties," and recording, which shears sight from sound but is relatively available and safe, is a genuine one. Though Brown chose not to address them, the other major music media—radio, print, and film—complicated his categories. Radio gave "live" sound but no sight. Print could provide sight but no sound. Film could reconnect sight with sound and could be distributed as widely as the other media, but, as Sam Donahue pointed out in the quotation that began this chapter, the reconnection of sight to sound in film was not innocent or transparent. Together all of these media, including a wide variety of performance situations, formed the territory for the segregated look of swing, and the people dedicated to changing that look to reflect something like Brown's vision carefully exploited each medium's unique qualities.

Precisely because they did not make the "mix" visible, records were the initial step toward institutionalizing mixing in swing.[16] In 1933, the independently wealthy record producer, critic, and social activist John Hammond, set up his first recording dates with Benny Goodman, then a well respected freelance musician. According to Hammond's autobiography, "the most effective and constructive form of social protest" he could think of was "to bring recognition to the Negro's supremacy in jazz."[17] Consequently, he wanted Goodman to record with a mixed band. Hammond recalls Goodman responding: "If it gets around that I recorded with colored guys, I won't get another job in this town."[18]

Hammond acquiesced to Goodman's fears, which he felt were well founded, but after producing enough successful records in the depression-stunted market, Hammond collected the power in the industry to arrange mixed sessions, including dates with Goodman backing Billie Holiday and Ethel Waters and playing with pianist Teddy Wilson and saxophonist Coleman Hawkins. (That one of Hammond's mixed sessions was released under the imprimatur of "The Chocolate Dandies" indicates the vestigial power of the visible in sound recording. From a present-day perspective this naming may seem "ironic,"[19] but in 1933 it had multiple, nonironic purposes: it invoked what Theodor W. Adorno derided as "'black jazz' as a sort of brand-name" and avoided the possibility of invoking anxiety about cultural miscegenation.[20])

In mid-1934, Goodman formed the first version of the big band that would eventually make him famous; its personnel were white, but much of its music was charted by the black arrangers Fletcher Henderson, Edgar Sampson, and Jimmy Mundy. Arrangers, like the personnel for a recording, may place their indelible stamp on a piece of music, but they are invisible. A year later, at a private jam session that might have defined Sterling Brown's vision of a jazz democracy, Goodman got reacquainted with Teddy Wilson, and in July 1935 the mixed Goodman trio cut its first records.

When the Goodman band took its first big step toward stardom, selling out the Palomar Ballroom in Los Angeles for two months in the late summer of 1935, the trio still existed only as a recording unit, never seen in public. It took another year for Goodman to make it visible. The next spring, Goodman and his drummer Gene Krupa (the third member of the trio) sat in with the Fletcher Henderson Orchestra at a "tea dance" held at the Congress Hotel in Chicago by the Rhythm Club, a group of white, socialite jazz fans. It marked, Goodman thought, "the first time, probably, that white and colored musicians played together for a paying audience in America."[21] The Rhythm Club booked the Goodman band for a similar show late in 1936, and under some pressure from the club's promoters, Goodman included the trio on the bill. No one complained about the mixing onstage and the show was a success. Thereafter, the trio was a regular fixture of Goodman's show, live and on the radio, and it was later expanded to a quartet by including Lionel Hampton.

The trio and quartet, however, were special instances. They played separately from the band as a discrete part of the show. In a 1937 photo essay on the Goodman band, *Life* used the caption for a photograph of Wilson to explain: "Negro pianist Teddy Wilson has many a White admirer. Because mixed bands are not the rule in New York, Wilson is not the regular pianist but steps up twice during each evening to play in a mixed quartet."[22] Furthermore, Wilson had been handpicked—"discovered"—by John Hammond because, in addition to being a great pianist, he was easy for whites to accept. Wilson was from a middle-class background and, in Hammond's estimation, "had the bearing, demeanor, and attitude toward life which would enable him to survive in a white society. . . . He not only had the talent to make it in any surroundings, but the mental and emotional equipment to do so."[23] These qualities, along with his restrained, graceful, and highly polished piano style, made Wilson a perfect match for Goodman's professorial bearing and precise playing and a perfect foil for Gene Krupa's flamboyance. As the 1937 *Life* pictures show, when Hampton, an energetic vibraphone player, joined to make the quartet, the visual "mix" was racially and attitudi-nally balanced: two exhibitionist percussionists, one white and one black, and two introspective melodists, one white and one black, all making beautiful music together—under carefully controlled and contained cir-cumstances that bent but did not entirely break "the rule" of common experience and expectation.

By the end of 1937 the Goodman band, including the trio and quartet, was nationally famous. All its units had made large-selling, critically re-spected records, had been featured regularly on the radio, and had been widely written about. The band had been in several movies, and the quar-tet had been in one, *Hollywood Hotel* (1938). It had toured the country, in-cluding the South, and encountered very little "unpleasantness" because of its racial mix.[24] At this point, the Goodman outfit—a small industry of its own—did three things simultaneously to further alter the look of jazz: It (1) mixed the full band (2) for a Carnegie Hall concert program that (3) responded explicitly to the transactional history of the music. According to Irving Kolodin, the impulse for the concert was explicitly historical: "the 'King of Jazz' in the previous decade (Paul Whiteman) had done it; why not the 'King of Swing' in the present (1930) one?"[25] It was implicitly racial-political.

Whiteman, who was still popular in the late thirties, had risen to fame in the twenties as the major proponent of "sweet" or "symphonic" jazz. Though he did use several black arrangers, his bands never in-cluded black players.[26] Further, his public, visual presentations consis-tently erased the African American contribution to jazz. His famous Aeolian Hall and Carnegie Hall concerts in 1924 began with a brief his-tory, "The True Form of Jazz," that burlesqued early jazz by making fun of the Original Dixieland Jazz Band, a white group from the teens, and ended with the premiere of Gershwin's *Rhapsody in Blue.* His autobiog-raphy begins with the sentence, "Jazz came to America three hundred years ago in chains" but beyond the first chapter makes no mention of African Americans and contains an illustration titled "Everybody Every-where" that shows jazz being created by tiny Whiteman figures in cos-tumes from Spain, Great Britain, Germany, France, and India![27] In his 1930 film, *King of Jazz,* an animated section called "The Melting Pot of Jazz" also excludes African Americans.

At the Goodman Carnegie Hall concert the regular band, the trio, and

47–50.
Benny Goodman,
Gene Krupa,
Lionel Hampton,
and Teddy Wilson
as pictured in *"Life
Goes to a Party,"*
Life 1 November 1937.

47

48

49 and 50 *(below)*

the quartet dominated the show. But at two important points in the program the band was replaced by a mixed, all-star line-up. The first instance
of this came in a section called "Twenty Years of Jazz," which pastiched
white (Original Dixieland Jazz Band, Beiderbeck, Ted Lewis) *and* black
(Louis Armstrong, Ellington) jazz and employed three key members of
the Ellington Orchestra. The second was a jam session using six members of the Count Basie band (including Basie and Lester Young) and
one of the Ellington men; here, significantly, the black players outnum-
bered the white players onstage, shifting the established ratios of racial
mixture in the Goodman band's mixed jazz.

This Carnegie Hall concert—unlike Whiteman's symphonic jazz concert—forwarded jazz's claim as an art on its own "popular" terms. The
program was dance music, though no one danced. On the one hand, this
just officialized for a night one common reaction to the Goodman band:
"Standing and listening is what most Goodman fans do for more than
half a typical Madhatten Room evening," *Life* had reported in 1937.[28]
On the other hand, by anchoring its audience in Carnegie Hall's seats, by
disallowing even the potential for the distraction of dance, the Goodman
concert ensured that its audience quite literally saw jazz's own "artistic"
terms not just as "popular" but also as racially mixed.

The Carnegie Hall concert, which was successful in drawing a sell-
out crowd and in garnering national media attention, accelerated both
mixing in jazz and jazz's claim to be an art. When Krupa left Goodman
in 1938, Lionel Hampton joined the band on drums. In 1939 Fletcher
Henderson played piano for the band. In 1940 Sid Catlett, Charlie Christian, John Simmons, and Cootie Williams all joined the band.[29] A few
other bands mixed: Artie Shaw hired Billie Holiday. Charlie Barnet employed Frankie Newton and Lena Horne over the next few years. Gene
Krupa employed Roy Eldridge in the early forties and had him sing
a mixed-race and mixed-gender duet with Anita O'Day on "Let Me
Off Uptown" (represented in a 1942 soundie of the same title). From
the other side of the color line, Fletcher Henderson hired several white
players, though he claimed that in the South they had sometimes been
forced to wear blackface.[30] Still, Horne's hiring by Barnet in 1941, well
before she was a national star, was unusual enough to be headline news
for the *Chicago Defender,* which noted that she was the "third vocalist
[ever] to be employed by a white band"—and which also noticed when
Horne did not tour the South with Barnet and when she quit due to

"trouble encountered in the so many lily white spots where the band played."[31]

In 1938, John Hammond held the first of two "Spirituals to Swing" concerts at Carnegie Hall, both sponsored by leftist political organizations. The first concert featured an all-black roster, but the second, held in 1939, concluded with a mixed Goodman sextet—a progression that at once asserted the black sources of swing and suggested that ultimately a racially mixed outcome sprang from these sources.

Also in 1938, Cafe Society opened downtown with an explicit commitment to racial mixing on the bandstand and, more notably, in the audience. Previous to this, audiences had certainly been racially mixed at times, but such mixing had mostly taken place in black neighborhoods and had been tinged with a one-way sense of the exotic; now the flow of color could (in a small way) reverse, moving from Harlem to downtown. The Cafe Society held its own Carnegie Hall concert in 1941, and in 1943 Duke Ellington initiated a series of yearly concerts at Carnegie Hall, saying, in a *Time* review, "The Negro is not merely a singing and dancing wizard but a loyal American, in spite of his social position. I want to tell America how the Negro feels about it."[32] Swing was becoming simultaneously popular, "artistic," and insistent about racial politics.[33]

At the same time, the jam session was becoming a national myth, and jazz criticism, previously the domain of slumming classical critics, industry papers, and small specialty publications, was moving into the mainstream. The late thirties saw the publication of the first books of jazz history and criticism—often larded with photographs documenting the mixed evolution of jazz[34]—and a wide array of general interest periodicals began to review jazz. For instance, in January 1937 *Reader's Digest* reprinted an essay from *The Delineator* called "It's Swing!." This piece typifies much mainstream, popularizing writing on swing from this period. It emphasizes racial mixing in the music at its origins in turn-of-the-century New Orleans ("Negro, white—they jammed together") and asserts the importance of the jam session for swing players, while avoiding any uncomfortable mention of present-day mixing. It presents the music as serious: the audience members "have come here not to dance, but to listen." It promotes Louis Armstrong (not undeservingly) to the "King of Swing," demoting Goodman to the "Swingmaster." Nonetheless, Armstrong, a perspiring exotic "in a state of profound agitation," needs to be identified for the writer by a kindly, Rochester-like waiter:

"Yes, suh, boss. That boy is Louis Armstrong."[35] For all its errors and offenses, essays like this one increased swing's public exposure and kept relevant terms—race, popularity, art—in wide view.

Media activity surrounding swing peaked in the years between 1943 and 1945. In its February 1943 issue, *Esquire* selected a mixed "All-American" jazz band. All-star bands were common to specialty magazines like *down beat* and to African American newspapers like the *Defender,* but in a magazine that boasted a circulation of seven hundred thousand, this was new. The same year *Look* hired Leonard Feather, then a writer and editor well known in the jazz press, to do capsule record reviews. Feather concentrated on jazz and, for the next two years, carefully balanced his column between records by black and white musicians, all of whom were shown in tiny photos next to each of Feather's paragraphs. (From a current perspective this may seem insignificant, but entire issues of the magazine would go by without showing any "other" American face besides those accompanying Feather's reviews.[36]) Later in 1943, *Look* and *Life* each published photo essays entitled "Jam Session."[37] Both showed black and white players, but, unlike the *Look* essay, which was a series of individual portraits from a wide array of venues, Gjon Mili's *Life* piece documented a mixed session the photographer had set up at his loft. Each of Mili's photographs showed various mixtures of whites and blacks playing and listening. Unlike the writer for the 1937 *Life* piece on the Goodman band, the anonymous writer of the accompanying text for "Jam Session" felt comfortable leaving this fact unremarked.

Esquire again selected an All-American band in 1944, but that year it also assembled this mixed band onstage at the Metropolitan Opera House, broadcast the show live on the radio, and recorded it on V-disk for the troops overseas. The editorial for the issue recounted "The Upward Journey of Hot Jazz, from the Junkshops to the Met," and boasted that "this will be the first time that American Jazz has invaded that innermost sanctum of musical respectability."[38] The magazine also made jazz a regular part of each issue in 1944, adding columns by Feather and Paul Eduard Smith and publishing the first of its *Jazz Yearbooks.* The next year *Esquire* topped itself by staging and coordinating for radio broadcast three concerts on a single night: Louis Armstrong played from New Orleans, Benny Goodman's mixed quintet played from New York, and the Ellington Orchestra, augmented by various other All-American

51. Gjon Mili's lead photo from "Jam Session,"
Life 11 October 1943.

award winners, played from the Philharmonic Auditorium in Los Angeles. As a grand finale, musicians from all three places jammed with one another over the radio — the ultimate democratic, American jam session, technologically joining races, regions of the country, and masters from different genres of jazz. Perhaps in this instance it was appropriate that this feat could only be "seen" in the listeners' imaginations — imaginations prepared by slow years of gradualist assimilation to see racially mixed, "concert" jazz as the look of American music, a look as fluid and varied as the sound of the music itself.

Leonard Feather's explanation of the 1945 All-American awards, however, suggests that not even the imaginations of swing *fans*, let alone the mainstream "American" imagination, was yet so developed in its vision of jazz. "Why didn't Harry James and Jimmy and Tommy Dorsey win anything?" Feather asked himself rhetorically. His answer gives a sense

of the visual, racial politics of the dominant jazz discourse at the end of
the swing era:

> I'm glad you asked that. It brings me to the point that this ballot is based
> on musical values, *not* on commercial success. . . .
>
> Further, our experts are free from race prejudice. In polls in which jazz
> fans do the voting, the majority of winners is usually white. In our ballot,
> the overwhelming majority is Negro; not because anybody is anti-white
> or pro-Negro, but because most of the great jazzmen today happen to be
> colored.[39]

Art—"musical value"—was at stake, and, according to Feather, musical
values had no intrinsic color, though commercial values, which reflected
for Feather the values of (white) consumers, did.

In the September 1944 issue of *Esquire,* Feather had asked a group of
black jazz players a pointed question: "How have Jim Crow tactics affected your career?" Teddy Wilson's response, grounded in the mechanics of making a living, showed in detail how white prejudice continued,
despite high-profile mixed bands, to control the sight of jazz across the
full range of industrial forms of music:

> The whole time I was with Benny Goodman's Quartet, from 1935 to
> 1939, there was no significant trouble. I lost some movie work when they
> wanted me to do the recording for a musical sequence in *Big Broadcast of
> 1936* but have a white musician substitute for me when they shot the pic-
> tures. I refused to do that. The following year Benny made *Hollywood Hotel*
> for Warners and they did photograph the Quartet, all of us wearing the
> same uniform and no suggestion of segregation. But the scene was shot in
> such a way that they could cut it out in movie houses down South.
>
> When I got a big band together in 1939 I found out more about how Jim
> Crow works against musicians. They had an equal rights law in Pennsyl-
> vania, and promoters were scared to hire colored bands because it might
> attract Negro patrons and they'd be risking lawsuits by refusing them ad-
> mittance. That means that where a white band doing a road tour out of
> New York could break it up into short, convenient transportation jumps,
> a colored band could not break the journey until it got to Pittsburgh, the
> first town large enough to hold a strictly colored dance.
>
> Of course, the biggest handicap is in radio. A lot of the best locations
> with network wires, like the Astor and the Pennsylvania [a room Wilson *had*
> worked with the Goodman Quartet] and the New Yorker Hotel, don't hire
> Negro bands, and the commercial radio shows are almost entirely impos-

sible because the sponsors are afraid their product would be boycotted by white Southerners if they hired a colored outfit. Radio and records are the life-blood of a band, so that means that a colored band has to rely mainly on records.[40]

A year earlier in Los Angeles, Norman Granz, a young film editor at MGM, had begun his own work on the racial-political, artistic-commercial nexus of jazz. Building on a decade of work by people like Hammond, Wilson, Goodman, Henderson, and Feather and working in the wartime boom rather than the Depression, Granz could be explicit about his motives: "I get mad easily—about racial discrimination . . . and *Jazz at the Phil* [JATP, Granz's organization] is a good way to do something about it. Jazz is ideal to use in promoting better race relations because the American Negro has contributed so much to the history of jazz. You can't begin to understand jazz without, at the same time, beginning to understand the Negro and his contributions to our culture."[41] He also could be bolder about the effect jazz was supposed to have *off* the bandstand. As Feather and Wilson's comments suggest, mainstream American audiences resisted both mixed bands and mixed audiences, with the limited mixing that was taking place on records and in performances seldom being reflected, and certainly not being amplified, in the make-up of audiences.

Beginning with the first jam sessions he organized and extending through two decades of JATP concerts, tours, and records, Granz applied three rules: The musicians he hired would be paid well; there would be no dancing at his events; and there could be no segregation on either the bandstand or in the audience.[42] The first of these rules responded to exploitative club owners and promoters. The second institutionalized a trend that was already familiar from other attempts to establish jazz as an art, a concert music. The third rule was most important because it recognized the limitations of previous efforts to mix the look of jazz—efforts that had relied on an optimistic trickle-down theory of cultural-social change. Granz's third rule attempted to ensure consumption as an act of resistance to racist conventions; it tried to direct attention both to the relation of individual consumers to the producers of the music they consume *and* to the relations between individual and perhaps different consumers of the same musical product.

JATP evolved as a complex, market-driven and market-responsive answer to a racist situation, just as at the same time bebop was developing, in part, "as a profound criticism of the failure of swing's ecstatic hopes for a modern America rooted in pluralism and individualism."[43] Bebop, especially in its early stages, turned to local and exclusivist modes of production and upped the musical ante with an insistence on virtuosic and "authentic" black invention.[44] JATP concentrated on national (later, international), inclusive, and conjunctive elaborations of jazz, on "mass-producing" and mass-marketing a sort of "swing-bop" fusion, especially to the young.[45] Bop was explicitly oppositional and disjunctive, frustrated by the unfair terms of "assimilation" in America and refusing to play the game. JATP, which would eventually include most of the great bebop players, was also oppositional, but it wanted to change the rules of assimilation, to alter what assimilation would look like, and to shift the ground for the meaning of the term.

It was as these developments took place that Granz assembled the cast and crew of *Jammin' the Blues*—including Lester Young, John Simmons, and Sid Catlett, black musicians who had played in high-profile mixed groups and jam sessions, Barney Kessel, a white apprentice of black guitarist Charlie Christian and a veteran of mixed bands, and Gjon Mili, photographer of mixed jam sessions. Seen in the arc of attempts to mix and aestheticize the look of jazz, *Jammin' the Blues* functions as the first national advertisement for the JATP ideology of oppositional inclusion and progressive consumerism.

Change the Look and Slip the Yoke?

Of course, *Jammin' the Blues* was not the first Hollywood film to represent jazz. Jazz musicians had been seen on screen since before the introduction of sound, and by 1944 the sight and sound of swing bands were a regular part of musicals; the Count Basie band, for example, appeared in five musicals filmed in 1943.[46] *Jammin' the Blues* was not the first film to show a mixed band: Mae West had sung with the Ellington band in *Belle of the Nineties* (1934); Martha Raye (in blackface) had sung with Louis Armstrong in *Artists and Models* (1937); the Goodman quartet appeared in *Hollywood Hotel* (1938); and in *To Have and Have Not,* a film that *Jammin' the Blues* was billed with, Lauren Becall sang with a mixed band fronted by Hoagy Carmichael. And *Jammin' the Blues* was not the first film to attempt to represent jazz in an "artistic" way or as a self-conscious art: the short *Yamekraw* (1930) illustrated James P. Johnson's tone poem for orchestra, jazz band, and chorus with expressionist imagery familiar from German film, King Vidor's *Hallelujah!,* and stage productions like *Porgy* (1927) and its more famous musical version, *Porgy and Bess* (1935, revived 1941); in another short, *Symphony in Black* (1934), the Ellington orchestra played a nine-minute "symphony," also intercut with expressionist images, for a white, concert-hall audience.

Still, in 1944, Leonard Feather summarized how most jazz fans probably felt about Hollywood's representation of the music: "In the movies —you find [jazz] all too seldom. The bands that get the biggest film breaks generally aren't jazz outfits and even when they are, their presentation is usually inadequate. As for small groups, Hollywood has virtually ignored them."[47] Feather never specified his standards of adequacy or excellence for the representation of jazz on film, but the blueprint for a "legitimate" musical he elicited from Sam Donahue can serve as a guide. An adequate representation of jazz would focus on the music and musicians, avoiding "illogical" intrusions, whether of spectacle ("jitterbug dancers") or narrative ("chicks bursting into song in the middle of a forest"), and it would record the audio and the visual tracks simultaneously, fusing "real and spontaneous" sight and sound. Feather's more general critical standards help fill out these guidelines: The jazz itself should be "real"—challenging and demanding art, based on musical rather than commercial values. The players should be credited for their work. And the casting should avoid racial discrimination, recognizing at the same time that "most of the great jazzmen today happen to be colored."

Neither Donahue's blueprint nor Feather's fondness for Louis Armstrong's "delightful screen personality and natural acting ability" suggest a desire to apply any sort of simple "documentary" aesthetic to representing jazz on film.[48] Though it was used in seemingly countless shorts and many features, neither Donahue nor Feather discussed Hollywood's most common convention for filming swing—"canned" performance, or putting a band on a set and letting it "play" (to prerecorded sound) directly to the camera. Presumably, then, they had little use for this convention, which seldom captured the energy or the visual "showmanship" of the music.[49] In the early forties, the ideal vision of jazz on film for Donahue, Feather, and jazz players and fans in general was probably the long-rumored Orson Welles biopic of Louis Armstrong, a narrative, feature-length, A-quality production that would have united the consummate "artists" of Hollywood and jazz.[50]

By these standards—or hopes—no worthy tradition of jazz on film existed in 1944. None of the films I have mentioned, despite their interest and importance, focused on jazz or jazz musicians. At best the music was incidental to the narrative, used to give depth to a character, like Mae West's Ruby Carter in *Belle of the Nineties,* or a location, like Martinique in *To Have and Have Not.* At worst, regressive, racist representation recuperated a progressive visual representation of the music; for example, in *Hollywood Hotel* a blackface number precedes the appearance of the Goodman quartet. Films that did focus on the lives of "jazz" musicians, like *Blues in the Night* (1941) and *Birth of the Blues* (1941), indulged in what could be called the Whiteman effect, erasing the African American contributions to jazz and making the blues the province of performers like Bing Crosby and Mary Martin.[51] The 1934 musical *Murder at the Vanities* depicts this erasure in its most extreme form when an enraged classical conductor machine-guns the elegantly uniformed Ellington orchestra after they impress "his" audience; this murder, which is ostensibly part of the show, is not the murder of the film's title. Otherwise, Hollywood placed black musical performers in segregated, "Jim Crow" specialty numbers—the position of the Basie band in all its 1943 musicals[52]—or in completely segregated films like *Yamekraw, Stormy Weather* (1943), or *Cabin in the Sky* (1943).

The concerns of African American activists and intellectuals and the standards of the liberal, largely white discursive community of jazz fans conjoined (though not always perfectly) across dissatisfaction with these Hollywood film conventions. After decades of specific, localized protests and general complaint in the black press, in 1942 the NAACP held its national conference in Los Angeles and used the occasion to pressure Hollywood to more adequately represent African Americans.[53] Two years later, the sociologist Lawrence Reddick, analyzing the movies as "one index to what the American people have come to believe about the Negro," anatomized the nineteen "principal stereotypes of the Negro in the American mind," among them the natural-born musician, the perfect entertainer, and the uninhibited exhibitionist.[54] Reddick felt that in the years since *Gone With the Wind* Hollywood had improved its depiction of blacks, but he was still deeply dissatisfied with Jim Crow films, which were by definition "false and objectionable," and with the continued reliance on "the usual roles given to Negro actors that call for types . . . [including] various jazz musicians."[55] Jackie Lopez, the writer who reviewed *To Have and Have Not* and *Jammin' the Blues* for the *Chicago Defender,* opened her piece by referring to this continuing struggle: "The stiff lipped complaining we've been tossing Hollywood way may have some bearing on the fact that the movie town is viewing the race with new eyes."[56]

Jammin' the Blues responded to and attempted to reformulate the conventions used for representing jazz and African American musicality, even as it could not escape them. It attempted to (re)envision jazz as an art and an entertainment, as specifically African American and generally (mixed) American, as private and public, exclusive and inclusive, as spontaneous and practiced, ephemeral and commodifiable. It tried to do all this in three songs.

The opening of *Jammin' the Blues* announces the film's difference from standard Hollywood product of the same period using several means. The most obvious is the comprehensive head credits, which list all the players names in big, graphically bold type. This was uncommon recognition for any musician who was not a popular, "name" star—a vocalist or bandleader, usually. ("That we should ever live to see the day!" was Charles Emge's response in *down beat*.) The credits assure the musicians' possession of their performances, disperse the "authorship" of the film, and attempt to ensure its "authenticity," its veracity. For uninitiated viewers, the credits serve to individuate the players and suggest that the blues were no longer an anonymous (Negro) folk music or the domain of Bing Crosby. For viewers in the know, the credits link the film to the discourse about jazz, investing it with a certain documentary power by drawing on an alternative firmament of stars. Within this alternative star system, *Jammin' the Blues* used some of the biggest names: In the 1944 *down beat* poll Lester Young (tenor sax) and Sid Catlett (drums) placed first in their respective categories; Jo Jones (drums) followed Catlett, and Barney Kessel (guitar) was seventh in his category.[57] Catlett won the *Esquire* All-American gold award in 1943, 1944, and 1945, and Young won an *Esquire* silver award in 1945.[58] In short, the credits of *Jammin' the Blues* announce the democratic, contributory nature of these blues and assert that this music is made by specific, excellently qualified individuals.

The symbolic currency of the stars of *Jammin' the Blues* would have run deep for jazz fans and for other musicians. Young, Catlett, and Jones were the elder statesmen of the blues as a musical discipline. Catlett had played with virtually everyone; Young and Jones were members of the great Basie band. Musically, they self-consciously bridged the gap between swing and bebop, innovating and listening to others' innovations but stubbornly reminding younger players of the great value of what had come before.[59] And Young particularly, with his coded styles of speech and fashion, was an icon, "the first black musician to be publicly recognized not as a happy-go-lucky entertainer, à la Armstrong, but as an artist of the *demi-monde* whose discontents magnified those felt in general by his race."[60]

The brief voice-over introduction, which immediately follows the credits, reveals the tension between Hollywood conventions and resistant impulses for representing jazz that *Jammin' the Blues* works within and tries to work through: "This is a jam session. Quite often these great artists gather and play—ad lib—hot music. It could be called a midnight symphony." On the one hand, this voice is familiar from other Hollywood shorts, documentaries, and newsreels—the voice of God, the voice of white authority, preceding and framing what the audience sees and hears. On the other hand, this voice is different, both in what it says and in how and when it says it. The credits have subtly displaced the voice, diminishing its ability to fully name what the audience will experience. Further, the combination of the image and the sound (a slow, soft piano vamp, supported by bass and drums), both of which are continuous and uncut at this point in the film, pulls the voice into an already existing flow that has an attraction of its own.

The voice-over begins in an authoritative, definitive mode: "This is a jam session." The subtext is something like, "You've read about and seen pictures of jam sessions, now see and hear a *real* one."[61] Then it moves to a description of "great artists" who "quite often" "gather and play—ad lib—hot music." Within the context of popular discourse about jazz, this description is complex: the players the audience is about to hear and see are "great artists"—not "folk artists" or "Negro artists." The failure to specify that the players are black violated Hollywood and standard journalistic conventions of representation in 1944,[62] and the iterative "quite often" implies repetition and practice. Nonetheless, these artists also create their art spontaneously, "ad lib." In other words, their art utilizes one of the principal qualities of entertainment. Hollywood musicals often worked to incorporate art into entertainment, but the voice in *Jammin' the Blues* works from the opposite direction to incorporate entertainment into art.[63] The use of "hot music"—in the words of *down beat,* "Jazz-dom's term for one of its proudest boasts: the ad lib solo playing of its crack musicians"[64]—instead of the common words "jazz" and "swing" indicates the noncommercial yet exciting aspect of the music. Shifting to the conditional mode for its last sentence, the voice reiterates this combination: "It could be called a midnight symphony." *This* artistic form takes place outside the constrictive boundaries of polite conven-tion. This sentence claims "hot music" as a "symphonic," artistic form, but it also admits a cliché—"midnight"—that is dense with both roman-tic and potentially racist significations. Then the voice leaves off and lets the artists "speak" for themselves.

The body of *Jammin' the Blues* substantiates the difference that its opening sequence claims. Midway through the voice-over, the camera still lingers on the abstract image that was under the credits—two con-centric white ovals slightly off-center on a saturated black field with an occasional wisp of white smoke moving past them. As the voice-over ends, the camera draws back slowly, and at the same time the circles begin to tilt, revealing that they are the key-lit brim and crown of a saxo-phone player's pork-pie hat; the player draws his reed to his lips and joins the song; the camera continues to draw back, showing that the player holds a burning cigarette between the index and middle fingers of his right hand, even as they work the valves of his horn. The opening ab-straction has turned into a most detailed representation. (As soon as the abstraction became recognizable as a hat, jazz aficionados would have known they were seeing Lester Young, whose pork pie was as iconic in jazz as Chaplin's bowler was in film. Then they would have recognized the odd angle at which Young held his horn. Finally, the most dedicated, the same people who stood along the front of the bandstand wherever the Basie band played, may have begun to try to catch his fingerings and his fashions.) Only after the camera has reframed its subject to show his seated figure surrounded by inky darkness is there a cut to another angle.

This opening sets the photographic strategy for the film. The image moves back and forth between medium and long shots and extreme close-ups, focusing on the visible materiality of the process of making hot music: the surfaces of instruments and clothing—of ties, trousers, shoes, and hats; the small motions of hands and fingers on valves, keys, and strings; furrowed brows and distended cheeks and tiny gestures of com-

52 and 53. Establishing shots of the bands in "Midnight Symphony" and "Jammin' the Blues" in *Jammin' the Blues* (1944).

munication. Sometimes these images are connected through disjunctive cuts, returning the image briefly to the level of abstraction or juxtaposing various individuals with one another or the group; other times tracking and reframing link a detail to a larger image of the whole scene, an individual soloist to the group.

The setting never intrudes because there is none—only apparently limitless blackness or whiteness surrounding the players. *Jammin' the Blues* rejects the architectures of both professional and "folk" musical performance—theaters, bars, levees, barns—common to Hollywood films. Instead, it creates an undifferentiated space defined by shadow and light, a space that encourages the viewer to concentrate on the music but also encourages the viewer perhaps even more to see the ways musicians look as they make their music.[65] If the jam session from the Goodman band's 1938 Carnegie Hall concert or if the "technological" jam session

from *Esquire*'s 1945 All-American broadcast could have found ideal locations—ones not constrained by the visible meanings of the concert hall
or the invisibility of radio—those locations would probably have looked
something like the space of *Jammin' the Blues*.

The sound, which had no apparent relation to the abstract image under
the titles but was suddenly bound to the image when the abstraction
turned into Lester Young, continues firmly to relate to the image for the
remainder of the film. As was standard Hollywood practice, most of the
images were shot to prerecorded, playback sound. Norman Granz (credited as the film's "technical director" because he recorded all the music)
took extraordinary care, however, to minimize the effects of this disjuncture. Charles Emge reported in his *down beat* review that

> Granz had phonograph recordings made of the solos so that the boys could
> take them home and memorize them. . . .
>   Drum solos are especially difficult to synchronize. Good results were
> obtained by Granz by recording some of the more complicated passages,
> such as "rolls," on the set during shooting and dubbing these sections into
> the track.[66]

This practice came as near as Hollywood would probably allow to the
live recording-while-shooting that Sam Donahue thought would make
musical film look and sound "real and spontaneous."

Jammin' the Blues is not a narrative, so there are no story events to
intrude on the presentation of the music.[67] Instead, the main organizing principle of *Jammin' the Blues* is addition, expressed both aurally and
visually. The first, slow number ("Midnight Symphony" [MS], which begins under the credits) is followed by a medium-tempo, vocal rendering
of the standard, "On the Sunny Side of the Street" [SSS], which is followed by the concluding, up-tempo instrumental ("Jammin' the Blues"
[JTB]).[68] The image track matches this increase in tempo on the sound
track with an increase in the tempo of the editing.[69] MS uses a quintet
line-up (the rhythm trio plus tenor sax and trumpet); SSS uses a sextet
(rhythm trio, guitar, tenor sax, and voice); and JTB uses a septet (rhythm
trio, guitar, two tenor saxes, and trumpet). So an increasing instrumental
depth and complexity accompanies the music's increasing tempo.

The visual track parallels this increasing musical complexity and density in three ways. First, with one exception, the visual track accurately
records these line-ups, resulting in increasingly "crowded" compositions.

54 and 55. Establishing shots of the bands in the three numbers of *Jammin' the Blues*.

(The exception is SSS, where, though the guitar is clearly audible, we see no guitarist. I will interpret this absence later.) Second, the film adds a new photographic effect with each song. SSS adds silhouette to the chiaroscuro established in MS, and JTB adds multiple exposure. Finally, beginning in SSS, the film adds an additional space. In MS all the players clearly occupied the same space, but in SSS Lester Young is shown away from his compatriots. This new space, while it seems as "real" as the film's primary space, has a phantasmagoric quality in that shots from Young's position show Marie Bryant (the vocalist) sitting alone, even though the master shot shows her in the midst of the rhythm players. JTB fills this same phantasmic space with a pair of jitterbugging dancers.

But, if *Jammin' the Blues* is not organized narratively, neither is it a typical Hollywood canned performance. Coincident with its additive organization, *Jammin' the Blues* posits an evolving relationship between

56 and 57. "Imagined" spaces in "On the Sunny Side of the Street" and "Jammin' the Blues" from *Jammin' the Blues*.

its performers and the camera. When the film begins, the musicians are not arrayed frontally, as if playing for an implied audience, but in a sort of loose circle or U. The camera has the mobility to seek them out and peer at them from most any angle or distance, but none of the players look directly at the camera, at the viewer; rather, the musicians seem to serve as their own audience. In sss, Marie Bryant, the singer, seen in tightly framed close-up, looks obliquely past the camera—but not directly at it. The fact that she is singing increases a sense of address, but the shot-reverse-shot editing (the same editing used to show conversations in films with dialogue) variously shows her addressing the bassist and then Lester Young.[70] sss does contain two quick insert shots, however, one of the pianist and one of the bassist looking directly at the camera. jtb begins with a master shot showing the three horn players standing in line, making the band appear more frontally aligned, gives the aggressive,

58. Illinois Jacquet at the climax of "Jammin' the Blues."

59. Jo Jones's direct address of the camera at the end of *Jammin' the Blues*.

overblown, upper-register tenor sax of Illinois Jacquet the last and longest solo played directly to the camera, and concludes with the drummer, Jo Jones, smiling directly at the camera and acknowledging the audience with a nod.

As it gains aural and visual speed and density, *Jammin' the Blues* also moves from the oblique abstractness of its opening to a direct, concrete, (self-)referential close. The players move from the unsmiling introspection of Lester Young to the grinning extroversion of Jo Jones. And as the musicians play more and more intensely and more and more directly to the camera, the film creates an additional imaginative space in which it finally places a pair of jitterbugging dancers, forging a possible point of entry for an audience. Through its careful organization, *Jammin' the Blues* attempts to transform its viewers from outsiders to insiders, from voy-

60. Title card from
Dixieland Jamboree
(1945).

61. Eunice Wilson
and the Five
Racketeers from
Dixieland Jamboree.

eurs and eavesdroppers to acknowledged audience members and possible participants.

For comparison, consider another Warner Bros. musical short, *Dixieland Jamboree* (1945). Here the title and production credits appear over a drawing of white-gloved hands playing a banjo and attended by thick lips and rolling eyes, all apparently held together by an invisible body. This image alludes directly to blackface minstrelsy and is repeated, in some variation, in virtually every Hollywood film dealing with minstrelsy or with black musicians. Music ranging from spirituals to Tin Pan Alley accompanies a rapid montage of images of stevedores, field hands, "happy darkies," a blackface performer, and out-takes from *Jammin' the Blues.* Over this a stentorian voice intones:

"Always music has been an intimate part of a people's existence. And in America, the Negro has given to music a newer, greater significance, attaining a superb perfection, a pulsating, inescapable style. Talented with the gift of rhythm and a spontaneity of improvisation, the American Negro has fused the past with the present to create an art that is characteristic of our time, dancing, singing, and playing such music that swings the whole world to the matchless rhythm of the Five Racketeers and Eunice Wilson."

Wilson and the Racketeers (a vaudeville blues singer and a novelty quintet) appear in a canned performance in front of a backdrop of watermelon slices. The film goes on to show canned performances by the Three Whippets (a dance team), Adelaide Hall (a "sentimental" singer), the Nicholas Brothers (dancers), and Cab Calloway (commercial jazz).

In slightly different order and without the Calloway number, the body of this film was released in 1936 as *All-Colored Vaudeville Show,* but in 1945 Warner Bros. recycled it, adding Calloway and the "ethnographic" voice-over. While *Dixieland Jamboree* does not claim to be about any specific type of music but rather about black music and blackness in general, it nonetheless shows the regressive representations of black performers and music that *Jammin' the Blues* would have been seen against. That *All-Colored Vaudeville Show* could return as *Dixieland Jamboree* speaks volumes about Hollywood's sensitivity to African American concerns; what is more, Warner Bros. was considered one of the most sensitive studios.[71] It vividly illustrates why critics like Lawrence Reddick were wary of Hollywood depictions of blacks as musicians and entertainers. Moreover, by using images appropriated from *Jammin' the Blues,* *Dixieland Jamboree* makes the importance of context clear: Flanked by images of men loading cotton and barefooted youngsters playing kazoos, a few brief seconds of Lester Young accompanied by a trumpet playing a variation on "Dixie" hardly seems special. The words of the voice-over, the programmatic assemblage of the music, and the careless mixture of images work very differently—and toward different ends—from their equivalents in *Jammin' the Blues.* And the canned performances, with images often poorly matched to sound, have seemingly nothing in common with the performances in *Jammin' the Blues.*

Yet, for all their important differences, *Dixieland Jamboree* and *Jammin' the Blues* have similarities that reveal the limits of the latter films' escape from Hollywood conventions. The carefully deployed iconography, space, organization, and pattern of address of *Jammin' the Blues* would have been available for negative, ungenerous readings, especially in the context of the racist image creation that *Dixieland Jamboree* represents. Even as it draws together the individuality and collectivity of the musicians, the space in *Jammin' the Blues* suggests hermeticism, complete interiority, and a divorce from any "organic" public. The film's organization leads to exhibitionist gestures that are closer to Cab Calloway's commercial entertainment than concentrated, "artistic" musicianship.[72] This pattern is amplified by the shifts in the film's address and iconography. While the film initially challenges the viewer to understand and make sense of the cultural forms it represents, it ends by easing the challenge, directly addressing the audience, and presenting images of the jitterbugging couple, which Sam Donahue named as Hollywood's primary method of "covering up" black bands, and the grinning black man. This last image in particular—especially as embodied in Louis Armstrong's performance persona—was probably the most widely disseminated image of black musicianship in America, and it had become a key image in the reformulation of the look of midforties jazz, an image associated with the "tomming" that bebop formed itself against. Writing about Miles Davis, who codified on trumpet the cool playing style Lester Young originated on tenor sax, Quincy Troupe recalled the meaning of *not* smiling for an audience: "Besides the magisterial, deep-cool hipness of his musical language, the aspects of Miles that affected me most were his urbane veneer and his detached sure sense of himself as royalty, as untouchable in a touch everything world. . . . Mile's refusal to grin in front of white audiences like so many other black entertainers made a statement to me."[73] Troupe's words could be reformulated to describe the opening of *Jammin' the Blues* but not its close.

Perhaps the aspect *Jammin' the Blues* has most in common with *Dixieland Jamboree*, and with other Hollywood representations of jazz, is the fact that it makes jazz look like an *unmixed* music—the fact that it appears to be, though it is not, a Jim Crow film. Given the trajectory of racial mixing traced in the first half of this chapter, and given the places of many of *Jammin' the Blues*'s key collaborators in that trajectory, this fact marks a disappointing compromise. The nuances of this compromise are important, however, for what they reveal about the recalcitrance of Hollywood conventions and about strategies for chipping away at that recalcitrance—and the presumed recalcitrance of the "American" mind these conventions represented.[74]

62–64. Stills of transition from black to white background in *Jammin' the Blues*.

Jammin' the Blues does include the white guitar player Barney Kessel, but his "inclusion" is carefully managed. According to Charles Emge in *down beat:* "Mr. Studio objected to the appearance of a white musician with Negroes. Of course, he didn't object personally, but it just wouldn't go with Southern audiences. Granz was asked to eliminate Barney Kessel or to get a Negro guitarist to 'fake' his playing in the picture. Granz refused but had to be satisfied with photography that hides the fact that Kessel is white from all but the most discerning eyes."[75] In fact, Granz settled for both more and less in his struggle with "Mr. Studio." Before Kessel ever appears (in JTB, the film's closing tune), Kessel's presence is first—and exclusively—*audible* on the soundtrack during SSS.

"On the Sunny Side of the Street" is *Jammin' the Blues*'s central and most familiar song. In light of the knowledge of Kessel's veiled inclusion in SSS, the visuals chosen to accompany the song seem to allegorize the lyric about "crossing over" and moving from the "shade" into the sun. At the start of the number a dissolve moves through "the reflection of a singer [Marie Bryant] on the ebony mirror of a piano top"[76] and changes the color of background from the black of MS to white. When the camera cuts from its close-up of Bryant to an establishing shot, it centers the frame on an empty chair (see Fig. 54). The absent but audible Kessel arrives as a ghost, an unused chair and a pale wash of (his) color suffusing *Jammin' the Blues*'s only popular song.

In 1944, crossover was not yet a term used to designate music that was successful with both blacks and whites—or, more precisely, music played by blacks and popular with blacks that then became popular with whites. According to Henry Louis Gates and Gerald Early, however, the trope of crossing over had long been rich with meaning in African American discourses: It signified death, passing for white,[77] "both a pure rebirth and a mongrelized synergism," and "the weight of one's previous location bearing down on where you are now."[78] But the "dead" person in *Jammin' the Blues,* the person with the invisible body (which in Ralph Ellison's terms would be passing for black), the person who should not consort (before institutionally imagined, "southern" eyes) with the "other" race and who represented musical-social mongrelization was white. When Hollywood erased African Americans in mixed bands (or in its narratives of American life), it made the illusion complete by replacing them with white stand-ins. Kessel's absent presence in SSS is more complex: it refuses Hollywood convention (even if the convention would have played

65 and 66. Stills of
Barney Kessel in
Jammin' the Blues.

in reverse); it sounds as a small testimony to the black jazz musicians who
disappeared from the sight of the mainstream audience as jazz struggled
to cross over and become a respected "American" art; and it stands as a
reminder of the power of whiteness in America.

Ultimately Kessel does "appear" during the film's eponymous last
song, deep in the shadows at the edge of the frame (see Fig. 55), multiply exposed, and in extreme close-up. Kessel's fragmented and obscured
image in JTB serves as the coded visible sign of the film's—and jazz's—resistance to Hollywood conventions, a sign available only to the most "discerning eyes" (eyes that would presumably have accompanied knowledgeable ears). For those able to read the code, Kessel's veiled inclusion
in the film reverses standard notions of minority/majority and the typical tokenism of mixing in predominantly white bands. It recalls Leonard
Feather's casual formulation—"most of the great jazzmen today happen

to be colored"—but suggests that, nonetheless, jazz should not be categorized only as "Negro" or "colored," a category that the mainstream could use too easily to dismiss or exoticize the music. In the headline for a story written to accompany its review of *Jammin' the Blues, Ebony* magazine deciphered the code for its readers: "Jamming Jumps the Color Line."[79]

Recounting her experience of *Jammin' the Blues* at the State and Lake Theater in downtown Chicago, the *Chicago Defender* reviewer Jackie Lopez was rhapsodic: "For those ten minutes you held on to the armrests of your seat, and you were saying to yourself over and over again: 'This is art. This is art.' Just a ten minute dose of really fine jazz. . . ."[80] To Lopez the film, along with its feature-length companion, *To Have and Have Not,* indicated "Hollywood has potentialities," that it could see that black people are "like anyone else." James Agee in *The Nation* found *Jammin' the Blues* "one of the few musical shorts I have ever got even fair pleasure out of hearing, and the only one . . . which was not a killing bore to watch." But where Lopez saw art, Agee saw pretense and "middlebrow highbrow" artiness.[81] He was not interested in the color of the cast, which he did not mention. Agee was a minority of one among the reviewers of *Jammin' the Blues.* The other reviewers applauded the film in terms less breathless than but similar to Lopez's, and aside from the writers in *down beat* and *Ebony,* most, like Lopez, described what they saw (and heard) as a "Negro" film. In an unsigned capsule review for *Time,* Agee joined the majority, while pointing out that the film's "new," "artistic" qualities were new only by Hollywood standards; Agee also took this opportunity to point out that the cast was not all-Negro, and he named most of the players.[82]

Agee's critical stuttering and Lopez's hopeful excitement are symptomatic of the tensions and contradictions *Jammin' the Blues* was trying to mediate. On the one hand, "art" proves that black people are like everyone else—except, in order for the art to be made (on film, at any rate), black people could not *be* with anyone else, at least not in America. (*To Have and Have Not* does show mixing, which impressed Lopez, though she pointed out, recasting the title's chiasmus, that the film was set in Martinique.) On the other hand, in Agee's formulation (which he had made explicit in his 1944 essay "Pseudo-Folk"), the striving for "art" reduces black people to everyone else, corrupting and decaying the true "folk" nature of the Negro.[83] Finally, such positions, incorporated and enforced by Hollywood, left little room for the types of negotiation *Jammin' the Blues* was attempting.

The categories *Jammin' the Blues* partakes of and tries to fuse mark the complexity of the film's project, the complexity of music as a social-cultural, visual and aural representation, and the contradictions of America as a "community" in the midforties. *Jammin' the Blues* worked to emphasize at once the creativity and humanity of African American musicians, to be color blind, and to be racially mixed, but it did this work at a moment when such simultaneity was not yet widely acceptable. The film's careful orchestration (and compromise) of these multiple desires allowed it to be made in Hollywood and made it available and exciting to a wide audience. But, despite many hopes, the complexity of these desires ensured that refinements, expansions, or even generic repetitions of *Jammin' the Blues*'s model for making jazz music visible on film would not be soon in coming.

Coda

I think the idea of a musical really struck a positive note with Columbia [Pictures]. I guess they know singing and dancing Negroes sell. —SPIKE LEE (on *School Daze*) (1988)

You know, when we did the preview of our movie *Hooray for Love,* which was sixty years ago, people came out of the audience and hugged and kissed us and said, "Oh, how wonderful," and blah blah blah, and I thought to myself, "How wonderful if it could be like this forever" . . . but it's sixty years later and I really haven't seen too many changes. —JENI LEGON (Bill Robinson's Dance Partner in *Hooray for Love*) (1998)

As we have seen, the aesthetic and commercial successes—qualified in each instance—of *Stormy Weather* and *Jammin' the Blues* did not spur expansion or imitation, or even particularly redirect the black-cast musical or musical short. Whether considered in the short term, which usually characterized the Hollywood studios' cyclical method of product (and genre) development, or in the relative long term, there followed from these films neither a series of reflections on black entertainers and entertainment in America nor further attempts at the respectfully inventive depiction of black musical performance. The wedges these films drove into thinking about apt depictions of black musical performance, both in the film industry and in the largest segment of its audience, were apparently too thin to create openings for anything more innovative than a *Nat "King" Cole Musical Story* "featurette" (1955), *St. Louis Blues,* or the interracial numbers in, for instance, *A Song is Born* (1948) and *High Society* (1956). Still, as studio-era, industrially integrated Hollywood began to collapse across the fifties and new models had yet to emerge, a keen-eyed (and -eared) observer might have been able to track down — and might have had some optimistic feelings about — *The Sound of Jazz* on TV in 1957 or *Jazz on a Summer's Day* in a few art cinemas in 1960, both of which were carefully racially integrated, artful documentaries indebted to *Jammin' the Blues*. The same observer might have felt (very) cautious optimism about the 1961 Hollywood film, *Paris Blues*, which elaborated, then belabored, and finally fumbled both the relationships between black and white jazz musicians (Paul Newman and Sidney Poitier) and between jazz and classical music.

Similarly, the provocative "failures" of the backstage, entertainment world explorations of *Swing!* and *The Duke is Tops* did not spawn race-film imitators. Music remained a crucial attraction of race films as they continued to be produced, with diminishing frequency, into the late forties. At least one African American–directed race film, Spencer Williams's *The Blood of Jesus* (1941), was an enduring financial success, is often considered a "classic" of sound-era race film, and can be thought of as a unique form of the musical.[1] As it's title makes clear, however, Williams's film had spiritual concerns rather than secular ones, and the rest of the race-film musicals, such as *Beware* (1945), *Hi De Ho* (1945), or *Boy! What a Girl* (1945), even when they did have a backstage aspect never engaged in explicit critical reflection as part of their generic workings. By the fifties, race film was an eviscerated, untenable category and the few works that did hew to the category were musical "revues" that tacked together recycled single-song shorts.[2] In the view of the off-Hollywood production companies that had attempted to cater to niche audiences (companies that had never been industrially integrated and thus were well positioned to exploit the era of studio disarray), the emerging teen audience may have been seen as replacing the "race" audience. And that teen audience — part of which may also have been seeking out *The Sound of Jazz, Jazz on a Summer's Day,* or *Paris Blues* — was treated now and again to its own comparatively integrated (or less segregated) musicals in rock 'n' roll movies like *Rock Around the Clock* (1956) and *Go, Johnny, Go!* (1958).

Around 1959, then, despite the dominance of *Porgy and Bess* in terms of money spent and earned, the formal attentions of reviewers and press agents, ability to inflect a larger market of spin-off products, and probably in terms of audience drawn into theaters, and with its old-fashioned (but culturally elite and approved) view of African Americans, which it distilled in its old-fashioned generic form, potential alternatives were becoming increasingly available. And after all, while *Porgy and Bess* may have dominated discursively in 1959, it also "failed." It seemed then that a social and cultural transformation was underway—and not just retrospectively for, say, Sidney Poitier and Harry Belafonte, who had finally broken through to mainstream film stardom; or for those buying and burning rock 'n' roll records; or for those who attended the Newport Jazz Festival; or for those who chose to sit-in at a lunch counter instead of (or in addition to?) going to the movies.

For this book there is no better sign of this transformation along with its turns and complexities than that in the arenas of America's public spaces many African Americans accompanied both their struggles for civil rights—and later their expressions of frustration at the limits that could not be broken by legal rights—with songs like "We Shall Overcome" and "Dancin' in the Streets." When the musical that consolidates and choreographs an imagery to both capture and renew these songs' initial (TV news) images *and* that provides them with a compelling narrative context to somehow "resolve" (in multiple romances, one supposes) the problems they symbolize can be written, filmed (staged and recorded, too), and be successful enough to be shown year in and out on TV (like *Show Boat*), and not just during Black History Month (like *Hallelujah!* and *Stormy Weather*), then . . . But that time clearly is not yet. And perhaps there is no better cultural sign that the U.S. civil rights transformation is incomplete than that such a musical seems so hard to imagine. At the same time, there may be no better sign that many Americans are still hoping for—and still trying to create—this transformation than that musical performance and stories about it—the musical—remain such vibrant locations of sociocultural production and argument.

Of course, the common wisdom is that the musical is dead, but the common wisdom is wrong.[3] More accurately, it is only right if it uses narrow definitions, usually drawn out of a canon of plays and films produced in the overlapping eras of Hollywood industrial integration and formal genre integration. Moreover, the common wisdom about the musical is probably most wrong in relation to African Americans.[4]

Though there was a decade-long pause between 1959 and the next wave of the predominantly black-cast musicals, neither the black musical performer nor the all or predominantly black-cast musical as a subgenre disappeared when *Porgy and Bess* sank, when old Hollywood became new Hollywood, or when new "randomized," "fragmented" forms, like music video, flourished on TV and in postmodern cinema. Far from it. In fact, since I was born in 1960, the thoughts that led me to this book arose not from my firsthand experience of *Hallelujah!, Stormy Weather,* or *Carmen Jones*—although I do very distinctly remember Louis Armstrong in *Hello, Dolly!* (1969). Rather, these thoughts came into being after seeing and then wondering what might be behind

— Sammy Davis, Jr., the Supremes, and the Jacksons on TV in the sixties and seventies.

— "Blaxploitation" films (*Cleopatra Jones* [1973] *not Carmen Jones*), which like many of my peers, I heard first via hits songs and soundtracks and saw later.

— Predominantly black-cast musicals like *Lady Sings the Blues* (1972), *Car Wash* (1976), *Sparkle* (1976), *The Wiz* (1978), *Beat Street* (1984), *Breakin'* (1984), *Krush Groove* (1985), *Tap* (1989), *The Five Heartbeats* (1991), and *What's Love Got to Do With It?* (1991).[5]

— Auteurist musicals interested in race like *Finian's Rainbow* (Coppola, 1968), *All That Jazz* (Fosse, 1979), *The Cotton Club* (Coppola, 1984), and the performance number that climaxes *The Color Purple* (Spielberg, 1985).

— Overtly or covertly integrationist—or even polyracial—pop musicals like *Fame* (1980), *Flashdance* (1983), *Purple Rain* (1984), *The Bodyguard* (1993), or, more recently, the nontraditionally cast remake of Rodgers and Hammerstein's *Cinderella* (1997, made for TV) and *Save the Last Dance* (2001).[6]

— Michael Jackson's struggle to get black images on MTV, which he finally did—big time—with the long form video, "Thriller" (1983); Janet Jackson's minimusical video, complete with Cyd Charrise, the Nicholas Brothers, and Cab Calloway, for "Alright With Me" (1989); Michael Jackson's de(con)struction of the "Singin' in the Rain" number in the controversial coda to "Black or White" (1991).[7]

— Most of Spike Lee's films, which take stabs—in the several senses of the word—at the musical.

This is a partial catalogue of the post–*Porgy and Bess* material that initially prompted this book. What I found behind this profusion was more than I had expected—enough to fill this volume, and enough to preclude detailed analysis herein of black musical performance and American musical film (and TV) since 1960. (The canny, Hollywood-trained reader will be forgiven for wondering if I'm preparing her or him for *Disintegrating the Musical II.*) But the history I found behind—and that was often directly referenced and sometimes signified upon in—the profusion of black musicality in the movies and TV that I grew up with has also led me to wonder how much the dis/integrated musical and the socioculture it interacts with had changed—or not.

The recent near simultaneous release of two films, Joel and Ethan Coen's *O Brother, Where Art Thou?* and Spike Lee's *Bamboozled*, suggest to me that others are wondering too. A brief consideration of these films' and filmmakers' surprisingly shared—yet startlingly different—wonderings might provide a clearer sense of the distance traveled (or not) since 1959 and will at least clarify the continuing cultural presence and work of the black musical performance in American musical film.

O, Where Art the Brothers?

In many respects *O Brother* and *Bamboozled* could not be much different. *O Brother* is set in a fabulously imagined Southern, rural past and is comic, affirmative, tightly crafted, and luminously photographed. It is also a musical of a kind that even formalist genre critics would recognize. Since *O Brother* carefully, if fancifully, motivates all its performances and uses "folk" music (more on this later), it might even be seen as a formally integrated musical. *Bamboozled* is set in a not very embellished Northern, urban present and is satiric, despairing, loosely assembled, and often muddily shot on digital video. It is not a musical in any traditional sense but is rather a drama about making a musical TV variety show. *O Brother,* whatever else it may be, is not controversial, which is in keeping with the aloof, quirky (some would argue, condescending) authorial image the Coen Brothers have cultivated. *Bamboozled* is calculatedly controversial—to the extent, even, that newspapers rejected its advertising images as racist—and this is in keeping with Spike Lee's authorial image as an engaged, critical (some would argue, opportunist) provocateur.[8] Certainly U.S. audiences treated the two films very differently. *Bamboozled* lasted barely two months in theaters and earned only about a quarter of its ten million dollar cost. *O Brother* ran for nearly six months and almost doubled its twenty-six million dollar cost. Not surprisingly, *O Brother* received more and generally very warm attention from critics and reviewers. *Bamboozled* also received some positive notice, but over all it received much less notice, most of it scathingly negative, and even its positive reviews were often heavily qualified.

But *O Brother* and *Bamboozled* also have substantial commonalities. Each film is interested in the phenomena of mass, recorded media, the making and dissemination of which are central to the plots of both. Related to this, each film is transfixed by the past, especially the recorded, mediated past and its importation into the (our) present. And each makes this fixation part of its form, both remaking moments from earlier films and sound recordings and literally incorporating older work. Further, each film pivots around how encounters with—recording by— forms of mass mediation transform its protagonists, though the process of transformation and its end result are profoundly different in each case.

In *O Brother,* the protagonists, all on the run from authority (prison, the devil), record a song at a small radio station in order to make some money and then go on their way. Unbeknownst to them, their song becomes a hit, and at the film's climax, still unaware of their fame, they reprise their hit, and their adoring audience saves them from their nemesis, which allows the hero to reestablish his social legitimacy and reunite with his wife. In *Bamboozled,* a TV writer and his assistant, desperate to be allowed to do better work, scheme to get released from their contracts by producing an offensive flop. They hire a pair of street performers to star in their show, which becomes a hit, and the offense they had expected to lead to their firing leads instead to an internecine bloodbath. So, in *O Brother* the media encounter—recording a song—transforms its protagonists into free men (and, indeed, keeps them alive), and it transforms its main protagonist, Ulysses Everett McGill (George Clooney), into a comic hero and comically upstanding, professional citizen. In *Bamboozled* the media encounter—being taped for TV—imprisons its protagonists in masks and stereotypes and ultimately transforms many of them, including the main one, Pierre Delacroix/Peerless Dothan (Damon Wayans), into corpses; no one is transformed into a hero.

My plot synopses and catalogue of differences and similarities leave out, however, that both *O Brother* and *Bamboozled* concern interracial groups, though again with very different emphases, and both are interested in how race gets represented in the confluence of image, song, and story. This interest gets distilled into the most iconic connection between

67. The white protagonists in blackface in *O Brother, Where Art Thou?* (2000).

O Brother and *Bamboozled:* each uses blackface—very differently. Blackface in *O Brother* is a throwaway effect. In *Bamboozled,* it is an obsession.

O Brother's interracial group—a benign and happy one—comes into being when three white escaped convicts, Everett, Pete (John Turturro), and Delmar (Tim Blake Nelson), pick up a black hitchhiker, Tommy Johnson (Chris Thomas King). Like his patronymic namesake, the bluesman Robert Johnson, Tommy has just sold his soul to the devil (who, he insists, was white) in exchange for guitar skills. Almost immediately, the group gets a chance to record a song for the blind engineer of a small radio station. Trying to second guess his (potential) producer's desires, Everett claims the three white men are black, accompanied by a white guitarist; when he discovers he has guessed wrong, he reverses himself, and "The Soggy Bottom Boys" flawlessly perform what will become their hit, "I am a Man of Constant Sorrow." That evening, after playing "Hard Time Killing Floor Blues" around their campfire, Tommy abandons his friends when it appears they will be arrested. After a series of misadventures, which include having to black up (though they do not deploy minstrel blackface conventions) in order to spring Pete from the chain gang, Everett, Delmar, and Pete find Tommy about to be lynched at a Ku Klux Klan rally. Instead of fleeing, as Tommy had done, the three blacked-up whites, overpower the Klan color guard. In the confusion caused by white men in blackface in Klan robes, they free Tommy. The reconstituted Soggy Bottom Boys escape to the cover of a political rally where, now in hillbilly beards, they are mistaken for the entertainment. They reprise "I am a Man of Constant Sorrow" and discover their fame. At the

same time, their performance reveals the corrupt heart of the local re-
form candidate and Klan wizard, who tries to whip up resentment with
his repeated cries of "They's integrated!" but who is instead run out of
town on a rail. Constructed as heroes by the incumbent governor, the
team goes on a quest to recover Everett's wedding ring from his home,
which is about to be flooded by the Tennessee Valley Authority. They
arrive to find their original jailer, who also matches Tommy's description of the devil, waiting to lynch them, but the flood washes them all
away. The quartet emerges unscathed (presumably the jailer/devil and
his compatriots were not so lucky), and Tommy even finds Everett's ring
in the roll top desk he happens to be floating on.

This is a delightful (and wildly shaggy) story, and among its many
delights is that it shows black and white musicality as interwoven. In
musical comedy tradition, Everett, Pete, Delmar, *and* Tommy can—and
emphatically do—play together and, hence, get along together (or perhaps it is vice versa). Their co-created music is both the symbol and
the substance of a social and cultural bond, and it begins to blur their
racial identities. When need be, the whites blacken (blacking up) and
the black whitens (donning a fake white beard and joining a "hillbilly"
band). With the aid of song, they leap the charged color divide, which
is symbolically reiterated in the convicts' classic black-and-white-striped
costume, as well as in Tommy's dark suit and white shirt. Moreover, when
the team's music has been "mass communicated" (in the film's terms)
in the blind (one of the film's themes) medium of recorded sound, it
can facilitate similar bonds among others, even in the sighted (and sited)
medium of live performance. Here it leads to the utopian moment when
a segregated, Depression-era, Southern audience defends integration. In
O Brother's comic world, the politicians watching this event unfold get
the drift of the lesson.

This reading could be accused of overstating the case for *O Brother*'s
concern with race, representation, and integration in (and through)
musicalized images. After all there are many other characters (e.g., Pete's
brother-in-law, Governor Pappy O'Daniel, Babyface Nelson, Everett's
wife, Penny) that consume as much screen time interacting with the escaped convicts as Tommy Johnson does. As with the Al Jolson films I analyzed in chapter two, however, *O Brother* uses careful narrative framing
to show that this seemingly marginal concern is central. *O Brother* begins
with a Christian song, "Po' Lazarus," performed by an all-black chain

gang as a slow tempo, polyrhythmic, polyvocal work song. When this number concludes, the camera moves to show Everett, Pete, and Delmar—apparently the only three white men who had been on the chain gang—escaping, accompanied nondiegetically by the spritely, solo-voiced, hobo song, "Big Rock Candy Mountain." In the penultimate scene—the near lynching of the collective—another group of black laborers (who are not in prison stripes and who therefore may or may not be prisoners) sings the down tempo, polyvocal Christian lament, "Lonesome Valley," as they dig graves. This formally matches and thematically recalls the opening—and the flood effects a second escape. The conclusion of the film shows Everett united with his wife and daughters, who sing "Angel Band." The final image of the film, however, is of another African American character—a blind soothsayer who travels by railroad handcart and who had, immediately after the convicts' escape, cryptically foretold their adventures. As the McGill family crosses a railway line, the camera, which had been tracking them as they walked, stops, allowing the McGills to leave the frame, and watches this man recede into the distance on his cart. At the same time, he is assigned the film's last line, which he picks up in song from Everett's daughters: "Oh bear me away on your snow white wings to my immortal home."

Black figures and voices, then, bracket *O Brother* as well as, in the character of Tommy, traversing its middle. And these imprisoned or isolated, yet connected figures make the case for the inescapable presence and importance of blacks in America—defacto, practical integration instantiated here in the industrial infrastructure of the railroad, for example—even as they suggest that the blithe, utopian integration of the body of the film is incomplete and far from fully accomplished. But considered carefully, even that utopian aspect of the narrative and its form complicates itself: Tommy Johnson is thinly drawn; he abandons his friends; and he is wholly *instrumental:* he supplies the musical backdrop for his white compatriots (and when he performs his song, which shows he *can* sing, he performs alone and his work passes without comment from the others). He is instrumental also in providing his companions the occasion for their liberal heroism.

Joel Coen has been quoted as saying *O Brother* "is a valentine to the music."[9] It is certainly that, but one of its energizing forces is the differential complexity of that definite article: Is *the* music so unified, so defined? What would be at stake in such a unification? And what about the implied "folk" that stand, apparently, behind the music? *O Brother,* even (or maybe especially) with its nuanced probing of race and audiovisual representation, seemingly cannot help but find some folk more knowable, more definite and fully representable than others. Joel Coen has also dismissed the politics of *O Brother:* "The political undercurrent of the movie functions primarily for dramatic purposes, because the politics are frankly pretty primitive. The bad guys are racial bigots and KKK Grand Dragons, and the good guys are the heroes of the movie."[10] This may be so at the level of explicit politics, but it does not capture the film's conflicted-but-utopian, integrative-but-limited racial, musical, and cultural politics.

The Coens have suggested that they imagined *O Brother* as the film Preston Sturges's musical-comedy director John Sullivan (from *Sullivan's Travels* [1940], which *O Brother*'s title references) "might have made had he the chance to do an important film and had he been a big fan of country music."[11] Consequently, Sturges's film provides a useful gauge for the distance *O Brother* imagines U.S. culture has come in representing and confronting its race problems (and possibilities). Like *O Brother, Sullivan's Travels* also addressed issues of race, racial relations, and representation both directly—a late scene is set in a black church, where the congregation welcomes the white(!) chain gang to their movie night of Mickey Mouse cartoons by singing "Go Down Moses (Let My People Go)"—and indirectly—early, and much more briefly, a buffoonish black cook gets (comically?) hung by having his head poked through a bus roof and following that he gets whitefaced. Are these typifications being cemented or contested? *Sullivan's Travels* does not make a didactic point of clarifying these questions but instead allows them either to be ignored or to linger uncomfortably. At the end of *Sullivan's Travels,* John Sullivan, who had been yearning to make a serious film instead of a musical comedy, concludes that laughter is a socially good, unifying force (he does not mention music, but since he makes musicals, we can assume, I think, that he would include music as a social good, too). Sullivan was spurred to this conclusion by his experience in the black church, and his articulation of it is accompanied by a montage of laughing faces, many of which recall that scene. However, none of the faces in this montage are black. We know Sturges wanted to include some black faces in his montage, but his studio would not allow him to conclude his film with even this reference to blacks, this brief, purely formal moment of integration.

68. Man Ray /
Mantan (Savion
Glover) in blackface
in *Bamboozled*
(2000).

Sixty years later, the Coen Brothers *could*—and did—end their imagining of Sullivan's "important" movie with blacks and whites together,
singing the same song—but at the same time, traveling away from one
another.[12]

"Every Nigger is an Entertainer"?

If *O Brother* is an energetic and intricate "valentine" to (the) "folk" music,
to the musical, to the possibilities and limits of interracial collaboration
and representation in the United States, and to the unpredictable, and
therefore always conceivably liberating potentialities of "folk," popular,
and mass recorded cultures, then *Bamboozled* is a poison-pen letter. No
doubt many of the potential viewers of the film would have suspected
as much from *any* Spike Lee film, and *Bamboozled*'s title and advertising images could have only amplified such suspicions. That *Bamboozled*
intended to be harsh and didactic was clear the moment one saw its
posters featuring black performers in blackface, but as perhaps the black
blackface—or the infectious groove underneath Stevie Wonder's didactic opening song, "(We are a) Misrepresented People"—ought to indicate, *Bamboozled* is not simple, and its harshness may have pleasures of
its own.

One pleasure of *Bamboozled*, one it has in common with *O Brother*,
is its love of erudition, its skein of references that runs (in an exceedingly partial list) from Mark Twain to Ralph Ellison to James Baldwin,
from Bert Williams to Al Jolson to *Stormy Weather* to *Sunset Boulevard*

to *Network*. One way of looking at *Bamboozled* is as a game of referentiality, meaning, and connection. At stake in the game is nothing less than how to remember the past—indeed, to confront its mimetically recorded legacies over and again—while moving on, how to adjudicate appropriate and inappropriate, constructive and destructive pleasures, and how to judge the sociocultural effects of these pleasures. Such stakes might be most emphatic for the satirist-critic who can come to love what he hates by taking pleasure in expressing his aggravation and for the (mass) cultural producer who can misrecognize his own work as it moves into the past-that-remains-present. To underscore this idea, late in the film we see a montage of racist "collectibles," which includes the box or board of an apparently vintage game called "Bamboozled"; close scrutiny of the credits reveals that "Bamboozled" is a contemporary painting. And to suggest that this game and its stake are quite serious, near the film's end one character pronounces a death sentence on another with the words, "You fucked up in the game now."

Bamboozled signals its concern with these complexities of interpretation and pleasure in a host of other ways as well. Most subtly, while the bulk of the film is shot on digital video, the protagonist Pierre Delacroix's black blackfaced variety show, "Mantan's New Millennium Minstrel Show," is lovingly and very crisply shot on super-16 millimeter. As a consequence, the minstrel show looks better and more attractive, at least in conventional cinematic terms, than its surrounding "reality." On the one hand, this supports one of *Bamboozled*'s critical claims: We (mainstream America?) like art and entertainment that are "better looking"— easier to perceive, brighter, clearer, lighter—than reality. On the other hand, *Bamboozled* does not dispute that there are attractions to high craft—a point it underscores both by lavishing considerable attention on its musical numbers and by using photographer David Levinthal's super-aestheticized images of racist collectibles in its end credit sequence.

More overtly, *Bamboozled* develops a virtual catalogue of instances of problematic approbation and mixed (and changing) motives: For instance, at auditions, Delacroix and his assistant and co-conspirator Sloan (Jada Pinkett) laugh in astonishment when one performer delivers a song entitled "Niggers is a Beautiful Thing"—and (but?) he gets the job. During the filming of the pilot episode of "Mantan's New Millennium Minstrel Show" an "applause" (later it becomes a "howl") sign prompts the stunned audience, which does as it is told, if a bit uncertainly. Immediately following this, Delacroix visits his father (Paul Mooney), who is a stand-up comic working his brand of raunchy, obscenity and "n-word" laced material in small black clubs, where the audience laughs uproariously; after the show, as the father drinks himself into a stupor, he instructs Delacroix with that old show biz cliché—memorably put to music in *Singin' in the Rain* and famously signified on in Ellison's *Invisible Man*—"always keep 'em laughing, son." At its next taping session, the minstrel show breaks through to spontaneous audience approval (and starts, apparently, to amuse even Delacroix and Sloan, who never intended it to be funny) with an homage to and updating of *Stormy Weather*'s indefinite talk. And when the show first airs, one member of a group of hip-hop militants, who loathe the show (as Delacroix initially intended *everyone* should), cannot suppress his mirth at a mock old-time tune, "You Ain't Never Seen No Nigger Play Fiddle Like This."[13] His compatriots bully him back into line, but not before he protests, "That shit is funny to me. . . . I find that shit funny."

Bamboozled then is well aware of—and a participates in—a desire to police representations and the pleasures audiences can draw from them (and the benefits their makers can reap), while also being aware of—and participating in—the elusiveness of representations and their pleasures. The critic J. Hoberman argues that *O Brother, Where Out Thou?* is too cool, too smug to allow itself even to imply that it might have pondered, say, inverting its story and making it focus on Tommy Johnson instead of Ulysses Everett McGill; it may be concerned with representations of race, but it is not concerned enough to allow itself to be unnerved. In contrast, *Bamboozled*'s excruciating multiple awarenesses do unnerve it, leading it to (in Hoberman's word) "chaos," to gaps, to connections it cannot quite bring itself to make but that are, nonetheless, symptomatic in their absence.[14]

The gap many critics of the film note is that between the explicit minstrelsy and stereotyping that Delacroix and Sloan research and build "Mantan's New Millennium Minstrel Show" out of and the apparent target of *Bamboozled*'s satire—namely the nonblackfaced, less clearly stereotyped (or, perhaps, stereotyped in the name of satire) black roles in more recent film and television shows. This gap is most manifest in the climactic (non)"number" of the film, a five-minute montage—a tape assembled by Sloan to show Delacroix "the shit [he's] contributed to"— of blackfaced numbers and egregious stereotypes. It begins with Stepin

Fetchit's blackface appearance in *Dimples* and goes on to include substantial portions of the blackface material I've analyzed in the first part of this book. But it does not include the indefinite talk scene from *Stormy Weather* or any of Micheaux's black blackface, and it does not include any of the black-cast material analyzed in the second part of this book. Nor does the final montage include anything from, say, the TV variety show "In Living Color" (1990–1994), which starred two of the key performers from *Bamboozled*, Damon Wayans (Delacroix) and Tommy Davidson (Womack/Sleep 'n' Eat) and which Spike Lee repeatedly criticized as neomistrelsy. *Nor* does it include—or explain precisely why it should not include—any images from Lee's own concert film, *The Original Kings of Comedy* (2000), despite the fact that a number of them, especially out of context (or recontextualized, as in *Bamboozled*'s montage) would seem to fit.

In fairness, Spike Lee does implicate—or at least explicitly place—himself and his earlier work in this tar baby of a film. Lee's name and his public position in an ongoing controversy around authority, language, and representation are invoked early in the film when a white TV network executive defends his use of the word "nigger" to Delacroix: "I don't give a good god damn what that prick Spike Lee says, . . . 'nigger' is just a word, and if [rapper] Ol' Dirty Bastard can use it every other word, why can't I?" Delacroix takes Lee's position, both with his boss and later in conversation with his father (who adds a corollary to his injunction to "leave 'em laughing"—"Every nigger is an entertainer"—and also this signifying nonanswer to Delacroix's question about why he uses "that word" so much: "I say nigger one hundred times every morning; it keeps my teeth white"). But later, caught up in the success of his show, as well as by his perverse desire to control something he has already so clearly lost control of, Delacroix uses the word in a skit and shares a laugh over it with his boss. What can the status or value of this (represented) pleasure be? Is Lee abandoning his earlier, publicly stated position? Or, rather, what relation does that position have to *Bamboozled*? How do black authorship of and authority over (self)representation(s) in mass media work here?

Lee is also implicated, though less overtly, in *Bamboozled*'s parodies of hip-hop TV commercials for "Da Bomb" malt liquor and "Tommy Hillnigger Ghettowear." Parallel to his work in film, Lee has cultivated a very active career directing TV commercials, and while his commercials fastidiously avoid the stereotypes and hypersexualization of *Bam-*

69 and 70. Comedian Bernie Mack mimicking a "stuttering," "slow" boy in *The Original Kings of Comedy* (2000), an image that bears a close relationship with the "jolly nigger bank," which *Bamboozled* uses as its distilled image of minstrelization.

boozled's parodies, they—particularly his early ones—played an important role in legitimating the black youth/hip-hop audiences both as a potential market for ads and as a symbol for reaching other groups. In his advertising work he has also regularly worked with corporations whose products (and marketing) have stirred controversy among black critics and in some black neighborhoods—for example, Nike, Anheuser Busch, and the navy.[15] Additionally, Lee's earliest films—*She's Gotta Have It* (1986), *School Daze* (1988), and *Do the Right Thing* (1989)—contributed to spreading the sexualized imagery that pervades his parodies, particularly the fixation on black female (hyper)sexuality and its mediated fetish, the black woman's ass, enthusiastically proffered for the close-up camera. When Lee's early films are considered in their contexts, it is clear that he has broader interests than *just* objectifying black women. However, the well known—and in Toni Cade Bambara's view, "pro-Afro

71 and 72. A butt from the "Doin' the Butt" number in *School Daze* (1988), an image that is amplified and satirized as "hip hop" advertising for "Da Bomb" malt liquor in *Bamboozled.*

esthetic"[16]—"Doin' da Butt" dance number from *School Daze,* Lee's black-revisionist college musical, was eminently excerptable, had a separate life as a music video, and seems to have sparked more extreme developments of the same theme in the music video genre, which in turn seem to lead to hip-hop advertising, which in turn leads to . . . *Bamboozled* and its ad parodies. As with *The Original Kings of Comedy*'s overlaps with the minstrel mask, "Da Butt" is not very far removed, when taken out of its context, from "Da Bomb."

But the idea of "removal," of a desire for distance from past practices and relations, can be turned on its head. While some connections seem as though they ought to be broken—and perhaps cannot be—other connections in *Bamboozled* seem as though they ought to be maintained— and cannot be. The street-performing partners that Delacroix and Sloan tap for "Mantan's New Millennium Minstrel Show," Womack, who is a

73. Man Ray / Mantan's "Dance of Death" in *Bamboozled* (note the pistol in extreme close-up in the left foreground).

comic MC and singer, and Man Ray (Savion Glover), a tap dancer, are the film's clearest representatives of this crisis, if only because they are at the center of the "game," the vortex of the storm. They first lose their connection to themselves, as they are blacked up (in lingering detail far beyond that of the standard transformations in Hollywood's blackface scenes) and assigned "new" names, Sleep 'n' Eat and Mantan. Of course, these names are not new at all; they are the performing names of iconic, stereotypic thirties and forties black character performers, Willie Best and Mantan Moreland.[17] Womack realizes their loss before Man Ray, and the two have a falling out, so they ultimately lose one another, despite Womack's repeated question (reminiscent of *The Duke is Top*'s theme song), "Do you remember me!?" Man Ray comes to agree with Womack and repudiates his blackface stardom, but he does so with the mode of expression that drew him to Delacroix's attention and that he used while blacked up: tap dance, a skill he learned (as did Savion Glover) from Jimmy Slyde and Lon Chaney, his elders and forebears. But Man Ray's (apparent) breaking of undesirable connections (e.g., with blackface and media commodification) and reassertion of desirable ones (e.g., himself, his [folk] art and its traditions) is illegible to the hip-hop militants (who are, the film suggests, neominstrels in their own right). Recalling the "playful" threat that concluded Oscar Micheaux's *Swing!*, they capture Man Ray and murder him on live TV, while he tap dances—much as Savion Glover danced in memorializing Gene Kelly and dis/integrating his "Singin' in the Rain" at the 1996 Academy Awards show.

When Womack leaves Man Ray, he argues that nothing has changed:

"It's the same bullshit . . . just done over." He then does an uncanny Stepin Fetchit imitation, "Yas sah . . . what you want from me, massa? Ah sing for ya . . . ah tap dance for ya . . . ah coon for ya . . . anything to make you laugh." But of course, something *has* changed. There can be a character like Womack in American film, a character who can be shown slipping his masks on and off, a character who can be in blackface and be shown refusing blackface. So in its fashion, *Bamboozled,* in contrast to *O Brother,* makes the case for a greater sociocultural distance covered since 1959. Not surprisingly, though, *Bamboozled* gives with one hand while taking with the other. The film's last line, delivered in voice-over from beyond the grave by Pierre Delacroix, reiterates his father's lesson, "Always leave 'em laughing." As he begins to laugh, Delacroix is joined by a canned laugh track that verges on hysteria—and calls to mind the similar building of laughter at the end of *Sullivan's Travels,* which perhaps suggests that if we have traveled any distance, it is only far enough to see that happy statements like "always leave 'em laughing" and the happy ends they imply are only the thinnest of coverings for despair.

Bamboozled is finally maddeningly equivocal—unequivocally equivocal, it would be fair to say—but that makes it a particularly excellent instance of the enduring problems and contradictions of racialized representation that I have worked to identify and analyze in this book. At the film's end, Man Ray is horribly, wrongly, melodramatically murdered—a murder that is also a musical number, and which tries to convey the difficulties and discomforts of filming, especially in an "entertaining" way, what Susan Gubar has called the "spirit murder" of misrepresentation. As he is about to be put to death, Man Ray pleads, "For what? Singin' and dancin'? I'm just hoofin', man." *Bamboozled* means to convince us that—particularly for African Americans—there is no such thing as "just" singin' and dancin'. I hope my analysis has convinced you that there never was.

Notes

Introduction: Disintegrating the Musical

1 Peter Noble, *The Negro in Films* (1948; reprint, Port Washington, N.Y.: Kennikat Press, 1969), 49.

2 For more on (inter)racial social-problem films—e.g., *Home of the Brave* and *Pinky*—see Ralph Ellison, "The Shadow and the Act" (1949), in *Shadow and Act* (New York: Vintage, 1972), 273–81; Michael Rogin, *Blackface, White Noise* (Berkeley: University of California Press, 1996); and Aaron Baker, "From Second String to Solo Star: Classic Hollywood and the Black Athlete," in Daniel Bernardi, ed., *Classic Hollywood, Classic Whiteness* (Minneapolis: University of Minnesota Press, 2001), 31–51. Donald Crafton claims that the first black-cast drama was *North of Dixie* (Paramount, 1929), but this film seems to have been lost (*The Talkies: American Cinema's Transition to Sound, 1926–1931* [New York: Scribner's, 1997], 403–6). The first still extant black-cast drama is *Bright Road* (MGM, 1953).

3 The musical is a peripheral presence in the five foundational texts of the contemporary study of African Americans in American film: Daniel Leab's *From Sambo to Superspade: The Black Experience in Motion Pictures* (Boston: Houghton Mifflin, 1975) dismisses the musical as a genre. Donald Bogle's popular and influential *Toms, Coons, Mulattoes, Mammies, and Bucks,* new third edition (New York: Continuum, 1994 [1973]) gives them only brief consideration. In his three volumes, *Slow Fade to Black: The Negro in American Film, 1900–1942* (New York: Oxford University Press, 1977); *Black Film as Genre* (Bloomington: Indiana University Press, 1978); and *Making Movies Black: The Hollywood Message Movie from World War II to the Civil Rights Era* (New York: Oxford University Press, 1993), Thomas Cripps provides more extensive and nuanced consideration of music and musical performance, especially in the late twenties and early thirties, but his focus on creating a broad sociocultural history precludes extensive formal analysis of a single genre. More recent books continuing the study of African Americans in sound film—Manthia Diawara, ed., *Black American Cinema* (New York: Routledge, 1993); Ed Guerrero, *Framing Blackness: The African American Image in Film* (Philadelphia: Temple University Press, 1993); Mark Reid, *Redefining Black Film* (Berkeley: University of California Press, 1993); Clyde R.

Taylor, *The Mask of Art: Breaking the Aesthetic Contract—Film and Literature* (Bloomington: Indiana University Press, 1998)—also continue the emphasis of the earlier studies on nonmusical and usually dramatic or serious genres.

4   For the standard version of this story, see Eileen Southern, *The Music of Black Americans: A History,* revised edition (New York: Norton, 1983).

5   [W. E. B. Du Bois], "*The Birth of a Nation:* An Editorial," *Crisis,* May–June 1915, 33.

6   [W. E. B. Du Bois], "Dramatis Personae," *Crisis,* October 1929, 342, 355–56, 358.

7   W. E. B. Du Bois, *The Souls of Black Folk,* in *Writings,* ed. Nathan Huggins (1903; reprint, New York: New American Library, 1986), 545. Du Bois reiterated his position many times in his essays and once again in book form; see *The Gift of Black Folk* (1924; reprint, Millwood, N.Y.: Kraus-Thomson Organization Limited, 1975). For one contemporary extrapolation of Du Bois's position, see, for example, Kalamu ya Salaam, "How We Sound Is How We Are," *African American Review* 29.2 (summer 1995): 181–82.

8   Langston Hughes, "Note on Commercial Art," *Crisis,* March 1940, 79.

9   The scholarly work addressing these issues has increased immensely in the last twenty-five years. Two foundational texts were Robert Sklar, *Movie-Made America: A Social History of American Movies* (New York: Random House, 1975) and David Bordwell, Janet Staiger, and Kristin Thompson, *The Classical Hollywood Cinema: Film Style and Mode of Production to 1960* (New York: Columbia University Press, 1985). My understanding has been most strongly influenced by Miriam Hansen's account of the conflicted and uneven development of the "new universal language" of spectatorship in the early classical era of Hollywood film; see *Babel and Babylon: Spectatorship in American Silent Film* (Cambridge: Harvard University Press, 1991). For a useful history of the rise of industrial-managerial integration, see Alfred D. Chandler, Jr., *The Visible Hand: The Managerial Revolution in American Business* (Cambridge: Harvard University Press, 1977).

10   W. E. B. Du Bois, "The Right to Work," in *Writings,* 1235–38. Adding critical significance to the NAACP board's move to fire Du Bois were the facts that he was a founder of the NAACP and the founding editor of *The Crisis.*

11   W. E. B. Du Bois, "Segregation in the North," in *Writings,* 1239–48. Du Bois's use of integration here is the first racial-social use of the word that I have found; it predates the OED's listed first use by fifteen years.

12 W. E. B. Du Bois, "The Board of Directors on Segregation," in *Writings*, 1252–54. This is not the first time, in this seemingly socioeconomic debate, that Du Bois had recourse to art. In "The Right to Work" he cites the robustness of Negro "art" both as evidence of African Americans' ability to build something of such ingenuity and integrity as his proposed "black market" and as inspiration for facing the unavoidable short term "cost" of this black cooperation. Here, in "The Board of Directors on Segregation," Du Bois makes plain that for him black art, before all other forms, means music.

13 For the best history of the general circumstances in which African Americans could see movies in this period see, Douglas Gomery, "Movie Theatres for Black Americans" in *Shared Pleasures: A History of Movie Presentation in the United States* (Madison: University of Wisconsin Press, 1992), 155–70.

14 F. Scott Fitzgerald, *The Last Tycoon* (New York: Scribner's, 1941), 92; negro is uncapitalized in the original. This fascinating figure would yield interestingly to Toni Morrison's analysis of "American Africanisms" in white-authored U.S. literature, a project well beyond the scope of this book. For our immediate purposes, though, part of Fitzgerald's protagonist's response to the "negro" is especially interesting: "They have pictures of their own" (93). Certainly Fitzgerald was aware of race film, then, and he implies that major Hollywood producers were as well.

15 Du Bois, "Segregation in the North," in *Writings*, 1246.

16 When he revisited *The Birth of a Nation* controversy in his autobiography, Du Bois reflected specifically on the problem of controlling film production and the challenges of criticizing mass media: "In combating this film, our Association was placed in a miserable dilemma. We had to ask liberals to oppose freedom of art and expression, and it was senseless for them to reply: 'Use this art in your own defense.' The cost of picture making and the scarcity of appropriate artistic talent made any such immediate answer beyond question" (*Dusk of Dawn: An Essay Toward an Autobiography of a Race Concept* [1940] in *Writings*, 730).

17 Malcolm X, as told to Alex Haley, *The Autobiography of Malcolm X* (New York: Ballantine, 1964), 99. The racially integrated movie theater in Michigan where young Malcolm recalled seeing *Gone With the Wind* seems also to have contributed a particularly bitter edge to his hatred of that film (32).

18 For a provocative argument about how sight, especially in the form of film, comes to influence the associational/representational "meaning" of sounds in music, see Simon Frith, *Performing Rites: On the Value of Popu-*

lar Music (Cambridge: Harvard University Press, 1996), 99–122. Later in the same work (see 123–44), Frith extends the discussion specifically to race and musical meaning but, surprisingly, has no recourse to film.

19 Bogle, *Toms, Coons, Mulattoes, Mammies, and Bucks,* xx. See also Donald Bogle, *Brown Sugar: Eighty Years of America's Black Female Superstars* (1980; reprint, New York: Da Capo, 1990) and *Dorothy Dandridge: A Biography* (New York: Amistad, 1997).

20 Samuel A. Floyd Jr.'s *The Power of Black Music: Interpreting Its History from Africa to the United States* (New York: Oxford University Press, 1995) is the most thoroughgoing recent attempt to define "black music." Floyd argues that black music is characterized by a "heterogeneous sound ideal," a phrase he borrows from Olly Wilson's studies of West African music; that it is resolutely communal, interactive, and participatory; and that these qualities are, in an important sense, qualities of performance rather than "text" (26–27, 151–52, 269–70; see also Frith, *Performing Rites,* 136–42). Floyd's analysis is very useful, but film also precisely breaks apart these crucial characteristics, constructing (through sound and picture editing, among other means) a performance, perhaps representing the communal and interactive and capturing the heterogeneous sound ideal, but also making impossible, in quite the sense Floyd means, participation, extended interaction, and heterogeneity.

21 Lewis Nichols, "*Oklahoma!* a Musical Hailed as Delightful," *New York Times,* 1 April 1943, 27.

22 John Chapman, "*Carmen Jones* Simply Superb Negro Adaptation of *Carmen,*" *New York Daily News,* 3 December 1943.

23 While race is left completely unmarked and unremarked within *Carmen Jones* (a fact I explore in some detail in chapter four), race and ethnicity (and racial-social integration) are carefully, if peripherally, incorporated into *Oklahoma!* The peddler, Ali Hakim, clearly marked as an ethnic, is integrated into the community—and whitened—when he marries Ado Annie. In contrast, when Will, a cowboy and, like Ali, a male comic foil, returns from Kansas City he sings of the bawdy pleasures the metropolis offers ("Ev'rythin's Up to Date in Kansas City") and then does a mysterious dance, which he explains thus: "That's rag-time. Seen a couple of colored fellers doin' it" (Richard Rodgers and Oscar Hammerstein II, *Oklahoma!* in *Six Plays by Rodgers and Hammerstein* [New York: Modern Library, n.d.], 16).

24 See, for example, Geoffrey Block, "The Broadway Canon from *Show Boat* to *West Side Story* and the European Operatic Ideal," *The Journal of Musicology* 11.4 (fall 1993): 525–44.

25 John Mueller, in his essay "Fred Astaire and the Integrated Musical,"

Cinema Journal 24.1 (1984): 28–40, comes up with a half dozen formal categories that might constitute "integration" in the narrative, feature-length film musical.

26   Richard Dyer, "Entertainment and Utopia," in *Genre: The Musical,* ed. Rick Altman (London: Routledge and Kegan Paul, 1981), 183.

27   Rick Altman, *The American Film Musical* (Bloomington: Indiana University Press, 1987), 16–89. See also Gerald Mast, *Can't Help Singin': The American Musical on Stage and Screen* (Woodstock, N.Y.: Overlook Press, 1987), 1–6, Jane Feuer, *The Hollywood Musical,* second edition (Bloomington: Indiana University Press, 1993), 50, 67–71, 94–96 and Dyer, "Entertainment and Utopia," 176–89.

28   Altman, *American Film Musical,* 290, and more generally, 272–327.

29   See Feuer, *Hollywood Musical,* especially 1–22, and Altman, *The American Film Musical,* 322.

30   For a specific analysis of how industrial integration *could* empower African Americans as well as ethnic Americans, see Lizabeth Cohen, *Making a New Deal: Industrial Workers in Chicago, 1919–1939* (New York: Cambridge University Press, 1990). Although I have explained the crisis of economic and racial-social integration in terms of African American experience, it was also a profoundly felt class and gender crisis for many white Americans from at least late 1929 until at least the end of World War II.

31   Feuer, *Hollywood Musical,* 87–122; Altman, *American Film Musical,* 360–64.

32   Mast, *Can't Help Singin',* 6, 7–24, and 35–38.

33   Dyer attributes this quotation to Brecht; see "Entertainment and Utopia," 189.

34   Altman, *American Film Musical,* 32, 340. Feuer works to complicate this monolithic sense of audience in her "Postscript for the Nineties" in the second edition of *Hollywood Musical* (123–45), and Altman, in bravely revisiting and revising his theory of genre (though not with reference exclusively to musicals), makes the fragmented and variegated audience central to his thinking; see Rick Altman, *Film/Genre* (London: BFI, 1999). For a related argument, see Janet Staiger, *Interpreting Films: Studies in the Historical Reception of American Cinema* (Princeton: Princeton University Press, 1992), 79–97. See also Steve Neale, *Genre and Hollywood* (New York: Routledge, 2000), which also champions a less formalist, text-driven genre theory.

35   Altman, *Film/Genre,* 99.

36   Feuer, *Hollywood Musical,* 124.

37   For a similar response to the idea of musical integration (as a formalized

symbol of social integration), but from a "queered" rather than raced perspective, see D. A. Miller, *Place for Us: Essay on the Broadway Musical* (Cambridge: Harvard University Press, 1998), 3.

38 These terms are Altman's from *American Film Musical,* 128–327.

39 For a sense of this, see David Meeker, *Jazz in the Movies,* enlarged edition (New York: Da Capo, 1981); Phyllis Rauch Klotman, *Frame by Frame: A Black Filmography* (1979; reprint, Bloomington: Indiana University Press, 1997); and Klotman and Gloria J. Gibson, *Frame by Frame II: A Filmography of the African American Image, 1978–1994* (Bloomington: Indiana University Press, 1997).

40 Hansen, *Babel and Babylon,* 125.

41 Willie Ruff, *A Call to Assembly: The Autobiography of a Musical Storyteller* (New York: Viking, 1991), 68.

42 Tommye Berry, "Kansas City Likes The Film, *Hooray for Love,*" *Chicago Defender,* 17 August 1935, 7.

43 The study of African American reception practices (especially historical reception practices) is still in its early stages. Mary Carbine documents and analyzes the interpenetration of live, black performance and the movies in " 'The Finest Outside the Loop': Motion Picture Exhibition in Chicago's Black Metropolis, 1905–1928," *Camera Obscura* 23 (May 1990): 9–42. Gregory Waller documents the same phenomenon for the same period, but on a citywide scale, in *Mainstreet Amusements: Movies and Commercial Entertainment in a Southern City, 1896–1930* (Washington, D.C.: Smithsonian Institution Press, 1995), and Alison Griffiths and James Lathan focus on a slightly earlier period in Harlem in "Film and Ethnic Identity in Harlem, 1896–1915," in *American Movie Audiences: From the Turn of the Century to the Early Sound Period,* ed. Melvyn Stokes and Richard Maltby, (London: BFI, 1999), 46–63. Dan Streible looks farther afield and at a period spanning the transition to sound in "The Harlem Theater: Black Film Exhibition in Austin, Texas: 1920–1973," in Diawara, *Black American Cinema,* 221–36.

As Miriam Hansen has argued, much theorizing of the film spectator has constructed too monolithic a figure. In her own work, Hansen finds evidence for a wider array of spectatorial practice during the silent era. She finds this evidence especially in the unique intersections of the live event(s) of filmgoing and the mechanically reproduced, homogenizing Hollywood movie. See *Babel and Babylon,* especially 1–125, and "Early Cinema, Late Cinema: Permutations of the Public Sphere," *Screen* 34.3 (autumn 1993): 197–210.

Hansen suggests that the coming of sound did further consolidate and homogenize the Hollywood film spectator, but my research suggests (extending Carbine) that this was not true in African American communities where music and live performance often overshadowed the film and continued to be crucial elements of the cinema program into the fifties and even the sixties. (Thomas Doherty argues that the silenced audience has been overemphasized in "This is Where We Came In: The Audible Screen and the Voluble Audience of Early Sound Cinema," in Stokes and Maltby, *American Movie Audiences*, 143–63.) Moreover, though my evidence for this is still largely anecdotal, it seems that many African American audiences have maintained, since the silent era, an "impolite," "loud," interactive and often explicitly critical relationship with U.S. movie screens. The *Defender* often ran articles chastising loud theater audiences; see also, Ralph Ellison, "The Shadow and the Act," in *Shadow and Act*, 273–81; James Baldwin, *The Devil Finds Work* (New York: Dell, 1976); and Gary Dauphin, "The Show: Sometimes the Audience Produces More Entertainment Than the Plotline," *Village Voice*, 21 November 1995, film special section, 10, 12.

44 Lerone Bennett, Jr., "Hollywood's First Negro Movie Star," *Ebony*, May 1959, 106. *Porgy and Bess* (in which his singing was dubbed) was not the only role in which Poitier sang. He also sang at the beginning and the ending of *The Defiant Ones* (1959), made almost simultaneously with *Porgy and Bess* and a film Poitier much preferred for its seriousness.

For the beginnings of an analysis of the unique forms of "black stardom," see Arthur Knight, "Star Dances: African American Constructions of Stardom, 1925–1960," in Daniel Bernardi, ed., *Classic Hollywood, Classic Whiteness* (Minneapolis: University of Minnesota Press, 2001), 386–414.

45 In constructing this brief analysis, I have drawn on the voluminous literature on Robeson and *Show Boat*. Most important have been, on Robeson, Martin Duberman's *Paul Robeson* (New York: Knopf, 1988), Richard Dyer's *Heavenly Bodies* (New York: St. Martin's, 1986), and the essays collected in Jeffrey C. Stewart, ed., *Paul Robeson: Artist and Citizen* (New Brunswick, N.J.: Rutgers University Press and The Paul Robeson Cultural Center, 1998); and on *Show Boat*, Miles Kreuger, *Show Boat: The Story of a Classic American Musical* (New York: Oxford University Press, 1977) and Lauren Berlant, "Pax Americana: The Case of *Show Boat*," in *Cultural Institutions of the Novel*, ed. Deidre Lynch (Durham, N.C.: Duke University Press, 1996), 399–422.

46 Carol Clover, "Dancin' in the Rain," *Critical Inquiry* 21.4 (summer 1995): 722–47.

1 Wearing and Tearing the Mask

1 The Scribe, "'Jazz Singer' Plays Metropolitan; Grand Theater Closed for Repairs," *Chicago Defender,* 12 May 1928, sec. 1, 10. The quarter-page advertisement in the 21 April 1928 *Pittsburgh Courier* (national edition, sec. 1, 12) for *The Jazz Singer*'s week at the Elmore Theater indicates that Chicago's exhibitors and African American journalists were not anomalous in their attention to this film.

2 Advertisement for the Metropolitan Theater, *Chicago Defender,* 20 October 1928, sec.1, 10.

3 Michael Rogin has reminded interpreters of *The Jazz Singer,* though, that there *is* a black performer in the film: Mary Dale's black maid, who appears briefly during a backstage scene. See Michael Rogin, *Blackface, White Noise: Jewish Immigrants in the Hollywood Melting Pot* (Berkeley: University of California Press, 1996), 92.

4 Rogin claims that "*The Jazz Singer* ended the use of blackface as [an] unself-conscious method of impersonating African Americans (as in *Birth of a Nation*) . . . [and] introduced to feature films blackface as conscious film subject"; *Blackface, White Noise,* 167. I have borrowed this usage of "veritable" from Jim Pines, *Blacks in Films: A Survey of Racial Themes and Images in the American Film* (London: Studio Vista, 1975). There is no comprehensive catalogue of Hollywood (or, more broadly, American) films that use blackface; I base my numbers on films that I have either seen or seen stills from, and I feel confident, consequently, that my estimates are conservative ones.

5 Eddie Cantor, as told to David Freeman, *My Life is in Your Hands* (New York: Harper and Brothers, 1928), 159. Though I will have more to say about Cantor in my next chapter, I hasten to add here that Cantor was not racist, at least not within his period's standards of what constituted racism. He was noted for his fairness in dealing with his African American colleagues; he almost always acknowledged Williams's influence and acclaimed his immense skill; and according to at least one source, Cantor shamed Gosden and Correll—better known as Amos 'n' Andy—into remunerating the black blackface comics Flournoy Miller and Aubrey Lyles for material they took from that team's routines (Olivette Miller in Yvette Smith, *Mo' Funny: Black Comedy in America* [New York: 12th Street Productions/HBO, 1993]). See also, Eddie Cantor, "Bert Williams—'The Best Teacher I Ever Had," *Ebony,* June 1958: 103–6.

6 Eric Lott, *Love and Theft: Blackface Minstrelsy and the American Working Class* (New York: Oxford University Press, 1993), 240n. The afterlife

of blackface is not only manifest in film. Blackface continued as a professional and semiprofessional live performance practice into the forties and, residually, into the fifties when it continued on TV and in live amateur programs, where it sometimes still appears. More recently, blackface has been reappearing in postmodern theatrical performances as a kind of after-afterlife.

7 In the series of essays leading to his book, *Blackface, White Noise* (1996), Michael Rogin can be seen working against the weight of assumptions about the early end of cinematic blackface. Over the course of four essays Rogin finds progressively later and less certain moments for the "end" of blackface in American movies. See Michael Paul Rogin, " 'The Sword Became a Flashing Vision': D.W. Griffith's *The Birth of a Nation*" in *Ronald Reagan, the Movie and Other Episodes in Political Demonology* (Berkeley: University of California Press, 1987), 227; "Blackface, White Noise," *Critical Inquiry* 18 (spring 1992): 450–51; "Making America Home: Racial Masquerade and Ethnic Assimilation in the Transition to Talking Pictures," *The Journal of American History* 79.3 (December 1992): 1054; " 'Democracy and Burnt Cork'," *Representations* 46 (spring 1994): 5.

Jim Pines in *Blacks in Films* finds all blackface performance after *The Jazz Singer* "decadent" and, hence, somehow unworthy of analysis (19; Rogin duplicates this logic in "Blackface, White Noise," 450–51). Gerald Mast in *Can't Help Singin': The American Musical on Stage and Screen* (Woodstock, N.Y.: Overlook Press, 1987) allows that blackface existed beyond the thirties but keeps it unduly tied to Jolson: "If movie blackface began with Jolson, it also ended with him. . . . The last blackface performance[s] in . . . Hollywood musical[s] [were] . . . in *The Jolson Story* (1946) and *Jolson Sings Again* (1949)" (89).

Joseph Boskin's *Sambo: The Rise and Demise of an American Jester* (New York: Oxford University Press, 1986) is the only study that campaigns steadily against "the neat historical iron[ies]" (Mast, 87) to which assumptions about the early end of cinema blackface give rise. See also, Susan Gubar, *Racechanges: White Skin, Black Face in American Culture* (New York: Oxford University Press, 1997), 53–94.

8 Rogin, "Blackface, White Noise," 451 n. 70. Two early examples of this elusive use of the term are John D. Silvera, "Still in Blackface," *Crisis*, March 1939, 76–77, and Dalton Trumbo, "Blackface, Hollywood Style," *Crisis*, December 1943, 365–67, 378. Silvera does briefly mention blackface as a continuing practice of the late thirties but generally uses the term to refer to stereotyped roles played by African Americans. Trumbo, despite discussing in some detail several films that featured blackface performances, focuses exclusively on stereotyped roles.

9 Ella Shohat, "Ethnicities-in-Relation: Toward a Multicultural Reading of American Cinema," in *Unspeakable Images: Ethnicity and the American Cinema,* ed. Lester D. Friedman (Urbana: University of Illinois Press, 1991), 223.

10 Carol Clover, "Dancin' in the Rain," *Critical Inquiry* 21.4 (summer 1995): 740.

11 Eileen Southern, *The Music of Black Americans: A History,* revised edition (New York: Norton, 1983), 92.

12 For what is still the best history of black minstrels—and minstrelsy in general—in the nineteenth century, see Robert Toll, *Blacking Up: The Minstrel Show in Nineteenth-Century America* (New York: Oxford University Press, 1974), especially 195–269. See also Henry Sampson, *Blacks in Blackface: A Source Book on Early Black Musical Shows* (Metuchen, N.J.: Scarecrow, 1980).

13 Stuart Hall, "What is This 'Black' in Black Popular Culture?" in *Black Popular Culture,* ed. Gina Dent (Seattle: Bay, 1992), 27.

14 See, for instance, Albert W. Davis, "Past Days of Minstrelsy," *Americana,* June 1912, 529–47.

15 James A. Jackson, "What Sort of People are Show Folks?" *Richmond Planet* 19 July 1930.

16 Carl Wittke, *Tambo and Bones: A History of the American Minstrel Stage* (Durham, N.C.: Duke University Press, 1930), 249.

17 This scrutiny was also part of the larger flurry of critical attention to American culture that had built across the twenties. For a social and cultural history that pays especially careful attention to race as a component of this scrutiny, see Ann Douglas, *Terrible Honesty: Mongrel Manhattan in the 1920s* (New York: Farrar, Straus and Giroux, 1995).

18 For a very useful and wide-ranging map of writing on blackface, both before and after the period I am focusing on here, see Lott, *Love and Theft,* especially 1–37. The black writers I attend to here were not the first to write about blackface. Lott analyzes an 1849 review of a black minstrel troupe by Frederick Douglass and considers ironic, subversive modifications of minstrel song lyrics in Martin Delany's *Blake* (1859–61).

19 Johnson, *Black Manhattan* (1930; reprint, New York: Arno, 1968), 87.

20 Ibid., 93.

21 Ibid., 93.

22 To further complicate this intricate picture, it's worth noting that poet-lyricist Johnson directly contributed, along with his brother J. Rosamond Johnson and their partner Bob Coles, to this second phase.

   Working from and extending Johnson, Ann Douglas suggests, "*Shuffle Along* was hailed by blacks and whites as a critical step away from minstrelsy and its coon songs toward a modern black musical art, yet in some ways its importance stems precisely from its *return* to minstrelsy. The so-called years of exile for the Negro performers [Johnson's assessment of the period 1910–1920] had resulted, not in a diminution of modern Negro musical art, but in a proud intensification and creative complication of it, and *Shuffle Along* signaled an audacious and self-conscious mining of the Negro musical's black-and-white minstrel roots" (*Terrible Honesty,* 378).

23 [W. E. B. Du Bois,] "Dramatis Personae," *Crisis,* October 1929, 342.

24 "Dramatis Personae," 342. Like Johnson, Du Bois was also very interested in the theater, and the performing arts more generally. However, Du Bois pursued his interests not by working as a theater professional but rather by organizing amateur consciousness-raising pageants and sponsoring community and little theater groups—all specifically addressed to black audiences.

25 W. E. B. Du Bois, [Untitled Eulogy], in Mabel Rowland, ed., *Bert Williams, Sons of Laughter: A Symposium of Tribute to the Man and to His Work . . .* (1923; reprint, New York: Negro Universities Press, 1969), 218. Williams himself actually did not smile much—his blackfaced stage persona was that of the sad clown, "Nobody" in the lyric of his most famous song. Du Bois also wrote of Williams's "genius," despite the horrors of minstrelsy, in "Drama Among the Black Folk," *Crisis,* October 1916, 169, and *The Gift of Black Folk* (1924; reprint, Millwood, N.Y.: Kraus-Thomson Organization Limited, 1975), 309–10.

26 Rowland, *Son of Laughter,* 217–18.

27 Ibid., 218.

28 See Douglas, *Terrible Honesty,* especially 31–107, for this hatred of masks. Douglas argues that this is a quality of the era, though one that had very different ramifications for blacks and whites.

29 George Santa, "Does Blackface Acting Exert a Magic Spell Over American Audiences?" *Richmond Planet,* 31 January 1931, 6. This piece is reprinted from the *Baltimore Afro-American,* but the original publication date is not indicated.

30 Santa, "Does Blackface?" 6.

31 Ann Charters, *Nobody: The Story of Bert Williams* (New York: Macmillan, 1970). See also Cantor, *My Life is in Your Hands,* 159–62.

32 Santa, "Does Blackface?" 6. According to Jolson's most thorough biographer, early in his career Jolson did explicitly imitate Williams, though after he had already started blacking up. See Herbert G. Goldman, *Jolson: The Legend Comes to Life* (New York: Oxford University Press, 1988), 34–40.

33 Santa, "Does Blackface?" 6.

34 A 1930 article in the *Chicago Defender* gives some sense of Amos 'n' Andy's early audience among blacks: "In reply to many inquiries concerning the racial identity of the popular radio comedy team of Amos 'n' Andy which have reached the *Defender* from its readers throughout the country the following information is given. Freeman F. Gosden, the Amos of the pair, and Charles J. Correll, Andy, are white men" ("Amos 'n' Andy Now in the Million Dollar Circle," 5 June 1930, 6).

For a broader sense of African Americans' changing receptions of Amos 'n' Andy, see Melvin Patrick Ely, *The Adventures of Amos 'n' Andy: The Social History of an American Phenomenon* (New York: Free Press, 1991).

35 Henry Brown, "Just Where Did 'Blackface' Comedy Get Its Start?" *Chicago Defender,* 31 December 1932, 11.

36 Ibid., 11.

37 The Varieties artist was Charles Matthews, who did blackfaced performances in the 1820s, and the stable hand was the black Jim Crow, whose song and walk/dance were appropriated in blackface by T. D. Rice.

Brown cites yet another piece on blackface, this one written by Theophilus Lewis, the drama critic for *Opportunity* magazine and the *New York Amsterdam News*. I have been unable to locate the essay to which Brown refers, but the density and relative accuracy of Brown's narrative suggests that Lewis's essay would be worth looking at.

As should be obvious by now, claims about the "origin(s)" of blackface are complex, controversial, explicitly political, and probably well beyond ever settling—they are mythic. For sophisticated though differing treatments of these myths see Lott, *Love and Theft* and Roger D. Abrahams, *Singing the Master: The Emergence of African-American Culture in the Plantation South* (New York: Pantheon, 1992).

38 Brown, "Just Where?" 11.

39 See Sampson, *Blacks in Blackface,* and Mel Watkins, *On the Real Side: Laughing, Lying, and Signifying* (New York: Simon and Schuster, 1994), 80–180. For an individual African American's account of his encounters with blackface, see Richard Grupenhoff, *The Black Valentino: The Stage and Screen Career of Lorenzo Tucker* (Metuchen, N.J.: Scarecrow, 1988), 20–21, 32–52.

40 See, for example, "To Open at Lafayette," a photograph of the husband and wife music and comedy team Butterbeans and Susie, with Butterbeans in blackface, *Chicago Defender,* 19 March 1927, sec. 1, 8, and "At Grand Next Week," a photograph of Dashin' Dinah and Eddie Lemons, with Lemons in blackface, *Chicago Defender,* 30 April 1927, sec. 1, 9.

41 "Chicago's Finest Theater to Open Doors Saturday," *Chicago Defender,*
    4 February 1928, sec. 1, 6.

    The *Defender* monitored the planning and construction of the Regal
    very carefully but also very contradictorily: See, for example, "Draw
    Color Line on Theater Building," *Chicago Defender,* 19 March 1927, sec. 1,
    2, which reports on segregated hiring practices during the construction
    of the theater thereby "giving evidence already of what the policy of its
    owners will be toward the color line," and "If You Can Name This New
    Theater, You'll Win a Prize," *Chicago Defender,* 5 November 1927, sec. 1, 1.

    The *Defender*'s editors were certainly right to give the Regal so much
    attention. It had a profound influence on the geography of South Side
    entertainment, shifting the center of attractions from the smaller, older,
    often individually (if not black) controlled attractions of "the Stroll" to
    a tonier neighborhood further south and east and into the hands of a
    large, white corporation. The historic importance of the Regal is marked
    in contemporary South Side Chicago by the New Regal, another old
    movie palace (still further south and east) that has been renovated as a
    community center for staging civic events, touring plays, and concerts.

42 Evangaline Roberts, "Garbage Goes Over Big This Week at Regal," *Chi-
    cago Defender,* 10 August 1929, sec.1, 9. Rogers had been a fixture on the
    South Side entertainment scene since before World War I; after his regu-
    lar run at the Regal, he had occasional engagements there while working
    as MC at the Golden Lily Cafe.

43 "2,500 Attend 38th Showing of Minstrels," *Chicago Defender,* 2 April
    1932, sec.1, 13; this charity minstrel show was held at the Savoy Ballroom,
    which was adjacent to the Regal and which, along with the Regal, cap-
    tured the biggest name black jazz bands whenever they toured. I have not
    been able to confirm the headline's seeming suggestion that this tradition
    began before the turn of the century.

44 See, for example, "Morgan Park Community Center has Minstrel Show,"
    Chicago Defender, 4 May 1929, sec. 1, 6; "Met Has a Minstrel Show,"
    Chicago Defender, 8 April 1933, sec. 1, 8, which suggests that the Metro-
    politan Theater, a cinema, did run a quasi-minstrel show for commercial
    purposes in spring 1933; Barbara Llorayne, "Those Amateur Minstrels
    Are Real Pros Now," *Chicago Defender,* 22 April 1933, sec. 1, 8; Dewey R.
    Jones, "Nation's Stars to Help Defender Benefit Show," *Chicago Defender,*
    29 April 1933, sec. 1, 1—this show was to benefit the Scottsboro boys
    and included Flournoy Miller, who was still performing in blackface; "By
    Their Acts, They Help Feed Poor At Christmas Time," *Chicago Defender,*
    18 December 1937, sec. 1, 13.

45 Marshall Stearns and Jean Stearns, *Jazz Dance: The Story of American Vernacular Dance* (New York: Macmillan, 1968), 244.

46 Ibid.

47 Grupenhoff, *Black Valentino*, 41.

48 The show on which I am basing this analysis is *The Harlem Follies*, a 1927 vehicle assembled to showcase Bessie Smith. Smith's husband was the show's producer, so it was controlled by African Americans, but Smith's attraction was such that the show played in both black and white theaters.

49 Stearns, *Jazz Dance*, 244; the Stearnses add that Garbage performed like Bert Williams.

50 Henry Louis Gates, Jr., *The Signifying Monkey: A Theory of African-American Literary Criticism* (New York: Oxford University Press, 1988), 109. Gates is analyzing the performance of Johnny Hudgins in a fragment of a 1927 Jean Renoir film, *Sur un air de Charleston*. For a feminist critique of Gates's analysis, see Tania Modleski, "Cinema and the Dark Continent: Race and Gender in Popular Film" in *Feminism Without Women: Culture and Criticism in a "Postfeminist" Age* (New York: Routledge, 1991), 126–29.

51 In investigating the "stereotype" in colonial discourse, Homi Bhabha argues that its main register for both colonizers and colonized is endless ambivalence; "The Other Question," *Screen* 24.6 (November/December 1983): 18–35. The stage names of "Garbage" Rogers and "Pigmeat" Markham distill this ambivalence, playing, as they do, with African American traditions of linguistic inversion (e.g., bad is good) to create a perpetual flicker between good/bad, negative/positive, and perhaps even masochism/sadism.

52 Thelma Lee Wallace, "Our Musical Shows," *Chicago Defender*, 29 October 1927, sec. 2, 2.

53 *Chicago Defender*, 14 February 1931, sec. 1, 6.

54 The claim that blackface was "habitual" has been a favorite one for explaining the continuance of black blackface. See, for example, Watkins, *On the Real Side*, 394.

55 The month after its report on Hudgins, the *Defender* printed a photograph of George Dewey Washington with a caption saying he had quit his "hobo" act. It is not clear that Washington was a blackface performer, but given that blackface was such a regular part of black comedians' repertoire, it seems likely that part of his hobo act was blackface and that Hudgins's renunciation of blackface was not entirely unique. The photograph is of the "new" Washington wearing a suit and playing a cello. "Drops Rags," *Chicago Defender*, 14 March 1931, sec. 1, 9.

56 Brown, "Just Where," 11.

57 There is some reason to believe that Hudgins returned to blackface. A 1942 article reports that Hudgins was in Europe from the mid-thirties through the beginning of World War II and, upon returning to the U.S. worked two years for "Silas Green from New Orleans," an old-fashioned minstrel show on perpetual tour of the South. "Johnny Hudgins, Yes Silent John, Is Back," *Chicago Defender,* 7 March 1942, 21.

58 J. Rogers "Folks We Can Get Along Without," *Chicago Defender,* 28 November 1936, sec. 1, 16.

59 Grupenhoff, *Black Valentino,* 42.

60 "Women's Minstrel Show Is Huge Success," *Chicago Defender,* 11 November 1939, sec.1, 16. According to the report, this was the third annual benefit for this cause; it is not clear whether the previous shows also used blackface.

61 John F. Szwed, "Race and the Embodiment of Culture," *Ethnicity* 2 (1975): 27.

62 In *On the Real Side* Watkins charts the connections between black music and humor; see 47, 77, 339, and 379. In his history of early Chicago jazz, William Howland Kenney sensitively analyzes the range of attractions black entertainments offered. He also claims, more specifically, "the most popular [white jazz] groups removed some of the moral onus from their music by mixing in liberal amounts of vaudeville humor." Since these white groups based their performances on a reverent attention to black jazz performance, it seems likely that the same could be said of black bands (*Chicago Jazz: A Cultural History, 1904–1930* [New York: Oxford University Press, 1993], 66).

63 It is also important to remember that black venues were almost always open to whites (the inverse was less often true) and that most "black" venues were owned and often managed by whites, so that black blackface nearly always had a (potential) double audience and function.

64 To place the Children's Home minstrel show in further, national-social, political, and cultural perspective, it's worth recalling that earlier in 1939, the great black contralto, Marian Anderson, had been denied access to the DAR's Constitution Hall in Washington, D.C. Prompted by the NAACP, Eleanor Roosevelt cosponsored Anderson in a free, Easter-Sunday concert in front of the Lincoln Memorial.

65 Ralph Cooper claims that he convinced Markham to give up blackface during their time together at the Apollo in the late thirties; see Ralph Cooper with Steve Dougherty, *Amateur Night at the Apollo: Ralph Cooper Presents Five Decades of Great Entertainment* (New York: HarperCollins, 1990): 112–14. (For more on Cooper see chapter five.) Ted Fox, in *Showtime at the Apollo* (New York: Da Capo, 1993), 165, claims Markham

finally gave up blackface in 1945. See also Watkins, *On The Real Side,* 394–95, and comedian Timmie Rodgers in Smith, *Mo' Funny.*

66   Francis S. Hatcher, "Assails Blackface Act in Theatre," *Chicago Defender,* 10 March 1945, sec. 1, 14.

67   Albert Murray, *Stomping the Blues* (1976; reprint, New York: Da Capo, 1982), 190.

68   Mel Watkins claims "Crackshot Hartley . . . continued blacking up until the early fifties, and may have been the last of the popular black circuit comedians to do so. By that time, however, few objected, since it was such an obvious anomaly" (*On the Real Side,* 395).

69   By 1929 blacks—especially urban blacks—would probably seldom see white blackface any place outside the movies, since it was by then restricted mostly to Broadway shows (e.g., Jolson and Cantor) or white amateur shows, neither of which were amenable (or perhaps particularly interesting) to black audiences. Earlier in the century, and in rural areas, this was not so strictly the case: In 1910 a white blackface performer worked in the black-owned Pekin Theater on Chicago's South Side (see Kenney, *Chicago Jazz,* 184, n5); about 1919 Lorenzo Tucker saw a white blackface medicine show performer in Tidewater, Virginia, and became intrigued with show business (Grupenhoff, *Black Valentino,* 21); making photographs for the Farm Security Administration in 1935, Ben Shahn captured a similar show, playing for a racially mixed audience, in Hudington, Tennessee (in these photographs, it is not clear whether the blackface performer is black or white; see Brooks McNamara, *Step Right Up* [New York: Doubleday, 1976], 114, 142).

2 "Fool Acts"

1   Eric Lott, *Love and Theft: Blackface Minstrelsy and the American Working Class* (New York: Oxford University Press, 1993), 6, 234–36; Lott, "White Like Me: Racial Cross-Dressing and the Construction of American Whiteness" in *Cultures of United States Imperialism,* ed. Amy Kaplan and Donald Pease (Durham, N.C.: Duke University Press, 1993), 474–82; and Michael Rogin, *Blackface, White Noise: Jewish Immigrants in the Hollywood Melting Pot* (Berkeley: University of California Press, 1996), 14.

2   Lott, "White Like Me," 474; see also *Love and Theft,* 6.

3   See James Weldon Johnson, *Black Manhattan* (1930; reprint, New York: Arno, 1968); Roger D. Abrahams, *Singing the Master: The Emergence of African-American Culture in the Plantation South* (New York: Pantheon,

1992); Robert Toll, *Blacking Up: The Minstrel Show in Nineteenth-Century America* (New York: Oxford University Press, 1974), LeRoi Jones [Amiri Baraka], *Blues People: Negro Music in White America* (New York: Morrow Quill, 1963); Henry Sampson, *Blacks in Blackface: A Source Book on Early Black Musical Shows* (Metuchen, N.J.: Scarecrow, 1980); Mel Watkins, *On the Real Side: Laughing, Lying, and Signifying* (New York: Simon and Schuster, 1994); Berndt Ostendorf, *Black Literature in White America* (Totowa, N.J.: Harvester, 1982); Kevin K. Gaines, *Uplifting the Race: Black Leadership, Politics, and Culture in the Twentieth Century* (Chapel Hill, N.C.: University of North Carolina Press, 1996); Nathan Irvin Huggins, *Harlem Renaissance* (New York: Oxford University Press, 1971); Harold Cruse, "The Creative and Performing Arts and the Struggle for Identity and Credibility" in *Negotiating the Mainstream: A Survey of the Afro-American Experience,* ed. Harry A. Johnson (Chicago: American Library Association, 1978), 47–102; and Ann Douglas, *Terrible Honesty: Mongrel Manhattan in the 1920s* (New York: Farrar, Straus and Giroux, 1995).

4   Douglas Gomery's chapter, "Theatres for Black Americans," in his *Shared Pleasures: A History of Movie Presentations in the United States* (Madison: University of Wisconsin Press, 1992), 155–70, is still the best general survey of the availability of movies for African American audiences, especially in the sound era. Gregory A. Waller's *Main Street Amusements: Movies and Commercial Entertainment in a Southern City, 1896–1930* (Washington, D.C.: Smithsonian Institution Press, 1995) and Kathryn H. Fuller's *At the Picture Show: Small Town Audiences and the Creation of Movie Fan Culture* (Washington, D.C.: Smithsonian Institution Press, 1996) provide useful and provocative social history of African American audiences in the silent era.

5   Rogin, *Blackface, White Noise,* 73–81. In theatrical minstrelsy, the reasons for not showing the transformation into blackface were pragmatic: It took too long to black up on stage and the spectacle was too small, too detailed. The minstrel parade, in which minstrel show performers not wearing blackface gave the public a free sample of their wares the afternoon before their show, may have implied the transformation. And of course, there were exceptions to my generalization: Ned Wayburn's *Minstrel Misses,* a New York roof garden revue, had seventeen women black up on stage (see "Midsummer Night's Entertainment," *The Theatre Advertiser,* n.d. [c. 1936], n.p.; held in "Blackface" clip file, Billy Rose Theater Collection, New York Public Library, Lincoln Center). See also my discussion of Amos 'n' Andy later in this chapter.

6   In reviewing *The Jazz Singer, New York Times* critic Mordaunt Hall spent

about a quarter of his column appreciating Al Jolson's transition into blackface: "One of the most interesting sequences of the picture itself is where Mr. Jolson as Jack Robin . . . is perceived as talking to Mary Dale [his girlfriend] . . . as he smears his face with black. It is done gradually, and yet the dexterity with which Mr. Jolson outlines his mouth is readily appreciated." "Al Jolson and the Vitaphone," *New York Times* 7 October 1927, sec. 4, 24.

7   As a genre, the musical might seem especially immune to this line of analysis. After all, what motivates any performance in a musical? Pleasure, magic, entertainment, utopian yearnings? Richard Dyer analyzes such questions in his essay, "Entertainment and Utopia," *Genre: The Musical,* ed. Rick Altman (London: Routledge and Kegan Paul, 1981), 175–89, suggesting that we can ask functional questions such as why should it be blackface performance that seemed—and apparently was —entertaining in these films? Two exceptions to my claim about the motivation for blackface performance are Fred Astaire's "Bojangles of Harlem" number in *Swing Time* (1936) and Eleanor Powell's stair dance in *Honolulu* (1939), both explicit tributes to Bill Robinson. For a reading of the former, see Susan Gubar, *Racechanges: White Skin, Black Face in American Culture* (New York: Oxford University Press, 1997), 88-90.

8   For a thorough analysis of anarchic comedy, though one that does not consider blackface or race in any detail, see Henry Jenkins, *What Made Pistachio Nuts? Early Sound Comedy and the Vaudeville Aesthetic* (New York: Columbia University Press, 1992).

9   Rogin, *Blackface, White Noise,* 148.

10 Ibid., 182; Rogin slightly overstates his case by claiming that "every blackface musical . . . shows the performer blacking up."

11 Ibid., 147.

12 Ibid., 119–20.

13 Ibid., 128; here Rogin is talking about more than just blackface films (though blackface films make up half his textual sample). Rogin often subsumes blackface into a larger category he calls "racial cross-dressing" in his work.

14 Ibid., 128, 196.

15 *The Jazz Singer* [1927], in *Souvenir Programs of Twelve Classic Movies 1927–1941,* ed. Miles Kreuger (New York: Dover, 1977), 8.

16 Ibid., 6–7. For a differing account of how Jolson came to black up, see Albert Goldman, *Jolson: The Legend Comes to Life* (New York: Oxford University Press, 1988), 35–36.

17 The story varies as to the directness of contact between Rice and the black man who inspires him, the attempted precision of Rice's imitation, and

the effect of Rice's imitation on his model, all of which can range from considerable to none; see Lott, *Love and Theft*, 55–62. For other versions of the origin of minstelsy, see W. T. Lhamon Jr., *Raising Cain: Blackface Performance from Jim Crow to Hip Hop* (Cambridge: Harvard University Press, 1998), and Dale Cockrell, *Demons of Disorder: Early Blackface Minstrels and Their World* (New York: Cambridge University Press, 1997).

18 Lott, *Love and Theft*, 57.

19 Ibid., 55–62.

20 Ibid., 56.

21 Lott has noted the tendency of the nineteenth-century stories of minstrelsy's origins to rely on the mechanisms of the form, "as if this . . . event generated or secreted 'naturally' the formal means appropriate to it"; see "Love and Theft: The Racial Unconscious of Blackface Minstrelsy," *Representations* 39 (summer 1992), 25.

22 Stuart Hall, "Encoding/Decoding" in *The Cultural Studies Reader,* ed. Simon During (New York: Routledge, 1993), 90–103.

23 Lott found only one example that combined his paradigms; see *Love and Theft,* 59–60.

24 *The Jazz Singer* souvenir program, 6.

25 Richard Dyer, "White," *Screen* 29.4 (1988): 44.

26 Pines, *Blacks in Films: A Survey of Racial Themes and Images in the American Film* (London: Studio Vista, 1975), 17, 19.

27 *The Jazz Singer* souvenir program, 7.

28 Rogin, *Blackface, White Noise,* 92.

29 Pines, *Blacks in Films,* 19.

30 From the opening shot, a very long, very mobile track through a crowded cafe, the film (directed by Lloyd Bacon) signals that, unlike some previous Warner Bros. talkies, it intends to impress its audience visually as well as aurally. For an analysis of *The Singing Fool* within the context of the Hollywood economy of the late twenties, see Douglas Gomery, "*The Singing Fool,*" in *Close Viewings: An Anthology of New Film Criticism,* ed. Peter Lehman (Tallahassee: Florida State University Press, 1990), 370–82.

31 This conundrum is amplified by the (implied) fact that Al is Jewish and Grace is a gentile, a reiteration of the situation in *The Jazz Singer* but without the complication of the disapproving patriarch.

32 By 1930 this depiction of a successful touring minstrel show was already a nostalgic fantasy. The enthusiastic reviewer for *Variety* suggested as much: "This picture has something that is now by itself in America, and that might be worth a strong plug in exploitation—a minstrel show. As stage ensemble, minstrelsy has about died out; it may be a circus to the

kiddies to let them see what their folks have seen—the minstrel show";
Bime, "*Mammy* [film review]," *Variety,* 27 March 1930.

33   Though it is not clear that the woman in the center is supposed to be the
other two women's mother, the logic of the joke implies it.

34   Jolson played in the stage version of *Big Boy* from 1924 to 1926—or
more accurately, version*s,* since as with many star-driven musicals of this
period the script and song list of this show changed frequently. He had
played a version of his "black" character, Gus, beginning with *The Whirl
of Society* in 1912 and continuing with four other very successful shows
before *Big Boy,* the character's last appearance. See the "stageography" in
Goldman, *Jolson,* 315–55.

35   See, for example, Buddy Mason, "Traveling the Rocky Road to Fame:
Raymond Turner Conquers Tremendous Obstacles to Achieve Success
in Movies," *Richmond Planet,* 21 June 1930, illustrated section, 1–2. The
pinnacle of this Horatio Alger story (New Mexico poverty, Hollywood
success, crippling illness, success regained) is Turner's appearance in *Big
Boy*—where, Mason claims, Turner is "a 'wow.'" What Mason doesn't
mention is that Turner's appearance is unbilled and lasts no more than
thirty seconds. The other black performers in *Big Boy* are on screen for
longer than Turner and are billed as the Monroe Jubilee Singers.

36   See Ed Guerrero, *Framing Blackness: The African American Image in Film*
(Philadelphia: Temple University Press, 1993), 25–26 for an argument
about how twists of such stock scenes can serve as "ideological breaks"
in an otherwise typical Hollywood film.

37   In this context, it may also be worth remembering that, in *Birth of a
Nation,* Gus is the name of the "black" (unselfconsciously blackfaced
white) who is lynched for having caused young Flora Cameron to kill
herself.

38   Rush, "*Big Boy* [film review]," *Variety,* 17 September 1930.

39   Goldman, *Jolson,* 195.

40   Metropolitan Theater advertisement, *Chicago Defender,* 1 November
1930, 8; Michigan Theater, Advertisement. *Chicago Defender,* 15 November 1930, 6. This booking pattern, which was not unusual but was also
not the norm, could suggest block-booking pressures, variable advertising patterns, a misguided theater programmer or, since Jolson was fading, Warner Bros.' attempt to maximize its income with a hard sell. But
it could also suggest anticipated demand. In Richmond, Virginia, the
National Theater advertized *Big Boy* as an incentive to African Americans to visit its "new colored balcony"; National Theater advertisement,
Richmond Planet, 16 August 1930, 4.

41 Melvin Patrick Ely, *The Adventures of Amos 'n' Andy: A Social History of an American Phenomenon* (New York: Free Press, 1991), 61–62.

42 See Donald Crafton, *The Talkies: American Cinema's Transition to Sound, 1926–1931,* History of the American Cinema, vol. 4 (New York: Scribner's, 1997), 408–9. See also Ely, *Adventures of Amos 'n' Andy,* 125.

43 Metropolitan Theater advertisement, *Chicago Defender,* 27 December 1930, 6; Michigan Theater advertisement ("return engagement by popular demand"), *Chicago Defender,* 18 July 1931, 8; Metropolitan Theater advertisement, 19 March 1932, 8—this ad notes that the engagement is for one night only and that *Check and Double Check* will be accompanied by a Cab Calloway short.

44 Ely, *Adventures of Amos 'n' Andy,* 104. Amos 'n' Andy, especially in their earliest incarnation as rural southerners about to migrate north did have occasional contact with whites (see Ely, 64–96)—there were whites in *Check and Double Check*—but this contact diminished over time. Until the forties, all the performers on the radio show were white.

45 See for example, Johnson, *Black Manhattan,* 116, 203, on Jolson's support for black songwriter Maceo Pinkard and black playwright Garland Anderson.

46 "Al Jolson Buys Film Rights to *Green Pastures,*" *Chicago Defender,* 6 June 1931, 7.

47 "Al Jolson's Offer for *Green Pastures* as Talkie is Refused by Producers," *Chicago Defender,* 13 June 1931, 7.

48 "Al Jolson Given the Lead in 1933 Edition of *Porgy,*" *Chicago Defender,* 9 December 1933, 8.

49 "Al Jolson Pleads for Lead in 'Emperor Jones' on Stage," *Chicago Defender,* 7 April 1934, 9. I have been unable to confirm that Jolson did play these roles on radio.

50 The only other film in the Jolson filmography that contains no blacks is *Say It With Songs,* which also contained no blackface. Later, in 1933, Jolson made a second film without any blackface performances, *Hallelujah, I'm a Bum!,* but United Artists did not promote the film. It found almost no audience and ended as Jolson's worst financial failure. The film did use the black actor Edgar Connor, but I have found no notice of this (nor even an ad for the film) in the black press; see Goldman, *Jolson,* 206–09, 212.

51 The *Wonder Bar* serialization began in the *Chicago Defender,* 26 May 1934, 10 and ran in five installments through 23 June. The only other instance I have noted of such an advertising campaign was for *I am a Fugitive from a Chain Gang.* (It is worth noting that Warner Bros. was

much more active than any other studio in advertising film in Chicago's black community during the thirties. This would change around World War II.) See also Metropolitan Theater advertisement, *Chicago Defender,* 23 June 1934, 8.

52 "Al Jolson Certain to Get Lead in Film's Pastures," *Chicago Defender,* 20 July 1935, 8.

53 "Al Jolson May Play 'De Lawd' On the Screen," *Richmond Planet,* 28 September 1935, n.p.

54 Rogin, *Blackface, White Noise,* 186.

55 Goldman, *Jolson,* 217, 289; Allen Woll, *Black Musical Theatre: From Coontown to Dreamgirls* (Baton Rouge: Louisiana State University Press, 1989), 164.

56 Ely, *Adventures of Amos 'n' Andy,* 160–93, narrates and analyzes this protest.

57 That this step was still very possible in the early thirties is shown in a letter Gershwin wrote to DuBose Heyward (author of *Porgy*): "I think it is very interesting that Al Jolson would like to play the part of Porgy, but I really don't know how he would be in it. Of course, he is a very big star, who certainly knows how to put over a song, and it might mean more to you financially if he should do it—provided that the rest of the production were well done. The sort of thing I have in mind is a much more serious thing than Jolson could ever do." Gershwin to Heyward, 29 March 1932, quoted in Woll, *Black Musical Theatre,* 164.

58 In the *Defender,* for example, the Metropolitan Theater ad for *Go Into Your Dance* appeared on the same page as an article that once more ridiculed Jolson for his aspiration to play De Lawd. See Malcolm B. Fulcher, "Writer Finds Race Plays Big Part in Pictures Now," *Chicago Defender,* 22 June 1935, 10.

59 Susan Gubar also analyzes this trope, though without reference to *Go Into Your Dance,* in *Swing Time* (1936), *Dixie* (1943), *A Double Life* (1947), and Lawrence Olivier's reflections on playing *Othello* (1965) in *Racechanges,* 90–94.

60 With the exception of "Hi-De-Ho in Your Soul" all the songs were written by the songwriting team of Harold Arlen and E. Y. Harburg.

61 William Keighly, the director of *The Singing Kid,* co-directed the Warners film of *The Green Pastures* the same year, which may also have contributed to the serious tone of this medley. "Spirituals to Swing" would become the title of a famous program of black music that would be staged at Carnegie Hall beginning in 1939. For more on the connection of the secular and the religious in black culture(s) see Albert Murray, *Stomping the Blues* (1976; reprint, New York: Da Capo, 1982), 23–42.

62 Rogin, *Blackface, White Noise,* 6.

63 The audience for *The Singing Kid* would have been expecting a duet of "You're the Cure" for two reasons: First, a closing duet is a convention of the musical. Second, and more specifically, they had already heard this song once before in the film as a duet between Al and Ruth's very young niece. The film disappoints both expectations.

64 Metropolitan Theater advertisement, *Chicago Defender,* 4 July 1936, 10; Michigan Theater advertisement, *Chicago Defender,* 11 July 1936, 10. Note also on this date and page the photograph of Pigmeat Markham wearing blackface and captioned "Harlem's Ace Comic." The build-up of Calloway as an important presence in *The Singing Kid* began early in the *Defender.* See "Calloway Is Star On Al Jolson Bill," *Chicago Defender,* 31 January 1936, 10; Harry Leavette, "Through Hollywood" [occasional column], *Chicago Defender,* 25 January 1936, 10 — this piece notes the casting of Calloway and other blacks in *The Singing Kid* and explicitly links "Goin' to Heaven on a Mule" with Jolson's desire to do *Green Pastures* and his interest in black performance; "Cab Does His Hi De Ho in Hollywood" [photo caption for still from *The Singing Kid*], *Chicago Defender,* 8 February 1936, 10.

65 Rogin, *Blackface, White Noise,* 196.

66 "'I Can't Believe That Al Jolson Would Humiliate Race,' Noble Sissle Writes," *Pittsburgh Courier,* 28 April 1938, 21.

67 *Pittsburgh Courier,* 7 May 1938, 20.

68 Eddie Cantor, as told to David Freeman, *My Life is in Your Hands* (New York: Harper and Brothers, 1928), 186–87.

69 I have found no mentions of Cantor, either positive or negative, during the thirties in the African American periodicals I have researched, though he does appear as a champion of radio desegregation in the forties. See, for example, "Cantor and Kaye Break Radio Rules to Star Negroes," *Ebony,* January 1943, 43.

70 When Garland got older, her performance style became a form of gender self-assertion that might be seen as paralleling Jolson's ethnic self-assertion and certainly caused her similar difficulties in maintaining her stardom.

71 See Regal Theater advertisement, *Chicago Defender,* 16 December 1939, 12; no playthrough dates at other South Side theaters were advertised.

72 There is considerable debate over whether Emmett authored "Dixie" and over whether it may have been black-authored. See Howard L. Sacks and Judith Rose Sacks, *Way Up North in Dixie: A Black Family's Claim to the Confederate Anthem* (Washington, D.C.: Smithsonian Institution Press, 1993).

73 At least one black critic had expressed scorn for an earlier Crosby film, *Birth of the Blues* (1941), because of its erasure of African Americans; see Al Monroe, "Swingin' the News" [column], *Chicago Defender,* 8 November 1941, 13. In *Birth of the Blues,* as in *Dixie,* Crosby overhears a group of black men singing and joins them; this time the men are prisoners as is Crosby, but Crosby gets out of jail, taking the music with him and never looking back. For a reading of this trope of the white overhearing, then joining, then surpassing the black source, see Krin Gabbard, *Jammin' at the Margins: Jazz and the American Cinema* (Chicago: University of Chicago Press, 1996), 64–100.

74 "Minstrel Shows: *Dixie* Traces History of Blackface Comedians," *Life,* 5 July 1943, 80, 83–84; "Race War in Detroit," 93–102. Both Rogin in *Black Face, White Noise* (195–96) and Gubar in *Racechanges* (79–81) provide readings of this confluence.

75 "South Sea Island Scandals," *Life,* 5 July 1943, 55.

76 *Rose of Washington Square,* a love story set at the turn of the century, ends with a surprising image that reveals how much was at stake in such protection. Tyrone Power, who plays a con man, gets arrested and handcuffed to another prisoner—a black man, the only African American to appear in the film.

77 *Jolson Sings Again* briefly addresses Jolson's "purchase" of a prize fighter. In a montage sequence, "Jolson"'s parents fill in their scrap book and an item comes up: "Jolson Buys Promising Young Heavyweight/Adds Rocky Samson to Fight Stable." The accompanying photo shows Samson to be white, and the following exchange ensues: Mother: "Buying a horse—that I understand, but buying a fighter, a human being, how is this poppa?" Father: "Foolishness—a tragedy, that's how it is. Our whole world is on fire. A Hitler swallows nations, millions of our people driven, tortured, killed like flies. You don't want to sing, alright—but horses, fighters . . ." [he slams the scrap book shut in disgust]. Immediately after this, Mamma is stricken with illness and dies, so the political aspect of this scene is recuperated into the wholly personal.

78 Ely notes that a similar phenomenon took place with *Amos 'n' Andy,* when African American critics worked to have the *Amos 'n' Andy* TV show—which used a black cast—canceled in the early 1950s (*Adventures of Amos 'n' Andy,* 1–10).

3 Indefinite Talk

1 Melvin Patrick Ely, *The Adventures of Amos 'n' Andy: A Social History of an American Phenomenon* (New York: Free Press, 1991), 160–93.

2 J. Rogers, "A 'Race-Hater' Tunes In," *Chicago Defender,* 21 November 1936, 16.

3 According to statistics in Henry T. Sampson, *Blacks in Black and White: A Source Book on Black Films* (Metuchen, N.J.: Scarecrow, 1977), 4, after a peak of thirty-two films in 1921, race film production dropped from eight in 1926 to three in 1927. Production rose slightly in 1928 but then leveled off at about three films a year (with a spike to seven in 1932) until 1937, when race production started to climb to its second highest peak of twenty-two films in 1940.

4 W. E. B. Du Bois, *The Souls of Black Folk* (1903) in *Writings,* ed. Nathan Huggins (New York: Library of America, 1986), 363–91. Double consciousness has been one of the most productive—and contested—ideas in twentieth-century African American thought. For a history of its working in "uplift" ideologies, see Kevin K. Gaines, *Uplifting the Race: Black Leadership, Politics, and Culture in the Twentieth Century* (Chapel Hill, N.C.: Univ. of North Carolina, 1996), and for a volume of essays that reflect on the concept's utility, see Gerald Early, ed., *Lure and Loathing: Essays on Race, Identity, and the Ambivalence of Assimilation* (New York: Allen Lane/Penguin, 1993).

5 For general overviews of Micheaux's biography and career, see Thomas Cripps, *Slow Fade to Black: The Negro in American Film, 1900–1942* (New York: Oxford University Press, 1977), 170–201, 309–48; Donald Bogle, *Tom, Coons, Mulattoes, Mammies, and Bucks: An Interpretive History of Blacks in American Film,* third edition (New York: Continuum, 1994), 101–16; Charlene Register, "Black Films, White Censors: Oscar Micheaux Confronts Censorship in New York, Virginia, and Chicago," in *Movie Censorship in American Culture,* ed. Francis Couvares (Washington, D.C.: Smithsonian Institution Press, 1996), 159–86; Pearl Bowser and Louise Spence, *Writing Himself into History: Oscar Micheaux, His Silent Films, and His Audiences* (New Brunswick, N.J.: Rutgers University Press, 2000); and J. Ronald Green, *Straight Lick: The Cinema of Oscar Micheaux* (Bloomington: Indiana Univ. Press, 2000).

6 For the most recent filmography (as well as information on all of Micheaux's writings), see Green, *Straight Lick,* 239–42, 271.

7 See, for example, Mark A. Reid, *Redefining Black Film* (Berkeley: University of California Press, 1993).

8 Daniel Leab, *From Sambo to Superspade: The Black Experience in Motion Pictures* (Boston: Houghton Mifflin, 1975). For Bambara and Bowser's comments, see Bestor Cram and Pearl Bowser, *Midnight Ramble: Oscar Micheaux and the Story of Race Movies* [film] (Boston: Northern Light Productions/American Experience/WGBH, 1994). For counter arguments see Green, *Straight Lick,* 118–21, and Tommy L. Lott, Review of Mark A. Ried, *Redfining Black Film, African American Review* 29.1 (spring 1995): 140–44.

9 Bogle, *Toms, Coons, Mulattoes, Mammies, and Bucks,* 115–16.

10 For instance, Jane Gaines has argued convincingly that *Within Our Gates* depends on—in the sense of being both a formal revision of and a response to—*The Birth of a Nation;* see "Fire and Desire: Race, Melodrama, and Oscar Micheaux" in *Black American Cinema,* ed. Manthia Diawara (New York: Routledge, 1993), 49–70.

11 See Donald Crafton, *The Talkies: American Cinema's Transition to Sound, 1926–1931* (New York: Scribner's, 1997), especially 63–88, and Henry Jenkins, *What Made Pistachio Nuts? Early Sound Comedy and the Vaudeville Aesthetic* (New York: Columbia University Press, 1992). Green also provides a close reading of *Darktown Revue,* largely congruent with mine, in *Straight Lick,* 151–55.

12 Thirteen widely touring shows from 1900 through 1936 bore the name "Darktown," shows associated with esteemed black performers such as Sissieretta Jones (aka Black Patti), Bob Coles, Salem Tutt Whitney and J. Homer Tutt. The most famous of these was *The Darktown Follies,* which ran from 1910 to 1916. Florenz Ziegfeld purchased the rights to and incorporated the finale of this show into the *Ziegfeld Follies,* and James Weldon Johnson singled it out in *Black Manhattan* (1930; reprint, New York: Arno Press, 1968) as the show that had brought greater attention to Harlem (173).

13 Johnson noted in *Black Manhattan* that the most powerful moment of the (white-produced) *Blackbirds of 1928* stage revue was "the singing in the burlesque of the wake scene in *Porgy* [the Heyward drama of 1928]. The burlesque scene was staged similarly to the original, even to the shadows on the wall. But instead of Spirituals the blues . . . were sung, and with an effect equally electric and almost as moving" (213).

14 Mel Watkins, *On the Real Side: Laughing, Lying, and Signifying* (New York: Simon and Schuster, 1994), 349.

15 Richard Dyer, "Entertainment and Utopia," in *Genre: The Musical,* ed. Rick Altman (London: Routledge and Kegan Paul, 1981), 176–89.

16 For another reading of *Ten Minutes to Live,* see bell hooks, "Micheaux's Films," in *Black Looks: Race and Representation* (Boston: South End,

1992), 133–44. I have found hooks's interpretation useful; in order to allow for the level of redemption she finds in the text, however, the film's blackface number has to go unmentioned, and, indeed, much of the film's narrative complexity/incoherence has to be straightened out. For other examples of doubling in Micheaux's work, see *Body and Soul* and *Swing!* On doubling as a theme in Micheaux's work see Green, *Straight Lick,* 41–56.

17 Tommy L. Lott, "Black Vernacular Representation and Cultural Malpractice," in *Multiculturalism: A Critical Reader,* ed. David Theo Goldberg (Cambridge, Mass.: Blackwell, 1994), 230–58.

18 See Cripps, *Slow Fade to Black,* 238–42, 266–94, and Bogle, *Toms, Coons, Mulattoes, Mammies, and Bucks,* 34–46.

19 Bogle, *Toms, Coons, Mulattoes, Mammies, and Bucks,* 43.

20 For a nearly rhapsodic African American review of an early Stepin Fetchit performance, see Alain Locke and Sterling A. Brown, "Folk Values in a New Medium" (1930) in *Black Films and Filmmakers,* ed. Lindsay Patterson (New York: Dodd, Mead, 1975), 25–29. I discuss this review of the Hollywood black-cast musical *Hearts in Dixie* (1928) in detail in chapter four.

21 For evidence of growing African American critical backlash against Fetchit starting in the late thirties, see Cripps, *Slow Fade to Black* and "Stepin Fetchit and the Politics of Performance," in *Beyond the Stars: Stock Characters in American Popular Film,* ed. Paul Loukides and Linda K. Fuller (Bowling Green, Ohio: Bowling Green State University Popular Press, 1990), 35–48.

22 They are named in the end credits as "the Two Black Dots," which shows the limits of their equality.

23 This claim is, not surprisingly, historically inaccurate, but connections between minstrelsy and stagings of *Uncle Tom's Cabin* were considerable and persistent, with Tom Shows becoming, essentially, minstrel shows after the Civil War. See Bruce McConachie, *Melodramatic Formations: American Theatre and Society, 1829–1887* (Iowa City: University of Iowa Press, 1992), and Eric Lott, *Love and Theft: Blackface Minstrelsy and the American Working Class* (New York: Oxford University Press, 1993), 211–34.

24 The fullest accounts of Miller and Lyles's career are in Henry Sampson, *Blacks in Blackface: A Source Book on Early Black Musical Shows,* (Metuchen, NJ: Scarecrow, 1980); Allen Woll, *Black Musical Theatre: From* Coontown *to* Dreamgirls (Baton Rouge: Louisiana State University Press, 1989); and Watkins, *On the Real Side.*

25 Watkins, *On the Real Side,* 263–64.

26 Miller and Lee's blackface is consistent with the late-period blackface of Jolson. It is not "realist" or verisimilar, but the exaggeration of the lips is slight and Miller and Lee do not seem to wear wigs. Their costumes are slightly ill-fitting and (in Miller's case) outdated and mismatched suits that are clean and in good repair; their shirts and ties appear to be a bit "loud" (insofar as black and white photography can indicate this); the most obvious comic elements of these costumes are black gloves (the extension to the hands of blackface), short pants, and, particularly in the case of Lee, shoes that are far too long.

27 Charles Keil, "Motion and Feeling through Music" (1966) and "Participatory Discrepancies and the Power of Music" (1987) in Keil and Steven Feld, *Music Grooves: Essays and Dialogues* (Chicago: University of Chicago Press, 1994), 54, 98. Feld's essay "Communication, Music, and Speech about Music" (1984), also collected in *Music Grooves,* has also influenced my analysis.

28 While directly about jazz, Paul F. Berliner's *Thinking in Jazz: The Infinite Art of Improvisation* (Chicago: University of Chicago Press, 1994) offers a more general account of African American alternative modes of education for performance that is useful for contextualizing Miller and Lee's art.

29 The number uses only three shots: a brief medium-long establishing shot, a medium shot, a medium-long shot that moves in to a medium shot and then out to a long shot at the conclusion of the turn. All three shots are from the position of an (unseen) theatrical audience. Aside from the costume and make-up and the jalopy, the mise-en-scene is minimal: even, unvaried lighting and a proscenium with a curtain.

30 The film, which creates a punctiliously all-black world, does not make this clear. Nonetheless, that all-black world recognizes that the larger world is not all black. At the beginning of the film, the first time Gabe presses Cousin Jake into service, when the limo pulls to the curb, one little boy says, "Must be General Pershing comin'," to which his friend replies, "Can't be—he's a blond." However, the tension between the all-black diegesis and the implied white diegesis (as well as the white nondiegetic frame) is such that it precludes showing any of the work Bill Williamson does in Hollywood, where—since *Stormy Weather* claimed to be a veiled biopic of Robinson—he should dance with a little white girl.

31 Michael Rogin, *Blackface, White Noise: Jewish Immigrants in the Hollywood Melting Pot* (Berkeley: University of California Press, 1996), 93–94.

32 In fact, what I am calling the superficial plot crisis has overdeterminations all its own—that, along with our expectations of the musical genre, is why it works. These overdeterminations, both racist and misogynist,

run along the lines of gender and class instead of race: Sharp-tongued, lower-class black women (Selina argues that the women should go on), too ignorant to see their own best interests beleaguer the black men who (despite their own character flaws) are trying to accomplish something that will be to everyone's benefit. It would certainly worth be analyzing *Stormy Weather* in these terms, but I cannot do so here.

4 Black Folk Sold

1   For more on (inter)racial social-problem films see "Introduction," note 2.
2   James Naremore, *The Films of Vincente Minnelli* (New York: Cambridge University Press, 1993), 51.
3   Rick Altman, *The American Film Musical* (Bloomington: Indiana University Press, 1987), 272–73.
4   Hollis Alpert, in *The Life and Times of* Porgy and Bess (New York: Knopf, 1990), 38–39, suggests that the novel is certainly set before World War I and, based on comparisons between the history of Charleston and events depicted in the novel, makes the case that Heyward probably intended to set it around 1911. That said, Alpert also provides evidence that Porgy was inspired by an actual person and some of his life's events—events that happened in 1924 (16–17).
5   DuBose Heyward, *Porgy* (1925; reprint, London: Jonathan Cape, 1928), 221.
6   Sporting Life is adapted from the character Sportin' Life (the name *Porgy and Bess* will readopt) in the novel but in the novel, Sportin' Life is driven from Catfish Row well before the story's conclusion.
7   DuBose Heyward, *Porgy,* 11; Dorothy Heyward and DuBose Heyward, *Porgy: A Play in Four Acts* (New York: Doubleday, Page and Co, 1927), n.p.
8   Heyward's introductory poem in *Porgy* captures his novel's ambiguous complex of southern liberalism and progressivism as well as its interest in—and construction of—the musical Negro:

> Porgy, Maria, and Bess
> Robbins, and Peter, and Crown;
> Life was a three-stringed harp
> Brought from the woods to town.
>
> Marvelous tunes you rang
> From passion, and death, and birth,

You who had laughed and wept
On the warm, brown lap of the earth.

Now in your untried hands
An instrument, terrible, new,
Is thrust by a master who frowns,
Demanding strange songs of you.

God of the White and Black,
Grant us great hearts on the way
That we may understand
Until you have learned to play. (7)

9   These white characters, who range from malevolent to benevolent
    (though not especially effective), were present in both versions of *Porgy*
    (in slightly greater numbers in the novel), and there, as in the musical,
    they play minor but powerful roles. In crucial ways, they shape the story:
    for example, because Porgy is jailed by an unsympathetic (though not
    malevolent—at least not initially) policeman, Bess is able to be lured
    away.

10 The photographs of the original cast of *Porgy and Bess* make it clear that a
    number of the performers were quite light skinned. In one photograph of
    the cast with their director, Rouben Mamoulian, an Armenian Jew, ap-
    pears darker than several of the cast, including Anne Brown, who played
    Bess; see Allen Woll, *Black Musical Theatre: From* Coontown *to* Dream-
    girls (Baton Rouge: Louisiana State University Press, 1989), 167. Because
    Porgy and Bess could tour to many regions where skin color mattered,
    ensuring the certainty of "race" on the stage was no small issue.

11 I base this claim on Alpert's survey of productions in *The Life and Times
    of* Porgy and Bess. Alpert notes two attempts—both recent and Euro-
    pean—to break with tradition in staging *Porgy and Bess*. A 1986 produc-
    tion in Glyndebourne made Porgy walk with crutches, which he discards,
    haltingly, as he heads for New York in the climax (329–30). "Most inno-
    vative" in Alpert's view was a 1988 production in West Berlin, the only
    one that did not set *Porgy and Bess* in the past and that used an abstract,
    "industrial art" setting (331).

12 While he does not credit *Porgy and Bess* with agency, historian Allen Woll
    has seen in *Porgy and Bess* an ironic symbol of the demise of black musi-
    cal theater in the thirties, the demise of a tradition that used black tal-
    ent both in front of and behind the stage curtain (though not usually
    black capital or control). Along with *Show Boat*, with its significant black
    roles, *Porgy and Bess*'s fortunes steadily rose across a period in which the

fortunes of black musical theater was in rapid decline. In *A Century of Musicals in Black and White: An Encyclopedia of Musical Stage Works By, About, or Involving African Americans* (Westport, Conn.: Greenwood, 1993), 393–415, Bernard L. Peterson suggests that there were 125 such shows in the decade 1910–1919; 362 from 1920–1929; 140 from 1930–1939; 46 from 1940–1949; 33 from 1950–1959.

13   In his review of the book for *Opportunity,* Cullen ended by writing, "READ *Porgy!*" ("*Porgy* [book review]." *Opportunity,* December 1925, 379). Sterling Brown organized a major essay around Heyward (among others), whom he described as "an honest artist"; see "Our Literary Audience," *Opportunity,* February 1930, reprinted in Angelyn Mitchell, ed., *Within the Circle: An Anthology of African American Literary Criticism from the Harlem Renaissance to the Present* (Durham, N.C.: Duke University Press, 1994), 69–78.

14   James Weldon Johnson, *Black Manhattan* (1930; reprint, New York: Arno, 1968), 211–12. Johnson also praises the novel in passing.

15   See for example Rob Roy, "*Porgy and Bess* More Than Opera/Roy: Acting and Not Music Sells This Gershwin Hit, He Finds," *Chicago Defender,* 22 February 1936, 11, and Rob Roy, "Best In Voice, Acting In *Porgy and Bess* Cast," *Chicago Defender,* 7 March 1936, 11.

16   See Alpert, *Life and Times of* Porgy and Bess, 123–24. The National management offered a compromise, one that had succeeded in mollifying the cast of *The Green Pastures* earlier in the thirties, namely, a segregated balcony, but the cast of *Porgy and Bess* refused. Alpert claims "hundreds" of African Americans attended these performances.

17   Edward Morrow, "Duke Ellington on Gershwin's *Porgy,*" *New Theatre,* December 1935, 5–6, reprinted in Mark Tucker, ed., *The Duke Ellington Reader* (New York: Oxford University Press, 1993), 114–17. Ellington's agent later claimed that Ellington was misquoted—and very upset; Richard Mack, "Duke Ellington—In Person," *Orchestra World,* May 1936, n.p., in Tucker, *Duke Ellington Reader,* 117–18. Like Ellington (who singled out John Sublett for praise) and Rob Roy in his February *Chicago Defender* piece, Hall Johnson implied that *Porgy and Bess* was a "good show" primarily because of its talented performers; see Hall Johnson, "*Porgy and Bess*—A Folk Opera," *Opportunity,* January 1936, 24–28.

18   "Nazis Criticize *Porgy and Bess,*" *Chicago Defender,* 17 April 1943, 19.

19   "Offensive 'Darky' Songs," *Chicago Defender,* 14 March 1942, 1. The "proper" orthography for this song title is, "I Got Plenty o' Nuttin'."

20   Ibid., 3.

21   Dean Gordon Hancock, " 'Dangerous Propaganda' Says This Critic of Planned Tour," *Chicago Defender,* 17 April 1954, 10. George Daniels, the

"pro" critic, focused entirely on aesthetics, especially the excellence of William Warfield and Leontyne Price in the leads and Cab Calloway as Sportin' Life; "Amusing Art, People The World Over Should See, Says Another," *Chicago Defender,* 17 April 1954, 10.

22 Rick Altman provides compelling visual evidence for the influence of Mamoulian's staging of *Porgy* on *Hallelujah!; American Film Musical,* 293–95. Thomas Cripps suggests that the author of *The Green Pastures,* Marc Connelly, a white playwright of light comedy who had never before evinced interest in black subjects, may have been directly inspired by the success of *Porgy;* "Introduction: A Monument to Lost Innocence," *The Green Pastures,* ed. Thomas Cripps (Madison: University of Wisconsin Press, 1979), 15.

23 Marvin Carlson, *Performance: A Critical Introduction* (New York: Routledge, 1996), 40–41.

24 Donald Crafton provides clear evidence, drawn from the trade press, of the many hostile forces in Hollywood, in the ranks of exhibitors, and, at least in the perceptions of the exhibitors, among white audiences that *Hearts in Dixie*'s foreword would have been trying to assuage; see *The Talkies: American Cinema's Transition to Sound, 1926–1931* (New York: Scribner's, 1997), 402–17.

25 Thomas Cripps provides a useful overview of the critical response to the film, which he characterizes as mostly positive, in *Slow Fade to Black: The Negro in American Film, 1900–1942* (New York: Oxford University Press, 1977), 240–42. For an exception, see Maurice Dancer, "Manhattan Critic Reviews New All-Colored 'Talkie' Film," *Pittsburgh Courier,* 9 March 1929, section 3, 1.

26 Elmer Anderson Carter, "Of Negro Motion Pictures," *Close Up* 5.2 (August 1929), 119. Not incidentally, *Porgy* provides the larger benchmark against which Carter measures the Hollywood's black cast output.

27 For the following discussion, see Alain Locke and Sterling A. Brown, "Folk Values in a New Medium" [1930], in *Black Films and Filmmakers,* ed. Lindsay Patterson (New York: Dodd, Mead, 1975), 25–29.

28 After Locke and Brown, *Hearts in Dixie* has not been treated in much aesthetic critical detail, and most such assessments have been negative, deploring the carelessness Locke and Brown so prized. See, for example, Altman, *American Film Musical,* 290–91; and Donald Bogle, *Toms, Coons, Mulattoes, Mammies, and Bucks: An Interpretive History of Blacks in American Film,* third edition (New York: Continuum, 1994), 27–28. For a very brief positive assessment of the film, see Gerald Mast, *Can't Help Singin': The American Musical on Stage and Screen,* (Woodstock, N.Y.: Overlook, 1987), 90.

29 [W. E. B. Du Bois], "Dramatis Personae: *Hallelujah!*," *The Crisis*, (October 1929): 355.

30 Ibid., 358.

31 Ibid., 342, 355–56.

32 W. E. B. Du Bois, *The Souls of Black Folk*, in *Writings*, ed. Nathan Huggins (New York: Library of America, 1986), 363–71, 536–46.

33 [Du Bois], "Dramatis Personae," 355–56.

34 Ibid., 356.

35 The only other films that come close to *Hallelujah!* in this regard are *Birth of a Nation* and the 1934 *Imitation of Life*.

36 An unnamed "Harlem leader" quoted in Daniel J. Leab, *From Sambo to Superspade: The Black Experience in Motion Pictures* (Boston: Houghton Mifflin, 1975), 94.

37 Cripps, *Slow Fade to Black*, 250–51.

38 "Protest Film Showing," *Chicago Defender*, 31 August 1929, 9. The paper had earlier reported on the film's dual—and thus implicitly segregated—premiere at both a downtown and a Harlem theater; "*Hallelujah!* to Have Double Opener in New York," *Chicago Defender*, 17 August 1929, 9.

39 "*Defender* Will Give 100 Free Tickets to *Hallelujah!*," *Chicago Defender*, 11 January 1930, 1; "5,422 Words Captures First Prize," *Chicago Defender*, 25 January 1930, 1; "Critic Calls *Hallelujah!* 'Best Film,'" *Chicago Defender*, 11 January 1930, 9; Ace, "*Hallelujah!* Discloses Talents of Actors," *Chicago Defender*, 1 February 1930, 10. For comparison, see the coverage of *Hearts in Dixie*, which had none of these features, in *Chicago Defender*, "*Hearts in Dixie*, Film of Song and Pathos, Plus Good Vodvil, Is Offered at Regal, 6 July 1929, 9; Evangaline Roberts, "*Hearts in Dixie* on Screen and Stage Brings Out Large Crowds to Regal Theater," 13 July 1929, 9. Certainly one thing this distinction suggests is that MGM had a more aggressive, and perhaps more progressive, publicity department than Fox.

40 Ace, "*Hallelujah!* Discloses Talents of Actors," 10.

41 Ibid., 10.

42 All references are to the *Chicago Defender*. When they write from outside Chicago, I indicate the correspondent's location, since this gives some sense of the *Defender*'s extraordinary reach. D. J. Russell (Windsor, Ontario), "He Likes *Hallelujah!*," 8 February 1930, 14; M. H. Eliot, "When to Laugh," 15 February 1930, 14; "We Are a Proud Race" [lead editorial], 1 March 1930, 14; Mrs. Fleetwood M. McCoy, "*Hallelujah!* a 'Work of Art,'" 1 March 1930, 14; Dennis A. Bethea, M.D. (Hammond, Ind.), "He OK's *Hallelujah!*," 8 March 1930, 14; Clara Robnet (Detroit), "In Defense of *Hallelujah!*," 8 March 1930, 14; Will A. Middleton (Dallas), "*Hallelujah!* Down South," 29 March 1930, 14.

43 All references are to the *Chicago Defender*. The direct quotations are from DeWill Suggs, "*Hallelujah!*," 15 February 1930, 14. Clarence J. McGivens, "A Comparison," 15 February 1930, 14, and "*Hallelujah!* Again," 26 April 1930, 14. McGivens may have felt compelled to write twice because of *Hallelujah!*'s long run on the South Side. *Hallelujah!* had advertised bookings from the beginning of February to the end of April; in contrast, *Hearts in Dixie*'s South Side run was contained entirely (at least in terms of advertised dates) in the month of July.

44 *A Prince of His Race* was a product of Colored Players, which according to Cripps (*Slow Fade to Black* 195–97) was a white-controlled company with a black front.

45 See Jessica H. Howard, "*Hallelujah!:* Transformation in Film," *African American Review* 30.3 (fall 1996), 441–51, for a formal, textual reading that considers *Hallelujah!* in some of the same terms as my reading but comes to substantially different conclusions.

46 This forward is adapted from a program note that accompanied the play. See Johnson, *Black Manhattan,* 219.

47 Ibid., 218–24.

48 J. A. Rogers, "*The Green Pastures* and Other Ruminations," *New York Amsterdam News,* 13 April 1935, 8. For more on the black reception of *Green Pastures,* see Thomas Cripps, *Making Movies Black: The Hollywood Message Movie from World War II to the Civil Rights Era* (New York: Oxford University Press, 1993), 81–82.

49 Ibid., 8.

50 In the source for *The Green Pastures,* Rourke Bradford's *Ol' Man Adam an' His Chillun* (1928), God was a "stereotype southern planter." Accounting for De Lawd's appearance in *The Green Pastures,* Mr. Deshee the Sunday school teacher explains, "When I was a little boy, I used to imagine he [God] looked jes' like our ol' preacher, de Reverend Mr Dubois." It is difficult to imagine that New York intellectual Marc Connelly, who wrote the play and screenplay, was not aware of the potential meaning of this choice of name.

51 Johnson, *Black Manhattan,* 218.

52 John Pittman, "The Duke Will Stay on Top!" [Interview with Duke Ellington from unidentified source, probably San Francisco, August 1941] in *The Duke Ellington Reader,* 149.

53 For more on *Jump for Joy,* see Edward Kennedy Ellington, *Music is My Mistress* (New York: Doubleday, 1973), 175–204; and Michael Denning, *The Cultural Front: The Laboring of American Culture in the Twentieth Century* (London: Verso, 1996), 309–19.

54 Cripps, *Making Movies Black,* 83.

55 C. E. Chapman, "Dallas, Texas Gets Premiere of Picture *Cabin in the Sky*," *Chicago Defender,* 20 February 1943, 18. This is just one of five film-related pieces—including an MGM ad—on this page.

56 Al Monroe, "Swingin' the News," *Chicago Defender,* 6 March 1943, 18. Monroe's column appears immediately below a piece of publicity boiler-plate re-announcing (and justifying) the Dallas premiere. Monroe would later report with enthusiasm that *Cabin in the Sky* would have a dual Chicago premiere at a downtown theater and at the South Side's Regal; "Swingin' the News, *Chicago Defender,* 3 April 1943, 18.

57 Rob Roy, "Even Lena Horne Gets Red Light, He Writes," *Chicago Defender,* 26 June 1943, 18. Roy's review followed the film's first Chicago run.

58 Ramona Lewis, "*Cabin* Picture Called Insult," *New York Amsterdam News,* 12 June 1943.

59 Naremore, *The Films of Vincente Minnelli,* 171.

60 Rex Ingram quoted in "*Cabin in the Sky* Invades Chicago This Week," *Chicago Defender,* 8 May 1943, 19.

61 Adam Knee, "Doubling, Music, and Race in *Cabin in the Sky*" in *Representing Jazz,* ed. Krin Gabbard (Durham, N.C.: Duke University Press, 1995), 193–208.

62 Malcolm X, as told to Alex Haley, *The Autobiography of Malcolm X* (New York: Ballantine, 1964), 99.

63 In comparison *Hallelujah!* runs 106 minutes, *The Green Pastures* 93, *Cabin* 99, *Carmen Jones* 105, and *Porgy and Bess* 138.

64 William Grant Still, "William Grant Still Tells of Screenland's Many Tricks," *Chicago Defender,* 13 February 1943, 18–19.

65 Lawrence F. LaMar, "Brand Story of *Stormy Weather* Retake as False," *Chicago Defender,* 3 April 1943, 19; "Bill Robinson to Sue Papers for *Stormy Weather*," and Al Monroe, "Swingin' the News," *Chicago Defender,* 17 April 1943, 18.

66 "Think Race Riots Hurt Negro Films," *Chicago Defender,* 31 July 1943, 18.

67 Cripps, *Making Movies Black,* 85.

68 Robin D. G. Kelley, "The Riddle of the Zoot: Malcolm Little and Black Cultural Politics During World War II," in *Malcolm X: In Our Own Image,* ed. Joe Wood (New York: St. Martin's, 1992), 154–82.

69 John Chapman, "*Carmen Jones* Simply Superb Negro Adaptation of *Carmen*," *New York Daily News,* 3 December 1943.

70 Undated (probably late 1944) clippings in the *Carmen Jones* file in the Billy Rose Theatre Collection of the New York Public Library indicate there were protests in Louisville and St. Louis.

71 "*Carmen Jones*," *Time,* 1 November 1954, 98.

72 Al Monroe, "*Carmen Jones* Entertainment Plus," *Chicago Defender,*

13 November 1954, 14; Hilda See, "*Carmen Jones* Pix More Sensational than Legit-er" *Chicago Defender,* 2 October 1954, 32. See's piece first enthuses about *Carmen* but for its second half recounts an interview with a film producer about the challenges of getting large budget, black-cast films distributed.

73 Rob Roy, "Warning to 1955: Your Predecessor Was a Ball!" *Chicago Defender,* 1 January 1955, 15; Roy explicitly linked *Carmen Jones* to *Cabin in the Sky* and *Stormy Weather,* as did many other critics, like Bosley Crowther of the *New York Times;* see "*Carmen Jones* Finds American Types Singing Foreign Opera Score," *New York Times,* 31 October 1954, section 2, 27. The *Defender* itself serves as a good index of some of what was happening to black America in the fifties: the paper was contracting both in force and scope, even as the neighborhood it served was simultaneously growing in size and contracting in the range of goods and services it offered.

74 "An Angry 'Prof Doodle' Hits Rob Roy's Claims for '54," *Chicago Defender,* 8 January 1955, 14.

75 James Baldwin, "*Carmen Jones:* The Dark is Light Enough" (originally "Life Straight in De Eye," 1954) in *The Price of the Ticket: Collected Nonfiction, 1948–1985* (New York: St. Martin's/Marek, 1985), 107. Baldwin also connects *Carmen Jones* to the two 1943 musicals, which he says were "bogus but rather entertaining . . . [because] at least one could listen to the music" (109).

76 Ibid., 112.

77 See William Barlow, *Lookin' Up at Down: The Emergence of Blues Culture* (Philadelphia: Temple University Press, 1989), 250–324.

78 Krin Gabbard, *Jammin' at the Margins: Jazz and the American Cinema* (Chicago: University of Chicago Press, 1996), 99–100.

79 "Start Work on the *Porgy and Bess* Pix," *Chicago Defender,* 2 October 1943, 19.

80 Bosley Crowther, "*Carmen Jones.*"

81 Monroe, "*Carmen Jones* Entertainment Plus," 14.

82 Hilda See, "Bess, sans Catfish Row, Out as Pix, Scribe Says," *Chicago Defender,* 2 April 1955, 32.

83 David Horn, "From Catfish Row to Granby Street: Contesting Meaning in *Porgy and Bess*," *Popular Music* 13.2 (1994): 168. Horn argues that a 1989–1990 attempt to stage a concert version of *Porgy and Bess* in Liverpool "represents the first time . . . that these two main debates . . . have found themselves in direct contact" (168). Hilda See's piece, and debates around the film more generally, suggest Horn is hearing an echo as an origin.

84 Almena Lomax, "Notes to Showfolk," *Los Angeles Tribune*, 15 August 1958.

85 Lerone Bennett, Jr., "Hollywood's First Negro Movie Star," *Ebony*, May 1959, 106.

86 See Era Bell Thompson, "Why Negroes Don't Like *Porgy and Bess*," *Ebony*, October 1959, 54, and Harold Cruse, *The Crisis of the Negro Intellectual: A Historical Analysis of the Failure of Black Leadership* (1964; reprint, New York: Quill, 1984) 100–104.

87 James Baldwin, "On Catfish Row" (1959) in *Price of the Ticket*, 177–81.

88 Bell, "Why Negroes Don't Like *Porgy and Bess*," 54.

89 Cruse, *Crisis of the Negro Intellectual*, 103.

90 For a detailed analysis of these recordings in their relation to the Goldwyn film, see Arthur Knight, " 'It Ain't Necessarily So That It Ain't Necessarily So': African American Recordings of *Porgy and Bess* as Film and Cultural Criticism," in *Soundtrack Available: Essays on Film and Popular Music*, eds. Pamela Robertson Wojcik and Arthur Knight (Durham, N.C.: Duke University Press, 2001), 319–46.

5 "Aping" Hollywood

1 For the best work to date on race film, see Thomas Cripps, *Black Film as Genre* (Bloomington: Indiana University Press, 1978) and Jane Gaines, "*The Scar of Shame*: Skin Color and Cast in Silent Film Melodrama," *Cinema Journal* 26.4 (summer 1987): 3–21, "Fire and Desire: Race, Melodrama, and Oscar Micheaux," in *Black American Cinema*, ed. Manthia Diawara (New York: Routledge, 1993): 49–70, and *Fire and Desire: Mixed Race Movies in the Silent Era* (Chicago: University of Chicago Press, 2001); and bell hooks, "Micheaux's Films," in *Black Looks: Race and Representation* (Boston: South End Press, 1992), 133–44. Considerable recent work on race film focuses on Micheaux and especially on his work in the silent era; see for example, J. Ronald Green, *Straight Lick: The Cinema of Oscar Micheaux* (Bloomington: Indiana University Press, 2000); and Pearl Bowser and Louis Spence, *Writing Himself into History: Oscar Micheaux, His Silent Films, and His Audiences* (New Brunswick, N.J.: Rutgers University Press, 2000). For a barbed exchange over the purposes and possibilities of interpreting and evaluating Micheaux's films, see J. Ronald Green, " 'Twoness' in the Style of Oscar Micheaux," in *Black American Cinema*, 26–47 and Thomas Cripps, "Oscar Micheaux: The Story Continues," in *Black American Cinema*, 71–79.

For two other studies of race musicals (broadly construed), see Adam Knee, "Class Swings: Music, Race, and Social Mobility in *Broken*

Strings," in *Soundtrack Available: Essays on Film and Popular Music,* ed. Pamela Robertson Wojcik and Arthur Knight (Durham, N.C.: Duke University Press, 2001, 269–94); and Adrienne Lanier-Seward, "A Film Portrait of Black Ritual Expression: *The Blood of Jesus,*" in *Expressively Black: The Cultural Basis of Ethnic Identity,* ed. Geneva Gay and Willie L. Barber (New York: Praeger, 1987), 195–212.

2 Though her arguments were published too recently to allow me to take them into full consideration, Anna Everett also works to recover Miller, along with many other black critics; see *Returning the Gaze: A Genealogy of Black Film Criticism, 1909–1949* (Durham, N.C.: Duke University Press, 2001).

3 Loren Miller, "Uncle Tom in Hollywood," *Crisis,* November 1934, 329.

4 David Bordwell, "Part One: The Classical Hollywood Style, 1917–60," in David Bordwell, Janet Staiger, and Kristen Thompson, *The Classical Hollywood Cinema: Film Style and Mode of Production to 1960* (New York: Columbia University Press, 1985), 3–11.

5 Miller, "Uncle Tom in Hollywood," 336.

6 According to the data reported in Henry T. Sampson's *Blacks in Black and White: A Source Book on Black Films* (Metuchen, N.J.: Scarecrow, 1977), 3–4, only three black-cast films were produced in 1933 and only two were produced in 1934. In 1937 seven black-cast films were made; in 1938 this number doubled, and production climbed for the next two years before tailing off with the coming of war. Whites controlled at least the finances of most of the companies producing these films.

7 Miller, "Uncle Tom in Hollywood," 336.

8 For the discussion to follow, see Loren Miller, "Hollywood's New Negro Films," *Crisis,* January 1938, 8–9.

9 Ibid., 9, my emphasis.

10 *Stevedore* was staged by the radical socialist Theater Union in New York. The play follows two plots. The first involves a racist attempt to frame a black man—any one will do—for the alleged rape of a white woman. The second involves management attempts to use racism to break the New Orleans dockworkers' union. These plots converge in the character of Lonnie Thompson, a black stevedore who attempts to bring blacks into the union and who consequently becomes the subject of the frame-up. After Thompson is assassinated by reactionary white union busters, the play ends with Thompson's black neighbors and the white unionists joining forces and mounting the barricades against the racist and capitalist mob. See Paul Peters and George Sklar, *Stevedore* (New York: Covici-Friede, 1934).

11 Miller, "Hollywood's New Negro Films," 9.

12 "Nor is this an argument that Negro actors should portray only Negro characters. There is no reason, except for the limitations of popular prejudice, why Negro actors should not portray Irishmen or Frenchmen as white American actors do"; ibid., 9.

13 Richard Dyer suggests that "white power secures its dominance by seeming not to be anything in particular." He argues further that "the invisibility of whiteness colonizes the definitions of other norms—class, gender, heterosexuality, nationality and so on—[but] it also masks itself as a category. White domination is then hard to grasp in terms of characteristics and practices of white people"—even when these characteristics and practices are specifically and consistently represented by, for instance, the Hollywood cinema as *white* (as opposed to black, or any other "color"). Richard Dyer, "White," *Screen* 29.4 (autumn 1988), 44, 46.

14 Miller, "Hollywood's New Negro Films," 9.

15 Ibid., 8.

16 Henry Louis Gates Jr., *Figures in Black: Words, Signs, and the "Racial" Self* (New York: Oxford University Press, 1987), xxiv.

17 Henry Louis Gates Jr., *The Signifying Monkey: A Theory of African-American Literary Criticism* (New York: Oxford University Press, 1988), xxi, 89–124.

18 Houston A. Baker Jr., *Modernism and the Harlem Renaissance* (Chicago: Univ. of Chicago Press, 1987), 86.

19 The advance publicity for *The Duke is Tops,* as reported in an unsigned *Chicago Defender* piece, emphasizes this relation between capital and quality: "The film . . . is said to be Ralph Cooper's [the film's star's] best. Upwards of $250,000 was spent to produce *The Duke is Tops*"; "*The Duke is Tops* on Way to Regal," *Chicago Defender,* 3 September 1938, 9. A more likely, though still generous, estimate of the cost of this film would be around twenty thousand dollars. For a discussion of the economics of race film production, see Daniel Leab, *From Sambo to Superspade: The Black Experience in Motion Pictures* (Boston: Houghton Mifflin, 1975), 180–84.

20 "Nina Mae On Coast For A Cinema Spot/*Hallelujah!* Star Given Rousing Reception By Performers," *Chicago Defender,* 17 September 1938, 8. This article refers to Cooper as the "general manager" of Million Dollar. It also serves to illustrate the active remembering and reminding black film could call forth: *Hallelujah!* had been released in September 1929.

21 Hurl., "*The Duke is Tops* [film review]," *Variety,* 20 July 1938.

22 *Chicago Defender,* 3 September 1938, 8.

23 Any number of music or jazz encyclopedias provide good basic outlines of Ellington's career, but here I have relied especially on Eileen Southern,

Biographical Dictionary of Afro-American and African Musicians (West-port, Conn.: Greenwood, 1982), 125–26. See also Max Harrison's section, "Jazz" (especially "Jazz Composition I") in Paul Oliver, Max Harrison, and William Bolcom, *The New Grove Gospel, Blues and Jazz, with Spirituals and Ragtime* (New York: W. W. Norton, 1986).

24 For a thorough discussion of Duke Ellington on film, see Krin Gabbard, *Jammin' at the Margins: Jazz and the American Cinema* (Chicago: University of Chicago Press, 1996), 160–203.

25 *Chicago Defender,* 6 August 1938, 8. Later in the year the *Defender* reported that a group of Cincinnati women were organizing a Ralph Cooper fan club; see "Organize Cooper Fan Club," *Chicago Defender,* 26 November 1938, 10.

26 See Ralph Cooper with Steve Dougherty, *Amateur Night at the Apollo: Ralph Cooper Presents Five Decades of Great Entertainment* (New York: HarperCollins, 1990); Cripps, *Slow Fade to Black,* 328–36; and Leab, *Sambo to Superspade,* 175–79. Cooper asserts that he both wrote and directed *The Duke is Tops,* but I have found no evidence to support his claim. The *Variety* review of *The Duke is Tops* notes Cooper's previous career as an MC but also suggests the limits of his previous celebrity— "outside Metropolitan boundaries [his name] can't mean much."

27 See Lena Horne and Richard Schickel, *Lena* (New York: Limelight, 1986); and Gail Lumet Buckley, *The Hornes: An American Family* (New York: Knopf, 1986). One important family acquaintance was Walter White, the executive secretary of the NAACP from 1934 to 1955. White had a personal commitment to changing the roles of blacks in American—specifically Hollywood—films and in the early forties he strongly encouraged Horne to pursue her career in Hollywood; see Horne and Schickel, 131, Buckley, 148–98, and Cripps, *Slow Fade to Black,* 349–89.

28 *Chicago Defender,* 29 October 1938, 10.

29 See advertisements in the 1938 *Chicago Defender:* 3 September, 8 (Regal Theater); 10 September, 9 (Regal Theater); 19 November, 10 (Michigan Theater); and 10 December, 10 (Park Theater). The Regal also employed an unusual advertising strategy for *The Duke is Tops,* one the theater reserved for what it deemed major attractions (Fats Waller or, oddly, *Gone With the Wind,* for instance). It placed two ads: one specifically for the film, the other for additional current or forthcoming features and bands.

30 See Metropolitan Theater advertisement in the *Chicago Defender,* 5 November 1938, 10. It is impossible to say with certainty that *Swing!* never returned to Chicago because only four theaters in the Black Metropolis advertised regularly in the *Defender:* the Regal, the Metropolitan, the Park, and the Michigan. *Defender* advertisements or copy in-

dicate that there were at least several other theaters operating (perhaps intermittently) on the South Side in 1938, for instance the New Fern Theater, the World Playhouse, and the Avenue Theater (see the New Fern ad, 23 April, 8; "Josephine Baker Stars In Film," 30 July, 8; and the Avenue ad 12 November, 10). And the *Film Daily Year Book of Motion Pictures* for 1938 lists twenty theaters that could be considered within the confines of Bronzeville.

31 Though Goodman was a respected swing player, this pattern duplicates that of the previous decade, when Paul Whiteman, rather than Jelly Roll Morton or Louis Armstrong, became the "King of Jazz." The history of the creating and naming of types of jazz, at least in myth, is a history of attempts to evade appropriation, and Swing arose to replace jazz when the latter term was fully appropriated by whites like Whiteman. Perhaps not incidentally, Ralph Cooper claims in *Amateur Night at the Apollo* that "historians are correct to conclude that the WMCA live broadcasts of my show gave the mass white audience its first exposure to 'the new sounds of black swing music' " (98).

32 Two of these shows—*Strut Miss Lizzie* (1922) and *Dixie to Broadway* (1924)—were attempts to capitalize on the success of Noble Sissle's and Eubie Blake's hit *Shuffle Along* (1921–1922). The third, *Put and Take* (1921) was developed before *Shuffle Along* and apparently attempted to avoid egregious minstrelization; a *Variety* reviewer responded, "Here the colored folks seem to have set out to show the whites that they're just as white as anybody. They may be just as good, but they're different, and, in their entertainment they should remain different, distinct and indigenous"; the show closed in two weeks after protests about a "colored company" playing in New York's Town Hall Theater. See Allen Woll, *Dictionary of the Black Theater: Broadway, Off-Broadway, and Selected Harlem Theater* (Westport, Conn.: Greenwood, 1983), 53, 131 and 159. See also Henry T. Sampson, *Blacks in Blackface: A Source Book on Early Black Musical Shows* (Metuchen, N.J.: Scarecrow, 1980), 369–70.

33 *New York Age* 10 May 1938, as quoted in Leab, *Sambo to Superspade,* 193. See also Cripps, *Slow Fade to Black,* 323–24 and 426, notes 23 and 24, and Leab, 190–93 for more general indications of the neglect Micheaux's films faced in the industry press and the hostility they aroused in the African American press. For other credits for the performers in *Swing!* (especially Alec Lovejoy, Carmen Newsome, Amanda Randolph, and Dorothy Van Eagle) see Phyllis Rauch Klotman, *Frame by Frame: A Black Filmography* (Bloomington: Indiana University Press, 1997), 658, 666, 671, 683.

Adding to Micheaux's persistent "image" problems, may have been the white businessmen with whom he associated. During the early and midthirties Frank Schiffman was the vice-president and secretary of Micheaux Film Corporation. Schiffman was the manager of the Apollo Theater and was notorious for his inequitable and racist treatment of African American performers; Cooper credits Schiffman's behavior, in part, with driving him away from his work at the Apollo. See Cooper, *Amateur Night at the Apollo,* 103–23; Cripps, *Slow Fade to Black,* 323; and Green, *Straight Lick,* 104–22.

34 See "The Motion Picture Production Code of 1930," reprinted in Garth Jowett, *Film: The Democratic Art* (Boston: Little, Brown, 1976), 468–72.

35 Rick Altman, *The American Film Musical* (Bloomington: Indiana University Press, 1987), 16–27.

36 For an alternative reading of *The Duke is Tops,* see Clyde Taylor, "Crossed Over and Can't Get Black," *Black Film Review* 7.4 (n.d.): 23–27; on *Swing!,* see Green, *Straight Lick,* 104–6, 118–23.

37 Hurl., *"The Duke is Tops."*

38 In 1935 Micheaux made a film entitled *Lem Hawkin's Confession* and, though this is not the place for it, a further understanding of *Swing!* might result from an intertextual reading of these two films.

39 Micheaux had earlier used this doubling technique in his best-known film, *Body and Soul* (1927), casting Paul Robeson in two roles—though Robeson's two characters are supposed to be clear opposites.

40 Jane Feuer, *The Hollywood Musical,* second edition (Bloomington: Indiana University Press, 1982), 22–47.

41 Gerald Mast, *Can't Help Singin': The American Musical on Stage and Screen* (Woodstock, N.Y.: Overlook, 1987), 232.

42 In a comic but symbolic vein that might be seen as a distillation of what Baker means by mastery of form, *The Duke is Tops* uses a white cat as its bad luck charm during its middle section. For more on the TOBA circuit see Sampson, *Blacks in Blackface.*

43 Baker, *Modernism and the Harlem Renaissance,* 63.

44 Miller, "Hollywood's New Negro Films," 9.

45 "Bei Mir Bist Du Schöen" was written in Yiddish by Jacob Jacobs, with music by Sholom Secunda for the 1933 Yiddish musical "I Would If I Could." The English lyrics were written for the Andrews Sisters in 1937 by Sammy Cahn and Saul Chaplin.

46 I have not been able to find any information on this song.

47 Baker, *Modernism and the Harlem Renaissance,* 20.

48 Altman, *American Film Musical,* 45.

6 *Jammin' the Blues*

1 Leonard Feather, "Jazz Symposium," *Esquire,* July 1944, 95.

2 [James Agee,] "Jammin' the Blues," *Time,* 25 December 1944, 50; James Agee, "Films," *The Nation,* 16 December 1944, 753; "Speaking of Pictures . . . Mili's First Movie is Skillfully Lighted Jam Session," *Life,* 22 January 1945, 6–8; Leonard Feather, "Jazz is Where You Find It," *Esquire,* May 1945, 95; Hermine Rich Isaacs, "Face the Music: Films in Review," *Theatre Arts,* December 1944, 725; Charles Emge, "On the Beat in Hollywood," *down beat,* 1 December 1944, 6; Jackie Lopez, "Is Hollywood Yielding?" *Chicago Defender,* 24 March 1945, 20; "Jam Session in Movieland," *Ebony,* November 1945, 6–7.

3 Whitney Balliet, "Pandemonium Pays Off," *The Sound of Surprise: Forty-Six Pieces on Jazz* (New York: Da Capo, 1978), 6; Ernie Smith, "Film," *The New Grove Dictionary of Jazz,* vol. 1, ed. Barney Kernfeld (London: MacMillan, 1988), 382; David Meeker, *Jazz in the Movies,* enlarged edition (New York: Da Capo, 1981), entry 1637; Frank Driggs and Harris Lewine, *Black Beauty, White Heat: A Pictorial History of Classic Jazz, 1920–1950* (New York: William Morrow, 1982), 268.

4 For an analysis of the uses of the "audio-visual disjuncture" in recorded music, see John Corbett, "Free, Single, and Disengaged: Listening Pleasure and the Popular Music Object," *October* 54 (Fall 1990): 79–101.

5 Evan Eisenberg, *The Recording Angel: Explorations in Phonography* (New York: McGraw-Hill, 1987), 11–33.

6 A 1945 General Electric advertisement plays on this quality of music, especially as it is mediated through mass culture: Under a full-color image of the lady in the tutti-frutti hat, a headline shouts, "Carmen Miranda's voice in natural color—a thrill only FM radio captures!" Under a smaller, black-and-white image of Miranda, a tiny caption reads: "Conventional radio—lacks color and richness. Something is missing." What is missing, of course, is not the full range of Miranda's singing voice but the spectacle of her *colorful* image, needed to lend credence to her "ethnic" voice; *Look,* 6 February 1945, 2.

7 Andrew Ross, "Hip and the Long Front of Color," in *No Respect: Intellectuals and Popular Culture* (New York: Routledge, 1989), 67–68.

8 For detailed examinations of these discursive shifts see David Stowe, *Swing Changes: Big Band Jazz in New Deal America* (Cambridge: Harvard University Press, 1994); Lewis A. Ehrenberg, *Swingin' the Dream: Big Band Jazz and the Rebirth of American Culture,* (Chicago: University

of Chicago Press, 1998); and Bernard Gendron, "Moldy Figs and Modernists: Jazz at War (1942–1946)," in *Jazz Among the Discourses,* ed. Krin Gabbard (Durham, N.C.: Duke University Press, 1995), 31–56.

9 LeRoi Jones [Amiri Baraka], *Blues People: Negro Music in White America* (New York: Quill, 1963), 181.

10 Ibid., 182.

11 Eric Lott, "Double V, Double-Time: Bebop's Politics of Style," *Callaloo* 11.3 (summer 1988): 597.

12 Ibid., 599; by "militancy," Lott means both social action, like the formation of Congress of Racial Equality (CORE), and asocial action, like the riots of the early forties.

13 Jones, *Blues People,* 188; young whites were also nonconformist, Baraka notes, but they always had a choice.

14 Sterling A. Brown, "Spirituals, Blues, and Jazz," *Jam Session: An Anthology of Jazz,* ed. Ralph J. Gleason (New York: G. P. Putnam's Sons, 1958), 26. Brown's vision was not new, though it was more concrete than many other descriptions of jazz as a democratic art; see, for example, J. A. Rogers, "Jazz at Home," in *The New Negro: Voices of the Harlem Renaissance,* ed. Alain Locke (1925; reprint, New York: Atheneum, 1992), 216–24. For a scathing countervision of jazz as "pseudo-democratic," see Theodor W. Adorno, "On Jazz," trans. Jamie Owen Daniels, *Discourse* 12.1 (fall–winter 1989–90): 45–69.

15 It is important to remember that, before the introduction of the LP in the late forties, records carried little of the visual information (whether in the form of illustrations and photographs or in forms suggested by liner notes and musician credits) that became common beginning in the fifties.

16 The events I discuss throughout this section are not important because they were momentous "firsts"—none of them were. Rather, they are important because they were attempts to change conventions within the music industry and to make previously local, isolated practices appear "popular," normal, and regular.

17 John Hammond with Irving Townsend, *John Hammond on Record* (New York: Summit Books, 1977), 68. James Lincoln Collier's *Benny Goodman and the Swing Era* (New York: Oxford University Press, 1989) has been invaluable for specifying the chronology of mixing in the Goodman band.

18 Hammond, *John Hammond on Record,* 136; "this town" was New York City.

19 Collier, *Benny Goodman,* 107.

20 Adorno, "On Jazz," 52.

21 Benny Goodman and Irving Kolodin, *The Kingdom of Swing* (New York: Frederic Ungar, 1939), 210.

22 "*Life* Goes to a Party: To Listen to Benny Goodman and His Swing Band," *Life*, 1 November 1937, 121.

23 Hammond, *John Hammond on Record*, 116.

24 This word is Goodman's; Goodman, *Kingdom of Swing*, 229. It refers only to direct harassment and does not include the routine humiliations of segregation, like separate and inferior accommodations for touring black musicians, that Wilson and Hampton experienced. Also see Collier, *Benny Goodman*, 173–76.

25 Irving Kolodin, album liner notes for Benny Goodman, *Live at Carnegie Hall*, Columbia 40244.

26 Gerald Early, "On *Good Morning Blues: The Autobiography of Count Basie*," in *Tuxedo Junction: Essays on American Culture* (New York: Ecco, 1989), 281.

27 Paul Whiteman and Mary Margaret McBride, *Jazz* (New York: J. H. Sears, 1926), 1. For the program of the Aeolian Hall concert, see 100–102.

28 "*Life* Goes to a Party," 121; *Time* had noticed the same phenomenon a year earlier in "Whoa-ho-ho-ho-ho-ho!," 20 January 1936, 35.

29 None of these integrated bands were visually documented as thoroughly as the trio or quartet, and as far as I know, none of them were ever filmed.

30 Leonard Feather, "Jazz Symposium," *Esquire*, September 1944, 93.

31 "Joins White Band," *Chicago Defender*, 4 January 1941, 1; "Leana [*sic*] Horne, Song Stylist in Town," *Chicago Defender*, 15 February 1941, 13; Al Monroe, "Swingin' the News," *Chicago Defender*, 19 April 1941, 12. See also, Al Monroe, "Mixing's the Thing, Lena Horne, Richmond, Cootie and Others Say," *Chicago Defender*, 16 August 1941, 10.

32 "Duke of Jazz," *Time*, 1 February 1943, 44.

33 Probably the best-remembered musical manifestation of this trend was Billie Holiday's performing and recording of "Strange Fruit"—an account of a lynching—beginning in 1939.

34 See for example, Frederic Ramsey Jr. and Charles Edward Smith, eds., *Jazzmen* (New York: Harcourt, Brace, 1939).

35 Holman Harvey, "It's Swing!" *Reader's Digest*, January 1937, 99–102.

36 When Feather was replaced in 1945, the reviews began to address a wider range of music, and the photos were replaced with line drawings meant to represent the music in question, rather than a specific musician.

37 "Jam Sessions," *Look*, 24 August 1943, 64–66; "Jam Session," *Life*, 11 October 1943, 117–24. In December 1944 *Esquire* followed suit with "Jam Session: At Cafe Society Downtown," 107–114.

38 "Editorial: The Upward Journey of Hot Jazz, from the Junkshops to the Met," *Esquire,* February 1944, 6.

39 Leonard Feather, "All-American Jazz Ballot, 1945," *Esquire,* February 1945, 102.

40 Leonard Feather, "Jazz Symposium," *Esquire,* September 1944, 93. Wilson misremembered which *Big Broadcast* he was excluded from — it was 1937, not 1936. This is significant only because, among the three *Big Broadcast* films, 1937 was the last of the three and the only one not to include black performers.

41 "Jazz at the Philharmonic," *Senior Scholastic,* 7 April 1947, 36.

42 For more on Granz, JATP, and its various spin-offs see Balliet, "Pandemonium Pays Off," 3–10; Leonard Feather, "The Granzwagon," in *From Satchmo to Miles* (1972; reprint, New York: Da Capo, 1984), 173–85; John McDonough, "Norman Granz: JATP Pilot, Driving Pablo Home," *down beat,* October 1979, 30–32 and "Pablo Patriarch: The Norman Granz Story Part II," *down beat,* November 1979, 35–36, 76; Francis Newton [Eric Hobsbawm], *The Jazz Scene* (1959; reprint, New York: Da Capo, 1975), 182–85; Raymond Horricks, "Clef/Verve: A Company Report," in *Profiles in Jazz: From Sidney Bechet to John Coltrane* (New Brunswick, N.J.: Transaction, 1991), 173–81.

43 Ehrenberg, *Swingin' the Dream,* 237.

44 The initial insularity of bebop was partially economic and extramusical: the music developed during the first musician's union recording ban, of 1942–1943. This insularity, however, was also iconoclastic intention. Stories abound of the difficulty and strangeness of the music (many would say "noise") at Minton's and Monroe's in Harlem — weird rhythms and times, difficult keys and odd ("wrong") harmonies with obscure melodies. Less consistent are accounts of the motives of the innovators' intentions. Many writers say the innovators did not want to be "ripped off" by whites; others say they did not want to be ripped off by commercializers (who would most likely have been white). The difference between these accounts is subtle, but Ralph Ellison, who adheres to the latter account, makes a point that suggests the difference is important: "there was no policy of racial discrimination at Minton's"; "The Golden Age, Time Past," in *Shadow and Act* (New York: Vintage, 1972), 212.

45 The first term in quotations is from Balliet, "Pandemonium Pays Off," 3; the second is from Barney Kernfeld, "Swing-Bop Combos," in *The Blackwell Guide to Recorded Jazz,* ed. Kernfeld (Cambridge, Mass.: Blackwell, 1991), 349–50. Kernfeld sees this hybrid as one defined by common elements of band size and instrumentation, which small swing groups (like the Goodman trio, quartet, and sextet) and bebop groups shared, and

by the melding of swing's "tunefulness" with bebop's "rhythmic complexity" and speed.

46 This was the Basie band's big Hollywood year. The films are *Stage Door Canteen, The Hit Parade of 1943, Reveille With Beverlie, Crazy House,* and *Top Man.* For thorough study of the interactions of jazz and film, see Krin Gabbard, *Jammin' at the Margins: Jazz and the American Cinema* (Chicago: University of Chicago Press, 1996).

47 Leonard Feather, "Jazz is Where You Find It," *Esquire,* July 1944, 95.

48 Ibid., 95.

49 On the early development of this convention, see Charles Wolfe, "Vitaphone Shorts and *The Jazz Singer,*" *Wide Angle* 12.3 (July 1990): 58–78. For insight into how some jazz players felt about "showmanship" during the mid-forties, see Paul Eduard Miller, "Jazz Symposium," *Esquire,* October 1944, 95.

50 "Orson Welles to Star Satchmo," *Chicago Defender,* 30 August 1941, 12; Feather, "Jazz Is Where You Find It," 95. In fact, this biopic was to be a condensed history of jazz and was one proposed section of the aborted *It's All True.* For more on Welles as a proponent of jazz as a racially mixed art, see Dave Dexter, *Jazz Cavalcade: The Inside Story of Jazz,* with a foreword by Orson Welles (1946; reprint, New York: Da Capo, 1977), 170–71, 212–13.

51 In his regular "Swingin' the News" column in the entertainment section of the *Chicago Defender,* Al Monroe noted this quality of *Birth of the Blues*—"The premiere in Memphis last Friday was nauseating to those who read between the lines while all those movie folk paraded and spoke"—and suggested renaming the film "The Development of the Blues"; Al Monroe, "Swingin' the News," *Chicago Defender,* 8 November 1941, 13.

52 An unsigned *Defender* article about the 1939 musical *St. Louis Blues* hints at how this convention looked to many African Americans: "Miss Sullivan [a jazz singer known for "swinging" folk songs like "Loch Lomond"] does not only do specialty numbers in the film. She is as important to the story as is lovely Dorothy Lamour and Lloyd Nolan. She is introduced early in the picture and remains throughout the entire entertainment"; "Maxine Sullivan Is Regal [Theater] Screen Star," *Chicago Defender,* 8 April 1939, 10. While it is true that Sullivan appeared throughout the film, she played the usual maid role.

53 The most complete account of the NAACP's intervention in Hollywood is Thomas Cripps, *Slow Fade to Black: The Negro in American Film, 1900–1942* (New York: Oxford University Press, 1977), 348–89. For an example of protest in the black press, see Earl J. Morris, "Hollywood Ignores Black

America," *Pittsburgh Courier,* 28 May 1938, 20, and Morris "Should the Negro Ban White Motion Pictures?" *Pittsburgh Courier,* 24 September 1938, 21.

54 L. D. Reddick, "Educational Programs for the Improvement of Race Relations: Motion Pictures, Radio, the Press, and Libraries," *The Journal of Negro Education* 13 (summer 1944): 368–9, 369n.

55 Ibid., 380.

56 Jackie Lopez, "Is Hollywood Yielding?" *Chicago Defender,* 24 March 1945, 20.

57 "Spivak Gets Crown From TD [Tommy Dorsey], Duke Wins[,] Bing Is New Voice," *down beat,* 1 January 1945, 13.

58 Robert Goffin, "*Esquire*'s All-American Band," *Esquire,* February 1943, 74; Goffin, "*Esquire*'s All-American Jazz Band," *Esquire,* February 1944, 29; Leonard Feather, "All-American Jazz Ballot, 1945," 28.

59 For rhapsodic appreciations of Young and Jones, lavishly illustrated with photographs, see Albert Murray's *Stomping the Blues,* produced and art-directed by Harris Lewine (1976; reprint, New York: Da Capo, 1982).

60 Francis Davis, "Lester Leaps In: The Difficult Life of the First Jazz Modernist," *Times Literary Supplement,* 12 June 1992, 16; clearly the term "public" here needs to be carefully qualified.

61 In 1944 Columbia released a musical called *Jam Session.* I have not been able to see this film. David Meeker claims that the black players in the mixed Charlie Barnet band "do not appear on camera, as white actors sat in their places"; *Jazz in the Movies,* entry 1629.

62 A passage from a short story by Harlem Renaissance writer Rudolph Fisher demonstrates the power of this convention by noting the power of inverting it: "And [in North Carolina] there were occasional 'colored' newspapers from New York: newspapers that mentioned Negroes without comment, but always spoke of a white person as 'So-and-so, white.' That was the point. In Harlem black was white." "The City of Refuge," in *The New Negro,* ed. Alain Locke, 58.

63 For examinations of the ideology of entertainment in the musical see Jane Feuer, "The Self-reflective Musical and the Myth of Entertainment," and Richard Dyer, "Entertainment and Utopia," both in *Genre: The Musical,* Rick Altman (London: Routledge, 1981), 160–174, 176–89; see also Feuer, *The Hollywood Musical,* 2d edition (Bloomington: Indiana University Press, 1993).

64 Mike Levin, "Separating the Righteous Jazz: Critic Proposes to View Records According to Grouping in Styles," *down beat,* 11 May 1942, 14. For a less honorific account, which sees hot jazz as an "artistic" fantasy bribe for the bourgeois intelligentsia, see Adorno, "On Jazz," 51.

65 This space developed out of intersecting technical, aesthetic, and informational concerns in Gjon Mili's photographic work. Mili was "fast motion" photographer; he used the same stroboscopic technology that creates images of bullets piercing apples. Just as in those famous photos, Mili's photos use plain backgrounds to focus on the uncanniness of "frozen" motion. In this regard, the photos in "Jam Session" are uncharacteristic. For a more typical example of his work see Mili's photo essay, "The Lindy Hop," *Life,* 23 August 1943, 95–103.

66 Emge, "On the Beat in Hollywood," 6.

67 The lack of narrative in *Jammin' the Blues* is not simply due to its brevity. In the only available book-length work on shorts, Leonard Maltin notes that "a conflict existed in the method of making musical shorts; one school of thought believed the camera should be set up and the performers should perform, period. The other school favored having a story line and working in the musical numbers as part of an overall plot"; see *The Great Movie Shorts* (New York: Crown, 1972), 211.

68 Both "Midnight Symphony" and "Jammin' the Blues" were "unpublished" pieces, which meant they were "written" in rehearsals and recording for the soundtrack; consequently, audiences could not have been familiar with these songs. Though the makers of *Jammin' the Blues* could not have known it when they were recording their version, "On the Sunny Side of the Street" would be very familiar to audiences, courtesy of the million-selling record of the song made by Tommy Dorsey late in 1944.

69 Empirically this is not strictly so: The average shot length in MS is twelve seconds (2:59/15 shots), in SSS eight (3:05/23), and in JTB ten (4:08/23). However, JTB uses seventeen set-ups, while SSS uses only ten, and this constant reframing and reorienting adds to the speedy feel of the final tune.

70 Claudia Gorbman points out that "Songs require narrative to cede to spectacle, for it seems that lyrics and action compete for attention"; *Unheard Melodies: Narrative Film Music* (Bloomington: Indiana University Press, 1987), 20. Since Gorbman is most interested in narrative music, which does not compete for attention, she leaves this insight unexplained, but I take it that songs compete for attention because we feel, in some way, that they address us in ways instrumental music does not.

71 Reddick, "Educational Programs," 379.

72 During the fifties, this became the general criticism of the JATP concert style; see Feather, "The Granzwagon," 179, and Balliet, "Pandemonium Pays Off," 8.

73 Quincy Troupe, "Up Close and Personal: Miles Davis and Me," *Conjunc-*

tions 16 (1991), 80. For an account of the changing meanings of Louis Armstrong in African American communities, see Gerald Early, " 'And I Will Sing of Joy and Pain for You': Louis Armstrong and the Great Jazz Traditions," in *Tuxedo Junction,* 291–300.

74 For an analysis of Hollywood's distorted reflection of (white) American racial-cultural norms, see Thomas Cripps, "The Myth of the Southern Box Office: A Factor in Racial Stereotyping in American Movies, 1920– 1940," in *The Black Experience: Selected Essays,* ed. James C. Curtis and Lewis L. Gould (Austin: University of Texas Press, 1970), 116–44.

75 Emge, "On the Beat in Hollywood," 6. Of all the other reviews of *Jammin' the Blues,* only *Ebony* and *Time* noted that the film had a mixed cast, and only *Ebony,* like *down beat,* complained about the fact that this mixture was obscured.

76 Isaacs, "Face the Music," 725.

77 Henry Louis Gates Jr., "The Same Difference: Reading Jean Toomer, 1923–1982," in *Figures in Black: Words, Signs, and the "Racial" Self* (New York: Oxford University Press, 1987), 200.

78 Gerald Early, "Introduction," in *Tuxedo Junction,* xiii.

79 "Jamming Jumps the Color Line," *Ebony,* November 1945, 8–9.

80 Lopez, "Is Hollywood Yielding?," 20.

81 Agee, "Films," 753.

82 [Agee], "Jammin' the Blues," 50.

83 James Agee, "Pseudo-Folk," *Partisan Review* 11.2 (spring 1944): 219–23.

Coda: Bamboozled?

1 For more on *The Blood of Jesus* see Thomas Cripps, *Black Film as Genre* (Bloomington: Indiana University Press, 1978), Adrienne Lanier-Seward, "A Film Portrait of Black Ritual Expression: *The Blood of Jesus,*" in *Expressively Black: The Cultural Basis of Ethnic Identity,* ed. Geneva Gay and Willie L. Barber (New York: Praeger, 1987), 195–212; and Armond White, "On Spencer Williams" in *The Resistance: Ten Years of Pop Culture that Shook the World* (Woodstock, N.Y.: Overlook, 1995), 106–8.

2 These were "soundies" and "telescriptions," each of which were canned performances of single songs meant for either a short-lived visual juke box or for use in early, content-hungry television.

3 As I write, this common wisdom is being revisited and variously reasserted or contested in light of the new (overt) musical, *Moulin Rouge* (2001). See, for example, Jesse Green, "How Do You Make a Movie Sing?," *New York Times Magazine,* 13 May 2001, 24–27, and Armond

White, *"Moulin Rouge," New York Press* 14.22 (online edition *www.nypress.com/14/22/film/film3.cfm,* 3 June 2001).

4 The other obvious exception to the common wisdom is animated children's films.

5 On *Car Wash,* see Richard Dyer, "Is *Car Wash* a Black Musical?" in *Black American Cinema,* ed. Manthia Diawara (New York: Routledge, 1993), 93–106.

6 In the *Cinderella* remake, black pop singer Brandi played the title role, which required changing certain of Hammerstein's lyrics that equated beauty with whiteness or ordinary "white" features; Whitney Houston played the Fairy God Mother, and the royal family was interracial and interethnic.

7 On "Thriller," see Kobena Mercer, "Monster Metaphors: Notes on Michael Jackson's *Thriller*" in *Welcome to the Jungle: New Positions in Black Cultural Studies* (New York: Routledge, 1994), 33–51, and on "Black or White," see Carol Clover, "Dancin' in the Rain," *Critical Inquiry* 21.4 (summer 1995), 745–47; and Lauren Berlant, *The Queen of America Goes to Washington City: Essays on Sex and Citizenship* (Durham, N.C.: Duke University Press, 1997), 210–18.

8 *O Brother* as a musical is also more surprising coming from the Coens than *Bamboozled*'s interest in the genre is coming from Lee. Before *O Brother,* the Coens had not shown much explicit interest in the genre (though there was a musical number in their film immediately previous, *The Big Lebowski* [1998]). Lee on the other hand has made one film that has advertised itself as a musical, *School Daze* (1988), and has made a fictional musical biopic, *Mo' Better Blues* (1990), and most of his other films contain at least important musical passages, if not full blown numbers (e.g., the color interval in the park in *She's Gotta Have It* [1986], the credit sequence and the "shout out" in *Do the Right Thing* [1989], or the homage to *Carmen Jones* in *Girl 6* [1996]). Lee also frequently mentions the musical in interviews.

9 Quoted in Robert K. Oermann, liner note to *O Brother, Where Art Thou?* soundtrack recording (Mercury Records, 2000), n.p. This note also details the many different names—"folk," "country," "old time"—that the various collaborators use to (try to) name the music of the film.

10 Joel Coen, as quoted in *The Guardian,* 19 May 2000, cited in James Mottram, *The Coen Brothers: The Life of the Mind* (Dulles, VA: Brassey's, 2000), 157.

11 Ibid.

12 Evidence of Sturges's original intention, as well as some discussion of Paramount Studio's attempts to get him to cut the entire scene in the

church can be found in *Five Screenplays by Preston Sturges,* ed. Brian Henderson (Berkeley: University of California Press, 1985), 683. For a fuller reading of *Sullivan's Travels* that helped shape mine, see Kathleen Moran and Michael Rogin, " 'What's the Matter with Capra?': *Sullivan's Travels* and the Popular Front," *Representations* 71 (2000): 106–34. Yet another way in which we might see the ending of *O Brother* as qualified is by remembering that even in the mid-thirties it was acceptable for blacks and whites to perform together as long as the white was young and the black old, like Shirley Temple and Bill Robinson.

13 This song, like the rest of the music, is played by the minstrel show's house (funk) band, which always appears dressed in prison stripes. Here *Bamboozled* might be said to throw away the music *O Brother* so dwells on and loves, just as *O Brother* throws away the blackface that *Bamboozled* so dwells on and, apparently, loathes.

14 J. Hoberman, "100 Years of Solitude," *Village Voice,* 20–26 December 2000.

15 For a scathing critique of Lee's advertising work, see Paul Gilroy, *Against Race: Imagining Political Culture beyond the Color Line* (Cambridge: Harvard University Press, 2000), 242–43; Gilroy is more generally concerned about what he understands as a tyranny of the visual in U.S., Western, and increasingly global culture, a tyranny, in his view, in which motion pictures play a large role.

16 Toni Cade Bamabara, "Programming with *School Daze,*" in *Five for Five: The Films of Spike Lee* (New York: Stewart, Tabori and Chang, 1991), 50. In leveling her serious, but painstakingly constructive, feminist critique of the film, Bambara calls it "a house-divided pageant," a musical that works against itself and the expectations of the genre (47).

17 Then again, Man Ray—a name this character may have chosen for himself (like the "X" in Malcolm X), is not a new name, either. Rather, it is also the name of the modernist photographer famed for, among many other works, his "Noire et blanche" (1926), a matched pair of inverted black and white photos of a white woman's face and a black, West African mask.

Bibliography

All references to the *Chicago Defender* and the *Pittsburgh Courier* are to the city editions of those newspapers.

Abrahams, Roger D. *Singing the Master: The Emergence of African-American Culture in the Plantation South.* New York: Pantheon, 1992.

Ace. "*Hallelujah!* Discloses Talents of Actors." *Chicago Defender,* 1 February 1930, 10.

Adorno, Theodor W. "On Jazz." Trans. Jamie Owen Daniels. *Discourse* 12.1 (fall–winter 1989–90): 45–69.

Agee, James. "Films." *The Nation,* 16 December 1944, 753.

[———.] "Jammin' the Blues." *Time,* 25 December 1944, 50.

———. "Pseudo-Folk." *Partisan Review* 11 (1944): 219–23.

Albright, Alex. "Micheaux, Vaudeville, and Black Cast Film." *Black Film Review* 7.4 (n.d.): 6–9, 36.

"Al Jolson Buys Film Rights to *Green Pastures.*" *Chicago Defender,* 6 June 1931, 7.

"Al Jolson Certain to Get Lead in Film's *Pastures.*" *Chicago Defender,* 20 July 1935, 8.

"Al Jolson Given the Lead in 1933 Edition of *Porgy.*" *Chicago Defender,* 9 December 1933, 8.

"Al Jolson Gives Morris 'Lowdown'; 'Hurt To My Heart.'" *Pittsburgh Courier,* 7 May 1938, 20.

"Al Jolson May Play 'De Lawd' On the Screen." *Richmond Planet,* 28 September 1935.

"Al Jolson Pleads for Lead in 'Emperor Jones' on Stage." *Chicago Defender,* 7 April 1934, 9.

"Al Jolson's Offer for *Green Pastures* as Talkie is Refused by Producers." *Chicago Defender,* 13 June 1931, 7.

Allen, Robert C. *Horrible Prettiness: Burlesque and American Culture.* Chapel Hill, N.C.: University of North Carolina Press, 1991.

Allen, Robert C., and Douglas Gomery. *Film History: Theory and Practice.* New York: Knopf, 1985.

"All Race Movie Opens on Sunday." *Chicago Defender,* 29 October 1938, 10.

Alpert, Hollis. *The Life and Times of* Porgy and Bess. New York: Knopf, 1990.

Altman, Rick. *The American Film Musical.* Bloomington: Indiana University Press, 1987.

———. *Film/Genre.* London: British Film Institute, 1999.

————, ed. *Genre: The Musical.* London: Routledge, 1981.

"Amos 'n' Andy Now in the Million Dollar Circle." *Chicago Defender,* 5 June 1930, 6.

"An Angry 'Prof. Doodle' Hits Rob Roy's Claims for '54." *Chicago Defender,* 8 January 1955, 14.

"At Grand Next Week." *Chicago Defender,* 30 April 1927, sec. 1, 9.

Attali, Jacques. *Noise: The Political Economy of Music,* trans. Brian Massumi. Minneapolis: University of Minnesota, 1985.

Avenue Theater. Advertisement. *Chicago Defender,* 12 November 1938, 10.

Babington, Bruse, and Peter William Evans. *Blue Skies and Silver Linings: Aspects of the Hollywood Musical.* Manchester: Manchester University Press, 1985.

Baker, Houston A., Jr. *Modernism and the Harlem Renaissance.* Chicago: University of Chicago Press, 1987.

Baldwin, James. "*Carmen Jones:* The Light is Dark Enough." 1954. In *The Price of the Ticket: Collected Nonfiction, 1948–1985,* 107–12. New York: St. Martin's/Marek, 1985.

————. *The Devil Finds Work.* New York: Dell, 1976.

————. "On Catfish Row." 1959. In *The Price of the Ticket: Collected Nonfiction, 1948–1985,* 177–81. New York: St. Martin's/Marek, 1985.

Balio, Tino. *Grand Design: Hollywood as a Modern Business Enterprise, 1930–1939.* History of American Cinema, vol. 5, ed. Charles Harpole. New York: Scribner's, 1993.

Balliet, Whitney. "Pandemonium Pays Off." In *The Sound of Surprise: Forty-Six Pieces on Jazz,* 3–10. New York: Da Capo, 1978.

Bambara, Toni Cade. "Programming with *School Daze.*" In *Five for Five: The Films of Spike Lee,* 47–55. New York: Stewart, Tabori, and Chang, 1991.

Banes, Sally. *Writing Dancing in the Age of Postmodernism.* Hanover, N.H.: Wesleyan University Press, 1994.

Barlow, William. *Lookin' Up at Down: The Emergence of Blues Culture.* Philadelphia: Temple University Press, 1989.

Barrios, Richard. *A Song in the Dark: The Birth of the Musical Film.* New York: Oxford University Press, 1995.

Bennett, Lerone, Jr. "Hollywood's First Negro Movie Star." *Ebony,* May 1959, 100–108.

Berlant, Lauren. "Pax Americana: The Case of *Show Boat.*" In *Cultural Institutions of the Novel,* ed. Deidre Lynch, 399–422. Durham, N.C.: Duke University Press, 1996.

————. *The Queen of America Goes to Washington City: Essays on Sex and Citizenship.* Durham, N.C.: Duke University Press, 1997.

Berliner, Paul F. *Thinking in Jazz: The Infinite Art of Improvisation.* Chicago: University of Chicago Press, 1994.

Bernardi, Daniel, ed. *The Birth of Whiteness: Race and the Emergence of the U.S. Cinema.* New Brunswick, N.J.: Rutgers University Press, 1996.

———, ed. *Classic Hollywood, Classic Whiteness.* Minneapolis: University Press of Minnesota, 2001.

Berry, Tommye. "Kansas City Likes The Film, *Hooray for Love.*" *Chicago Defender,* 17 August 1935, 7.

Bethea, Dennis A. "He OK's *Hallelujah!*" *Chicago Defender,* 8 March 1930, 14.

Bhabha, Homi. "The Other Question." *Screen* 24.6 (November/December 1983): 18–35.

"Bill Robinson to Sue Papers for *Stormy Weather.*" *Chicago Defender,* 17 April 1943, 18.

Bime. "*Mammy.*" Film review. *Variety,* 27 March 1930.

"Blind Wife Sues Cooper, Film Star." *Chicago Defender,* 6 August 1938, 8.

Block, Geoffrey. "The Broadway Canon from *Show Boat* to *West Side Story* and the European Operatic Ideal." *The Journal of Musicology* 11.4 (fall 1993): 525–44.

———. *Enchanted Evenings: The Broadway Musical from* Show Boat *to Sondheim.* New York: Oxford University Press, 1997.

Bogle, Donald. *Brown Sugar: Eighty Years of America's Black Female Superstars.* 1980. Reprint, New York: Da Capo, 1990.

———. *Dorothy Dandridge: A Biography.* New York: Amistad, 1997.

———. *Toms, Coons, Mulattoes, Mammies, and Bucks: An Interpretive History of Blacks in American Films.* Third edition. New York: Continuum, 1994.

Bordwell, David, Janet Staiger, and Kristin Thompson. *The Classical Hollywood Cinema: Film Style and Mode of Production to 1960.* New York: Columbia University Press, 1985.

Boskin, Joseph. *Sambo: The Rise and Demise of an American Jester.* New York: Oxford University Press, 1986.

Bowser, Pearl, and Louise Spence. "Identity and Betrayal: *The Symbol of the Unconquered* and Oscar Micheaux's 'Biographical Legend.'" In *The Birth of Whiteness: Race and the Emergence of the U.S. Cinema,* ed. Daniel Bernardi, 56–79. New Brunswick, N.J.: Rutgers University Press, 1996.

———. *Writing Himself into History: Oscar Micheaux, His Silent Films, and His Audiences.* New Brunswick, N.J.: Rutgers University Press, 2000.

Breon, Robin. "*Show Boat:* The Revival, the Racism." *The Drama Review* 39.2 (summer 1995): 86–105.

Brown, Henry. "Just Where Did 'Blackface' Comedy Get Its Start?" *Chicago Defender,* 31 December 1932, 11.

Brown, Sterling A. *Negro Poetry and Drama and The Negro in American Fiction.*
1937. Reprint, New York: Atheneum, 1969.

———. "Our Literary Audience." *Opportunity,* February 1930. Reprinted in
*Within the Circle: An Anthology of African American Literary Criticism from
the Harlem Renaissance to the Present,* ed. Angelyn Mitchell, 69–78. Durham,
N.C.: Duke University Press, 1994.

———. "Spirituals, Blues, and Jazz." *Jam Session: An Anthology of Jazz,* ed.
Ralph J. Gleason, 12–26. New York: G. P. Putnam's Sons, 1958.

Buckley, Gail Lumet. *The Hornes: An American Family.* New York: Knopf, 1986.

Burns, Ben. *Nitty Gritty: A White Editor in Black Journalism.* Jackson: University of Mississippi Press, 1996.

"By Their Acts, They Help Feed Poor at Christmas Time." *Chicago Defender,*
18 December 1937, sec. 1, 13.

"*Cabin in the Sky* Invades Chicago This Week." *Chicago Defender,* 8 May
1943, 19.

"Calloway Is Star on Al Jolson Bill." *Chicago Defender,* 31 January 1936, 10.

"Cantor and Kaye Break Radio Rules to Star Negroes." *Ebony,* January 1943, 43.

Cantor, Eddie. "Bert Williams—'The Best Teacher I Ever Had.'" *Ebony,* June
1958: 103–6.

———, as told to David Freeman. *My Life is in Your Hands.* New York: Harper
and Brothers, 1928.

Cantwell, Robert. *When We Were Good: The Folk Revival.* Cambridge: Harvard
University Press, 1996.

Carbine, Mary. "'The Finest Outside the Loop': Motion Picture Exhibition
in Chicago's Black Metropolis, 1905–1928." *Camera Obscura* 23 (May 1990):
9–42.

Carby, Hazel. *Race Men.* Cambridge: Harvard University Press, 1998.

Carlson, Marvin. *Performance: A Critical Introduction.* New York: Routledge, 1996.

"*Carmen Jones.*" *Time,* 1 November 1954, 98.

Carter, Elmer Anderson. "Of Negro Motion Pictures." *Close Up* 5.2 (August
1929): 118–22.

Chandler, Alfred D., Jr. *The Visible Hand: The Managerial Revolution in American Business.* Cambridge: Harvard University Press, 1977.

Chapman, C. E. "Dallas, Texas Gets Premiere of Picture *Cabin in the Sky.*"
Chicago Defender, 20 February 1943, 18.

Chapman, John. "*Carmen Jones* Simply Superb Negro Adaptation of *Carmen.*"
New York Daily News, 3 December 1943.

Charters, Ann. *Nobody: The Story of Bert Williams.* New York: Macmillan, 1970.

"Chicago's Finest Theater to Open Doors Saturday." *Chicago Defender,* 4 February 1928, sec. 1, 6.

Clover, Carol. "Dancin' in the Rain." *Critical Inquiry* 21.4 (summer 1995): 722–47.

Cockrell, Dale. *Demons of Disorder: Early Blackface Minstrels and Their World.* New York: Cambridge University Press, 1997.

Cohen, Lizabeth. *Making a New Deal: Industrial Workers in Chicago, 1919–1939.* New York: Cambridge University Press, 1990.

Cohen, Ralph. "History and Genre." *NLH* 9.2 (winter 1986): 203–18.

Collier, James Lincoln. *Benny Goodman and the Swing Era.* New York: Oxford University Press, 1989.

Cooper, Ralph, with Steve Dougherty. *Amateur Night at the Apollo: Ralph Cooper Presents Five Decades of Great Entertainment.* New York: Harper-Collins, 1990.

Corbett, John. "Free, Single, and Disengaged: Listening Pleasure and the Popular Music Object." *October* 54 (1990): 79–101.

Crafton, Donald. *The Talkies: American Cinema's Transition to Sound, 1926–1931.* History of the American Cinema, vol. 4, ed. Charles Harpole. New York: Scribner's, 1997.

Cram, Bestor, and Pearl Bowser. *Midnight Ramble: Oscar Micheaux and the Story of Race Movies.* Boston: Northern Light Productions/American Experience/WGBH, 1994.

Cripps, Thomas. *Black Film as Genre.* Bloomington: Indiana University Press, 1978.

———. "The Death of Rastus: Negroes in American Films Since 1945." *Phylon* 28.3 (fall 1967): 267–75.

———. "The Films of Spencer Williams." *Black American Literature Forum* 12.4 (winter 1978): 128–34.

———. *Making Movies Black: The Hollywood Message Movie from World War II to the Civil Rights Era.* New York: Oxford University Press, 1993.

———. "The Myth of the Southern Box Office: A Factor in Racial Stereotyping in American Movies, 1920–1940." In *The Black Experience: Selected Essays,* ed. James C. Curtis and Lewis L. Gould, 116–44. Austin: University of Texas Press, 1970.

———. "Oscar Micheaux: The Story Continues." In *Black American Cinema,* ed. Manthia Diawara, 71–79. New York: Routledge, 1993.

———. "'Race Movies' as Voices of the Black Bourgeoisie: *The Scar of Shame* (1927)." In *American History/American Film: Interpreting the Hollywood Image,* ed. John E. O'Connor and Martin A. Jackson, 39–55. New York: Unger, 1979.

———. *Slow Fade to Black: The Negro in American Film, 1900–1942.* New York: Oxford University Press, 1977.

———. "Stepin Fetchit and the Politics of Performance." In *Beyond the Stars:*

Stock Characters in American Popular Film, ed. Paul Loukides and Linda K. Fuller, 35–48. Bowling Green, Ohio: Bowling Green State University Popular Press, 1990.

Cripps, Thomas, ed. *The Green Pastures.* Madison: University of Wisconsin, 1979.

"Critic Calls *Hallelujah!* 'Best Film.'" *Chicago Defender,* 11 January 1930, 9.

Crowther, Bosley. "*Carmen Jones* Finds American Types Singing Foreign Opera Score." *New York Times,* 31 October 1954, section 2, 1.

Cruse, Harold. "The Creative and Performing Arts and the Struggle for Identity and Credibility." In *Negotiating the Mainstream: A Survey of the Afro-American Experience,* ed. Harry A. Johnson 47–102. Chicago: American Library Association, 1978.

———. *The Crisis of the Negro Intellectual: A Historical Analysis of the Failure of Black Leadership.* 1967. Reprint, New York: Quill, 1984.

Cullen, Countee. "*Porgy.*" Book review. *Opportunity,* December 1925, 379.

Dancer, Maurice. "Manhattan Critic Reviews New All-Colored 'Talkie' Film." *Pittsburgh Courier,* 9 March 1929, sec. 3, 1.

Daniels, George. "Amusing Art, People The World Over Should See, Says Another." *Chicago Defender,* 17 April 1954, 10.

Dates, Jannette L., and William Barlow, eds. *Split Image: African Americans in the Mass Media.* Washington, D.C.: Howard University Press, 1990.

Dauphin, Gary. "The Show: Sometimes the Audience Produces More Entertainment than the Plotline." *Village Voice,* 21 November 1995, film special sec., 10, 12.

Davis, Albert W. "Past Days of Minstrelsy." *Americana,* June 1912, 529–47.

Davis, Francis. "Lester Leaps In: The Difficult Life of the First Jazz Modernist." *Times Literary Supplement,* 12 June 1992, 16.

"*Defender* Will Give 100 Free Tickets to *Hallelujah!*" *Chicago Defender,* 11 January 1930, 1.

Denning, Michael. *The Cultural Front: The Laboring of American Culture in the Twentieth Century.* London: Verso, 1996.

Dennison, Sam. *Scandalize My Name: Black Imagery in American Popular Music.* New York: Garland, 1982.

Dent, Gina, ed. *Black Popular Culture.* Seattle: Bay Press, 1992.

Derrida, Jacques. *The Gift of Death.* Trans. David Wills. Chicago: University of Chicago Press, 1995.

———. *Given Time I: Counterfeit Money.* Trans. Peggy Kamuf. Chicago: University of Chicago Press, 1992.

DeVeaux, Scott. *The Birth of Bebop: A Social and Musical History.* Berkeley: University of California, 1997.

Dexter, Dave. *Jazz Cavalcade: The Inside Story*, with a foreword by Orson Welles. 1946. Reprint, New York: Da Capo, 1977.

Diawara, Manthia, ed. *Black American Cinema*. New York: Routledge, 1993.

Doane, Mary Ann. *The Desire to Desire: The Woman's Film of the 1940s*. Bloomington: Bloomington University Press, 1987.

Doherty, Thomas. "This Is Where We Came In: The Audible Screen and the Voluble Audience of Early Sound Cinema." In *American Movie Audiences: From the Turn of the Century to the Early Sound Period*, ed. Melvyn Stokes and Richard Maltby, 143–63. London: BFI, 1999.

Dorman, James H. "Shaping the Popular Image of Post-Reconstruction American Blacks: The 'Coon Song' Phenomenon of the Gilded Age." *American Quarterly* 40.4 (December 1988): 450–71.

Douglas, Ann. *Terrible Honesty: Mongrel Manhattan in the 1920s*. New York: Farrar, Straus and Giroux, 1995.

"Draw Color Line on Theater Building." *Chicago Defender*, 19 March 1927, sec. 1, 2.

Driggs, Frank, and Harris Lewine. *Black Beauty, White Heat: A Pictorial History of Classic Jazz, 1920–1950*. New York: William Morrow, 1982.

"Drops Rags." *Chicago Defender*, 14 March 1931, sec. 1, 9.

Duberman, Martin Bauml. *Paul Robeson*. New York: Knopf, 1988.

[Du Bois, W. E. B.] "*The Birth of a Nation*: An Editorial." *Crisis*, May–June 1915, 33.

———. "Drama Among the Black Folk," *Crisis*, October 1916, 169.

[———.] "Dramatis Personae." *Crisis*, October 1929, 342, 355–56.

———. *The Gift of Black Folk*. 1924. Reprint, Millwood, N.Y.: Kraus-Thomson Organization Limited, 1975.

———. *The Souls of Black Folk*. In *Writings*, ed. Nathan Huggins. 357–547. New York: New American Library, 1986.

———. *Writings*, ed. Nathan Huggins. New York: New American Library, 1986.

———. Untitled Eulogy for Bert Williams. In *Bert Williams, Son of Laughter*, ed. Mabel Rowland. 217–18. 1923. Reprint, New York: Negro Universities Press, 1969.

"*The Duke is Tops* on Way to Regal." *Chicago Defender*, 3 September 1938, 9.

"Duke of Jazz." *Time*, 1 February 1943, 44.

Dyer, Richard. "Entertainment and Utopia." In *Genre: The Musical*, ed. Rick Altman, 176–89. London: Routledge and Kegan Paul, 1981.

———. *Heavenly Bodies*. New York: St. Martins, 1986.

———. "Is *Car Wash* a Black Musical?" In *Black American Cinema*, ed. Manthia Diawara, 93–106. New York: Routledge, 1993.

————. *White.* New York: Routledge, 1997.

————. "White." *Screen* 29.4 (autumn 1988): 44–64.

Early, Gerald. *Tuxedo Junction: Essays on American Culture.* New York: Ecco, 1989.

————, ed. *Lure and Loathing: Essays on Race, Identity, and the Ambivalence of Assimilation.* New York: Allen Lane/Penguin, 1993.

"Editorial: The Upward Journey of Hot Jazz, from the Junkshops to the Met." *Esquire,* February 1944, 6.

Ehrenberg, Lewis A. *Steppin' Out: New York Nightlife and the Transformation of American Culture, 1890–1930.* Chicago: University of Chicago Press, 1981.

————. *Swingin' the Dream: Big Band Jazz and the Rebirth of American Culture.* Chicago: University of Chicago Press, 1998.

————. "Things to Come: Swing Bands, Bebop, and the Rise of a Postwar Jazz Scene." In *Recasting America: Culture and Politics in the Age of the Cold War,* ed. Lary May, 221–45. Chicago: University of Chicago Press, 1989.

Eisenberg, Evan. *The Recording Angel: Explorations in Phonography.* New York: McGraw-Hill, 1987.

Eliot, M. H. "When to Laugh." *Chicago Defender,* 15 February 1930, 14.

Ellington, Edward Kennedy. *Music is My Mistress.* New York: Doubleday, 1973.

Ellison, Ralph. *Going to the Territory.* New York: Vintage, 1986.

————. *Shadow and Act.* New York: Vintage, 1972.

Ely, Melvin Patrick. *The Adventures of Amos 'n' Andy: A Social History of an American Phenomenon.* New York: Free Press, 1991.

Emge, Charles. "On the Beat in Hollywood." *down beat,* 1 December 1944, 6.

Engle, Lehman. *The American Musical Theater.* Revised edition. New York: Collier Books, 1975.

Everett, Anna. *Returning the Gaze: A Genealogy of Black Film Criticism, 1909–1949.* Durham, N.C.: Duke University Press, 2001.

Eyman, Scott. *The Speed of Sound: Hollywood and the Talkie Revolution, 1926–1930.* New York: Simon and Schuster, 1997.

Fauset, Jessie. "The Gift of Laughter." In *The New Negro: Voices of the Harlem Renaissance,* ed. Alain Locke, 161–67. 1925. Reprint, New York: Atheneum, 1992.

Feather, Leonard. "All-American Jazz Ballot, 1945." *Esquire,* February 1945, 102.

————. "The Granzwagon." In *From Satchmo to Miles,* 173–85. 1972. Reprint, New York: Da Capo, 1984.

————. "Jazz is Where You Find It." Regular column. *Esquire,* July 1944, 95; May 1945, 95.

————. "Jazz Symposium." Regular column. *Esquire,* July 1944, 95; September 1944, 95.

Fehr, Richard, and Frederick G. Vogel. *Lullabies of Hollywood: Movie Music and the Movie Musical, 1915–1992.* Jefferson, N.C.: McFarland and Co., 1993.

Feld, Stephen. "Communication, Music, and Speech about Music." 1984. In Charlie Keil and Feld, *Music Grooves: Essays and Dialogues.* 77–95. Chicago: University of Chicago Press, 1994.

Ferber, Edna. *Show Boat.* 1926. Reprint, New York: Signet, 1994.

Feuer, Jane. *The Hollywood Musical.* Second edition. Bloomington: Indiana University Press, 1993.

———. "The Self-reflective Musical and the Myth of Entertainment." In *Genre: The Musical,* ed. Rick Altman, 160–74. London: Routledge, 1981.

Finson, Jon W. *The Voices That Are Gone: Themes in Nineteenth-Century American Popular Song.* New York: Oxford University Press, 1994.

Fisher, Rudolph. "The City of Refuge." In *The New Negro: Voices of the Harlem Renaissance,* ed. Alain Locke, 57–74. 1925; New York: Atheneum, 1992.

Fitzgerald, F. Scott. *The Last Tycoon.* New York: Scribner's, 1941.

"5,422 Words Captures First Prize." *Chicago Defender,* 25 January 1930, 1.

Floyd, Samuel A., Jr. *The Power of Black Music: Interpreting Its History from Africa to the United States.* New York: Oxford University Press, 1995.

"Folks We Can Get Along Without." *Chicago Defender,* 28 November 1936, sec. 1, 16.

Fox, Ted. *Showtime at the Apollo.* New York: Da Capo, 1993.

Freidberg, Anne. "A Denial of Difference: Theories of Cinematic Identification." *Psychoanalysis and Cinema,* ed. E. Ann Kaplan, 36–45. New York: Routledge, 1990.

Friedman, Lester D., ed. *Unspeakable Images: Ethnicity and the American Cinema.* Urbana: University of Illinois Press, 1991.

Frith, Simon. *Performing Rites: On the Value of Popular Music.* Cambridge: Harvard University Press, 1996.

Fulcher, Malcolm B. "Writer Finds Race Plays Big Part in Pictures Now." *Chicago Defender,* 22 June 1935, 10.

Fuller, Kathryn H. *At the Picture Show: Small Town Audiences and the Creation of Movie Fan Culture.* Washington, D.C.: Smithsonian Institution Press, 1996.

Gabbard, Krin. *Jammin' at the Margins: Jazz and the American Cinema.* Chicago: University of Chicago Press, 1996.

———, ed. *Representing Jazz.* Durham, N.C.: Duke University Press, 1995.

———, ed. *Jazz Among the Discourses.* Durham, N.C.: Duke University Press, 1995.

Gaines, Jane. *Fire and Desire: Mixed Race Movies in the Silent Era.* Chicago: University of Chicago Press, 2001.

———. "Fire and Desire: Race, Melodrama, and Oscar Micheaux." In *Black American Cinema,* ed. Manthia Diawara, 49–70. New York: Routledge, 1993.

———. "*The Scar of Shame:* Skin Color and Cast in Silent Film Melodrama." *Cinema Journal* 26.4 (summer 1987): 3–21.

Gaines, Kevin K. *Uplifting the Race: Black Leadership, Politics, and Culture in the Twentieth Century.* Chapel Hill, N.C.: University of North Carolina Press, 1996.

Garber, Marjorie. *Vested Interests: Cross Dressing and Cultural Anxiety.* New York: Routledge, 1992.

Gates, Henry Louis, Jr. *Figures in Black: Words, Signs, and the "Racial" Self.* New York: Oxford University Press, 1987.

———. *The Signifying Monkey: A Theory of African-American Literary Criticism.* New York: Oxford University Press, 1988.

Gay, Geneva, and Willie L. Barber, eds. *Expressively Black: The Cultural Basis of Ethnic Identity.* New York: Praeger, 1987.

Gendron, Bernard. "Moldy Figs and Modernists: Jazz at War (1942–1946)." In *Jazz Among the Discourses,* ed. Krin Gabbard, 31–56. Durham, N.C.: Duke University Press, 1995.

General Electric. Advertisement. *Look,* 6 February 1945, 2.

George, Nelson. *The Death of Rhythm and Blues.* New York: Dutton, 1988.

Gilman, Sander L. *Inscribing the Other.* Lincoln: University of Nebraska, 1991.

Gilroy, Paul. *Against Race: Imagining Political Culture beyond the Color Line.* Cambridge: Harvard University Press, 2000.

———. *The Black Atlantic: Modernity and Double Consciousness.* Cambridge: Harvard University Press, 1993.

Goffin, Robert. "*Esquire's* All-American Band." *Esquire,* February 1943, 74–75, 124.

———. "*Esquire's* All-American Jazz Band." *Esquire,* February 1944, 29.

Goldman, Herbert G. *Jolson: The Legend Comes to Life.* New York: Oxford University Press, 1988.

Gomery, Douglas. *Shared Pleasures: A History of Movie Presentations in the United States.* Madison: University of Wisconsin Press, 1992.

———. "*The Singing Fool.*" In *Close Viewings: An Anthology of New Film Criticism,* ed. Peter Lehman 370–82. Tallahassee: Florida State University Press, 1990.

Goodman, Benny, and Irving Kolodin. *The Kingdom of Swing.* New York: Frederic Ungar, 1939.

Gorbman, Claudia. *Unheard Melodies: Narrative Film Music.* Bloomington: Indiana University Press, 1987.

Green, Jesse. "How Do You Make a Movie Sing?" *New York Times Magazine,* 13 May 2001, 24–27.

Green, Ronald J. "Oscar Micheaux's Interrogation of Caricature as Entertainment." *Film Quarterly* 51.3 (1998): 16–31.

———. *Straight Lick: The Cinema of Oscar Micheaux.* Bloomington: Indiana University Press, 2000.

———. "'Twoness' in the Style of Oscar Micheaux." In *Black American Cinema,* ed. Manthia Diawara, 26–47. New York: Routledge, 1993.

Griffiths, Alison, and James Lathan. "Film and Ethnic Identity in Harlem, 1896–1915." In *American Movie Audiences: From the Turn of the Century to the Early Sound Period,* ed. Melvyn Stokes and Richard Maltby, 46–63. London: BFI, 1999.

Grossman, James R. *Land of Hope: Chicago, Black Southerners, and the Great Migration.* Chicago: University of Chicago Press, 1989.

Grupenhoff, Richard. *The Black Valentino: The Stage and Screen Career of Lorenzo Tucker.* Metuchen, N.J.: Scarecrow, 1988.

Gubar, Susan. *Racechanges: White Skin, Black Face in American Culture.* New York: Oxford University Press, 1997.

Guerrero, Ed. *Framing Blackness: The African American Image in Film.* Philadelphia: Temple University Press, 1993.

Gunning, Tom. "The Cinema of Attraction: Early Film, Its Spectator, and the Avant-Garde." *Wide Angle* 3 and 4 (1986): 63–70.

Hall, Mordaunt. "Al Jolson and the Vitaphone." *New York Times,* 7 October 1927, sec. 4, 24.

Hall, Stuart. "Encoding/Decoding." In *The Cultural Studies Reader,* ed. Simon During, 90–103. New York: Routledge, 1993.

———. "What Is This 'Black' in Black Popular Culture?" In *Black Popular Culture,* ed. Gina Dent, 21–34. Seattle: Bay, 1992.

"*Hallelujah!* to Have Double Opener in New York." *Chicago Defender,* 17 August 1929, 9.

Halliburton, Cecil D. "Hollywood Presents Us: The Movies and Racial Attitudes." *Opportunity,* October 1935, 296–97.

Hamm, Charles. *Putting Popular Music in Its Place.* New York: Cambridge University Press, 1995.

———. "The Theatre Guild Production of *Porgy and Bess.*" *Journal of the American Musicological Society* 40 (1987): 495–532.

Hammond, John, with Irving Townsend. *John Hammond on Record.* New York: Summit Books, 1977.

Hancock, Dean Gordon. "'Dangerous Propaganda' Says This Critic of Planned Tour." *Chicago Defender,* 17 April 1954, 10.

Handel, Leo A. *Hollywood Looks at Its Audience: A Report of Film Audience Research.* Urbana: University of Illinois, 1950.

Hansen, Miriam. *Babel and Babylon: Spectatorship in American Silent Film.* Cambridge: Harvard University Press, 1991.

———. "Early Cinema, Late Cinema: Permutations of the Public Sphere." *Screen* 34.3 (Autumn 1993): 197–210.

Harvey, Holman. "It's Swing!" *Reader's Digest,* January 1937, 99–102.

Hatcher, Francis S. "Assails Blackface Act in Theatre." *Chicago Defender,* 10 March 1945, sec. 1, 14.

Hazzard-Gordon, Katrina. *Jookin': The Rise of Social Dance Formations in African-American Culture.* Philadelphia: Temple University Press, 1990.

"Hearts in Dixie, Film of Song and Pathos, Plus Good Vodvil, Is Offered at Regal." *Chicago Defender,* 6 July 1929, 9.

Heyward, DuBose. *Porgy.* 1925. Reprint, London: Jonathan Cape, 1928.

Heyward, Dorothy, and DuBose Heyward. *Porgy: A Play in Four Acts.* New York: Doubleday, Page and Co, 1927.

Hoberman, J. "100 Years of Solitude." *Village Voice,* 20–26 December 2000.

hooks, bell. *Black Looks: Race and Representation.* Boston: South End, 1992.

Horn, David. "From Catfish Row to Granby Street: Contesting Meaning in *Porgy and Bess.*" *Popular Music* 13.2 (1994): 165–73.

Horne, Lena, and Richard Schickel. *Lena.* New York: Limelight, 1986.

Horricks, Raymond. "Clef/Verve: A Company Report." In *Profiles in Jazz: From Sidney Bechet to John Coltrane.* 173–81. New Brunswick, N.J.: Transaction, 1991.

Howard, Jessica H. "*Hallelujah!:* Transformation in Film." *African American Review* 30.3 (fall 1996): 441–51.

"Hudgins Cuts Black Face [*sic*], Proves Point." *Chicago Defender,* 14 February 1931, sec. 1, 6.

Huggins, Nathan Irvin. *Harlem Renaissance.* New York: Oxford University Press, 1971.

Hughes, Langston. "Note on Commercial Art." *Crisis,* March 1940, 79.

Hurl., "*The Duke is Tops.*" Film review. *Variety,* 20 July 1938.

Hyde, Lewis. *The Gift: Imagination and the Erotic Life of Property.* New York: Vintage, 1979.

" 'I Can't Believe That Al Jolson Would Humiliate Race,' Noble Sissle Writes." *Pittsburgh Courier* (national edition), 28 April 1938, 21.

"If You Can Name This New Theater, You'll Win a Prize." *Chicago Defender,* 5 November 1927, sec. 1, 1.

Isaacs, Hermine Rich. "Face the Music: Films in Review." *Theatre Arts,* December 1944, 723–27.

Jackson, James A. "What Sort of People Are Show Folks?" *Richmond Planet,* 19 July 1930.

"Jamming Jumps the Color Line." *Ebony,* November 1945, 8–9.

"Jam Session." *Life,* 11 October 1943, 117–24.

"Jam Session: At Cafe Society Downtown." *Esquire,* December 1944, 107–14.

"Jam Session in Movieland." *Ebony,* November 1945, 6–7.

"Jam Sessions." *Look,* 24 August 1943, 64–66.

"Jazz at the Philharmonic." *Senior Scholastic,* 7 April 1947, 36.

Jenkins, Henry. *What Made Pistachio Nuts? Early Sound Comedy and the Vaude-ville Aesthetic.* New York: Columbia University Press, 1992.

"Johnny Hudgins, Yes Silent John, Is Back." *Chicago Defender,* 7 March 1942, 21.

Johnson, Hall. *"Porgy and Bess—*A Folk Opera." *Opportunity,* January 1936, 24–28.

Johnson, James Weldon. *Black Manhattan.* 1930. Reprint, New York: Arno, 1968.

Johnson, Victoria E. "Polyphony and Cultural Expression: Interpreting Musical Traditions in *Do the Right Thing.*" *Film Quarterly* 47.2 (winter 1993): 18–29.

"Joins White Band." *Chicago Defender,* 4 January 1941, 1.

Jones, Dewey R. "Nation's Stars to Help Defender Benefit Show." *Chicago Defender,* 29 April 1933, sec. 1, 1.

Jones, LeRoi [Amiri Baraka]. *Blues People: Negro Music in White America.* New York: Quill, 1963.

"Josephine Baker Stars in Film." *Chicago Defender,* 30 July 1938, 8.

Jowelt, Garth. *Film: The Democratic Art.* Boston: Little, Brown, 1976.

Julien, Isaac, and Kobena Mercer. "Introduction: De Margin and De Center." *Screen* 29.4 (autumn 1988): 2–10.

Kauf. *"Hooray for Love."* Film review. *Variety,* 17 July 1935.

Keil, Charles. "Motion and Feeling Through Music." 1966. In Keil and Stephen Feld, *Music Grooves: Essays and Dialogues,* 53–76. Chicago: University of Chicago Press, 1994.

———. "Participatory Discrepancies and the Power of Music." 1987. In Keil and Stephen Feld, *Music Grooves: Essays and Dialogues,* 96–108. Chicago: University of Chicago Press, 1994.

———. *Urban Blues.* Chicago: University of Chicago, 1966.

Keil, Charles and Stephen Feld. *Music Grooves: Essays and Dialogues.* Chicago: University of Chicago Press, 1994.

Kelley, Robin D. G. "Notes on Deconstructing 'The Folk.'" *American Histori-cal Review* 97.5 (December 1992): 1400–1408.

———. "The Riddle of the Zoot: Malcolm Little and Black Cultural Politics During World War II." In *Malcolm X: In Our Own Image,* ed. Joe Wood, 154–82. New York: St. Martin's, 1992.

Kenney, William Howland. *Chicago Jazz: A Cultural History, 1904–1930.* New York: Oxford University Press, 1993.

Kernfeld, Barney, ed. *The Blackwell Guide to Recorded Jazz,* Cambridge: Blackwell, 1991.

Klinger, Barbara. "Digressions at the Cinema: Reception and Mass Culture." *Cinema Journal* 28.4 (summer 1989): 3–19.

———. "Film History Terminable and Interminable: Recovering the Past in Reception Studies." *Screen* 38.2 (summer 1997): 107–28.

Klotman, Phyllis Rauch. *Frame by Frame: A Black Filmography.* Bloomington: Indiana University Press, 1997.

Klotman, Phyllis Rauch, and Gloria Gibson. *Frame by Frame II: A Filmography of the African American Image, 1997–1994.* Bloomington: University of Indiana Press, 1997.

Knee, Adam. "Class Swings: Music, Race, and Social Mobility in *Broken Strings.*" In *Soundtrack Available: Essays on Film and Popular Music,* ed. Pamela Robertson Wojcik and Arthur Knight, 269–94. Durham, N.C.: Duke University Press, 2001.

———. "Doubling, Music, and Race in *Cabin in the Sky.*" In *Representing Jazz,* ed. Krin Gabbard, 193–208. Durham, N.C.: Duke University Press, 1995.

Knight, Arthur. " 'It Ain't Necessarily So That It Ain't Necessarily So': African American Recordings of *Porgy and Bess* as Film and Cultural Criticism." In *Soundtrack Available: Essays on Film and Popular Music,* ed. Pamela Robertson Wojcik and Arthur Knight, 319–46. Durham, N.C.: Duke University Press, 2001.

———. "Star Dances: African American Constructions of Stardom." In *Classic Hollywood, Classic Whiteness,* ed. Daniel Bernardi, 386–414. Minneapolis: University of Minnesota, 2001.

Kolodin, Irving. Album liner notes. Benny Goodman. *Live at Carnegie Hall.* 16 January 1938. Columbia 40244.

Krasner, David. *Resistance, Parody, and Double Consciousness in African American Theatre, 1895–1910.* New York: St. Martins, 1997.

Kreuger, Miles. *Show Boat: The Story of a Classic American Musical.* New York: Oxford University Press, 1977.

———, ed. *Souvenir Programs of Twelve Classic Movies, 1927–1941.* New York: Dover, 1977.

LaCapra, Dominick. "Comment [on Ralph Cohen]." *NLH* 9.2 (winter 1986): 219–21.

Lahr, John. "The Theatre: Mississippi Mud." *The New Yorker,* 25 October 1993, 123–26.

LaMar, Lawrence F. "Brand Story of *Stormy Weather* Retake as False." *Chicago Defender,* 3 April 1943, 19.

Lanier-Seward, Adrienne. "A Film Portrait of Black Ritual Expression: *The*

Blood of Jesus." In *Expressively Black: The Cultural Basis of Ethnic Identity,* ed. Geneva Gay and Willie L. Barber, 195–212. New York: Praeger, 1987.

Leab, Daniel. *From Sambo to Superspade: The Black Experience in Motion Pictures.* Boston: Houghton Mifflin, 1975.

"Leana [*sic*] Horne, Song Stylist in Town." *Chicago Defender,* 15 February 1941, 13.

Leavette, Harry. "Through Hollywood." Occasional column. *Chicago Defender,* 25 January 1936, 10.

Lee, Spike, with Lisa Jones. *Uplift the Race: The Construction of* School Daze. New York: Fireside, 1988.

Lehman, Peter, ed. *Close Viewings: An Anthology of New Film Criticism.* Tallahassee: Florida State University Press, 1990.

Levin, Mike. "Separating the Righteous Jazz: Critic Proposes to View Records According to Grouping in Styles." *down beat,* 11 May 1942, 14.

Levine, Lawrence W. *Black Culture and Black Consciousness: Afro-American Folk Thought from Slavery to Freedom.* New York: Oxford University Press, 1977.

———. "The Folklore of Industrial Society: Popular Culture and Its Audiences." *American Historical Review* 97.5 (December 1992): 1369–99.

———. *Highbrow/Lowbrow: The Emergence of Cultural Hierarchy in America.* Cambridge: Harvard University Press, 1988.

Lewis, Ramona. "*Cabin* Picture Called Insult." *New York Amsterdam News,* 12 June 1943.

Lhamon, W. T., Jr. *Raising Cain: Blackface Performance from Jim Crow to Hip Hop.* Cambridge: Harvard University Press, 1998.

"*Life* Goes to a Party: To Listen to Benny Goodman and His Swing Band." *Life,* 1 November 1937, 120–22, 126.

Llorayne, Barbara. "Those Amateur Minstrels Are Real Pros Now." *Chicago Defender,* 22 April 1933, sec. 1, 8.

Lock, Graham. *Blutopia: Visions of the Future and Revisions of the Past in the Work of Sun Ra, Duke Ellington, and Anthony Braxton.* Durham, N.C.: Duke University Press, 1999.

Locke, Alain, and Sterling A. Brown. "Folk Values in a New Medium." 1930. In *Black Films and Filmmakers,* ed. Lindsay Patterson, 25–29. New York: Dodd, Mead, 1975.

Locke, Alain, ed. *The New Negro: Voices of the Harlem Renaissance.* 1925. Reprint, New York: Atheneum, 1992.

Lomax, Almena. "Notes to Showfolk." *Los Angeles Tribune,* 15 August 1958.

Lopez, Jackie. "Is Hollywood Yielding?" *Chicago Defender,* 24 March 1945, 20.

Lott, Eric. "Double V, Double-Time: Bebop's Politics of Style." *Callaloo* 11 (1988): 597–605.

———. *Love and Theft: Blackface Minstrelsy and the American Working Class.* New York: Oxford University Press, 1993.

———. "Love and Theft: The Racial Unconscious of Blackface Minstrelsy." *Representations* 39 (summer 1992): 23–50.

———. "White Like Me: Racial Cross-Dressing and the Construction of American Whiteness." In *Cultures of United States Imperialism,* ed. Amy Kaplan and Donald Pease, 474–95. Durham, N.C.: Duke University Press, 1993.

Lott, Tommy L. "Black Vernacular Representation and Cultural Malpractice." In *Multiculturalism: A Critical Reader,* ed. David Theo Goldberg, 230–58. Cambridge, Mass.: Blackwell, 1994.

———. Review of Mark A. Reid, *Redefining Black Film. African American Review* 29.1 (spring 1995): 140–44.

Mack, Richard. "Duke Ellington—In Person." *Orchestra World,* May 1936, n.p. In *The Duke Ellington Reader,* ed. Mark Tucker, 117–18. New York: Oxford University Press, 1993.

Major, Clarence, ed. *Juba to Jive: A Dictionary of African-American Slang.* New York: Viking, 1994.

Maltin, Leonard. *The Great Movie Shorts.* New York: Crown, 1972.

Mason, Buddy. "Traveling the Rocky Road to Fame: Raymond Turner Conquers Tremendous Obstacles to Achieve Success in Movies." *Richmond Planet,* 21 June 1930, illustrated section, 1–2.

Mast, Gerald. *Can't Help Singin': The American Musical on Stage and Screen.* Woodstock, N.Y.: Overlook, 1987.

Mauss, Marcel. *The Gift: The Form and Reason for Exchange in Archaic Societies.* Trans. W.D. Halls. New York: Norton, 1990.

"Maxine Sullivan Is Regal [Theater] Screen Star." *Chicago Defender,* 8 April 1939, 10.

May, Lary. *The Big Tomorrow: Hollywood and the Politics of the American Way.* Chicago: University of Chicago Press, 2000.

———, ed. *Recasting America: Culture and Politics in the Age of the Cold War.* Chicago: University of Chicago Press, 1989.

Mayne, Judith. *Cinema and Spectatorship.* New York: Routledge, 1993.

McConachie, Bruce. *Melodramatic Formations: American Theatre and Society, 1820–1870.* Iowa City: University of Iowa Press, 1992.

McCoy, Mrs. Fleetwood. "*Hallelujah!* a 'Work of Art.'" *Chicago Defender,* 1 March 1930, 14.

McDonough, John. "Norman Granz: JATP Pilot Driving Pablo Home" *down beat,* October 1979, 30–32.

———. "Pablo Patriarch: The Norman Granz Story Part II." *down beat,* November 1979, 35–36, 76.

McGivens, Clarence J. "A Comparison." *Chicago Defender,* 15 February 1930, 14.

———. "*Hallelujah!* Again." *Chicago Defender,* 26 April 1930, 14.

McMillan, Terry, et al. *Five for Five: The Films of Spike Lee.* New York: Stewart, Tabori and Chang, 1991.

McNamara, Brooks. *Step Right Up.* New York: Doubleday, 1976.

Meeker, David. *Jazz in the Movies.* Enlarged edition. New York: Da Capo, 1981.

Meltzer, David, ed. *Reading Jazz.* San Francisco: Mercury House, 1993.

Mercer, Kobena. *Welcome to the Jungle: New Positions in Black Cultural Studies.* New York: Routledge, 1994.

"Met Has a Minstrel Show." *Chicago Defender,* 8 April 1933, sec. 1, 8.

Metropolitan Theater. Advertisements. *Chicago Defender,* 20 October 1928, sec. 1, 10; 1 November 1930, 8; 27 December 1930, 6; 19 March 1932, 8; 23 June 1934, 8; 4 July 1936, 10; 5 November 1938, 10.

Michigan Theater. Advertisements. *Chicago Defender,* 15 November 1930, 6; 18 July 1931, 8; 11 July 1936, 10; 19 November 1938, 10.

Middleton, Will A. "*Hallelujah!* Down South." *Chicago Defender,* 29 March 1930, 14.

"Midsummer Night's Entertainment." *The Theatre Advertiser,* n.d. [c. 1936], n.p.

[Mili, Gjon.] "The Lindy Hop." *Life,* 23 August 1943, 95–103.

Miller, D. A. *Place for Us: Essay on the Broadway Musical.* Cambridge: Harvard University Press, 1998.

Miller, Loren. "Hollywood's New Negro Films." *Crisis,* January 1938, 8–9.

———. "Uncle Tom in Hollywood." *Crisis,* November 1934, 329, 336.

Miller, Paul Eduard. "Jazz Symposium." *Esquire,* October 1944, 95.

"Minstrel Shows: *Dixie* Traces History of Blackface Comedians." *Life,* 5 July 1943, 80, 83–84.

Mitchell, Angelyn, ed. *Within the Circle: An Anthology of African American Literary Criticism from the Harlem Renaissance to the Present.* Durham, N.C.: Duke University Press, 1994.

Modleski, Tania. *Feminism Without Women: Culture and Criticism in a "Postfeminist" Age.* New York: Routledge, 1991.

Monroe, Al. "*Carmen Jones* Entertainment Plus." *Chicago Defender,* 13 November 1954, 14.

———. "Mixing's the Thing, Lena Horne, Richmond, Cootie and Others Say." *Chicago Defender,* 16 August 1941, 10.

———. "Swingin' the News." Regular column. *Chicago Defender,* 19 April 1941, 12; 8 November 1941, 13; 6 March 1943, 18; 3 April 1943, 18; 17 April 1943, 18.

Monson, Ingrid. *Saying Something: Jazz Improvisation and Interaction.* Chicago: University of Chicago Press, 1996.

Moran, Kathleen, and Michael Rogin. " 'What's the Matter with Capra?':
    Sullivan's Travels and the Popular Front." *Representations* 71 (2000): 106–34.
"Morgan Park Community Center has Minstrel Show." *Chicago Defender,*
    4 May 1929, sec. 1, 6.
Morris, Earl J. "Hollywood Ignores Black America." *Pittsburgh Courier,* 28 May
    1938, 20.
———. "Should the Negro Ban White Motion Pictures?" *Pittsburgh Courier,*
    24 September 1938, 21.
Morrow, Edward. "Duke Ellington on Gershwin's *Porgy.*" *New Theatre,*
    December 1935, 5–6. In *The Duke Ellington Reader,* ed. Mark Tucker, 114–17.
    New York: Oxford University Press, 1993.
Motram, James. *The Coen Brothers: The Life of the Mind.* Dulles, Va.: Bras-
    sey's, 2000.
Mueller, John. "Fred Astaire and the Integrated Musical." *Cinema Journal* 24.1
    (1984): 28–40.
Murray, Albert. *Stomping the Blues.* 1976. Reprint, New York: Da Capo, 1982.
Murray, James P. *To Find an Image: Black Films from Uncle Tom to Superfly.*
    Indianapolis, Ind.: Bobbs-Merrill, 1973.
Naremore, James. *The Films of Vincente Minnelli.* New York: Cambridge Uni-
    versity Press, 1993.
National Theater. Advertisement. *Richmond Planet,* 16 August 1930, 4.
"Nazis Criticize *Porgy and Bess.*" *Chicago Defender,* 17 April 1943, 19.
Neale, Steve. *Genre and Hollywood.* New York: Routledge, 2000.
———. "Questions of Genre." *Screen* 31.1 (spring 1990): 45–66.
"Negroes Movie-Conscious; Support 430 Film Houses." *Motion Picture Herald,*
    24 January 1942, 33–34.
New Fern Theater. Advertisement. *Chicago Defender,* 23 April 1938, 8.
Newton, Francis [Eric Hobsbawm]. *The Jazz Scene.* 1959. Reprint, New York:
    Da Capo, 1975.
Nichols, Lewis. "*Oklahoma!* a Musical Hailed as Delightful." *New York Times,*
    1 April 1943, 27.
"Nina Mae on Coast for Cinema Spot *Hallelujah!* Star Given Rousing Recep-
    tion by Performers." *Chicago Defender,* 17 September 1938, 8.
Noble, Peter. *The Negro in Films.* 1948. Reprint, Port Washington, N.Y.:
    Kennikat, 1969.
North, Michael. *The Dialect of Modernism: Race, Language, and Twentieth-
    Century Literature.* New York: Oxford University Press, 1994.
"Offensive 'Darky' Songs At Last Get Long-Awaited Boot Out of [Washington,
    D.C.] Schools." *Chicago Defender,* 14 March 1942, 1.
Oliver, Paul, Max Harrison, and William Bolcum. *The New Grove Gospel, Blues
    and Jazz, with Spirituals and Ragtime.* New York: W. W. Norton, 1986.

Omi, Michael, and Howard Winant. *Racial Formation in the United States, from the 1960s to the 1980s.* New York: Routledge, 1986.

"Organize Cooper Fan Club." *Chicago Defender,* 26 November 1938, 10.

"Orson Welles to Star Satchmo." *Chicago Defender,* 30 August 1941, 12.

Ostendorf, Berndt. *Black Literature in White America.* Totowa, N.J.: Harvester, 1982.

Park Theater. Advertisement. *Chicago Defender,* 10 December 1938, 10.

Patterson, Lindsay. *Black Films and Filmmakers.* New York: Dodd, Mead, 1975.

Peters, Paul, and George Sklar. *Stevedore.* New York: Covici-Friede, 1934.

Peterson, Bernard L., Jr. *A Century of Musicals in Black and White: An Encyclopedia of Musical Stage Works By, About, or Involving African Americans.* Westport, Conn.: Greenwood, 1993.

Pines, Jim. *Blacks in Films: A Survey of Racial Themes and Images in the American Film.* London: Studio Vista, 1975.

Pittman, John. "The Duke Will Stay on Top!" [Unidentified source, ca. 1941.] In *The Duke Ellington Reader,* ed. Mark Tucker, 148–51. New York: Oxford University Press, 1993.

" 'Prof. Doodle' Hits Rob Roy's Claims for '54." *Chicago Defender,* 8 January 1955, 14.

"Protest Film Showing." *Chicago Defender,* 31 August 1929, 9.

"Race War in Detroit." *Life,* 5 July 1943, 93–102.

Ramsey, Frederic, Jr., and Charles Edward Smith, eds. *Jazzmen.* New York: Harcourt, Brace, 1939.

Ray, Robert B. *A Certain Tendency in the Hollywood Cinema, 1930–1980.* Princeton, N.J.: Princeton University Press, 1985.

Reddick, L. D. "Educational Programs for the Improvement of Race Relations: Motion Pictures, Radio, the Press, and Libraries." *The Journal of Negro Education* 13 (summer 1944): 337–89.

Regal Theater. Advertisements. *Chicago Defender,* 10 September 1938, 9; 16 December 1939, 12.

Register, Charlene. "Black Films, White Censors: Oscar Micheaux Confronts Censorship in New York, Virginia, and Chicago." *Movie Censorship in American Culture,* ed. Francis Couvares, 159–86. Washington, D.C.: Smithsonian Institution Press, 1996.

Rehin, George F. "The Darker Image: American Negro Minstrelsy through the Historian's Lens." *American Studies* 9.3 (1975): 365–73.

Reid, Mark A. *Redefining Black Film.* Berkeley: University of California Press, 1993.

Rhines, Jesse Algernon. *Black Film/White Money.* New Brunswick, N.J.: Rutgers University Press, 1996.

Richardson, Willis, ed. *Plays and Pageants from the Life of the Negro.* 1930. Reprint, Jackson: University Press of Mississippi, 1993.

Riis, Thomas Lawrence. *Just Before Jazz: Black Musical Theater in New York, 1890–1950.* Washington, D.C.: Smithsonian Institution Press, 1989.

Roach, Joseph. *Cities of the Dead: Circum-Atlantic Performance.* New York: Columbia University Press, 1996.

Roberts, Evangaline. "Garbage Goes Over Big This Week at Regal." *Chicago Defender,* 10 August 1929, sec. 1, 9.

———. *"Hearts in Dixie* on Screen and Stage Brings Out Large Crowds to Regal Theater. *Chicago Defender* 13 July 1929, 9.

Robnet, Clara. "In Defense of *Hallelujah!*" *Chicago Defender,* 8 March 1930, 14.

Rodgers, Richard, and Oscar Hammerstein II. *Oklahoma!* In *Six Plays by Rodgers and Hammerstein,* 1–84. New York: Modern Library, n.d.

Roediger, David R. *The Wages of Whiteness: Race and the Making of the American Working Class.* London: Verso, 1991.

Rogers, J. "A 'Race-Hater' Tunes In." *Chicago Defender,* 21 November 1936, 16.

———. "Folks We Can Get Along Without." *Chicago Defender,* 28 November 1936, 16.

Rogers, J. A. "*The Green Pastures* and Other Ruminations." *New York Amsterdam News,* 13 April 1935, 8.

———. "Jazz at Home." 1925. In *The New Negro: Voices of the Harlem Renaissance,* ed. Alain Locke, 216–24. 1925. Reprint, New York: Atheneum, 1992.

Rogin, Michael. "Blackface, White Noise." *Critical Inquiry* 18 (spring 1992): 417–53.

———. *Blackface, White Noise: Jewish Immigrants in the Hollywood Melting Pot.* Berkeley: University of California Press, 1996.

———. " 'Democracy and Burnt Cork.' " *Representations* 46 (spring 1994): 1–34.

———. "Making America Home: Racial Masquerade and Ethnic Assimilation in the Transition to Talking Pictures." *The Journal of American History* 79.3 (December 1992): 1050–1078.

———. *Ronald Reagan, the Movie and Other Episodes in Political Demonology.* Berkeley: University of California Press, 1987.

Ross, Andrew. *No Respect: Intellectuals and Popular Culture.* New York: Routledge, 1989.

Routt, William D., and Richard J. Thompson. " 'Keep Young and Beautiful': Surplus and Subversion in *Roman Scandals.*" *Journal of Film and Video* 42.1 (spring 1990): 17–35.

Rowland, Mabel, ed. *Bert Williams, Son of Laughter: A Symposium of Tribute to the Man and to His Work, By His Friends and Associates.* 1923. Reprint, New York: Negro Universities Press, 1969.

Roy, Rob. "Best In Voice, Acting In *Porgy and Bess* Cast." *Chicago Defender,*
  7 March 1936, 11.
———. "Even Lena Horne Gets Red Light, He Writes." *Chicago Defender,*
  26 June 1943, 18.
———. "*Porgy and Bess* More Than Opera / Roy: Acting and Not Music Sells
  This Gershwin Hit, He Finds." *Chicago Defender,* 22 February 1936, 11.
———. "Warning to 1955: Your Predecessor Was a Ball!" *Chicago Defender,*
  1 January 1955, 15.
Rubin, Martin. *Showstoppers: Busby Berkeley and the Tradition of Spectacle.* New
  York: Columbia University Press, 1993.
Ruff, Willie. *A Call to Assembly: The Autobiography of a Musical Storyteller.* New
  York: Viking, 1991.
Rush. "*Big Boy.*" Film review. *Variety,* 17 September 1930.
Russell, D. J. "He Likes *Hallelujah! Chicago Defender,* 8 February 1930, 14.
Sacks, Howard L., and Judith Rose Sacks. *Way Up North in Dixie: A Black
  Family's Claim to the Confederate Anthem.* Washington, D.C.: Smithsonian
  Institution Press, 1993.
Salaam, Kalamu ya. "How We Sound Is How We Are." *African American
  Review* 29.2 (summer 1995): 181–82.
Sampson, Henry T. *Blacks in Black and White: A Source Book on Black Films.*
  Metuchen, N.J.: Scarecrow, 1977.
———. *Blacks in Blackface: A Source Book on Early Black Musical Shows.*
  Metuchen, N.J.: Scarecrow, 1980.
Santa, George. "Does Blackface Acting Exert a Magic Spell Over American
  Audiences?" *Richmond Planet,* 31 January 1931, 6.
Schatz, Thomas. *Boom and Bust: The American Cinema in the 1940s.* History of
  American Cinema, vol. 6, ed. Charles Harpole. New York: Scribner's, 1997.
———. *The Genius of the System: Hollywood Filmmaking in the Studio Era.*
  New York: Pantheon, 1988.
———. *Hollywood Genres: Formulas, Filmmaking, and the Studio System.* New
  York: Random House, 1981.
Schuller, Gunther. *Early Jazz: Its Roots and Musical Development.* New York:
  Oxford University Press, 1968.
———. *The Swing Era: The Development of Jazz, 1930–1945.* New York: Oxford
  University Press, 1989.
Scott, Joan. "The Evidence of Experience." *Critical Inquiry* 17.3 (summer 1991):
  773–97.
Scribe, The. " 'Jazz Singer' Plays Metropolitan; Grand Theater Closed for
  Repairs." *Chicago Defender,* 12 May 1928, sec. 1, 10.
See, Hilda. "Bess, sans Catfish Row, Out as Pix, Scribe Says." *Chicago Defender,*
  2 April 1955, 32.

———. "*Carmen Jones* Pix More Sensational than Legit-er." *Chicago Defender,* 2 October 1954, 32.

Shohat, Ella. "Ethnicities-in-Relation: Toward a Multicultural Reading of American Cinema." In *Unspeakable Images: Ethnicity and the American Cinema,* ed. Lester D. Friedman, 215–50. Urbana: University of Illinois Press, 1991.

"Should *Porgy and Bess* Be Taken Abroad Is Question American Negroes Cannot Agree On." *Chicago Defender,* 17 April 1954, 10.

Silvera, John D. "Still in Blackface." *Crisis,* March 1939, 76–77.

Sklar, Robert. *Movie-Made America: A Social History of American Movies.* New York: Random House, 1975.

Smith, Ernie. "Film." In *The New Grove Dictionary of Jazz,* vol. 1, ed. Barney Kernfeld, 382. London: MacMillan, 1988.

Smith, Yvette. *Mo' Funny: Black Comedy in America.* New York: 12th Street Productions/HBO, 1993.

Snead, James. *White Screens/Black Images: Hollywood from the Dark Side,* ed. Colin McCabe and Cornel West. New York: Routledge, 1994.

Snyder, Robert. *The Voice of the City: Vaudeville and Popular Culture in New York.* New York: Oxford University Press, 1989.

Southern, Eileen. *Biographical Dictionary of Afro-American and African Musicians.* Westport, Conn.: Greenwood, 1982.

———. *The Music of Black Americans: A History,* revised edition. New York: Norton, 1983.

"South Sea Island Scandals." *Life,* 5 July 1943, 55.

"Speaking of Pictures . . . Mili's First Movie is Skillfully Lighted Jam Session." *Life,* 22 January 1945, 6–8.

"Spivak Gets Crown From TD [Tommy Dorsey], Duke Wins[,] Bing Is New Voice." *down beat,* 1 January 1945, 1, 13.

Stacey, Jackie. *Star Gazing: Hollywood Cinema and Female Spectatorship.* New York: Routledge, 1994.

Staiger, Janet. *Interpreting Films: Studies in the Historical Reception of American Cinema.* Princeton, N.J.: Princeton University Press, 1992.

"Start Work on the *Porgy and Bess* Pix." *Chicago Defender,* 2 October 1943, 19.

Stearns, Marshall, and Jean Stearns. *Jazz Dance: The Story of American Vernacular Dance.* New York: Macmillan, 1968.

Stein, Judith. "Defining the Race 1890–1930." In *The Invention of Ethnicity,* ed. Werner Sollers, 77–104. New York: Oxford University Press, 1989.

Stewart, Jeffrey C., ed. *Paul Robeson: Artist and Citizen.* New Brunswick, N.J.: Rutgers University Press and The Paul Robeson Cultural Center, 1998.

Still, William Grant. "How Do We Stand in Hollywood?" *Opportunity,* April–June 1945, 74–77.

———. "William Grant Still Tells of Screenland's Many Tricks." *Chicago Defender,* 13 February 1943, 18–19.

Stokes, Melvyn, and Richard Maltby. *American Movie Audiences: From the Turn of the Century to the Early Sound Period.* London: BFI, 1999.

Stowe, David. *Swing Changes: Big Band Jazz in New Deal America.* Cambridge: Harvard University Press, 1994.

Strieble, Dan. "The Harlem Theater: Black Film Exhibition in Austin, Texas: 1920–1973." In *Black American Cinema,* ed. Manthia Diawara, 221–36. New York: Routledge, 1993.

Sturges, Preston. *Five Screenplays by Preston Sturges,* ed. Brian Henderson. Berkeley: University of California Press, 1985.

Suggs, DeWill. "*Hallelujah!*" *Chicago Defender,* 15 February 1930, 14.

Szwed, John F. "Race and the Embodiment of Culture." *Ethnicity* 2 (1975): 19–33.

Taves, Brian. "The B Film: Hollywood's Other Half." In Tino Balio, *Grand Design: Hollywood as a Modern Business Enterprise, 1930–1939.* History of American Cinema, vol. 5, ed. Charles Harpole, 313–50. New York: Scribner's, 1993.

Taylor, Clyde. "Crossed Over and Can't Get Black." *Black Film Review* 7.4 (n.d.): 23–27.

———. *The Mask of Art: Breaking the Aesthetic Contract—Film and Literature.* Bloomington: Indiana University Press, 1998.

"Think Race Riots Hurt Negro Films." *Chicago Defender,* 31 July 1943, 18.

Thompson, Era Bell. "Why Negroes Don't Like *Porgy and Bess.*" *Ebony,* October 1959, 50–52, 54.

Todorov, Tzvetan. *The Fantastic: A Structural Approach to a Literary Genre.* Trans. Richard Howard. Cleveland, Ohio: Case Western Reserve University Press, 1973.

———. *Genres in Discourse.* Trans. Catherine Porter. New York: Cambridge University Press, 1990.

———. *Mikhail Bakhtin: The Dialogical Principle.* Trans. Wlad Godzich. Minneapolis: University of Minnesota Press, 1984.

Toll, Robert. *Blacking Up: The Minstrel Show in Nineteenth-Century America.* New York: Oxford University Press, 1974.

"To Open at Lafayette." *Chicago Defender,* 19 March 1927, sec. 1, 8.

Troupe, Quincy. "Up Close and Personal: Miles Davis and Me." *Conjunctions* 16 (1991): 76–93.

Trumbo, Dalton. "Blackface, Hollywood Style." *Crisis,* December 1943, 365–67, 378.

Tucker, Mark, ed. *The Duke Ellington Reader.* New York: Oxford University Press, 1993.

"2,500 Attend 38th Showing of Minstrels." *Chicago Defender,* 2 April 1932, sec. 1, 13.

Wallace, Michele. *Invisibility Blues: From Pop to Theory.* New York: Verso, 1990.

Wallace, Thelma Lee. "Our Musical Shows." *Chicago Defender,* 29 October 1927, sec. 2, 2.

Waller, Gregory A. *Main Street Amusements: Movies and Commercial Entertainment in a Southern City, 1896–1930.* Washington, D.C.: Smithsonian Institution Press, 1995.

Watkins, Mel. *On the Real Side: Laughing, Lying, and Signifying.* New York: Simon and Schuster, 1994.

Watkins, S. Craig. *Representing: Hip Hop and the Production of Black Cinema.* Chicago: University of Chicago Press, 1998.

"We Are a Proud Race." *Chicago Defender,* 1 March 1930, 14.

Weems, Robert E., Jr. *Desegregating the Dollar: African American Consumerism in the Twentieth Century.* New York: New York University Press, 1998.

White, Armond. "*Moulin Rouge.*" *New York Press,* 3 June 2001.

———. "On Spencer Williams." In *The Resistance: Ten Years of Pop Culture that Shook the World,* 106–8. Woodstock, N.Y.: Overlook, 1995.

Whiteman, Paul, and Mary Margaret McBride. *Jazz.* New York: J. H. Sears, 1926.

"Whoa-ho-ho-ho-ho-ho!" *Time,* 20 January 1936, 35.

Williams, Alan. "Is a Radical Genre Criticism Possible?" *Quarterly Review of Film Studies* 9.2 (spring 1984): 121–25.

Willis, Susan. "I Want the Black One: Is There a Place for Afro-American Culture in Commodity Culture?" *New Formations* 10 (spring 1990): 77–97.

———. "Memory and Mass Culture." In *History and Memory in African American Culture,* ed. Genevieve Fabre and Robert O'Meally, 178–87. New York: Oxford University Press, 1994.

Wittke, Carl. *Tambo and Bones: A History of the American Minstrel Stage.* Durham, N.C.: Duke University Press, 1930.

Wojcik, Pamela Robertson and Arthur Knight, eds. *Soundtrack Available: Essays on Popular Film and Music.* Durham, N.C.: Duke University Press, 2001.

Wolfe, Charles. "Vitaphone Shorts and *The Jazz Singer.*" *Wide Angle* 12.3 (July 1990): 58–78.

Woll, Allen. *Black Musical Theatre: From* Coontown *to* Dreamgirls. Baton Rouge: Louisiana State University Press, 1989.

———. *Dictionary of Black Theater: Broadway, Off-Broadway, and Selected Harlem Theater.* Westport, Conn.: Greenwood, 1983.

———. *The Hollywood Musical Goes to War.* Chicago: Nelson-Hall, 1983.

"Women's Minstrel Show Is Huge Success." *Chicago Defender,* 11 November 1939, sec. 1, 16.

Wonder Bar. Serialized story. *Chicago Defender,* 26 May 1934, 10; 2 June 1934, 8; 9 June 1934, 10; 16 June 1934, 10; 23 June 1934, 10.

Wynter, Sylvia. "Sambos and Minstrels." *Social Text* 1 (1979): 149–56.

X, Malcolm as told to Alex Haley. *The Autobiography of Malcolm X.* New York: Ballantine, 1964.

Index

Arthur Knight is Associate Professor of American Studies and English at the College of William and Mary. He is the coeditor, with Pamela Robertson Wojcik, of *Soundtrack Available: Essays on Film and Popular Music,* also published by Duke University Press.

Library of Congress Cataloging-in-Publication Data

Knight, Arthur.
Disintegrating the musical : Black performance and American musical film /
Arthur Knight.
p. cm.
Includes bibliographical references and index.
ISBN 0-8223-2935-2 (cloth : alk. paper) — ISBN 0-8223-2963-8 (pbk. : alk. paper)
1. African Americans in motion pictures.   2. Musical films—United States—
History and criticism.   I. Title.
PN1995.9.N4 K59   2002
791.43′6—dc21   2002002700